# Key Account Management

# Key Account Management

**The Definitive Guide**

## Second edition

Malcolm McDonald
and
Diana Woodburn

AMSTERDAM • BOSTON • HEIDELBERG • LONDON • NEW YORK • OXFORD
PARIS • SAN DIEGO • SAN FRANCISCO • SINGAPORE • SYDNEY • TOKYO
Butterworth-Heinemann is an imprint of Elsevier

Butterworth-Heinemann is an imprint of Elsevier
Linacre House, Jordan Hill, Oxford OX2 8DP, UK
30 Corporate Drive, Suite 400, Burlington, MA 01803, USA

First published as *Key Customers* 2000
This second edition published 2007

**British Library Cataloguing in Publication Data**
A catalogue record for this book is available from the British Library

**Library of Congress Cataloguing in Publication Data**
A catalogue record for this book is available from the Library of Congress

ISBN–13: 978–0–7506–6246–8
ISBN–10: 0–7506–6246–8

For information on all Butterworth-Heinemann publications
visit our web site at http://books.elsevier.com

Typeset by Charon Tec Ltd (A Macmillan Company), Chennai, India
www.charontec.com
Printed and bound in The Netherlands

07 08 09 10 11    10 9 8 7 6 5 4 3 2 1

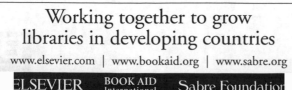

# Contents

# Foreword

I find it truly amazing that it is only in the past decade that key account management (KAM) has emerged as a major discipline in its own right. Even more surprising is that most business schools resolutely refuse to include it in their curriculum, preferring to stick with the perennial four 'Ps of marketing', which, whilst still relevant, are totally dependent on getting the strategy right for the new breed of powerful, global customers, who now demand seamless service from their suppliers in every country of the world where they operate.

Cranfield is a shining exception to the rule. In 1996 the first structured research was done on best practice key account management under the leadership of Professor Malcolm McDonald and Diana Woodburn. The current KAM Best Practice Research Club is a sophisticated extension of those exciting, earlier forays into best practice key account management.

The implications for suppliers of the enormous power of buyers today are felt across the entire corporate spectrum, and after a decade of research at Cranfield, we can now truly say that instigating best practice key account management implies a substantial programme of change management and simply cannot be achieved by tinkering with the salesforce.

The sequence of events is as follows:

1. Select the correct accounts to be included in the key account programme.

2. Categorize them according to their potential for helping us to grow our profits continuously.

3. Analyse their needs.

4. Develop strategic plans for and with each of them.

5. Get buy-in from all functions about their role in delivering the agreed value propositions. This involves IT, manufacturing, logistics, HR, finance, operations and R&D. This way, these functions will be customer-driven.

6. Get the right organization structure to serve the selected key accounts' needs.

7. Get the right people and skill sets in the key account team.

8. Implement the plans on an annual basis.

9. Measure the success of the plans, particularly in respect of whether they create shareholder value added.

10. Reward individuals and teams for their success.

Malcolm McDonald and Diana Woodburn have done a remarkable job in capturing all their research and practical experience in this excellent book and I commend it to you.

Martin Lamb
*Chief Executive*
*IMI plc*

# Acknowledgements

We are extremely grateful to Beth Rogers, now of Portsmouth Business School, who for many years helped us with our research and our thinking. Her part in earlier versions of this book, and particularly her work on the origins of key account management, was invaluable. We would like to acknowledge the contribution of Professor Tony Millman on the original key account management research report, back in 1996. Special thanks are due to him for his enthusiasm for the topic. His previous work, and that of Dr Kevin Wilson, was invaluable in creating frameworks for understanding the development of supplier/customer relationships.

Our thanks are due to other colleagues for their help and support: particularly to Dr Sue Holt, for allowing us to include some of her research; to Professor Nigel Piercy of Warwick Business School, for stimulating our thinking on several topics; to Dr Nikala Lane for her contribution to the section on teams; and to Professor Lynette Ryals for her overall support. Huge thanks are due to Steve Doubleday and Peter Mouncey for their major contribution to the editing process. We should certainly not forget our spouses for their endless forbearance during the writing process.

Lastly, too numerous to mention individually, are all the practitioners and their companies who have helped to develop our understanding of key account management, shape our thinking and validate our ideas: through the Cranfield KAM Best Practice Research Club, its focus syndicates and other practitioner forums, through participation in research and in KAM development consultancy projects, and through help with the case study insights distributed throughout the book.

# The purpose of this book

To help the time-starved reader, we have started each chapter with a 'Fast Track' for those who want a rapid reprise of the content before you delve deeper into the chapter or, indeed, skip to another chapter that contains material relating to your immediate priority. All the Fast Tracks have been compiled into one integrated section at the end of the book, so you can start or finish with the complete helicopter overview.

As this is a book designed for thinking practitioners, we have avoided filling the text with academic references, but we have added a list of items for further reading around each chapter, included at the end of the book.

The expression 'caveat emptor' (beware buyer) has been turned completely on its head during the past 10 years, so that 'caveat vendor' (beware seller) is now the norm. Customer power, particularly in over-supplied Western economies, is here to stay, hence the growing importance of key account management as a topic on the agendas of all companies, big or small.

This book represents state-of-the-art best practice, based on a decade of in-depth research into global best practice key account management from both supplier and customer perspectives, which has shown that, among other findings:

- Key account management is a strategic approach distinguishable from account management or key account selling. It should be used to ensure the long-term development and retention of strategic customers.

- Key account management is high profile, but difficult to do well.

- Key account management is appropriate to several types of relationships, but is most clearly manifest when supplier and customer have a mutually recognized partnership and a degree of trust.

- There are often mismatches between the way suppliers and customers perceive each other and their relationship, so careful communication and vigilance are vital.

- Regular monitoring of the profitability of individual customers by suppliers provides crucial information, but is quite rare because customer profitability is difficult to measure.

- Key account managers need a broad portfolio of business management skills to deal with interdependent or integrated customer relationships.

- Key account management has structural implications for selling companies. Interdependence and integration can only be achieved where the key account manager has a considerable degree of control over resources and decision making.

This book proposes ways of dealing with these findings, taking the reader to a level whereby he/she can implement solutions. It is intended to help key account strategists and key account managers to capture and develop a scientific basis for their company's practice. The scope of key account management is widening and it is becoming more complex. For key account management to be successfully implemented, there is an urgent need to develop reliable diagnostic tools and measures of performance that support strategic marketing decisions. The skills of professionals involved in key account management at strategic and operational levels need to be constantly updated and developed. So this book demonstrates how key account management can be implemented, and describes the elements of best practice that can be adopted by all types and sizes of organization.

### Chapter 1: The crucial role of key account management

This chapter sets key account management in the context of a dramatically changing business environment where increasingly complex relationships have altered the nature of marketing, and imposed an urgent need for greater understanding and more appropriate treatment of key relationships.

### Chapter 2: Selecting and categorizing key customers

We explain how to select and categorize the most appropriate accounts to target for key account management, which arguably means that this chapter is the most important in the whole book. Your KAM programme can be fatally flawed by making the wrong decisions at this stage.

### Chapter 3: Relationship stages

There is a clear hierarchy of key account relationships increasing in complexity and intimacy with the customer. Understanding where you are is crucial to adopting the right behaviour towards the customer.

### Chapter 4: Developing key relationships

Important relationships should not be left to develop on their own. Application of the right tools and techniques can help you get to the level to which you aspire with more speed and confidence.

### Chapter 5: The buyer perspective

Needless to say, buyers have their own view of key supplier relationships, and not necessarily the one the supplier would like. Ignorance of their perspective leads to complacency, inertia and disappointment, so understanding it is mandatory, however unwelcome.

### Chapter 6: Key account profitability

Profitability belongs to customers much more than to products. Since customers and customer behaviour cause cost as well as revenue, real customer profitability must be measured. It is not easy but, again, ignorance is foolhardy.

### Chapter 7: Key account analysis

This chapter examines how to analyse key accounts in order to establish and prioritize their needs.

### Chapter 8: Planning for key accounts

We introduce the processes for and the tools and techniques of key account planning. We describe how to set objectives and strategies for each targeted key account, and how to measure their profitability.

### Chapter 9: Processes – making key account management work

While key account plans are intrinsic to key account management, a plan is only a plan until it is implemented. Most companies' processes are not set up to deliver the promises of key account management but, like many initiatives, the devil is in the implementation.

### Chapter 10: The role and requirements of key account managers

Key account managers can fulfil one of four roles in managing the customer relationship, which, depending on the complexity of the relationship, may or may not involve leading a dedicated team. Each role has its own set of competences and attributes which should be understood in matching the right key account manager with each key account.

### Chapter 11: Organizing for key account management

There is no perfect structure for key account management as it is essentially a cross-boundary activity, though some structures are less KAM-friendly than others. This chapter looks at how key account management can be positioned in the organization and some of the issues that arise.

### Chapter 12: The origins of key account management

The evolution of the buyer/seller relationships is described. Key account management and partnership sourcing are seen to provide stepping stones towards integrated value management.

Innumerable tomes have been written about the importance of customer focus and getting close to customers. There can be no closer focus than 'the segment of one'. Whilst all customers are important, there is a danger in spreading scarce resources too thinly and achieving little of the real intimacy required by those few customers who can help us make significant progress towards our long-term objectives. The dilemma, then, is which customers to include in the key account management programme.

The growing complexity of business-to-business markets, which are in a state of metamorphosis from chains of value to integrated recipes of value, presents a great challenge.

All the indications are that in business-to-business marketing, key account management is not so much an option, but a customer expectation.

This book is designed to provide a route through this most difficult of terrains. It is a route map that has emerged from the authors' extensive research into the practice of global key account management with some of the world's leading companies. Although there is still much to learn, we believe readers will find this book representative of the very best of best practice.

*Professor Malcolm McDonald*
*Diana Woodburn*
*Marketing Best Practice*

# Before you read this book!

Just to give you an idea of your start point, try completing the two questionnaires below before you read further. The first questionnaire is designed to establish the current position of your organization on key account management, overall and on the 10 fundamental requirements of a successful KAM programme. The score profile will show you areas of existing strength and areas in need of serious attention. Try it with other people in your organization and see if they hold the same view.

The second questionnaire is aimed at your individual position, since most readers of this book will have had at least some experience of managing key accounts. Be as honest as you can – no-one is looking!

Come back to this page after you finish reading the book and repeat the questionnaires. Your view may change as you learn more about what key account management really means, in practice, and your personal scores may change too, if you have picked up some of the ideas in the book and implemented them.

## 1. How well developed is key account management in your organization?

Score out of 10: 0 = not at all; 10 = best practice.

| Does KAM in your organization have: | Before reading the book | After reading the book |
|---|---|---|
| A role in achieving the strategic vision | | |
| High profile support from senior management | | |
| Buy-in from appropriate organizational framework inc. teams | | |
| Careful selection of appropriate customers | | |
| Deep understanding of key customers and their strategies | | |
| Well-grounded, analysis-based customer plans | | |
| Customised offers, service or costs | | |
| Excellent, well-rounded key account managers | | |
| Excellent communications | | |
| Supportive, effective, dependable processes | | |
| Total | | |

## 2. How well do you know your key accounts?

Score out of 10: 0 = not at all; 10 = best practice.

| Do you know: | Before reading the book | After reading the book |
|---|---|---|
| Your key customer's segments/products and how you add value to them? | | |
| The customer's strategic plan? | | |
| The customer's financial health (ratios etc.)? | | |
| The customer's business processes (logistics, purchasing, production etc.) | | |
| What the customer values/needs from its suppliers? | | |
| Your company's proportion of the customer's spend? | | |
| Which of your competitors the customer uses, why, and how it rates them? | | |
| How much attributable (interface) costs should be allocated to your customer? | | |
| The real profitability of the account? | | |
| How long it takes to make a profit on a major new customer? | | |
| Total | | |

# List of figures and tables

**Figures**

**Tables**

# 1 The crucial role of key account management[1]

## Fast track

For a decade, the authors have been researching global best practice in the domain of account management, sponsored by many of the world's leading companies. The following topics in particular have been the focus of our research:

- **Key account selection**: Only a few selected customers can be included in the key account programme.

- **Classification of key accounts**: Derogatory labels like A, B, C, or gold, silver, bronze should be avoided at all cost.

- **Key account profitability**: The power of customers and their increased purchasing power has led to greater demands on the services of their suppliers. Unfortunately, many traditional accounting systems are incapable of accurately capturing all of the associated costs of dealing with major customers. Consequently, many suppliers are acting in ignorance of which customers make or lose them money.

- **Key account needs analysis**: A deep understanding of the customer's business is essential to success.

- **Strategic planning for key accounts**: Just as a three- to five-year strategy is essential for any business, so strategic plans for selected customers, signed off by the customers themselves, are also critical to success.

- **Roles and skills of key account managers**: Selling and negotiation skills are no longer sufficient on their own.

- **Other issues**: Information technology, organization structure and internal marketing all contribute to creating successful key account programmes.

The challenges that all organizations face today are:

- **Market maturity**: In most sectors, mature markets have transferred power from suppliers to customers, as suppliers compete for a share of a decreasing number of customers.

[1] For readers interested in discovering more about the origins and growth of key account management, there is a brief history in Chapter 12 of this book.

- **Globalization**: Market maturity has led to an increasing number of industries in which only a handful of truly global companies dominate the landscape. Hence, any supplier who cannot offer a seamless service in every part of the world where the customer operates, will not win the business.

- **Customer power**: With their new-found power, customers are increasingly looking to selected suppliers to give them competitive advantage by product and process development.

All these developments mean that suppliers have to be much more stringent in their key account selection criteria. They must allocate their scarce resources intelligently across their customer base, taking account of the risks associated with different kinds of customers in order to build continuous shareholder value added.

**In this chapter**

# Introduction

Back in 1996, the authors started a research club in Cranfield University School of Management because it was obvious even then that the power had been transferred from suppliers to customers. Customers were exercising their new-found power by dropping suppliers who did not live up to their expectations and by forcing down prices from other suppliers.

This apocryphal story about the buying director of General Motors was never denied: He called his suppliers together in Detroit and announced that they were all to drop their prices by 20 per cent and asked for questions. One brave chief executive officer of a supplying company told the GM buying director that his technology was years ahead of any competitor, was already 20 per cent cheaper than his competitors and that he could not reduce his prices by 20 per cent. The GM buying director asked his commissionaires to escort this supplier out and announced that his company would never deal with GM ever again. He then asked for further questions!

Whilst no doubt the story has been embellished over the years, you will instantly recognize this particular type of obnoxious bullying buyer and the reality is that you sometimes need to deal with them because of their size. Nonetheless, there is an appropriate way of handling such customers so that the relationship is still profitable and this will be covered in Chapter 7.

The problem back in 1996 was that no business schools anywhere in the world had bothered to do any research into the transfer of power from supplier to customer, so the authors established a research club based in Cranfield with the sole purpose of researching global best practice in the domain of key account management. By 2006, this research club has been going for 10 years and has systematically researched best practice, not just on the supply side, but also on the customer side. This dyadic research approach was essential because, even back in 1996, it was obvious that supplier delusions about customer relationships were rife. Over the intervening years, the following topics have been the focus of our research:

### Selecting key accounts

For readers interested in discovering more about the origins and growth of key account management, there is a brief history in Chapter 12 of this book.

The authors have, as recently as 2005, heard a director of a major telecommunications company claim that they had 1000 key accounts! The chief executive of a health care company claimed that they had 200 key accounts.

Such numbers are, of course, totally ridiculous. A moment's thought will reveal that any supplying company has limited capacity to commit cross-functional resources to selected customers. Each of us has hundreds of friends, but we only have capacity to devote real quality time and love to a handful – maybe four or five.

The same principle applies to companies, who must decide extremely carefully which major customers they are prepared to allocate this scarce resource to. This issue is expanded on in Chapter 2.

### Categorizing key accounts

Even today, the authors hear of suppliers classifying their key accounts using fatuous labels like A, B, C or gold, silver and bronze. Imagine a call centre operator letting it slip that they were dealing with a C or a bronze customer! The mind boggles over such derogatory, supplier-centric labels. A more suitable and customer-friendly type of categorization is provided in Chapter 2.

## Key account profitability

Our research reveals that about 85 per cent of Western European companies do not know whether they make or lose money from their biggest customers. They *think* they know, but most do not.

One of the authors used to be marketing and sales director of Canada Dry. Thirty years ago, two major retailers used to each buy about 3 million dozen bottles of ginger ale each year. One of these customers insisted on daily, just-in-time, store-by-store delivery, resulting in major stock-holding and delivery problems. They also insisted that the salesforce called daily to carry out merchandizing. Finally, they took about 145 days credit. The other retailer, taking a similar amount of products, asked for stocks to be delivered centrally to their warehouse for them to carry out their own deliveries. They did not insist on merchandizing and paid their accounts in 45 days. Yet, the accounting system calculated that both customers were equally profitable, as it allocated overhead costs on the basis of volume bought.

We have enjoyed activity-based costing (ABC) for over 20 years, yet most companies still have not learned the lesson that it is the cost of dealing with the customer after the 'product has left the factory' that causes either profit or loss. Even today, most companies still do product profitability and marmalade their fixed costs to customers based on turnover, thus penalizing customers who are inexpensive to service and rewarding customers who are expensive to service.

> Most companies still do product profitability and marmalade their fixed costs to customers.

## Customer needs analysis

Readers would surely agree that suppliers must really understand the needs of their customers and amend their approach accordingly. Alas, this certainly was not the case back in 1996 and is still largely untrue today. When key account managers are trained to sell volume and are paid accordingly, they have little interest in giving up substantial amounts of time and energy in researching the processes, organizational intricacies, financial details, etc. of their customers. But without such an investment they will never be able to align their offers with their customers' needs.

## Strategic planning for key accounts

This latter point is obviously related to the issue of preparing strategic plans for key accounts. The authors were recently running a key account management (KAM) workshop for a blue-chip supplier of expensive equipment for hospitals. On being told that one hospital had a multimillion pound budget for such equipment, we asked about the supplier's

> The good thing about not having a strategy is that failure comes as a complete surprise and is not preceded by a long period of worry and depression!

strategic plan for this hospital. Alarmingly, we were told that there was only a one-year forecast and budget. We were reminded of the famous saying that the good thing about not having a strategy is that failure comes as a complete surprise and is not preceded by a long period of worry and depression! Having strategic plans covering a period of at least three years, agreed with the customer, is a major factor in successful and profitable relationships, yet even today little exists beyond supplier-centric forecasts and budgets.

### Roles and skills of key account managers

It was surprising to say the least, that little was known in 1996 about the roles and required skill sets of key account managers. Amongst other things, we supervised a major doctoral thesis on this topic, so we can speak with great authority on what world class key account managers should be doing and what skill sets they require.

### Other issues

Other areas for our research efforts included the role of IT, organizational structures, measuring KAM effectiveness, communications, cultural issues, all of them covered extensively in this book.

The point we are making is that the material presented in this book is based on a decade of in-depth research into global best practice KAM and is, therefore, unlike most other books on the topic, which tend to rely on anecdotal or second-hand evidence for the assertions that are made. This is the reason we feel comfortable in describing this book as 'the definitive guide for practitioners', as the research club has been sponsored over the years by some of the most famous companies in the world and over 2 million euros have been invested in it.

## 1.1   Pressures that have led to growth in customer power

### 1.1.1   Summary of the pressures

> The characteristic and techniques of KAM were not extensively explored apart from the need for a dedicated salesforce beyond the 1990s.

As we have indicated in our introductory comments, whilst sales and marketing strategists have for some time been convinced that effective KAM leads to increased sales, heightened profitability and improved sales productivity, the characteristics and techniques of KAM were not extensively explored, apart from the need for a dedicated salesforce beyond the 1990s. The impetus behind this unprecedented interest in the dynamics and mechanics of KAM comes from an awakening to the need to address changes in both the context and constructs of marketing.

The marketplace today is a different world from that which we have known before and the rules of engagement have evolved significantly. Such rapid and radical transformation warrants attention.

With hindsight, we can easily recognize those pressures in the business environment that have led to the ascendancy of KAM as a separate and significant discipline. These pressures were initially identified in a research report published by Cranfield and the Chartered Institute of Marketing entitled *Marketing, the Challenge of Change* (McDonald *et al.*, 1994) and are described in the following sections (Sections 1.1.2–1.1.5).

### 1.1.2 Rapid change

Time has become a major determinant of competitive advantage. The drive towards lean production systems has increased interdependency in supply chains. Any company that is complacent will be quickly overtaken. Ironically, the shorter the opportunity for success, the more important it becomes for companies to think strategically and for the long term. In so doing, the potential for minimizing the risks inherent in rapidly changing markets through supply chain partnerships is often an attractive option. The symptoms and challenges in responding to rapid change are listed in Table 1.1.

> Any company that is complacent will be quickly overtaken.

| Symptoms | Challenge |
|---|---|
| Compressed time horizons | Ability to exploit markets more rapidly |
| Time-based competition | Process excellence and flexibility |
| Shorter product life cycles | More effective new product development |
| Shorter technology life cycles | More investment in skills and understanding of applications and technology |
| Transient customer preferences | Flexibility in approach to markets, accuracy in demand forecasting, and optimization in price setting |
| Increasingly diverse business area | Cultural sensitivity |

**Table 1.1**
Responding to rapid change

Managers understand that, for a product or service to be commercially advantageous to the provider, value must be added faster than cost. The concept has been labelled 'lean supply' by purchasing professionals. Lean supply involves the study of the entire supply flow from raw materials to consumer as an integrated whole.

In theory, effective supply flow is an absolute. In practice, companies just have to keep applying continuous improvement to be leaner than the competition. Adopting an approach in which the supplier and customer are joint guardians of the value in transit is vital. Examination of the value in transit demands that both the supplier and customer open their 'books' and facilitate two-way assessment in order to optimize performance. There should be no blame and excuses.

Lean supply practice also lends itself to sharing some costs critical to mutual success.

Lean supply practice also lends itself to sharing some costs critical to mutual success. Joint research and development, joint merchandizing, integrated logistic and electronic data interchange (EDI) are just a few examples of the opportunities available for making things happen better, cheaper and faster.

This concept is equally applicable to service industries.

### 1.1.3 Process refinement

Companies must be flexible, not just to raise customer satisfaction but to avoid waste and loss.

Company activities have shifted away from producing predefined products or services towards having the capability to produce creative solutions for customer requirements. Companies must be flexible, not just to raise customer satisfaction, but to avoid waste and loss. The symptoms and challenges in refining the process are listed in Table 1.2.

**Table 1.2**
Refining the process

| Symptoms | Challenge |
|---|---|
| Move to flexible manufacturing and control systems | Project orientation to deal with micro-segmentation |
| Materials substitution | Means to shift from single transaction focus to the forging of long-term relationships |
| Developments in technology (such as microelectronics and robotics) | More investment in skills to realize the potential of technology innovations |
| Concentration on core business | Embrace opportunities for suppliers to run non-core aspects of customer's business |
| Quality focus | Widespread involvement in quality initiatives |
| Collaborative working practices | Create greater customer commitment |

The prerequisite for process redesign is access to information across organizational boundaries. Without that exchange of information, no streamlining can be achieved. Buyer–seller partners are increasingly sharing common databases. The obvious example is stock management. If point of sale data is transferred to commonly held databases of stock information, the suppliers of logistics services and goods can make sure that retail outlets are always fully stocked with the fastest moving lines. That enables everybody to make more money through the consumers obtaining what they want when they want it. Buyers and sellers also need to examine their current activities together in order to explore and optimize processes.

The output of process redesign (or re-engineering) should be enhanced customer value.

The output of process redesign (or re-engineering) should be enhanced customer value. Customers want quality through attention to detail. Any customer wanting to initiate new quality indicators with a supplier is more likely to do so if there is a strong element of trust and partnership. The closeness of customer relationships can be greatly enhanced through collaboration, both across and between organizations. Joint planning initiatives and coordinated working practices can be used to create mutual understanding, benefit and commitment.

Our way of depicting how organizations receive goods and services, add value and sell them into their end-user markets is Professor Michael Porter's value chain. Figure 1.1 depicts the standard Porter value chain model for a manufacturing organization and Figure 1.2 depicts a value chain for a service organization.

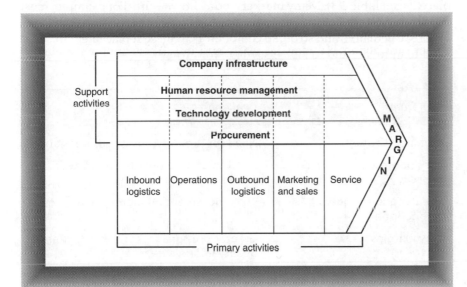

**Figure 1.1**
The value chain.

**Figure 1.2**
Internal value chain: service companies.

Within these models, companies will have functional specialists working together, ensuring a consistent and integrated approach to the development of value.

### 1.1.4 Redefining the marketplace and pleasing the customers

A product/market life cycle is the aggregate sales at a point in time of all goods or services which satisfy the same or similar needs in a market.

As well as the need to respond to rapid change through the refinement of processes, there is a need to recognize the changing nature of the marketplace itself (Table 1.3). Many markets today are mature. For example, most people in Western Europe have cars, washing machines, dishwashers, televisions, calculators and so on, so competitors in these replacement markets need to innovate and to look elsewhere for growth.

**Table 1.3**
Redefining the marketplace

| Symptoms | Challenge |
|---|---|
| Commoditization | Need for product/process differentiation |
| Lack of growth and over-capacity | Need to achieve growth within key accounts |
| Greater and stronger competition | Customer retention more vital than ever |
| Low margins | Greater pressure for cost reduction and quality improvement |
| Saturated markets | Need for new market creation and stimulation |
| Downsizing | Need to apply resource where it can deliver most value to customers |

**Market maturity**

Figure 1.3 illustrates the impact of market maturity on the key elements of business management. A product/market life cycle is the aggregate sales at a point in time of all goods or services which satisfy the same or similar needs in a market. The final column clearly illustrates the danger of allowing products and services to degenerate into commodities, with price availability and costs representing the only determinants of success. It is this danger more than any other that forces suppliers to pay more attention to key customers' specific requirements as a means of securing effective differentiation.

The fact that most industry-to-industry product/service markets in the developed world are mature has clearly propelled the development of KAM. Suppliers know that they can only grow at the expense of a competitor and the obvious first option is to prise more of existing customers' business away from the opposition by means of account penetration. Highly professional KAM can facilitate the achievement of this objective.

| Key characteristics | Unique | Product differentiation | Service differentiation | Commodity |
|---|---|---|---|---|
| Marketing message | Explain | Competitive | Brand values | Corporate |
| Sales | Pioneering | Relative benefits distribution support | Relationship based | Availability based |
| Distribution | Direct selling | Exclusive distribution | Mass distribution | 80 : 20 |
| Price | Very high | High | Medium | Low (consumer controlled) |
| Competitive intensity | None | Few | Many | Fewer, bigger international |
| Costs | Very high | Medium | Medium/low | Very low |
| Profit | Medium/high | High | Medium/high | Medium/low |
| Management style | Visionary | Strategic | Operational | Cost management |

**Figure 1.3** The product/market life cycle and market characteristics.

---

## Case study insight

### IMI's response to market maturity

IMI was until recently a 'metal bashing' company based principally in the Midlands in the UK. Their Board redefined their market boundaries into five 'platform businesses' which they could dominate, put much of their manufacturing in South America and China, and began developing close relationships with selected global customers. As a result, they are now one of the most profitable companies in the world.

---

When inflation and growth were high in Western economies, companies enjoyed a comfort zone, which masked inefficiency. Now, most economies are experiencing low inflation and in many sectors across the world, prices are falling. In such a climate there is no room for complacency. Business can only be won by being better than competitors and taking market share from them. Product, process and people improvements are imperative.

> Business can only be won by being better than competitors and taking market share from them.

### Customer power

The change within the business environment that is having the most dramatic impact on the development of KAM is the new-found expertise and power of customers and consumers in exercising choice (Table 1.4). Customer empowerment is not just a cultural change emanating from the growing popularity of adopting a customer focus, it is a consequence of mature markets. Nowadays, customers know that they can demand more

> Nowadays, customers know that they can demand more from suppliers because suppliers must seek to retain customers.

**Table 1.4**
Pleasing the
customer

| Symptoms | Challenge |
|---|---|
| Customers more demanding and more knowledgeable | Quality and traceability favour supply chain partnerships |
| Purchase behaviour strategic rather than tactical | A strategic and sympathetic approach to selling is required |
| Concentration of buying power | Selling companies need to add more value to succeed |
| Higher expectations | A greater investment and closer relation to the customer is required |
| Customer identity and role more complex | Need to better manage the complexities of multiple market channels |

Suppliers who cannot meet the geographical scope and consistent outputs demanded by global customers are rationalized off lists of preferred suppliers.

from suppliers because suppliers must seek to retain customers – not just to maintain profitability, but also to stay in business.

Customer power manifests itself in many ways. For example, there is the considerable concentration of industry, most recently on a transnational scale, which has made big customers even bigger (Figure 1.4). However, bigger customers do not necessarily mean more business opportunity. Suppliers who cannot meet the geographical scope and consistent outputs demanded by global customers are rationalized off lists of proposed suppliers. Customers want sophisticated solutions, which means that winning customer accounts can be very costly. It also means that retaining customers, which requires ongoing investment, is critical in achieving long-term profitability (Figure 1.5).

Sales to the top five customers as a percentage of total supplier sales over 25 years.
*Source*: Adapted from Wilson, 1998

**Figure 1.4**
Concentration of buying power in industries.

Costs of the front line (sales, service, trade promotions, etc. over 15 years).
Interface costs per customer (adjusted for inflation) – supplier to the print industry.

*Source*: Adapted from Wilson, 1998

**Figure 1.5**
Cost of servicing
the customer.

---

## Case study insight

### Key Industrial Equipment's response to the danger of commoditization

Key Industrial Equipment is a specialist distributor of specialist products offering thousands of categories. In addition to having to offer a comprehensive range, the company has received industry recognition for innovation and service. It offers extremely rapid delivery, electronic data interchange and will take on the assembly of parts if the customer requires it. In discussions with customers, they place the emphasis on end-to-end value rather than on unit price.

---

The customer may have always been hailed as king but, not being a very well-informed monarch, the king was often at the mercy of his 'subjects' (suppliers). The rising power of consumer pressure groups and the popular media have changed all that. They have wrested power from companies and vested it in the ultimate users of their products and services. End-customers expect a great deal of respect, which is now often contractually assured in some sort of charter document. The logical extension of this consumer-driven scenario is cooperation between all organizations delivering value in the flow of supply from raw materials to the consumer. The concept of adding value is significant. Consumers will soon leap-frog any links in the supply chain that they feel do not add value.

Customers need raw materials to be converted into what they can use, taken to where they need them and presented to them for choice. Which company in the supply chain does any of these is irrelevant. Consumer champions are also casting a critical eye over the whole supply chain in

Consumers will soon leap-frog any links in the supply chain that they feel do not add value.

the new millennium for ethical and environmental reasons. Trusted brand names have to ensure that their values are passed up the supply chain.

Consumers today know more about supply chains than might ever have interested them 10–20 years ago.

Consumers today know more about supply chains than might ever have interested them 10–20 years ago: they see it as relevant to the end-product they obtain. The idea of companies working together with their suppliers in order to deliver more value to the end-consumer is an attractive one, a matter of common sense. This is particularly pertinent to businesses which operate across national boundaries where the value chain is exceedingly complex and cultural sensitivities must be respected.

### 1.1.5   Globalization

The globalization of business has had many side-effects, including a greater interdependency between global customers and suppliers who have the capability to meet each other's increasingly complex needs (Table 1.5). These suppliers also realize the extent to which they can grow with their key customers if they consistently succeed in meeting their customers' expectations cost-effectively.

**Table 1.5** Coping with globalization

| Symptoms | Challenge |
|---|---|
| Industry players undifferentiated | Restructuring to achieve wider scope (restructuring of domestic operations to compete internationally) |
| Greater and stronger competition | Customer retention more vital than ever |
| Lower margins | Greater pressure for cost reduction and quality improvement |
| Greater customer choice | Need to customize offers |
| Larger and more complex markets | Need to become customer-focused in larger and more disparate markets |

Figure 1.6 shows that as industries mature, the end-result is often only a handful of truly global companies dominating an industry. Hence, there are only 10 car companies in the world and four firms of accountants, whilst in the UK, for example, four supermarkets account for about 80 per cent of all fast-moving consumer products.

### 1.1.6   Implications

The impact of all these changes – the imperative of keeping pace with rapid change, the requirement of refining processes, the necessity of redefining the character of the marketplace, the need for satisfying increasingly sophisticated customers/consumers and the obligation of facing the growing scope and scale of competition – has reverberated through the business relationship itself. It has encouraged KAM away from the traditional

**Figure 1.6**
Evolution of market maturity.

construct of a single relationship between salesperson and buyer, and towards the concept of strategic customers, where key customers command attention on vital statistics measuring more than simply their size.

---

**CHECKPOINT**

**Pressures on businesses today**

- Do you know how the pressures described above affect your company?

---

We see an increasing number of companies starting to build models of account attractiveness, matching their resources to the profit and status of any potential given customer or prospect. We also witness increasing professionalism among purchasers and decision-making units in buying companies as they evaluate the longer term value offered by suppliers (the quality of products, processes and people) rather than solely the price deal.

## 1.2   Why understanding relationships is so important

The relationship between two organizations has an existence beyond the obvious types of interaction, such as product and service adaptation, operational delivery and underlying strategy. All of these contribute to the nature and development of the relationship as well as depending on it (Figure 1.7). The intercompany relationship is affected by these interfaces and may also buffer turbulence arising from them. It is the 'glue' that binds companies together more or less closely and the medium through which interactions take place to deliver action.

*The intercompany relationship is the 'glue' that binds companies together.*

**Figure 1.7**
The relationship
as a medium.

Clearly, understanding the nature and potential of the customer relationship is critical in assessing opportunities and managing business development. We need to know where we stand now with our customer and what further engagement might entail. We will also need a sound appreciation of their market position, and internal strengths and constraints (see Chapter 7).

Understanding key relationships is both important and challenging because:

● the risks are ambiguous and the stakes are high,

● supplier–buyer interactions are already complex and lie at the heart of major change, and

● key relationships operate at different levels which require different behaviours.

### 1.2.1   Relationship risks

One of the primary reasons for developing relationships is risk reduction. There are risks associated with building close relationships with key customers as well as risks associated with not building them. In theory, there should be less chance of relationship breakdown where there is joint commitment, barriers to exit and mutual understanding and trust (see Chapters 3 and 4). However, while these attributes may appear highly desirable, they actually carry risks of their own. For example:

● The risk of being vulnerable to opportunism and not obtaining a satisfactory saving or return on investment in the relationship.

● The risk of committing to one partner at the exclusion of others and 'backing the wrong horse'.

● The risk of misunderstanding the relationship and failing to achieve reciprocal security.

### 1.2.2  Satisfactory return

The major question must be 'If we put time, effort and money into developing closer relationships with our trading partners, will they be more profitable?' The answer is not clear-cut, though it may be summed up as 'Yes, possibly, but not automatically'.

There is ample evidence from numerous sources indicating that suppliers have great difficulty in measuring the real profitability of their customers. Traditionally, accounting systems have used a geographical or business unit and/or product basis of analysis and customer cost accounting has been rudimentary. Substantial costs such as special customized developments, high-level, intercompany contacts and various additional services are very rarely allocated to individual customers. Thus, real customer profitability is difficult to analyse in practice and these intrinsic difficulties are compounded by inherent challenges to internal vested interests.

> Traditionally, customer cost accounting has been rudimentary.

Alarmingly, although few suppliers can assess the profitability of individual key accounts accurately, many suspect that, ultimately, they lose money on them. While Chapter 6 explores this problem in greater detail, the issue is introduced here to highlight some fundamental points.

- Close relationships with key accounts have substantial cost implications.

- The mismanagement of just a few large accounts can be potentially (disastrously) loss making.

- Customer relationships should be carefully selected and prioritized for the prudent investment of scarce resources (see Chapter 2).

---

**CHECKPOINT**

**Customer profitability**

- Do you know the profitability of individual customers?

---

The cost of building close, sophisticated, groundbreaking, new relationships should not be underestimated. Frequent, multilevel, multifunction communication alone represents a considerable expense. Further, relationships development usually entails investment in initiatives such as joint marketing, new restructuring, electronic commerce, staff retraining and stockholding. All too often the cost of pursuing a closer relationship is not anticipated and properly quantified.

> All too often the cost of pursuing a closer relationship is not anticipated and properly quantified.

Firmness can pay off handsomely: one loss-making company, admittedly with dominant shares in its core markets, implemented 'an aggressively upward pricing policy' with great success and achieved a return to excellent profits within two years.

### 1.2.3 Implications of joint commitment

In many cases, the commitment of the buying company is greater than that of the selling company (although the latter would not see it this way). Where it does not make sense to multisource a product or service, the buying company may be obliged to adopt a sole supplier. Meanwhile, the selling company will continue to supply other customers. The buying company must ensure that it has made the right choice, not only in relation to the matter at hand, but also because its decision will be a statement to other suppliers.

Similarly, a selling company's key customers may demand supplier exclusivity, preventing the supplier from broadening its customer base by serving the customers' competitors. The practice of exerting such pressure has generally been accepted by advertising agencies, for example, while other sectors have resisted it. However, the growth in the number of customers of considerable size has meant that this practice is increasingly tolerated.

> At this level of relationship, there may not be any room for parallel relationships, even for the selling company.

The range of functions and initiatives involved in the relationship may reach a point where significant company-level backing is required which cannot be satisfied simply by allocating more resources, people and time. At this level of relationship, there may not be any room for parallel relationships, even for the selling company. For example, if two competing companies were developing similar new products at the same time using a shared supplier, the supplier would find it exceedingly difficult to work with both customers in the same way. Confidentiality might be hard to guarantee, as might be the origins of a research breakthrough. If the supplier and each of the buying companies were to approach the marketplace together, the fact that the company is offering products together with two different partners might confuse consumers.

However, by choosing to work with a single business partner, both supplier and buyer are consciously excluding others and declaring that the decision is right for them. Both companies want a partner they can work with and benefit from. 'Backing the right horse' for a strategic-level relationship need not be as much of a gamble as backing a real horse if the pre-existing relationship is well understood and well managed.

### 1.2.4 Misconception and disappointment

There is a common misconception that closer relationships will automatically bring greater profits. The reality is not so simple. The inability of companies to measure profitability accurately or realistically gives cause for confusion. However, it would appear that relationship stage, maturity and business success are linked: closer key relationships are widely considered more successful than relatively distant key relationships according to a range of accepted success and financial indicators (Figure 1.8). Nevertheless, a substantial minority of relationships do not conform to this 'rule' and it would be a mistake to assume that developing any relationship will automatically bring success or that relationships which are not developed to closer levels are failures. This was clearly demonstrated in the Cranfield/*Financial Times* research report (McDonald and Woodburn, 1999).

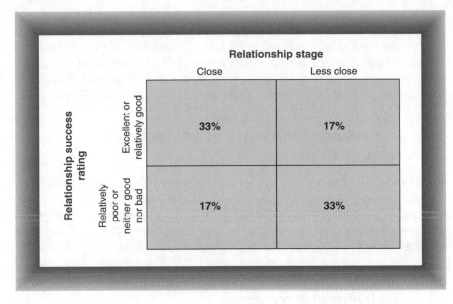

**Figure 1.8**
Relationship
closeness versus
relationship success.

A number of these non-conformists represent successful relationships that are not particularly close for good reasons. For example, if the product or service purchased is not a core item and does not offer opportunities for deriving differential benefit, the customer may naturally decide that a simple purchase with minimal support is adequate. Any extra attention or additional services lavished on the customer might be accepted, but not necessarily valued. From the supplier's perspective, an attempt at forced intimacy would be a mistake in this case and the business should be serviced with efficiency and a positive attitude, but not much more.

*From the supplier's perspective, an attempt at forced intimacy would be a mistake.*

### Case study insight

'I do not think suppliers would benefit from getting any closer to us: quite the reverse. We are a very "taking" company and it would not do them any good.' (Retailer)

It is not uncommon for some key relationships to be close, but to be considered unsuccessful and/or unprofitable. They may be intransigent situations into which companies have been cornered, perhaps by a determined buyer, optimistic key account manager or poorly written contract.

The fact that relationships can reach higher levels of intimacy and still prove unsuccessful should make companies wary of selecting the right relationships to develop in the first place as well as managing them extremely carefully (see Chapter 2). Part of that selection process should be an assessment of the relationship's current stage of development and the buyer's and supplier's respective degrees of commitment.

*Customer relationships, whether key accounts or otherwise, should be examined objectively and developed deliberately in line with company aims and capabilities.*

There is yet a further danger: that of sliding imperceptibly, by numerous smaller steps, into a relationship that the company has failed to anticipate, which has implications that they are unprepared for or cannot recognize. Logically, the development of key customer relationships should be a strategic process linked into the design and implementation of overall business strategy. Surprisingly, this critical connection is often overlooked. Customer relationships, whether key accounts or otherwise, should be examined objectively and developed deliberately in line with company aims and capabilities.

## 1.3 Increasing complexity of key account relationships

Relationships with key customer are not only complex, but increasingly so. For top customers, the simple model of 'I, salesperson, sell; you, buyer, get' only applies in certain circumstances. Few, if any, major business initiatives are now developed on this axiom. So why have things changed and how has this made key account relationships more complex?

### 1.3.1 The consolidation of customers into large, multidivisional companies

Key customer relationships often involve major corporations as both suppliers and customers. Because an amorphous mass is impossible to motivate and measure, most large companies introduce subdivisions into their businesses and the larger these companies become, the more entities they will contain. In many cases, a supplier will do business with more than one entity within the client company. While such a multiple interface offers potential benefits in terms of developing an inside track to new business with other parts of the organization, it may also incur undesirable costs. For example, there may be an obligation to service uneconomical parts of the business, involvement in internal competition, downward price levelling and additional communication costs.

### 1.3.2 The consolidation of customers leading to the adoption of dual roles: the customer may be 'competitor' as well as 'client'

The situation in which a customer is also a competitor and sometimes a supplier as well arises more frequently.

As companies consolidate, the situation in which a customer is also a competitor and sometimes a supplier as well arises more frequently. Obviously, this intertwining of relationships and roles complicates behaviour. Takeovers that juxtapose competitors inappropriately are a common cause of terminated key account relationships. However, some companies struggle on and learn to live with ambivalence, perhaps because industry consolidation leaves them with very little choice of customer or supplier. The potential for internal and external conflict is heightened and management of the relationship becomes evidently more strained.

### 1.3.3 The development of global businesses that demand global supply

Global customers requiring global supply and service add additional complexity to the task of managing relationships effectively. Problems which are easily identified but not easily resolved originate from differences in terms of language, culture, zone and geography, making the servicing of pan-global operations a tough challenge for even the fittest of suppliers. The prevalence of knowledgeable and powerful country managers helps somewhat, but the scope and size of the task remains formidable. In addition, new infrastructure may be required to service markets previously outside the supplier's sphere of activity which now fall within its global contract, meaning more new partners, languages and cultures to assimilate into the relationship.

### 1.3.4 The accelerating pace of change, particularly as new IT reshapes markets

Information technology, in particular electronic commerce, is forcing huge changes in the way companies work and how their markets operate. As always, there is a lag between the availability of the new technology which is possessed by the enlightened few and mass uptake with full-scale revision of the basic practices and processes. While it is not yet clear what the ultimate impact of IT development will be for business, it is already evident that many companies will have to make huge adjustments very quickly as customers adapt to electronic commerce and demand similar immediacy and intimacy from their existing suppliers.

> It is already evident that many companies will have to make huge adjustments very quickly as customers adapt to electronic commerce.

### 1.3.5 The emphasis on strategic alliances as a fast and flexible, but less clear-cut, approach to growth

New needs may be satisfied on both sides of the relationship by the creation of a strategic alliance with another company, which has strength in a specific area rather than through the development of existing internal expertise and physical assets. Selling companies may find themselves supplying third-party associates of their customers instead of their customers directly. They may also be supplying customers alongside other suppliers who may have been selected by them or by the customer. As supply chain management reaches further up- and downstream, more complex relationships are being formed involving more participants. Communication is likewise complicated and, because strategic alliances are often forged as a fast and flexible response to market change, opportunities for misunderstanding and confusion abound.

---

**Case study insight**

**Customer perspective**

'We deal with our suppliers on product development, marketing and ordering, but our warehouse is managed for us by Tibbett & Britten, so suppliers deal with them on inbound logistics.'

---

With today's flattened management structures, cross-functional teams are encouraged to take part in the activities traditionally allocated to lower levels of responsibility, including direct customer contact and decision making. Key customer relationships put more people and more functions in direct contact with the customers or supplier than ever before.

While the internal interactions required to drive the machine which actually delivers the customer promise are discussed later in Chapters 3 and 4, it is already abundantly clear that relationships and, in particular, key account relationships are undoubtedly complicated by the increased quantity and variety of contact with the customer.

## Summary

The external context in which buyer–seller relationships exist is becoming increasingly extensive and complex. Change drivers include the rapid pace of change, the refinement of processes, market maturity, heightened customer power and the globalization of business. At the same time, the internal, organizational context is also changing, removing traditional delineations of remit and responsibility. Conditions are more conducive to 'partnering' between suppliers and customers and, hence, the nature of marketing has altered. Marketers are moving away from a traditional transaction focus towards a customer focus. Thus, there is a pressing need for finding ways of describing relationships as a basis from which to understand them better and build them stronger – and this has led to the ascendancy of KAM.

# 2 Selecting and categorizing key customers

## Fast track

Choosing the customers that your company wants to treat as key accounts ought not to be too hard, certainly when compared with some of the difficult cultural and structural issues that arise from key account management. However, many companies approach the task in a rather casual fashion first time around, and only later realize how many onward decisions are driven by their selection of key customers, and how awkward it may be to unpick inappropriate choices.

The key customers you seek should be those that are aligned to your corporate strategy and will therefore make a major contribution to its achievement. If they do not, who will? So your portfolio of key accounts should contain these customers, and only these customers. If you dilute it with customers with dissimilar agendas, which will not respond particularly favourably to your strategies, you will be unable to demonstrate sufficiently positive results from the key account management programme, and you risk sinking the whole initiative. Undoubtedly, there will be pressures to include unsuitable accounts, but they must be resisted. Counter such pressures by adopting an objective criteria-based process, and applying it rigorously.

Whatever the size of the organization, there seems to be an almost universally appropriate number of key accounts, which is probably between 15 and 35, with 5 and 50 as the outer limits. Certainly, anything with three digits is too many. In fact, the process of selection and categorization starts with deciding, more or less, how many key accounts your company can handle.

The identity of the customer deserves careful attention. It not only determines how the customer will score against the criteria, and hence how much resource it should receive, but it also has implications about how it should be managed. Customers should be identified in their terms, not carved up according to the supplier's structure, unless it is well matched with the customer's.

Selection criteria should be chosen and their importance weighted by a senior management group, and then rolled out to be scored to people who know the customer. These criteria are applied to assess the customer's attractiveness to your company, and the data are then used on the vertical axis of the key account selection/categorization matrix to build a picture of your portfolio of customers.

To complete the picture, you need the customer's view of you as a supplier, in their terms. Obviously, that will be different for each customer, and you must resist the urge to apply a standard set of criteria on the horizontal axis. If you did that, it would only be a reflection of what you think of yourselves, and would not represent their views and differences at all. You would also, in effect, be saying that these customers are all the same and all want the same things, which is contrary to the whole philosophy of key account management, apart from being patently untrue.

The matrix identifies four kinds of key customers, to which it is appropriate to offer four generic strategies that should guide the specific strategies that are developed for each customer individually:

1. Star key customers – investment for growth

2. Strategic key customers – strategic investment

3. Status key customers – proactive maintenance

4. Streamline key customers – management for cash.

The systematic assessment approach described in this chapter enables suppliers to build a portfolio view of their customers that drives many further insights, decisions and expectations about them, which is much more realistic and powerful than the key customer lists that many suppliers use. We will refer to it frequently in the rest of this book.

**In this chapter**

## Introduction

The selection of key customers that a company makes has a crucial effect on the success of its key account programme and the perception of its success. Unless the key customer portfolio performs better than groups of customers not receiving the same level of investment, why would a company continue with it? Any customers who do not respond positively are diluting the results and endangering the whole programme.

The task of categorizing customers needs to be carried out methodically and thoroughly. It will probably take more effort than suppliers expect, but the importance of getting it right cannot be overestimated. All kinds of onward decisions depend on it, from what resource the customer receives, to who should be appointed to manage them, and what expectations may be set for them. Companies failing to tackle the task of selection and categorization properly should expect to fail at key account management.

This chapter gives clear guidelines on how to go about the process, to be applied carefully and systematically.

## 2.1 Why is choosing the right customers so important?

### 2.1.1 Fulfilling corporate strategy

Key customers must be those that will make a substantial contribution to the fulfilment of your strategic vision.

Key customer selection is one of the most important decisions that suppliers face in key account management (KAM). Whether key customers currently represent 20 per cent or 80 per cent of your business, they should, by definition, be business leaders – leaders in your business, and/or leaders in their own sectors as well. The key customers to which you give special attention must be those that will make a substantial contribution to the fulfilment of your strategic vision, so making the right choices is critical.

If you fail to choose appropriately, your portfolio is likely to contain a mixed bag of big names, old friends and difficult/over-demanding customers which is not going to take your business anywhere, never mind the vision of the future that you have mapped out. Your other customers are typically smaller and more often driven by their markets than leading in them, and it is very unlikely that they can fulfil both their own part in your strategy and make up for what the key accounts fail to deliver. So to achieve corporate objectives, you must select the right key customers.

Choosing key customers is one of the most important decisions in KAM, and also one of the earliest.

Although choosing key customers is one of the most important decisions in KAM, and also one of the earliest, some companies believe that their key customer portfolio is a 'given', and appear to avoid making the decision at all. In essence, they are saying that their biggest customers now are also their best, and will always be so. This is a very dangerous assumption, and should be challenged and investigated objectively. Look for phrases like 'We don't need to do that – our key customers choose themselves' and 'It's obvious – we all know who they are anyway.' Check your selection process against the list below.

---

### CHECKPOINT

**Is your key account selection process:**

1. Focused on current results rather than the longer term?

2. Selecting too many customers?

3. Based on poor and/or largely internal information?

4. Opaque, unaudited and easily manipulated?

5. Succumbing to internal political pressure to include unsuitable accounts?

6. Producing an unbalanced portfolio (see Section 2.3.1)?

7. Not differentiating enough between customers?

8. Not helping to assess potential new key accounts?

---

Given the importance of selecting the right key customers, it is something of a puzzle to work out why many suppliers make such a poor job of it. Although enlightened companies understand the need for rigour and care in making their choices, the selection process is still, in many companies, approached rather casually and intuitively. It is only further down the line, when some of the consequences begin to bite, that suppliers realize their mistake. Numerous companies have had to backtrack with some very large customers when they realized that they could not – or did not want to – deliver on their promises of special treatment.

Real key account management requires suppliers to deliver customized, innovative strategies to individual customers, and that capacity is seriously limited in any company, however large. Obviously, if there are not going to be many key accounts, then choosing all the right ones and none of the wrong ones is crucial to success.

> Choosing all the right ones and none of the wrong ones is crucial to success.

### 2.1.2  Selecting for superior returns

It quickly becomes clear that KAM and key customers will be a major pull on resources. If they are not, then it will be just a cosmetic programme, soon to be discredited by customers and your own organization alike. However, when your company is investing in customers, it will be expecting better performance from these customers than it receives from the rest of its customer base, whether in terms of growth, increased margins or some other contribution to profit.

The customers picked out for special treatment should be those who will give a superior yield in the future. Ultimately, that is how your Board will judge whether the approach is successful, and more worthy of their investment than, say, buying more equipment, more staff training or more advertising. Otherwise, why bother?

It follows that including any customers in your selection who do not respond to KAM could bring down the whole initiative, because the overall return on investment will be the poorer because of them (see Chapter 6 on key account profitability). In fact, while you are working hard with the 'right' accounts to increase shareholder value, the 'wrong' accounts can destroy shareholder value just as fast, by taking all they are given and doing exactly what they would have done anyway. BOC described these customers as the ones that 'want-it-all-but-don't-want-to-pay-for-it' (or can't).

> Including any customers in your selection who do not respond to KAM could bring down the whole initiative.

Even if you did a good job on selection at the outset, unless you have a process for deselecting key customers as well as choosing them, then your company will inevitably have accumulated some poor performers a few years into KAM. The portfolio should be reviewed with relegation and promotion in mind on an annual basis. Obviously, performance will be examined more frequently, but customers should not be selected, deselected and reselected on a quarterly basis. They do not appreciate this kind of fickle behaviour and are inclined to respond negatively.

---

**CHECKPOINT**

**Make sure that the selection process is:**

- based on valid, forward-looking criteria
- objectively applied
- resistant to political pressures
- dynamic.

---

Sensibly, underperforming customers should be identified at a regular, annual review, and then put 'on probation' for the next 12 months. Whether you decide to tell them in advance, or just observe what happens during the year, depends on your relationship with the account. Some companies are quite clear with their customers about what they have to do to become a key account, and therefore what they will have to do to stay as a key account. Others find this approach uncomfortable, and apply a mix of more subtle hints and negotiations.

Nevertheless, if no response is received, or you see that none is achievable, then restrictions should be placed on the resources accessible to the customer. Of course, you need to remember that these customers probably still give your company substantial business, so resource restriction needs to be accomplished with tact – but nevertheless, it must be done.

### 2.1.3  How many key accounts?

There is a ceiling to any supplier's capacity for intimacy.

Why would key customers spend their time with you if they did not expect significantly special treatment from their key relationships? Genuine KAM reaches deep inside a company to come up with the kind of breadth of offer and innovation that these customers seek. It requires a considerable change from traditional ways of working and, even if that is achieved, the capacity of a supplier to deliver this kind of treatment profitably is not infinitely expandable. There is a ceiling to any supplier's capacity for intimacy, which needs to be recognized. Hiring an extra bunch of key account managers to go out and be nice to customers does not shift the ceiling – but it may bring the house down!

Big companies with big customer databases often talk about their key customers as the 'top 100' or 'top 200', or even the 'top 300'. We can assume these have been badly chosen (usually just on past sales volume) and are inadequately served, certainly below the level expected by a key customer. As suppliers realize the limitations on their capacity to support key customers properly, they invariably tighten up on the numbers admitted to the portfolio.

Numbers of genuine key customers may range from about 12 to 50 (Figure 2.1). They may stretch from extremes of 5 to 75, but usually those at the

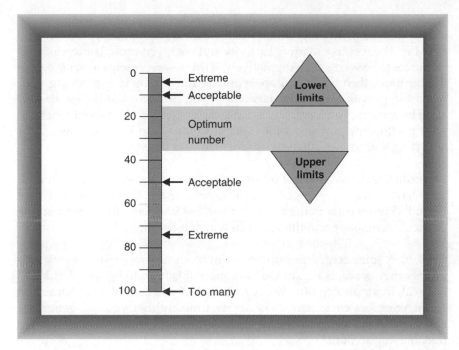

**Figure 2.1**
Key account numbers.

upper end of this range are actively working to reduce the number. In fact, about 50 key customers seemed to be the ceiling for successful KAM in even the largest corporations. The optimum number of key customers, i.e. that most commonly observed in companies running successful KAM programmes, is somewhere between 15 and 35.

Your company should balance the number of key customers it can handle with a number that represents enough business potential to make the initiative and the effort involved worthwhile. Adopt too many key customers, and

> The optimum number of key customers is somewhere between 15 and 35.

> Your company should balance the number of key customers it can handle with number that represents enough business potential to make the initiative and the effort involved worthwhile.

## Case study insight
### Controlling numbers in the portfolio

A global company started with a portfolio of 18 key accounts, which crept up to 34 over time. Results were outstanding – growth was double that of the rest of the customer base at no loss of gross margin. As the programme had been so successful, a decision was taken to roll out the programme to the 'top 250'. Unfortunately, the company could not cope with individual treatment for this number of key customers. Not only were the expectations of the new key accounts disappointed, but delivery of value to the existing portfolio began to break down as well. The supplier had to back-track on the status of most of the new key customers (who were nonetheless big and valuable customers) and was eventually left with 72 on its list, still more than it could handle well. The episode left a legacy of cynical customers and staff that will take some time to overcome.

you risk falling down on internal and external commitments, with a strong chance that the KAM programme will die a messy death. Adopt too few, and KAM will be seen as a marginal activity and not given enough attention and resources to be successful. Alternatively, if this few represents a major part of the business, then while you are reducing the risk by strengthening your relationships with these critical customers, you are also exacerbating the situation by growing your company's dependency on them. You should increase your portfolio by growing some other customers into key accounts and/or attracting segments of smaller customers to your business.

Nevertheless, it makes sense for novices to err on the side of caution until they have some experience to use as a benchmark. Somewhere between 15 and 35 is often about the right number, but it will finally depend on the particular company and the sector in which it operates.

Curiously, some companies do not seem to know exactly how many customers they count as key. In that situation, it is hard to believe that KAM is a real, living strategy in the organization. If you cannot even name and count your key customers, it is highly unlikely that you are genuinely managing them as key accounts, or that they will know and believe that they are key accounts.

## 2.2 Selection criteria

### 2.2.1 Identifying customers

Obviously, the potential of customers is fundamental in selecting them to be key accounts and, equally obviously, you cannot assess their potential

---

**Case study insight**

**Clarifying a key customer's identity**

Here is a discussion about the identity of a customer at the beginning of a customer selection workshop:

'So which key customer are we talking about here?'
'Nokia.'
'Is that all of Nokia?'
'Yes.'
'All of Nokia, including televisions, mobile phones, and any other divisions.'
'Oh no, not all that, it's the mobile phone division. Our sister companies deal with the rest.'
'So it's all of Nokia mobile phones, worldwide.'
'No, because we only deal with Western Europe. We have companies in Asia Pacific and the Americas which deal with those areas.'
'OK, so the customer as far as you are concerned is actually all the business units of Nokia mobile phones that buy in Western Europe?'
'Yes.'

until you have described the identity of the customer you are considering, which includes defining its boundaries. The identity of the customer is often simply assumed to be self-evident, but that can be dangerous.

In that case, the real identity of the customer was quickly clarified, but often this simple question provokes a lot more debate, either because it has never been clearly defined, or because it challenges the status quo in terms of who 'owns' various parts of the customer. Quite often, suppliers cut up the 'carcass' of the customer and hand out a limb to everyone in the family, but each separate piece is never going to have as much potential as the whole and, besides, maybe the arms and legs work together! In summary, beware of making artificial divisions of the customer ahead of rating them as a potential key customer; you can do that later, if you must.

> Beware of making artificial divisions of the customer ahead of rating them as a potential key customer.

Consider the case above: if Nokia moved manufacturing from Finland to Malaysia, it would inevitably result in a decline in business for the Western European part of this supplier. So, if Nokia is identified as the Western European part only, and if such a move were expected, it is unlikely to be accorded key account status by its current 'owner'. But treating the segment leader accordingly would be most unwise for the global supplier as a whole. Figure 2.2 illustrates the need for clarity when defining the customer. It can have a major impact on the extent to which you see true key account potential.

| Global, all divisions £500 m | Global, one division £300 m | One region, one division £100 m |

**Figure 2.2**
The importance of defining the customer clearly.

In fact, defining a customer in such a way is a figment of the supplier's organization, and often does not reflect the customer in its own terms. Sometimes suppliers justify the arrangement in terms of the customer's supposed purchasing history: 'They only buy from their office in this region, so it fits well with our structure.' But is that true? Do they buy in this way because you made them? When did you last check?

So even identifying key customers can be a complex issue, and because it can have far-reaching implications, it should receive proper consideration at an early stage in a KAM programme. Failure to do so can, at worst, result in

---

### Case study insight

#### Revealing a customer's true identity

One company saw limited potential in a customer who had been on their books for six/seven years, with fairly regular levels of business handled by a regional salesman. When he researched the customer properly he discovered:

- The customer was a global market leader in its field.

- It had 19 other sites in the UK which the company had not recognized.

- All of the other sites were buying from the supplier's competition.

This customer can be defined as one site with minimal growth potential (following on from the last six/seven years) or as 20 sites with huge potential, albeit with a strongly entrenched competitor. The former is not a key account, the latter may well be.

---

some very wrong and costly decisions and, even at best, it may mean that work done on evaluation and planning will have to be repeated when it is realized that the wrong customer identity and scope has been used.

### 2.2.2 Choosing selection criteria

> Your selection criteria should identify the customer's potential ... not just what they are delivering today.

Your selection criteria should identify the customer's attractiveness in terms of its potential for your company, not just what it is delivering today. Best practice companies work with a three-year timeframe, and some with longer. If you overemphasize current size or even current profit, you will put too much resource into those whose life cycle with you is maturing, and you will under-resource those who can grow. This is all too common, but under-resourcing growth is a serious problem when most companies (and their investors) quite rightly judge their performance on growth.

---

### CHECKPOINT

#### Avoid overemphasizing current performance by:

- Thinking about cases where you have grown customers and look at what it was about those customers that enabled success – did they have anything in common?

- Focusing on the customer – their potential, their position in their marketplace, their strategy – more than on your company and its current yield from the customer.

- Looking for customer characteristics and strategies that are aligned with your strategy – you will be investing in strategies that support their needs, and your alignment should win customer preference.

---

Try to involve a range of senior managers in arriving at your selection criteria, not key account managers themselves: these customers represent the future of your company, so you need a balanced, strategic and unbiased view. Indeed, the debate they will have is itself invaluable in uniting cross-functional views of what makes a 'good' key customer.

Having collected a large number of sets of selection criteria, we observed that they fall into three main categories, as shown in Figure 2.3. These all relate to specific, individual accounts. However, there is also a fourth, rather different, category, which contains criteria that represent characteristics of customers that are deemed to be 'for the good of the company', such as 'reference point' or 'innovation partner'. Such criteria are valuable if they are applied with caution and restraint, but often they seem to be a proxy indicator or excuse for customers who are particularly unrewarding financially. Suppliers may need reference customers and innovation partners, but only a few and, even then, they should not have to lose money on them.

**Figure 2.3**
Three types of selection criteria.

Suppliers should aim to have a balanced spread of criteria which will reflect not only how much business the customer could offer (outcome-based criteria), but how much business the customer is likely to offer (needs-based criteria), which is another matter, and how profitable it could be (attribute-based criteria), which is another matter again, as illustrated in Table 2.1. For each criterion, from any category, two important questions remain.

- How important is each in the view of your company and how should it be weighted to represent its relative importance?

- How can you measure customers against your criteria: what metrics should be collected?

**Table 2.1**
Characteristics of three types of categorization criteria

**1. Customer outcome-based criteria**
These are the criteria that come to mind first. They are generally:

● 'Hard' or quantitative factors, i.e. they can be unambiguously defined and objectively measured

● Outcomes that represent the business which suppliers like you could do with the customer; like:
  – purchases
  – margin
  – contribution
  – profit

● Factors that reflect the customer, independent of your company:
  – customer size/turnover
  – growth in customer's markets
  – spend with any supplier on goods and services from the category into which they put your company

**2. Customer needs-based criteria**
Customer needs-based criteria suggest the likelihood that your company in particular will retain the business, and are therefore:

● Aligned to your company strategy specifically

● Representative of the chance of your company securing and retaining the business (because your strategy will be aligned with the customer and you will be differentiated and supportive of their strategy)

● Qualitative but should be quite specific and are still measurable

● Factors that reflect your strategy, and are therefore different for each supplier; examples are:
  – global presence
  – dedication to compatible platforms
  – importance of low customer churn in their business

**3. Customer attribute-based criteria**
Customer attribute-based criteria represent what the relationship might be like and are therefore:

● Indicators of whether the business will be successful and profitable

● Perhaps 'softer' than either of the other two categories, but can still be quantitatively assessed

● Factors about how the customer may behave in relationships (which is not necessarily the same as in the relationship you have with them currently), like:
  – central decision-making structure
  – right attitude to relationships
  – prepared to pay for value
  – prepared to invest in relationships

---

**CHECKPOINT**

**Review your selection criteria:**

- Do they differentiate between customers?

- Are they stated clearly and unambiguously and can they be consistently interpreted by others?

- Are they measurable?

- Do they include a mix of 'hard' factors and 'soft' factors?

- Are there between four and seven in number?

---

### 2.2.3 Applying selection criteria

Rating and scoring customers in this way allows suppliers to compare customers who may be quite different, through bringing each back to a numerical score that reflects their differences, but still enables valid comparisons to be made. One customer may score well on potential size, but its attractiveness is genuinely reduced by its attitude to relationships, which will have an impact on the business. Another customer may be smaller, but is better to work with, and its overall score may turn out similar to the larger customer. Indeed, the profit each delivers to the supplier in the end may well be similar, which is what the score should represent.

Figure 2.4 shows how selection criteria are applied. Suppliers should aim to have no more than seven, and preferably fewer, which are chosen,

| Account attractiveness criteria | Relative importance weighting | Account A | | Account B | | Account C | |
|---|---|---|---|---|---|---|---|
| | | Rating (0–10) | Score (weight × rating) | Rating (0–10) | Score (weight × rating) | Rating (0–10) | Score (weight × rating) |
| | | | | | | | |
| | | | | | | | |
| | | | | | | | |
| | | | | | | | |
| | | | | | | | |
| | | | | | | | |
| | | | | | | | |
| | | | | | | | |
| | | | | | | | |
| | | | | | | | |
| Total | 100 | Total | | Total | | Total | |

**Figure 2.4** Account attractiveness assessment for selection as a key customer.

defined and weighted by senior management. These criteria are then rolled out to other staff who will rate the customers against them. Potential key customers are rated against the criteria and their ratings multiplied by the weighting to arrive at a score on each criterion. The total of the scores is the customer's overall attractiveness score. At an early stage, run a reality check with a few likely candidate customers, to see whether the relative scores turn out as expected. If they do not, do not necessarily make changes to the criteria or the weightings; establish whether, although the results are surprising, they also make good sense on closer examination.

In order to get as much consistency in rating as possible, the criteria will need to have measurements and scales attached to them. Ratings should be drawn up on a linear, 10-point scale:

- From the least acceptable for any key account, rating zero
- To the best that is anticipated, anywhere, in three years' time (or whatever time horizon is appropriate), rating 10 points.

Table 2.2 shows two examples, one of a quantitative criterion and one of a qualitative criterion rated against short scenarios. Each of your criteria needs to be supplied to the people scoring the customers with a definition and scale like these.

**Table 2.2**
How to scale and score selection criteria: examples

| *Example of quantitative criterion* | | *Example of qualitative criterion* | |
|---|---|---|---|
| *'Potential relevant spend in three years' time'* | *Rating* | *'Approach to risk and value sharing with suppliers'* | *Rating* |
| <£25 m | 0 | Takes win/lose approach | 0 |
| £25–49 m | 1 | | |
| £50–74 m | 2 | Prepared to work outside contract | 2 |
| £75–99 m | 3 | | |
| £100–124 m | 4 | Prepared to consider innovative solutions | 4 |
| £125–149 m | 5 | | |
| £150–174 m | 6 | Partnering: risk equally shared | 6 |
| £175–199 m | 7 | | |
| £200–224 m | 8 | Risk and reward equally shared | 8 |
| £225–249 m | 9 | | |
| £250 m+ | 10 | Trust-based open-book partnerships | 10 |

The process of key customer selection should be as objective and informed as possible – that is one of the main reasons for using a clear and criteria-based approach. So, while senior management should certainly be instrumental in determining the selection criteria, they should not rate and choose the customers. They rarely have a sufficiently close involvement to have the extensive, balanced and current knowledge required – but they might think they do!

At the same time, although key account managers should not misrepresent their customers in order to squeeze them into the portfolio, the temptation is there and many fall into it. To combine customer knowledge and objectivity, roll out the task of rating customers against the criteria to several people in each case, not just the key account manager. Other functions that have customer contact, like customer service, logistics and accounts, should be included.

However, arriving at a set of relative attractiveness scores does not yet confirm the identity of your key customers: their views need to be taken into account as well. The next section describes how.

> Senior management should not choose the customers.

## 2.3  Categorizing key customers

### 2.3.1  The key account selection matrix

Listing the customers that your company finds most attractive is not the end of key account selection – it is more like the beginning. Whether the customer will respond to KAM depends on their view of your company, and it would be ridiculous to ignore it. It is also dangerous to assume you know what that view is, without even talking to the customer about it.

The matrix in Figure 2.5 effectively captures these two views: yours of the customer (on the vertical axis), and theirs of you (on the horizontal axis), expressed in terms of your relative business strength with them (see Section 2.3.2). The size of the shaded circles can be used to represent the volume of business – either the customer's potential spend on the category of goods or services you supply (in three years' time) or their current spend with your company. A simple software package, Key Account Selection Matrix (KASM) can produce this matrix view from your data.

The key account selection matrix is, in fact, a four-box adaptation of the matrix developed by GEC, which is normally applied to markets rather than individual customers. It suggests that different customers, at different stages of their life cycle with the supplier, will therefore require and respond to different approaches. In managing these key accounts, it is useful to group them according to the way you intend to treat them and what you can expect from them, as well as understanding them as individual customers. The matrix identifies four groups, all of which are nevertheless key customers, and deserve complimentary titles.

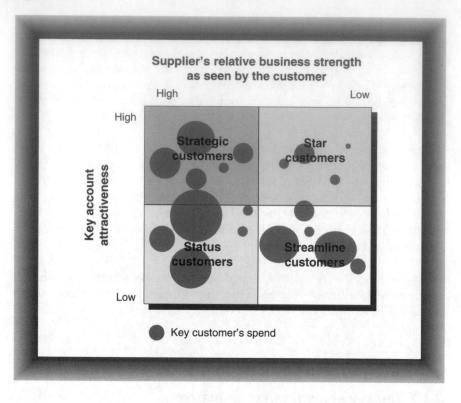

**Figure 2.5**
The key account selection matrix.

### Star customers

| | |
|---|---|
| Attractiveness: | high |
| Relative business strength now: | low |
| Life cycle stage: | start-up/development |
| Strategic approach: | invest for growth |
| Expectation: | substantial growth in volume/sales |
| Net free cash outflow: | present neutral/negative |

These are the strategic customers of the future. They probably do not do a lot of business with you at the moment, but analysis shows that they are the kind of customer that is aligned with your strategy and has good potential too. They do not rate your company highly, because: (a) they do not know what you have to offer, (b) they do know what you have to offer, but it does not actually suit their needs. If the reason is (a), you have a job of communication to do, but if it is (b), you have serious development and change work on your hands, and you will need to investigate the business case carefully before taking it on. In both cases, investment is required to change your position: probably more to change the offer than to execute the communication required.

## Strategic customers

| | |
|---|---|
| Attractiveness: | high |
| Relative business strength now: | high |
| Life cycle stage: | deep, close relationship |
| Strategic approach: | strategic investment |
| Expectation: | growth in volume/sales and profits |
| Net free cash flow: | positive, optimized rather than maximized |

The most innovative and important projects should be developed with these customers. Your company has a large amount of their business, but you continue to find ways of developing it further together. You make money from the customer, but you should also be investing on an on-going basis to bring new value to them, and even to expand the market through what you can offer together. Suppliers need a deep and multilevel relationship with such customers, requiring multiskilled key account managers to handle the relationship and the business.

## Status customers

| | |
|---|---|
| Attractiveness: | low |
| Relative business strength now: | high |
| Life cycle stage: | maturing |
| Strategic approach: | proactive maintenance |
| Expectation: | stable profits |
| Net free cash flow: | very positive |

These are very likely to be your strategic customers of the past: you have a great relationship, but you judge that their market or their business is not going to grow, so while they form a hugely important role in paying everyone's salaries and dividends today, they cannot deliver your strategic vision of the future. You need to treat them well, without lavishing your most innovative and exclusive ideas on them. At the same time, manage the cost base carefully to make sure profits are maximized, and that the excellent relationship you have does not allow them to draw down resources that they cannot repay.

## Streamline customers

| | |
|---|---|
| Attractiveness: | low |
| Relative business strength now: | low |
| Life cycle stage: | mature |
| Strategic approach: | manage for cash |
| Expectation: | low price, low gross margin |
| Net free cash flow: | positive |

These customers are the ones who constantly query the price, who negotiate on everything. Indeed, there may be less polite names you would like to call them. However, they are key customers because they give you a lot of business, and your company may feel that it needs the volume, or something else these customers can give you. Otherwise, why do it? There may come a time when you feel that you are prepared to resign the business, but until then suppliers should manage the costs very carefully, and make sure that the gross margin is positive, even if it is not large.

The position of the customer in the matrix suggests the outcome of some important decisions about them: on investment, management and pricing, for example. But as one key account manager commented on the exercise of constructing the matrix, 'It's an objective and transparent process. It should get better buy-in from everyone. There won't be any disputing that some customers aren't worth the effort.'

### 2.3.2 Relative business strength

Relative business strength represents the customer's view of your company as a supplier relative to the best competitor, whoever that may be in its view, and however it may view the merits of that competitor (rather than how you would see them). Since this evaluation is designed to capture the customer's point of view, it is important that the customer decides:

- the criteria
- the importance of the criteria
- how your company is viewed against the criteria
- how your best competitor is viewed against the criteria.

Second-guessing the customers' views is only the first step towards finding out what they really think.

In order to take a first cut of candidate key customers, however, you may decide to second-guess the customers' views, but this is only the first step towards finding out what they really think. However, it is legitimate to make a preliminary attempt at the customers' view based on the best analysis and evaluation you can do, in order to identify the customers whose attitudes should be explored further.

It is the essence of KAM that each customer is different, which includes understanding that each has different criteria for suppliers.

Try putting yourself in their position and considering what you, as this particular customer, would seek from a supplier for your kind of business. There will some essential performance requirements, and there will be some 'softer' factors, which will probably be to do with the customer's strategy and how you might help them (or not); what your company is like to work with; and what added value you bring them. However, research (Woodburn and McDonald, 2001) has shown that suppliers frequently mistake what customers care about and the extent to which they care about it, so you should realize that nothing is better than asking them. That will take time and money, hence the reason for a preliminary assessment to identify which customers should be investigated in depth.

It follows, therefore, that each key customer will have a different set of criteria, even compared with others in the same sector. Indeed, it is the essence of KAM that each customer is different and is worthy of being addressed on an individual basis, which includes understanding that each has different criteria for suppliers, and dealing with these differences. While applying a uniform set of criteria is entirely appropriate on behalf of one company (e.g. as in your account attractiveness criteria), it is entirely inappropriate on behalf of any more than one company (e.g. as in the customers' relative business strength criteria for suppliers).

Yet suppliers do exactly that, rationalizing it as 'keeping things simple' or, in reality, 'making life easy for ourselves' (even at the expense of common sense and success). In spite of that, many suppliers impose criteria supposedly representing the customer's view, which usually represent their own ideas of what worthwhile performance looks like, and apply it to all key customers. At a stroke, they have eliminated the opportunity to understand the customer's unique set of requirements. There seems little excuse for this nonsense (especially when there is uncomplicated software to help). Figure 2.6 shows an example of one customer's supplier criteria, which will clearly differ from another customer's.

| Headline criteria | Breakdown | Score 0–5 |
|---|---|---|
| Assured supply | Product quality management<br>Supply management | |
| Values/trust-based business relationship | Teamwork<br>Openness, honesty, fair play | |
| Management excellence | Quality management<br>Environmental management<br>Management depth | |
| Low cost – best value | Competitive validation<br>Process optimization<br>Financial strength | |
| System player | Communication<br>Best practices<br>Customer satisfaction | |
| Technical competencies | Health & safety<br>Product consistency | |
| Overall score | | |

**Figure 2.6**
One global customer's statement of its requirements of its suppliers.

To complete your preliminary assessment of key customer candidates:

- Identify the set of criteria that each customer would use, taking into account its pressures, its markets, its strategies, its performance requirements and its expectations of suppliers.

This table alone, completed for each customer, provides excellent guidelines on what to do to make progress with the customer.

- Give the criteria the weighting you think the customers would, bearing in mind that customers generally rate soft factors like 'easy to do business with' higher than suppliers rate them.

- Estimate their rating of your company against each criterion, based as far as possible on their current perceptions, not what you think they ought to be. You may think they misunderstand, or are ignorant or unfair, but the score should still reflect what they themselves would put down in real research.

- Estimate their rating of the best competitor on the same basis, and on any competitors who have distinctively different approaches. If you have no direct competitor in this customer, rate the best supplier of any goods or services that the customer is using.

- Complete the table in Figure 2.7.

| Customer: | | | | | |
|---|---|---|---|---|---|
| Suppliers' business strengths | Relative importance weighting | Your company | | Best competitor: ............... | |
| | | Rating (0–10) | Score (weight × rating) | Rating (0–10) | Score (weight × rating) |
| | | | | | |
| | | | | | |
| | | | | | |
| | | | | | |
| | | | | | |
| | | | | | |
| Total | 100 | Total | | Total | |
| | | Difference: | | | |

**Figure 2.7**
Relative business strength for comparative supplier evaluation.

This methodology brings customers' appraisals of your company to a series of scores that, while based on different criteria, can nevertheless be compared on a numerical basis. Obviously, a high score and a positive difference versus the best competitor says that as far as that customer is concerned, your company is excellent compared with the options available to it. A low score and a negative difference versus the best competitor indicate a poor perception from the customer, which has a better alternative supplier available. This table alone, completed for each customer, provides excellent guidelines on what to do to make progress with the customer.

The results of this exercise should be matched with the results of the customer attractiveness exercise and plotted in the matrix in Figure 2.5, which is then used as the basis for the provisional selection of key customers. However, before finalizing the key account portfolio, you must go and verify your assumptions with the customer, ideally through neutral third parties. In fact, best practice companies go and ask customers for their point of view even though what they hear may be uncomfortable at times, but poor companies just go on guessing.

### 2.3.3  Rebuffs and exits

**Rebuffs**

Only reciprocated relationships are real relationships. So you may want to put 'desire to have a relationship' with your company as an account attractiveness criterion. However, 'desire to have a relationship' is more like a killer 'make-or-break' clause than an account attractiveness criterion. Used as a criterion in account attractiveness assessment, the customer could score low on that count but still score high overall if it performed well on most other criteria. It could look like a company that must be in your key customer portfolio, being treated as a development or strategic account. That would be a nonsense, though, if it refused to have a relationship with your company. The best way to treat the issue is to rate the attractiveness of the customer independently of its 'desire to have a relationship' with your company, and then consider afterwards whether it wants the relationship, or could be persuaded to want it, as a final decision on how to deal with it.

Ultimately, however wonderful you think a customer is, if it does not want a relationship, and is most unlikely to change in the foreseeable future, there is no point in selecting it as a key customer. It may be that it is perfectly aware of what you have to offer, but is highly satisfied with a competitor which suits it very well, and has no intention or need to make any changes. Alternatively, it may be that its company philosophy keeps suppliers at arms' length. For whatever reason, if 'prepared to trade, no closer relationship allowed' is its settled view, including it in your key account group is futile.

The judgement would be different from that in which the customer does not have much relationship with you now, but would potentially be prepared to have a closer relationship if you positioned your company correctly. In the former case, it is assumed that you will get no opportunity to work towards that situation: in the latter, it is believed that it would respond, given the right approach.

**Exits**

In order to manage a customer portfolio, it must be possible to retire accounts as well as adopt them. Most suppliers find this difficult, and end up with unmanageable portfolios because inappropriate customers have never been cleaned out. But while these customers sit in the customer portfolio, they take up resources without making the level of response that justifies their staying.

> Only reciprocated relationships are real relationships.

> Most suppliers end up with unmanageable portfolios because inappropriate customers have never been cleaned out.

There are a number of reasons why customers may be inappropriately labelled as key:

- They are often very good customers who have been included because the supplier did not recognize its limitations in capacity for KAM and has simply selected too many (see examples in Figure 2.8).

- The supplier has overrated the customer's performance against selection criteria, and found out its mistake later.

- The customer over-represented its ability or willingness to respond to KAM treatment, whether inadvertently or by design, and is not delivering value to the supplier now nor will do in the foreseeable future.

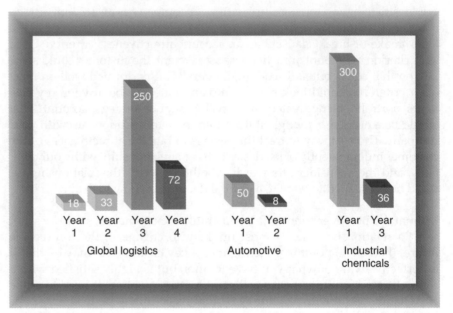

**Figure 2.8**
Reducing numbers
of key customers.

However the situation has arisen, it cannot be left unaddressed. There are two options for customers who should leave the portfolio: exit to the next tier down, or complete exit and loss of the business to the supplier.

- **Exit to next tier down**: Some companies opt not to tell the customer about its change of status, but carefully and slowly withdraw resources. Others are clear about it, in order to give the customer the chance to respond if it wants to remain a key account. The choice probably depends on relative power positions.

- **Complete exit**: Most suppliers find it difficult to let go of a major customer, even when it is clearly making a loss for them, and even when there was no other good reason for continuing to do business with them that gave any alternative value to the supplier. Sometimes letting such customers go can make a significant improvement to the supplier's profitability, but it should be regarded as a last resort, if the profitability cannot be turned round.

Whether a step down or a total separation, careful management of exits is an essential part of customer portfolio management.

Whether a step down or a total separation, careful management of exits is an essential part of customer portfolio management.

---

### Case study insight

**When losing customers put a stop to losing money**

Having had to make a major change in pricing strategy forced upon it by the marketplace, one supplier feared that it would lose some of its key customers. In fact, only a few of them walked away. The combination of the new pricing strategy and the disappearance of those few large, loss-making customers did wonders for the supplier's profitability, and over a fairly short space of time it moved up to the number two spot in the industry, from being number eight.

---

## 2.3.4 Categorization vs selection: portfolios vs lists

Treating your key customers as a list is a lot less appropriate than viewing them as a portfolio, as in the matrix shown in Figure 2.9. First, it is often assumed that once they are 'on the list', they have passed some kind of test and should now all receive the same approach and resource: an idea which this chapter hopes to have dismissed by now. Second, lists are generally seen as having a top and a bottom, so the notion creeps back in that there are customers at the top of the list who are the 'best', and almost inevitably, they are those with the biggest current turnover. Thus your carefully applied criteria-based process is bypassed and frustrated, and in so doing, your company loses a lot of good KAM practice aimed at optimizing the return on effort. Third, decisions about key customers on a list are commonly made on a case-by-case basis, often on individual contracts rather than via a proper view of the key customer group. As a result, there is a danger that the performance of the group will depend on a series of unconnected decisions and hence is likely to be suboptimal. In particular,

**Figure 2.9**
Unidimensional list vs multidimensional portfolio.

the longer term is likely to be traded off against the short term, and the short term may be compromised as well.

A supplier should be focused on the performance of its portfolio of key customer relationships, like a share portfolio.

Suppliers should focus on the performance of their portfolio of key customer relationships, like a share portfolio. When the customer is seen as a member of a portfolio, temporary shortfalls in some customers can be consciously balanced against returns from others. Managing key customers as a portfolio ensures that the supplier maintains a balance between those making a contribution through net cash outflow now, and those who will in the future. When customers are managed as individuals only, there is more pressure to maximize returns from each of them at any given time, which may be inappropriate and even detrimental to their growth in the longer term.

---

### CHECKPOINT

**To have real portfolio management in place you need:**

1. Customer categorization: a view of key customers as a group, subcategorized according to their potential.

2. Forecasting: an ability to forecast outcomes and model the responses to different levels of resource, given the customer's position in the portfolio.

3. Value-based prioritization: a process that compares the potential values of customers, and agrees customer priorities based on strategy and balance in the portfolio.

4. Resource allocation: a process of allocating resources in line with strategy and the optimization of the portfolio.

---

Some companies claim to manage their key customers as a portfolio but, digging deeper, they have none of the essential processes in place to achieve it. They have a view of the portfolio as a picture, but no more than that: they have not operationalized that view, so they cannot benefit from it.

### 2.3.5 Allocating scarce resources

In any sensibly managed company resources are made scarce, in order that those available should be used most economically. Key customers have the potential to eat up huge amounts of resource, so any resource within their reach needs to be managed very carefully indeed. In fact, their reach goes well beyond the key account manager, who is, effectively, the conduit through which the customer accesses the supplier's resources.

Even when customers have passed the first hurdle and been admitted to the portfolio of key accounts, their consumption of resources should not be standardized, but should be determined by their anticipated potential. Choices still have to be made about who does, and who does not, get resource-intensive solutions and tailoring. Failure to make clear distinctions between key customers according to where you expect to get the best return results in inappropriate allocations.

In our research (Woodburn *et al.*, 2004), we discovered that misallocation of resources occurred for several reasons, mainly:

- Lack of individual customer strategy: No customer policy guidelines existed to indicate whether there was, or was not, an accepted desire to develop with that particular customer, against which the merits of specific proposals could be decided.

- Lack of commitment to strategy: In spite of having clearly categorized the customer, its treatment in practice might be quite different from that identified as strategically appropriate. One supplier said, 'We throw more at our worst key account than we do at any of the others, in spite of the relationship.'

- Poor implementation: No process existed to link together individual decisions into a consistent customer treatment. Resource allocation was a series of separate submissions decided on their individual merits.

> 'We throw more at our worst key account than we do at any of the others, in spite of the relationship.'

We should add 'application of key account managers' powers of persuasion and influence' to that list. It is the responsibility of all employees in a supplier to use its resources as wisely as possible, but one key account manager's words, 'You have to fight for your customer, don't you?', represent a very common view. However, you should not be 'fighting for your customer'. If it has been objectively decided and agreed that investing in your customer is not the best use of your company's resources, then you should not be trying to gain more than allocated. You will be destroying shareholder value and might reasonably be accused of acting in your own best interests rather than those of your company.

So you should not expect applause for engaging in that kind of battle. If you won it, you would then have put yourself in the position of having effectively guaranteed a performance superior to that of selected customers – not just a good performance – and even then, you might not be congratulated for robbing your company's strategic customers of resource. So it may be tempting to massage the figures to get your customer into the programme, or to grab resources if it remains outside, but consider very carefully before you do so.

> It may be tempting to massage the figures to get your customer into the programme, but consider very carefully before you do so.

---

### Case study insight

#### Allocating resource selectively in hi-tech

A global hi-tech supplier was renowned for the quality of its R&D people. As creative, blue-sky thinkers, they liked to pursue exciting ideas wherever they appeared. However, the supplier discovered that a lot of its R&D time was being spent with start-up companies, which had bright ideas but were poorly positioned to exploit its innovations commercially. Meanwhile, key customers were being starved of R&D resources, so they were not getting the innovative products they needed to feed their well-developed markets. The supplier introduced a policy that major R&D projects would only be offered to key customers in the future.

Some companies have good, objective, criteria-based processes for evaluating projects, contracts or requests for tender that they might attempt to win (although surprisingly many do not), but relatively few bring the customer dimension into the evaluation, even in the simple manner shown in Figure 2.10. As a result:

● Important information is not considered, which would be indicative of the chance of winning the bid and/or its success in terms of profitable fulfilment.

● Resources are tied up by less important customers and are not available to strategic customers when required.

Clearly, as Figure 2.10 suggests, good projects in good customers are ideal and, just as clearly, suppliers should avoid poor projects in poor customers. However, an apparently good project in a poor customer should be challenged because it may easily not turn out as well as expected with a difficult customer; equally, an apparently poor project in a good customer may be explored and improved within the kind of relationship that allows that to happen.

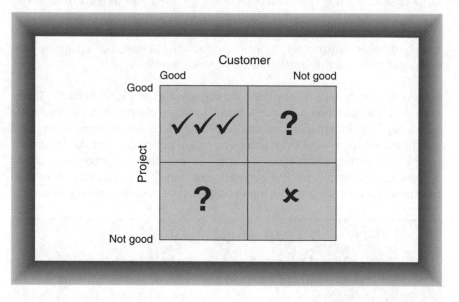

**Figure 2.10**
Adding the customer dimension to project approval.

## Summary

In summary, selection and categorization of key customers largely exist in order to ensure that resources are correctly allocated to them in line with your company's strategies, and with theirs. So your categorization needs to be backed by a sound and effective process that applies the categorization through identifying resource requirements, approving their allocation to certain customers and withholding them from others, and ensuring that these intentions are followed through in practice. Unless your company makes its categorization mean something, there is little point in doing it at all.

Selection of key accounts is often a contentious issue, as it obviously involves the non-selection of some customers that give the company substantial amounts of business currently, and/or customers that are important to particular individuals. People will fight to have these customers included; sometimes using internal politics, sometimes warping the data input to the selection process, or applying other means. You will need to be rigorous, vigilant and firm. There are a variety of onward effects of allowing the wrong customers onto the programme, all of them unfortunate and likely to bring the KAM initiative into disrepute.

In any case, as time goes on, there will be customers to take out of the key account portfolio, even if their selection was right at the beginning: their circumstances may have changed, or they may have made promises to respond that you now see they are not going to fulfil. Make sure you and colleagues consider the implications and process of relegation at the outset, so that you all recognize the necessity of relegation and agree how to approach it, before a specific customer is involved.

# 3 Relationship stages

Key account management (KAM) is very much concerned with managing the relationship with the customer, but remember that the relationship is a means to an end, that is, business development, and not an end in itself. Nevertheless, it is important to understand these relationships, which vary from simple, transactional forms to intimate and complex liaisons. There is a distinct hierarchy of relationship levels which describes the progression from the simple trading stage right up to a configuration that is only a short step away from a merger. Whatever level of relationship is reached, the requirements for efficient fulfilment of basic transactions remains, although a good relationship might allow a greater period of tolerance and assistance with poor performance than a simple, easy-to-exit relationship. Ultimately, however, a customer will have to buy from the supplier who gives them the offer they need, however good the relationship.

Both the key account manager and the supplier organization need to know what kind of relationship they have with each customer, and therefore what they can and cannot do with it. Suppliers generally have delusions of intimacy with the customer, and believe that they are one stage closer than the customer does. Since the essence of a relationship is reciprocation, then the supplier can only work with the level of relationship that both parties agree on.

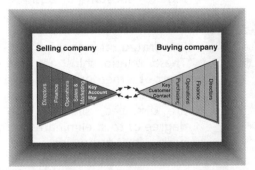

**Exploratory relationships**
Suppliers need to recognize potential key accounts from the outset and treat them as such. The bigger the customer, the longer it takes. Be prepared to be patient and manage internal expectations. Monitor the signals sent out rigorously.

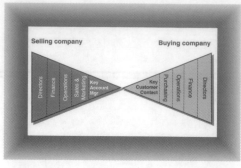

**Basic relationships**
This simple, transactional relationship has benefits of efficiency, clarity and resource control alongside its disadvantages of vulnerability to competition, fragility to change, potential for bias, limited understanding of each other and limited opportunity.

**Cooperative relationships**
To be regarded as a transitional stage, this stage is hard to control and likely to be losing money. It may be a necessary rite of passage, but not a stage to prolong. Key account managers are still 'out in the cold' and 'in the dark', and the supplier is not yet trusted, so the more positive feel has yet to be translated into real advantage.

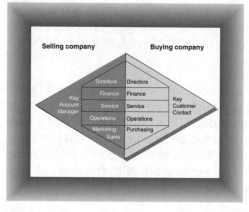

**Interdependent relationships**
This is the stage to which suppliers developing KAM normally aspire with the right kind of customer. These relationships involve trust, much more exchange of information, proactive strategies based on a much deeper understanding of the customer and opportunities for joint strategic planning leading to substantial business growth.

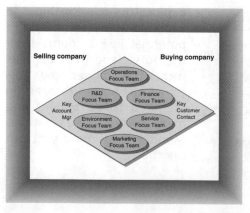

**Integrated relationships**
These relationships are just short of a merger. Boundaries between the two companies are dissolved, since a high degree of trust eliminates the need for protection. *Integrated* relationships are few in number because they take

a lot of dedicated resource, are not easy to put together, and tend to repel other customers in the same marketplace.

Even close relationships do not necessarily last forever, although there are some that have worked for decades. Disintegration may be driven by changes in the ownership or market position of either company, or by the supplier's failure to develop the relationship. Ultimately, the supplier has to be able to offer the customer what it wants, so a relationship, however good, cannot compensate if the supplier's product or service fails to meet the customer's needs.

## Introduction

Not surprisingly, relationships between complex suppliers and complex customers are likely to be complex too. They are made up from a web of people interacting with other people in the partner organization, which is not easy to manage. In addition, those relationships need to be supported by a web of internal relationships in order to respond to an ever-moving picture of the customer's needs, and to achieve effective and timely implementation.

Inevitably, these relationships will not be uniform, and quality and cooperation will vary with different people in different functions and different parts of the customer's organization at any given time. Nevertheless, it is possible to identify characteristic stages of relationship between two organizations that takes this variation into account. Several research groups have been able to describe levels of relationship, which the companies involved can also recognize.

Clearly, the way a relationship between two organizations works is different from the way a relationship between two people operates. A great deal has been written about interpersonal relationships elsewhere, so we have taken it as our job to discuss the relationship between two organizations. Parallels between person-to-person relationships and business-to-business relationships can certainly be drawn, but there are also major differences in how they should be managed and developed. This chapter describes the stages relationships can reach with key customers, while the next chapter discusses more specifically how they may be achieved.

## 3.1   Understanding key relationships

### 3.1.1   Why do you need to know?

In personal relationships, you behave differently towards different people according to how well you know them and what they mean in your life. If you treated your oldest friend with distant formality, he or she would be puzzled and upset: old friendships should be warm and relaxed, frank and open to new ideas. Similarly, if you treated an acquaintance like your postman or your child's teacher as an old friend, they would be equally puzzled and upset, or even offended and enraged by your familiarity. It is the same with intercompany relationships. If you have just started trading with a customer in a limited way, trying to involve the chief executive in a strategic planning workshop would be seen as unnecessary at best, and presumptuous at worst. Asking for inside information about the business may be greeted with suspicion, if yours is seen as a simple trading relationship, but it may be welcomed and even expected if you have a highly collaborative liaison with the customer.

You need to understand when you do not yet have the kind of relationship that entitles you to call on that amount of attention. Many customers have thousands of suppliers, so they have to prioritize their time very carefully (see Chapter 4). Your best plan is to:

- understand your current position in the relationship hierarchy,

- decide how far this relationship can go and how far you want it to go, and

- make a plan to move forward, matching your strategies to the stage you have reached.

Be aware of the fact that customers do not usually see the relationship in the same way as the supplier, particularly the key account manager (Figure 3.1). When we asked suppliers what level of relationship they had with a key

> Suppliers suffer from delusions of intimacy much more than customers.

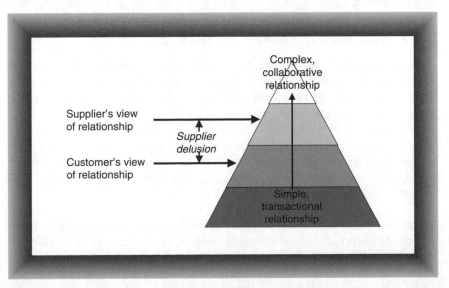

**Figure 3.1**
The relationship perception gap.

Only the reciprocated part of a relationship is effective. It follows that the rest is either an investment or a waste.

customer, and then asked their customers the same question, we found that the answers were almost always different. The supplier usually rated the relationship one level higher than the customer. But only the part of the relationship that is agreed by both sides can be real. If you think about it, you cannot be closer to me than I am to you. Of course, the reverse is true too, that your customer cannot be closer to you than you think you are to them but, in general, it is suppliers that suffer from delusions of intimacy much more than customers. In fact, only the reciprocated part of a relationship is effective. It follows that the rest is either an investment or a waste.

### Investing resource

It may be right to behave as if the relationship were more advanced than it is currently, in order to develop it to that higher level, provided that:

- you have calculated that the customer can and will respond,

- you are intentionally investing in the customer,

- you monitor the development of the relationship and the return from it, and

- you take action if progress is not achieved.

### Wasting resource

If you have somehow slipped into a stage of relationship which is one-sided and not moving forward, you should stage a cautious retreat:

- consider what you are doing that is not appreciated by the customer

- withdraw resources carefully to a more appropriate level.

The following sections describe the different stages of relationship in some detail to help you identify at what level you cooperate with your customers currently, and what that indicates in terms of your behaviour and opportunities.

### 3.1.2   The hierarchy of key relationships

For some time now, researchers have been aware of a hierarchy or ladder of relationships between suppliers and key customers (Scott and Westbrook, 1991; Dunn and Thomas, 1994; Millman and Wilson, 1996). Each group gave the stages slightly different names, but they are all clear that the focus of relationships of the lowest order is on transactions between the companies, while at the high end the focus shifts towards a highly collaborative approach to the relationship, in which the companies concentrate on combining their strengths to develop new, joint business initiatives that challenge existing boundaries.

Of course, the development of key relationships is a continuum rather than a series of step-changes, but different levels with different characteristics can usefully be identified. They can effectively be described as a pyramid, as in Figure 3.2. This way of looking at key account relationships suggests that each layer of the pyramid is built on the one below. As the relationship develops

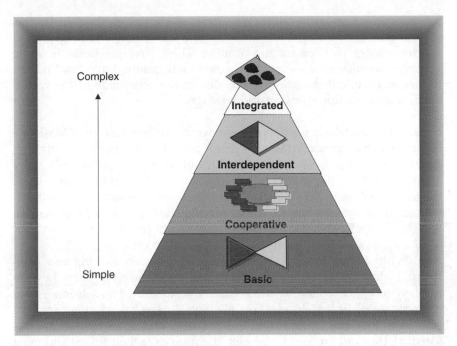

**Figure 3.2**
Hierarchy of key relationships.

to a higher, more intimate and more complex level, it still depends on the sustained satisfaction of needs at the lower levels and does not ignore those elements. They continue to form the base of the pyramid and of the relationship. A buying company, however closely involved with its supplier at a strategic level, still expects that its transactions will be carried out efficiently. Two characteristics define a watershed in supplier/customer relationships. Try the litmus test below for a quick check on where your relationships are.

---

### CHECKPOINT

#### For each of your key customers

1. Trust
   - Do they and their company trust you and your company?
   - Do you and your company trust them?

2. Mutual importance
   - Do both sides consider that they need each other and are important to each other, and are prepared to state that explicitly?

---

Trust implies that both companies believe that the other would not indulge in opportunism. Opportunism means taking advantage of the other, for example, maintaining or even increasing prices, assuming that the customer is ignorant of a cut in raw material costs which would actually enable a price cut. Trust, at least on the customer's side, does not really appear until the *interdependent* stage of relationship, which is the most common aspirational level beyond the *basic* stage. In addition, at lower levels of relationship the customer still sees that it can exit the

> Trust implies that both companies believe that the other would not indulge in opportunism.

relationship quite easily (although suppliers are rather shocked by this view and often do not share it), and only at the *interdependent* stage would it acknowledge its need for the supplier. These two questions therefore give you a quick idea of whether your relationships have reached the higher levels of collaboration or are still on the other side of the water-shed, at a transactional or transitional stage.

Portrayal of key relationship stages as a pyramid is reminiscent of Maslow's hierarchy of human needs (Maslow, 1943). Stated very simply, Maslow suggested that the needs of an individual could be positioned in a hierarchy according to the order in which they must be satisfied. At the lowest level, the individual has fundamental physiological requirements, such as food, water and warmth, and unless these are adequately fulfilled, the individual will show no interest in fulfilling other, less urgent needs.

At a slightly higher level, people have a need for safety and freedom from threat. If they are preoccupied with protecting themselves, then they are unlikely to be motivated by more esoteric issues, such as self-image, for example. At a yet higher level, people have a need for relationships that give them love and esteem from their fellows, and if this requirement is satisfied, they can proceed to develop themselves to their fullest and most creative potential. In other words, the motivation of individuals towards achievement at the higher levels of their capabilities requires underpinning by the satisfaction of more basic needs.

> The *basic* relationship requires the fulfilment of normal sustainable trading.

The development of key account relationships seems comparable with Maslow's scheme (Figure 3.3). At the lowest level, which can be compared

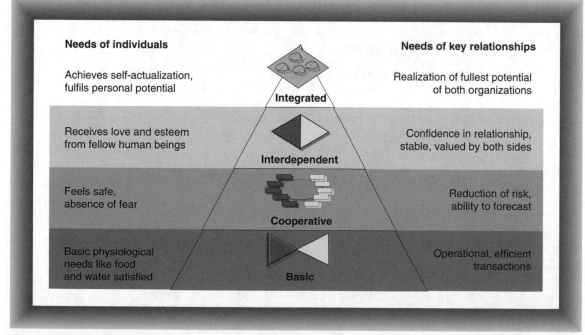

**Figure 3.3**   Needs of the individual compared with the needs of key relationships.

with the individual's physiological needs, the *basic* relationship requires the fulfilment of normal sustainable trading as a minimum; i.e. the efficient handling of transactions (orders, deliveries, payments and so on). If your company cannot manage ordinary transactions adequately it will, quite rightly, have little success in developing the business further.

At the *cooperative* stage, equivalent to Maslow's need for safety, relationships reach a point where the parties are, at least, no longer in constant fear of losing the relationship. Supplier and customer act in a cooperative way, rather than being constantly suspicious of or threatening towards each other. As the companies get to know each other better, they begin to understand each other's modus operandi and can predict the future, up to a point. It becomes possible to discuss forecasts of demand.

> At the *cooperative* stage, the parties are no longer in constant fear of losing the relationship.

The *interdependent* stage is perhaps equivalent to Maslow's need for 'love and esteem'. Both companies recognize their on-going relationship and this is reflected in their confidence and high regard for each other. Since neither company anticipates or considers termination of the relationship, both can adopt behaviour appropriate to longer term business development.

> The *interdependent* stage reflects both companies' confidence and high regard for each other.

At the highest or *integrated* level, the relationship is so close that the two companies act as a single entity without internal barriers although, by definition, it stops short of being an actual, legal merger. The companies trust each other and do not feel the need to operate protective measures against opportunism. The relationship can now be at its most creative, using the potential of both partners to develop innovative, mould-breaking strategies.

> At the *integrated* level, the two companies act as a single entity without internal barriers.

Relationships may start at the bottom of the pyramid and work their way up, but not always. Some will begin at a higher level, although it is hard to imagine companies entering into an *integrated* relationship without prior experience of each other. However, a fairly close relationship may exist from the outset if the product/service is very complex or customized, or particularly important to either or both companies. In those cases, the relationship may well spend longer at the pre-trading, or *exploratory*, stage.

Even among the elite group of customers selected by companies as 'key' accounts, the number of relationships that can be maintained at each stage becomes fewer as the level of complexity and collaboration increases. Logically, there is a limit to the number of close relationships that any company can sustain (see Chapter 2). Such relationships require the adaptation of standard offers and services, and the investment of time, money and people, especially people with sufficient seniority – and the supply of all of these is constrained.

Notably, *integrated* relationships are relatively rare, not just because of the resources they require. An *integrated* relationship with one customer in a marketplace, with all the commitment and joint activity that it implies, is likely to deter others from trading with the same supplier, as they, not unreasonably, fear that the best ideas, the latest developments and any exclusive offers will go to the customer with the *integrated* relationship. They suspect

> An *integrated* relationship with one customer is likely to deter others from trading with the same supplier.

Increasingly, companies linked together in integrated supply chains are appearing as the unit of competition.

they will receive second best, added to the danger of their commercial secrets leaking to their competitor. Major players are therefore likely to look for alternative suppliers with whom they can develop a similar position. Increasingly, rather than individual companies competing independently with each other, companies linked together in integrated supply chains are appearing as the unit of competition (Christopher, 2005).

---

## CHECKPOINT

### What kind of relationships do you have with your key customers, and how many of each kind do you have?

| Response | Score |
|---|---|
| Strongly agree | 4 |
| Agree | 3 |
| Disagree | 2 |
| Strongly disagree | 1 |

| *To what extent does this statement apply to the relationship?* | *Score* |
|---|---|
| Both companies would find ending our relationship difficult and complicated | |
| There is a real spirit of partnership and trust between our two companies | |
| Together we have produced long-term strategic plans for the development of our relationship | |
| Both companies have set up cross-functional teams of people dedicated to meeting the customers' needs | |
| People at all levels in the organization are in constant communication with each other | |
| Both companies acknowledge that the other is important to them | |
| Total | |

| Score | Relationship stage |
|---|---|
| 6–10 | Basic |
| 11–16 | Cooperative |
| 17–22 | Interdependent |
| 23–24 | Integrated |

NB: Remember, suppliers tend to overstate the relationship reached by one stage.

---

## 3.2  Stages in key relationships

### 3.2.1  *Exploratory relationships*

Where the potential importance of the relationship qualifies the customer as a future key account, it should be treated as such from the start.

The *exploratory* stage is the earliest stage of relationship development, before trading begins, so it could be described as a stage of investigation and development of understanding. Where the potential importance of the relationship qualifies the customer as a future key account, it should be treated as such from the start, and distinguished from the handling of the general run of new leads and prospects.

Failure to recognize potential key accounts early enough is a sad waste of opportunities. Unfortunately, some companies do not adapt their response to the potential, so they burn up resource in a relentless tendering process that delivers a uniform standard of mediocre bids, which are unnecessarily rich for straightforward customers and nothing like good enough for potential key accounts.

Needless to say, current key accounts can be lost, so the recruitment of replacements is critical. As major openings are few and infrequent, it is essential to approach promising prospects in the right way from the first contact, so *exploratory* KAM should be operated with those customers selected as 'key', and only those. Selection methods are described as part of the categorization approaches in Chapter 2. Ideally the same criteria should be used for selection as for categorization, but sometimes suppliers analysing their customers include criteria which can only be satisfied where there is actual business.

To decide whether a prospect qualifies for an *exploratory* relationship, the supplier should concentrate on customers which will support the achievement of its corporate strategy. For example, if the supplier's aim is to enter a new market segment, then it may target a well-regarded participant in the sector. Failing that, it should target a company which operates in a sector with similar issues, in order to tap into their knowledge of tackling those issues. If the supplier is attracted by the opportunity to learn from leading-edge customers, they should build their desires into the criteria they use for evaluating prospects, as in the example shown in Table 3.1.

| Key account selection criteria | Weight | Potential key account | |
|---|---|---|---|
| | | Rating (0–10) | Score (weight × rating) |
| Size: spend on products we offer | 35 | 8 | 280 |
| Strategic alignment: potential to use our planned product innovations | 25 | 7 | 175 |
| Rate of growth in their market(s) | 20 | 5 | 100 |
| One of top three suppliers in their marketplace | 10 | 8 | 80 |
| Has long-term relationships with suppliers | 10 | 6 | 60 |
| **Total** | 100 | | 695 |
| Minimum score to qualify as key account = 650 | | | |

**Table 3.1**
Criteria-based qualification of a potential key account

In an *exploratory* KAM relationship, the key account manager and the purchasing manager tend to keep the process of exploration very focused. They tightly control the amount of interaction with others in their organizations until a decision to work together has been reached. Typically, all communication will go through these two people so that they can monitor and control each exchange. They may interact on a regular basis, possibly over a long period of time, in order to bring the two organizations closer together. The *exploratory* relationship is represented diagrammatically in Figure 3.4.

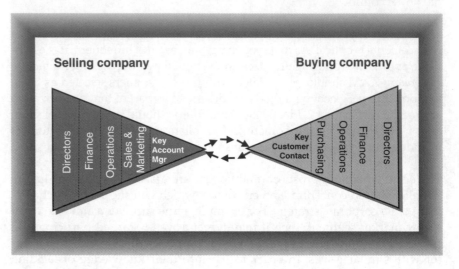

**Figure 3.4**
Exploratory KAM relationship.

At this stage, the companies have very little history of interaction or experience of each other, so they will be trying to form an opinion of each other, probably both on objective and subjective grounds. Like bats in the mating season, both seller and buyer are sending out signals and exchanging messages prior to the decision to get together. They will make judgements objectively based on the information they are given and, more subjectively, on 'signals' that may be generated directly by the other company, or indirectly by third parties. Reputations and signals are examined very carefully, and the impact of any event, communication or rumour can be magnified, sometimes disproportionately so.

On both sides, managing the signals transmitted and their implications needs to be a deliberate, conscious process and one supported by the whole of the organization. If the key account manager claims that his or her organization is flexible and responsive, then the purchasing manager will look for signs to support the truth of that assertion. Naturally, the claim will be discounted if, for example, instead of the tailored version promised, a standard service specification arrives with just a few suggestions as to how it can and cannot be changed to meet the specification.

At this initial stage of the relationship, the selling company will be courting the customer in order to explore its particular needs and aspirations; determine the size and scope of the opportunity; identify how it might differentiate itself from the current supplier; and understand how the decision on

> On both sides, managing the signals transmitted and their implications needs to be a deliberate, conscious process and one supported by the whole of the organization.

> Trust is a slow-growing and fragile seedling, which must be cultivated with care.

supplier selection will be made. Selling skills will be important, but care should be taken that pushing for short-term sales results does not destroy a larger, longer term relationship.

At the same time, the customer with an unfulfilled or underfulfilled need will be exploring the supplier's offer, capabilities and credentials, and quite possibly doing so with more than one supplier simultaneously. It is unlikely that either party will disclose truly confidential information at this stage, for trust is a slow-growing and fragile seedling, which must be cultivated with care.

The key account manager and the purchasing manager have to manage a difficult balancing act between investing enough to secure the business and using up too many resources speculatively. At this investigative stage, the major share of investment comes from the selling company, as the buyer asks for inspection visits, evidence of organizational capability, samples made to their specification, costings and other information which may not be readily available. All too often, the key account manager's requests for assistance in complying with these demands are seen by colleagues as an irritation and a secondary priority. Rather than being aligned supportively behind the key account manager, colleagues are busy pursuing other objectives.

> At this investigative stage, the major share of investment comes from the selling company.

---

### CHECKPOINT

#### For *exploratory* relationships

- Does the customer potentially qualify as a key account?
- Have you identified what you need to explore?
- Are all the signals the customer receives properly managed? By whom?
- Have you planned how to promote and back up your company's reputation?
- Has your company agreed how long it may need to work on developing this relationship and allocated resources to it?
- Have appropriate progress-tracking milestones been set?

---

### Case study insight

#### The consequences of misaligned views

The supplier's production manager saw his priority as hitting targets for a high volume of output and a low reject rate. He saw no good reason to compromise his targets by switching production equipment to developing samples for people who were not even customers yet. So production-quality samples promised to a prospective key customer were late: more than one deadline was missed and when the delivery eventually arrived, the supporting data were absent. By this time, the prospective customer had become sceptical about promises that real orders would be treated differently, and placed its business elsewhere.

Overcoming a lack of cooperation from other managers is one of KAM's greatest problems. The key account manager must have high-level status and/or top-level backing, and the implications of KAM must be made blatantly clear throughout the supplying organization. The stakes are too high to risk any unnecessary gaffes or avoidable mishaps that may prevent the relationship from ever getting beyond the *exploratory* stage.

### 3.2.2  Basic relationships

The *basic* KAM stage implies a relationship with a pronounced transactional emphasis.

*Basic* relationships are most like a traditional sales relationship, but they are still appropriate for a great many key customers. The *basic* stage implies a relationship with a pronounced transactional emphasis, in which the key account manager and purchasing manager are now in regular contact, although their organizations are still aligned behind them rather than alongside them. The standard trading management approach that both companies normally adopt will be applied, and no customized arrangements have been set up. The key account manager and the purchasing manager still expect all communication and exchanges to be channelled exclusively through them, so as yet no one else on either side has really developed a relationship with his or her opposite number. Figure 3.5 depicts a *basic* KAM relationship.

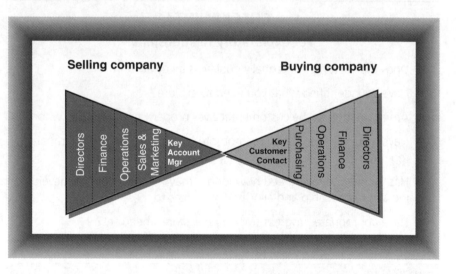

**Figure 3.5**
Basic KAM relationship.

Channelling interaction through a single point of contact should be efficient.

The interest level on both sides is limited, so the relationship is managed as efficiently as possible and, indeed, channelling interaction through a single point of contact should be efficient, even if it has other downsides. Responsibilities are normally clear, and communication and control simple, so overhead costs should be contained because the constriction of interaction between the two companies naturally curbs the amount of management time that each party can take up. Key account managers handling such relationships can have about five of them in their portfolio, so they have enough to do just responding to ordinary customer requests, without raising the activity level further. With everything going through the key account manager as the single channel of communication, he or she does not have the time to use up a great deal of extra cost or develop resource-hungry projects for the customer.

At the *basic* stage, neither party feels particularly committed to the relationship. The business is based on a stripped-down, simple exchange of money for goods and services that is not surrounded by extra systems and services valued by the customer which it would find awkward and inconvenient to surrender. The perception is that barriers to exit are low, especially on the buyer's side, and the key account manager is well aware of this. After all, the buyer is probably sourcing from a competitor simultaneously, so switching is not a big problem. The buying company may also use other suppliers of the same product/service in order to play one off against another.

In *basic* relationships the customer tends to be very focused on the price, which features heavily in discussions, negotiations and measurements of success. The key account manager is equally focused on his or her reward package, which is generally based on short-term volumes. With strong, short-term financial drivers in place on both sides, there is little room or appetite for relationship development and therefore for major growth. Supplier organizations do not seem to recognize the limiting effect of the incentives they commonly operate.

There is not a great deal of information shared in a *basic* relationship, partly because the emphasis on transactions limits the topics discussed, and partly because a foundation of trust between the two companies has not been established. If neither side is sufficiently well informed to be more proactive, then both parties will behave reactively, simply responding to situations as and when they arise. The level of exchanges is likely to be low generally, in terms of both quantity and quality. The volume of communication on operational subjects may be high, but this 'noise' level may be obscuring the fact that discussion on more important issues is not happening, and the supplier should not be misled into thinking this indicates a closer relationship than is really the case. The characteristics of a *basic* relationship are as follows:

- Transactional, emphasis on efficiency
- Driven by price, success measured by price
- Probably one of several suppliers
- Seen as easy to exit
- Single channel of communication
- Business relationship only
- Very little information sharing
- Reactive rather than proactive
- Driven by personal reward structures
- Standard organization.

> At the *basic* stage, neither party feels particularly committed to the relationship.

> With strong, short-term financial drivers in place on both sides, there is little room or appetite for relationship development and therefore for major growth.

**Table 3.2**
Advantages and dis-
advantages of *basic*
relationships

| Advantages | Disadvantages |
|---|---|
| Efficient | Seen as easy to exit |
| Simple | Driven by price |
| Clear objectives | Very little information sharing |
| Easier to control: standard approach single channel of communication | Reactive rather than proactive |
| Easier to measure | Overdependent on the relation-ship between two people |
| Key account manager skills more readily available | Open to biased view: coloured by principal contacts |
| | Easy to break up |
| | Hard to grow |

The most pressing problem is the vulnerability created by having only a single point of contact.

A *basic* relationship has its advantages and disadvantages (Table 3.2). It may deliver goods and services efficiently, but it is not robust, nor is it likely, for example, to create new opportunities in the marketplace or find major cost savings through process re-engineering. However, the most pressing problem is the vulnerability created by having only a single point of contact that may easily be opened up by the competition. This is a fairly superficial business relationship, devoid of any deeper commitment that might persuade a buyer to be tolerant of a mistake or to warn of impending threats.

Turnover of key staff is often cited as the reason for relationship breakdown.

Even if there were some kind of personal chemistry between the key account manager and the purchasing manager, should either person leave his or her job, that bonding would be lost. The successor might not be able or willing to continue the relationship and, indeed, successors often make a point of changing 'old' suppliers and bringing in those with which they are familiar. Turnover of key staff is often cited as the reason for relationship breakdown.

A *basic* relationship is indicated for large accounts that are aggressive price-fighters with no interest in added value, or no intention of paying for it.

A *basic* relationship is clearly not all bad, and in some circumstances it is the most appropriate. Because of its potential for efficiency, a *basic* relationship is indicated for large accounts that are aggressive price-fighters with no interest in added value, or no intention of paying for it. Some companies should always be treated in this way, because they adopt this stance in all their purchases. However, there are others who build closer relationships when purchasing their core inputs, but not when the product is not critical to them. Suppliers need to be able to recognize the difference, although it may be right to work within a *basic* relationship anyway.

However important the customer may be to the supplier, a genuinely closer relationship will not develop with a customer who is not prepared to reciprocate. In such circumstances, there is a ceiling to the level of relationship that can be attained, and any attempts to take it beyond this point are doomed to fail (see Chapter 4). Suppliers are wise to recognize this fact and avoid the fruitless investment of time, money and 'free gifts' in terms of extra services. Although the customer may happily accept an enhanced offer, it remains uncommitted, buying on price as usual. The supplier should only develop the relationship further if the customer meets strategic selection criteria, including a propensity to reciprocate.

A relationship can be very successful at the *basic* level, but it still may not be possible or advisable to develop it further, for a number of good reasons:

- The length of life of the relationship may be limited by changes pending in the environment in terms of legislation, technology, market, company ownership and so on.
- The buying company may be low-price focused and unresponsive to added value.
- The buying company may be known for supplier-switching behaviour.

In summary, a *basic* relationship is indicated when the overall lifetime value of the relationship is not expected to repay investment in terms of time, resources, customization and so forth. In order to decide whether and how the account should be developed and what objectives it should have, a deep understanding of the customer and the markets in which it competes will be needed.

If the relationship is at a *basic* stage just because it is new, then it may be effectively a trial time during which the selling company has to prove its ability to deliver its offer in an efficient manner. Buyers will obviously prefer to develop business with suppliers who have demonstrated that they can live up to minimum operational requirements. However, trial experience is not always possible, as in the case of major one-off contracts. As in the *exploratory* relationship, the supplier should be very aware of the signals it sends: even at this stage, it must always look like a supplier that has the potential to take on a greater role in the customer's business.

### 3.2.3   Cooperative relationships

The *cooperative* relationship becomes something akin to a network, albeit a fairly loose one. The key account manager and the purchasing manager work more closely together and now, in addition, the relationship involves a wider range of people and a wider range of interaction than before. Indeed, the people in the front line of transaction handling, that is to say, order processing and customer service, are generally in much more frequent contact with their counterparts than is the key account manager with the purchasing manager.

More people have an understanding and appreciation of the business than in *basic* KAM, though their contact may not be regular or frequent. Nevertheless, the growing web of involvement means that the business is better protected against the departure of the key account manager or the purchasing manager, but the major thread of the relationship still runs between the original two key players. Although the relationship begins to

*The growing web of involvement means that the relationship is better protected against the departure of the key account manager or the purchasing manager.*

draw in more people and harness more resource, it is not a highly organized state, so there are many things that can go wrong. The multifunction links of a *cooperative* relationship are represented in Figure 3.6, although they are shown in a much tidier way than they would be in reality.

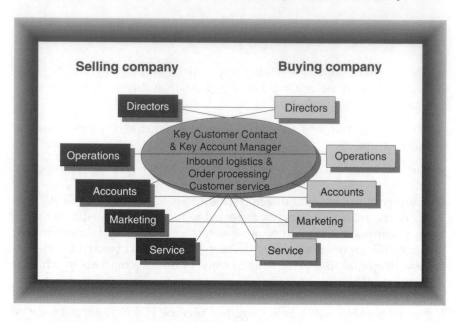

**Figure 3.6**
Cooperative KAM
relationship.

*Cooperative*
relationships are
messy and hard to
manage.

*Cooperative* relationships are messy and hard to manage. Clear lines of communication, responsibility and authority have not been established in *cooperative* relationships, and activity is at least uncoordinated, or even out of control. For example, you may find that just as you have sealed a sensitive deal with some people in the customer organization, your accounts receivable department has put the customer on 'stop' because they have exceeded their credit limit. Perhaps you did not tell accounts that this customer had a acquired a new status with the company and should be given a higher limit; or perhaps they do not know who is the key account manager, or even that one exists, and did not think of consulting you first.

At this stage, the supplier is looking for opportunities to add value for the customer, in order to develop the relationship, and the buyer adopts a positive and communicative attitude towards the supplier. The buyer may identify further opportunities to do business together or help you to solve operational problems that arise, rather than just passing them on. The underlying shape of the organization on either side does not change. The customer is still handled within the supplier's existing structure, and no significant organizational adaptations are normally made.

However, a social context begins to appear, often fostered by the selling company through organized events like golf days and trips to sports fixtures, or through smaller events like lunches and dinners. In the beginning, some of the most valuable gatherings are the more casual lunches or after-work get-togethers where people get to know each other in a more relaxed

---

**CHECKPOINT**

**Visualizing cooperative relationships**

Draw a model based on Figure 3.6 for each of your *cooperative* relation-ships. Put in the actual people and functions involved on both sides.

● Draw the central core of the relationship and the people on both sides who work together in it.

● Add the functions/people who have occasional contact as boxes round the outside of each organization.

● Draw lines between the boxes to show the links between them.

● Have you decided whether this relationship should move forward towards *interdependent* or backwards towards *basic*?

● Have you developed a plan to get this relationship under control and move it to the desired stage?

---

setting, having set work aside for a short period. This network brings new strength to the relationship. Participants become driven by a desire not to let personal contacts down, which is a far more effective motivation than formal statements of intent or customer charters. The key characteristics you might expect to see in a *cooperative* relationship are as follows:

● Selling company adds value to relationship

● May be preferred supplier

● Exit not particularly difficult

● Multifunction contacts

● Relationship still mainly with buyer

● Organization mainly standard

● Limited visits to customer

● Limited information sharing

● Forecasting, not joint strategic planning

● Not really trusted by customer.

Suppliers have more access to their key customers than they do in *basic* relationships, and that gives them more information with which to work. You may still feel that the amount of contact you get is not quite as much as you want (see Figure 3.7), and you know that there are other suppliers (possibly, but not necessarily, competitors) who get a much greater share of the purchasing manager's time. Like a climber reaching the first peak of a mountain range, the realization dawns that there are further, higher peaks to climb which were simply not visible before.

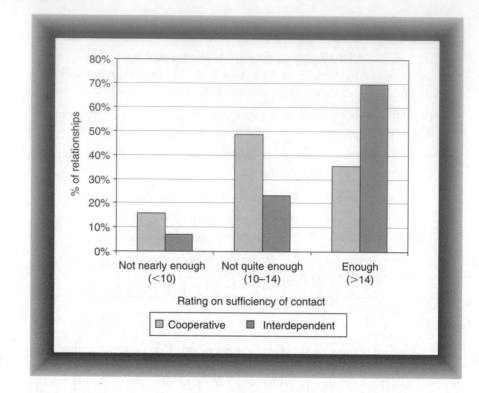

**Figure 3.7**
Contact between selling and buying companies.

The key account manager remains somewhat 'out in the cold' and 'in the dark'.

Visits to the customer continue to be limited by the time the purchasing manager is willing and able to devote to the type of product and supplier concerned. While information is shared across a broader range of topics than before, it is still confined to material that is fairly readily available. The supplier is not trusted sufficiently for the buyer to volunteer highly confidential information, and the key account manager remains somewhat 'out in the cold' and 'in the dark'. Joint strategic planning is not really possible and does not develop much beyond simple forecasts of price and volume. However, even forecasting constitutes useful progress compared with *basic* KAM, which may not offer medium term demand visibility, never mind demand security.

Exit is still not regarded as particularly difficult: inconvenient, possibly, but certainly not unthinkable.

Even at this stage, exit is still not regarded as particularly difficult; inconvenient, possibly, but certainly not unthinkable. The selling company has not achieved sole supplier status, and the buyer continues actively to scan the competitive landscape to make sure it is getting best value for money. The business is still very vulnerable to competitors, and another supplier with the inside track might gain advance information, for example, on new customer sites or new strategic directions, which is denied to a selling company at only a *cooperative* stage of relationship development. A competing supplier who has inside knowledge can work out an interesting and innovative proposition, long before the latter gets the same information.

So although a *cooperative* relationship has a positive feel, and is less defensive and more open than a *basic* relationship, some reserve remains; doors are opened, but not flung wide. More useful information is made available, but this does not include sensitive material, because the supplier is not really trusted by the customer. It is often at the *cooperative* stage that the real potential to progress the relationship is grasped, or lost. It is still an uphill task to break out of the cycle of limited information and limited capability to make better and more exciting offers to the customer.

It is still an uphill task to break out the cycle of limited information and limited capability to make better and more exciting offers to the customer.

*Cooperative* KAM can be a difficult stage, having lost the efficiency and control of *basic* KAM, but not having gained the benefits of openness and joint activity of *interdependent* KAM. Indeed, we believe many of the relationships with key customers that lose money for suppliers are at the *cooperative* stage (see Figure 3.8). At this stage, the supplier is probably spending a lot on the relationship, as the number of contact points and activities grows, but the customer is not yet ready to respond with a really substantial uplift in volume.

Many of the relationships with key customers that lose money for suppliers are at the *cooperative* stage.

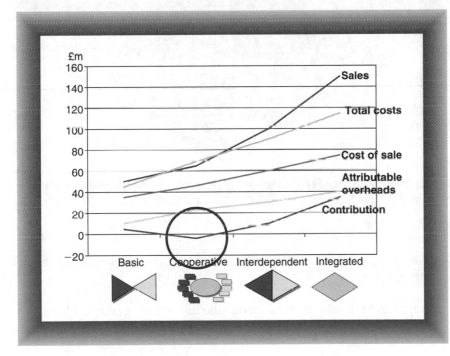

**Figure 3.8** Customer profitability and the relationship trap.

While making a loss on these relationships is not inevitable, they should certainly be challenged and their profitability be properly investigated and monitored. This view strongly suggests that sticking at a *cooperative* stage is not a good idea, so you should work to move the relationship forward as quickly as possible, or carefully take it back to *basic*.

### 3.2.4  Interdependent relationships

In an *interdependent* relationship, the organizations collaborate across a range of functions. Interactions are orchestrated and managed by, rather than channelled through, the key account manager and the purchasing manager, whose role is now to oversee the interfaces and ensure that nothing occurs which will discredit the partnership. The companies are locked into each other, not inextricably, though if the relationship were to end, retreat would be difficult and inconvenient. They may have set up various initiatives together, such as common working practices, shared product specifications and joint marketing activity, which would take considerable time and effort to unravel. Figure 3.9 shows how the two companies have become closely aligned, with direct function-to-function communication at all levels.

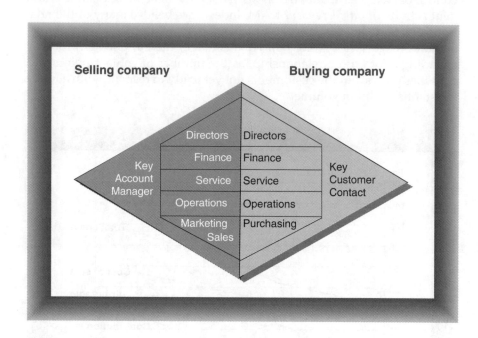

**Figure 3.9**
Interdependent
KAM relationship.

Remember, two characteristics of the relationship are critical in establishing the existence of an *interdependent* relationship:

Buyer and seller acknowledge the importance of each to the other.

● Buyer and seller both acknowledge the importance of each to the other.

● They trust each other.

If either of these is missing, then this is not an *interdependent* relationship. You need to bear in mind the optimism that generally leads key account managers to overestimate the relationship, because customers generally do not rate their commitment and trust at the same level as you do.

The management of this relationship is not at all like managing a *basic* or normal selling relationship. Instead of getting on and doing things him or herself, the key account manager needs to consider how to work through other people in the business, how to coordinate what they do, and how to gain an appropriate level of visibility of activity without drowning in communication and tasks. Often, this is unfamiliar and uncomfortable territory, but it is nevertheless what is required to do the job in these circumstances.

---

### CHECKPOINT

#### Visualizing interdependent relationships

Draw models based on Figure 3.9 for each of your *interdependent* relationships. Put in the actual people and functions involved on both sides.

- Have you explicitly stated how this relationship will be operated and managed?

- Have you aligned your company's functions and the people in them with the customers' functions and people, so they all know their counterparts?

- Does everyone know their role in this relationship?

- Do they understand what decision-making remit they have, and when it is and is not necessary to contact you?

---

There is a lot going on in this kind of relationship that cannot be left to casual, ad hoc contacts. We would expect that the selling company has now become the sole or first option supplier, at least, and the customer now regards the supplier as a strategic external resource. The two will actively share sensitive information and engage in joint problem solving. There is also a tacit understanding that experience and skills will be shared. The expertise of either, or both, companies may be directed towards product improvement, quality control procedures or administrative systems that underpin commercial transactions. A current focus will be the deployment of new e-commerce systems to streamline processes. The characteristics of *interdependent* relationships are as follows:

- Both acknowledge importance to each other

- Principal or sole supplier

- Exit more difficult

- Larger number of multifunctional contacts

- Developing social relationships

- Deep understanding of customer

- High volume of dialogue

- Streamlined processes

- Exchange of sensitive information

- Proactive rather than reactive

- Both sides prepared to invest in relationship

- Wider range of joint and innovative activity

- Joint strategic planning, focus on the future

- Development of trust.

The volume, quality and scope of information exchange increases considerably in an *interdependent* relationship, as more people in the selling company are talking to more people in the buying company. Strategic and sensitive material will be added to the information previously shared, which would have been more transactional and tactical in a *cooperative* relationship, and just transactional in a *basic* relationship. This new level of communication and interaction is a key driver at this stage of the relationship. The two companies develop a better understanding of each other in a business and organizational sense, and individuals build closer social relationships with people in the other company.

> The whole web of interaction and communication draws the two companies even closer together, like a positive gravitational pull.

The whole web of interaction and communication draws the two companies even closer together, like a positive gravitational pull. The two companies are reaching further into each other's internal environments and touching more points in the internal value chains. Team members from both companies often work together to lobby or gain senior management approval for a project. A selling company in an *interdependent* relationship is 'inside the magic circle', in contrast to the 'out in the cold' position those in *cooperative* relationships have to accept. Figure 3.10 shows the difference in information exchange between the two stages.

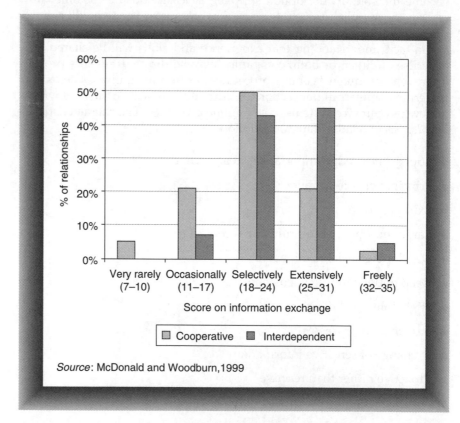

**Figure 3.10** Extent of information exchange between selling and buying companies.

Such is the level of maturity and understanding of both parties that each allows the other to profit from the relationship. Consequently, pricing should be long term and stable, perhaps even fixed, or varied to a formula that allows both sides to plan and removes the need for constant haggling/negotiating. Setting the expectations of both sides clearly and realistically at the outset is key to the building of successful relationships.

The level of maturity and understanding of both parties allows the other to profit from the relationship.

It is at this stage that what is arguably the most important benefit of excellent relationships with key accounts emerges: the opportunity for mutual cost reductions. At previous stages of relationship development the major opportunity for the selling company has been business development, but now, in addition, genuine cost savings also become available to both sides. In an *interdependent* relationship the companies are sufficiently well informed and familiar with each other to be able to work together closely to achieve those savings. Hence the emphasis on seriously nurturing a relationship that has reached the *interdependent* stage.

Arguably the most important benefit of excellent relationships with key accounts emerges: the opportunity for mutual cost reductions.

Companies in an *interdependent* relationship can focus on the medium and longer term future, rather than just the present and short term, and can adopt a more proactive than reactive approach to business development. Jointly conducted strategic planning begins to appear, though not in all cases. Where strategic planning is not collaborative, it is often due to the fact that the individual companies are still rather poor at strategic planning anyway.

A different attitude towards the relationship now exists. Senior managers have more confidence in the relationship's sustainability and value. They look more favourably on requests for investment into the development of the business, and are prepared to wait longer for the payback. Normally, financial managers demand a quick return on investment into customer accounts. They are much less comfortable about investing in a situation where they have little control over the use of funds (i.e. a customer) than they are with investing in their own people, plant or equipment. However, investing in a stable relationship should begin to look comparable with some of these other investments, especially if presented in appropriate terms, like a business case.

---

### CHECKPOINT

#### Talking to finance

- Do you know how to put together a business case for customers and customer projects?

- Did you put your last customer proposal to finance in terms of a discounted cash flow/net present value?

---

Mutual trust begins to develop, provided that, of course, each company has proved itself trustworthy. The key account manager and the purchasing manager must be vigilant and watch out for any opportunistic behaviour on the part of anyone in their own companies that might breach that trust. Trust must be nurtured at all times; it is hard won and easily lost.

Trust must be nurtured at all times; it is hard won and easily lost.

> **Case study insight**
>
> **Making the business case for finance in a global services company**
>
> One company reckoned it took a year to assemble and agree a proposal for investment with a customer. It took another year to deploy the money, making it at least two years before any return could possibly appear. In the initial stages of the KAM programme it was hard work to gain approval for such investment and little was granted. Then one key account manager worked closely with an accountant to put his proposals in sound financial terms and, with some reluctance, the proposal was accepted. After several projects with key customers, prepared in appropriate financial terms, the company was more comfortable with such projects and the key account managers were more comfortable with making them in the language of finance.

For example, if the selling company gains a raw material cost reduction, the production manager or product manager may decide to maintain prices to improve the profitability of the line, at least until the competition appears to be reducing their prices. That may be fine for the bulk of customers, but if key customers in an *interdependent* relationship are not informed of the cost reduction, they would see exclusion from sharing in the cost savings as opportunism on the part of the selling company, and react adversely.

Care must be taken to avoid breaches of trust inadvertently as well as deliberately, and to ensure that everyone is aware what constitutes a breach of trust in the customer's eyes. It is critical that all those involved with the relationship, in any respect, are aware of the way in which the particular customer should be treated in order to ensure that any action or decision will build, and not undermine, the position of trust achieved. *Interdependent* relationships are too precious to break accidentally.

### 3.2.5   *Integrated relationships*

The two parties come together to operate as a single entity to create value over and above what either could achieve individually.

In a few cases, it may be possible for the seller/buyer relationship to advance beyond a separated, albeit interdependent, partnership. In an *integrated* relationship the two parties come together to operate as a single entity, while maintaining their separate identities, to create value over and above what either could achieve individually. External boundaries as well as internal boundaries now fall away as the two companies realize that together they can accomplish feats previously unimaginable to either.

Integrated KAM involves working together in cross-boundary functional or project teams, as depicted in Figure 3.11. By this means the organizations become so intertwined that individuals may feel more affinity with their focus team than with their official employer. The borders between buyer and seller have become blurred. The teams, rather than either organization,

### Case study insight
#### Outsourcing a vital function

Fashion is a fast-moving and fickle industry that lives or dies by its latest collection. In order to concentrate on designing and producing new clothes, a leading fashion brand decided to focus its own people and resources on the supply side and to outsource the management of its warehouse and delivery logistics to a specialist company. This company employs the logistics director, although he is treated as if he were head of one of the manufacturer's own functions. He sits on the board and has the same access to information as any other director. The two companies keep very few secrets from each other, and the service is run on a completely open-book basis.

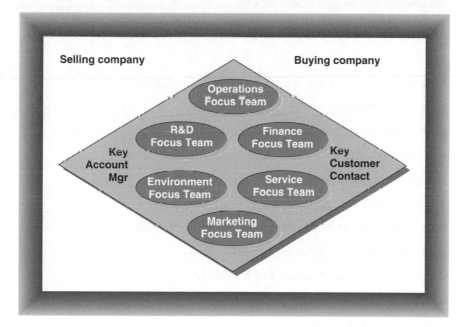

**Figure 3.11**
Integrated KAM relationship.

run the business, making decisions about their interactions with other teams according to the strategy they are implementing. Staff may even be based at the partner's premises, though not necessarily. If it came, exit would be traumatic at both personal and organizational levels.

The roles of the key account manager and the purchasing manager have fundamentally changed. The appearance of competent teams to handle day-to-day processes and develop specified projects enables these two people to assume a more strategic role, ensuring that the whole business is moving in a profitable and sustainable direction. Troubleshooting should have become a very minor part of their activity.

The focus teams may be functional, issue based or project based. They will meet regularly, or have their own communications networks if meeting is difficult, as in global relationships. Data systems will be integrated, information flow streamlined and barriers removed. A single business plan can now be produced, linking back into the planning processes of the two organizations. *Integrated* relationships are characterized by openness and transparency that allows everyone to get on with the job of creating new value for the relationship, rather than defending themselves against the other party.

More of the benefits that start to flow from an *interdependent* relationship can be realized now. There is greater confidence in the trustworthiness and commitment of both parties, which allows further disclosures such as transparent costing and openness on even the most sensitive subjects. The feeling shared by both companies that 'we are in this together' transcends normal defensive business behaviour. The characteristics of an interdependent relationship are as follows:

- Real partnership: complementary, mutually dependent
- Few in number
- Sole supplier, possibly handling secondary suppliers
- High exit barriers, exit is traumatic
- Individual organizations subsidiary to team socially
- Dedicated, cross-boundary functional/project teams
- Open information sharing on sensitive subjects
- Transparent costing systems
- Assumption of mutual trustworthiness, at all levels
- Abstention from opportunistic behaviour
- Lowered protection against opportunism
- Joint long-term strategic planning
- Better profits for both.

*The number of companies who have even one integrated relationship appears to be small.*

Each *integrated* relationship requires the dedication of considerable resource from both sides, and the number of customers with whom a company can have this kind of relationship must therefore be very few. In fact, the number of companies who have even one *integrated* relationship appears to be small.

*It would be difficult to operate two such relationships in parallel within the same market area.*

It would be difficult, in most cases, to operate two such relationships in parallel within the same market area. In fast-moving consumer goods especially, advertising agencies work closely with their major clients, often for a very long time, but they can only work with one such client in each sector. Top clients are unwilling to trust an agency that is working with a competitor, however much it claims to operate sealed cells inside its business.

Since both parties work so closely together in an *integrated* relationship, any opportunistic behaviour would be spotted very quickly. In fact, as the relationship will have established itself within both companies and its value will be generally accepted, the chances of anyone taking inappropriate decisions should be much less than at the lower level of relationship development.

Mutually transparent costing in this kind of relationship should not be mistaken for the approach used in some sectors, such as retail and car manufacturing, where powerful buyers have demanded open-book accounting from suppliers in a weak position, in return for continuing to do business at all. A liaison between unequals, in which certain aspects of a relationship are dictated by the more powerful partner, should not be confused with a genuinely open and collaborative relationship with a key account.

Overall, an *integrated* relationship offers the best chance of maximizing opportunities to cut costs, develop a broader business base, enhance expertise, make creative and innovative approaches to the market, and secure a long-term future. As relationships at the *integrated* stage cannot be numerous, they should be especially well chosen and very well managed.

### 3.2.6 Disintegrating relationships

At any time and at any stage, the relationship can fall apart. Breakdown may occur for one or more of a number reasons (Table 3.3), for example, a takeover of either company, that changes its position in the marketplace and means that it now competes with the other company in some way. Changes of key people, especially the principals engaged in the relationship; changes in structure, so that production is moved to another country; changes in culture, from added-value to lean; and indeed, many other changes, are potentially dangerous.

Price or product is rarely the reason for relationship breakdown.

| Change | Relationship | Performance |
|--------|--------------|-------------|
| Key personnel<br><br>Market positions<br><br>New culture, organization ownership | Key account manager's approach or lack of skills<br><br>Failure to forge multilevel links<br><br>Breach of trust<br>Complacency | Prolonged poor performance against agreed programme |

**Table 3.3**
Causes of *disintegrating* relationships

Price or product is not that often the reason for relationship breakdown. Ultimately, however, a customer will have to buy from the supplier who gives them what they need, however good the relationship, so suppliers cannot afford to be complacent about their core offer. Relationships facilitate business: they are not an end in themselves, and you should remember that they are not what the customer is buying.

Poor performance is much less often the cause of disintegration than might be supposed, at least, not from an *interdependent* relationship. In fact, if a supplier has built up a good relationship, then it may get a surprising amount of tolerance for poor performance, provided that the customer understands what the supplier is planning to do to remedy the situation, and sees that it is making every effort to implement the remedy.

More commonly, disintegration is caused by failure at the heart of the relationship, which depends very much on the key account manager. Some customers are quite clear with their supplier if they do not like their key account manager, and get a replacement, but others would rather give up on the relationship without explaining why. Customers are frequently frustrated by the inability of the key account manager or supplier organization, or both, to appreciate the vision of what they are trying to achieve and to be prepared to play a part in it, rather than just sell goods or services. In some cases this is a limitation of the key account manager, but in other cases it is the fault of a 'deaf' and complacent supplier.

So a failure to forge multilevel links with the customer may be the key account manager's fault, but it may equally be the fault of the supplier, which does not have and is not prepared to develop an interesting proposition for the customer that would warrant the attention of anyone other than the buyer.

The business developer who was ideal at the growth stage is unlikely to be the right person to manage a *disintegrating* relationship.

Disintegration can be sudden and followed by exit, or it may be prolonged through a return to a lower level of relationship where the companies continue to do business together, but on different terms. In any case, *disintegrating* KAM is a purely transitional stage, not a stable state, as any of the other stages can be. Given the complexity of some relationships and the variety of links involved, disengagement may take some time, so *disintegrating* KAM may last for quite a long while.

The key account manager's role may change to one of damage limitation. The business developer who was ideal at the growth stage is unlikely to be the right person to manage a *disintegrating* relationship.

## Summary

Understanding the nature of key relationships, and the behaviour of companies involved in them, is crucial to the profitable management of the business they represent. Without it, companies can easily attempt inappropriate strategies, which are unlikely to succeed. Failure may be expensive, both in terms of actual expenditure and lost opportunity.

Five stages of key supplier/customer relationships have been identified. To characterize the nature of the relationship from the point of view of either party, they are described as *exploratory* (precedes actual trading), *basic, cooperative, interdependent* and *integrated*. Relationships may develop progressively through each stage in turn, or they may not. They can also start at a fairly mature stage in certain circumstances where multi-sourcing is inappropriate, for example, or they can remain at any given level indefinitely.

Disintegration may occur at any stage, for a large number of reasons. More distant, less sophisticated relationships (*basic, cooperative*) are more vulnerable than closer relationships (*interdependent, integrated*), which is why suppliers, in particular, are often keen to develop them further. However, companies have a limited capacity for intimacy, partly because of the potentially heavy costs associated with key relationships, and they should choose very carefully the partners with whom they wish to develop close ties.

Suppliers at a lower stage of relationship development have to work hard to overcome the self-perpetuating cycle of being kept 'in the dark' and 'out in the cold'. Recognition of their current relationship position should at least help them to identify what action to take in order to break the pattern.

The key features of the five types of relationship are summarized in Table 3.4.

**Table 3.4** Summary of development stage characteristics

| Relationship feature | Exploratory | Basic | Cooperative | Interdependent | Integrated |
|---|---|---|---|---|---|
| Relationship emphasis | Research, reputation | Transactional and price | Mainly transactional but positive | Mutual and developmental | Open and strategically focused |
| Supplier status | One of several/many | May be one of several | Preferred | Principal or sole, possibly managing secondary suppliers | Sole, possibly primary |
| Ease of exit | Easy: not started trading | Easy | Not difficult, slight inconvenience | Difficult | High exit barriers, separation traumatic |
| Information sharing | Careful, as necessary | Very little, based around transactions | Limited | High volume, some sensitive | Open, even on sensitive subjects |
| Contact | Channelled through individual KAMgr | Channelled through KAMgr and Buyer | Close: KAMgr and Buyer, Logistics and Order Processing. Occasional: others | Close: all functions as necessary | Intimate: focus groups and teams |
| Access to customer | Customer request only | Limited | More, but not quite enough | Much more, enough | Constant, both sides |
| Adaptation of organization and processes | Standard | Standard | Mainly standard | Streamlining of processes, some organizational adaptation | Joint processes, new organization |
| Relationship costs | May be small or large. Speculative investment | Limited | Increasing for selling company, few savings if any | Major running costs and investment, offset by savings and more business | As for interdependent: probably larger sums but easier to identify |
| Level of trust | Exploring reputation and 'signals' | Neither trusted nor mistrusted | Not wholly trusted | Real trust developing, protective barriers lowered | Trustworthiness assumed at all levels |
| Planning | Variable | Little or none, probably only short-term forecasts if any | Forecasting rather than planning | Joint strategic planning, though not all cases | Joint strategic, long-term planning |
| Relationship potential | Important, to qualify as key account | Limited | Could be good, but not easy to win from here | Very good | Very good/excellent in revenue and profits |

# 4 Developing key relationships

Most companies embarking on key account management (KAM) are hoping to develop their customer relationships. We hope you will do so having first decided, very carefully, which ones are suitable for development – because some are not.

But what does deciding to develop a relationship mean? How do you know where to start? Charm has very limited leverage in corporate purchasing today and, indeed, the procurement department will make sure that it does not count for much. If you want to be a key supplier, much more tangible value is expected.

In fact, the way to a customer's heart is through its business – not your business. As a minimum, the customer expects its key suppliers to understand:

- Its marketplace
- Its strategies
- What its customers want
- How it adds value in its business
- Where it makes its money.

There are no shortcuts that are likely to last, so Chapters 7 and 8 give you a systematic process to gain the deep customer understanding you need, plus a process to help you come up with strategies that add value to the customer's business. Added value (for the customer, not necessarily for you) is what gains commitment. Your company is expected to bring an on-going stream of value propositions to the customer, and you cannot possibly do that without a real understanding of what adds value and why, where and when.

Customers classify suppliers according to the potential they have to bring value to their business, in terms of the supply-side market risk and their purchasing power. If what you have to offer is, in the customer's eyes, a commodity product delivered in a commoditized way, you are wasting your time trying to build a relationship. What would they gain? Customers, like suppliers, have a limited capacity for intimacy, and they will use what capacity they have where it gives them most advantage.

Given a strong foundation of customer understanding, relationship development can be accelerated through doing a good job of mapping the people inside the customer who matter to you, and deciding with whom you want to have your relationships. You should also decide who, in your organization, will be the 'owner' of that relationship – no key account manager can or should 'own' them all. Rather, it is the key account manager's job to encourage and build a balanced set of relationships from top to bottom of both organizations, supporting the supplier's staff in working out strategies to help their counterparts in the customer organization. Rather than responding to purely personal needs, ideally, they will be adding value to the contact's working life and area of the business, which is a more robust way to build a relationship anyway.

Many people seem to believe that relationships 'just grow', but if you have good business development strategies and adopt a process of applying them through good relationship development strategies, you should really be a winner with your customers. Try picking the features of an *interdependent* relationship and working on those alongside your business development strategies. The synergistic effect of the two together should give the relationship and its outcomes some real acceleration. Having achieved the relationship your company wants, there are a few traps to be avoided. They may seem obvious when simply stated but, sadly, they appear quite frequently:

- complacency
- lapses in integrity
- leaking profitability.

Relationships with key customers can and should be developed with purpose and with process (see Chapter 9). These relationships are too valuable and too risky to leave to any less focused approach.

**In this chapter**

# Introduction

Suppliers are keen to push their key account managers out of the office to develop relationships with customers, frequently overlooking the obvious fact that customers have a strong point of view of their own on whether it is worth spending time with your company or not. Not surprisingly, customers do not care whether the conversation would add value to your business. They are as short of resources as any other company, and they cannot afford to waste them in conversations that add no tangible value to their business.

So when key account managers do get in front of a customer, they need to have something interesting to say, which means they need a real and deep understanding of the customer's business, just as a beginning. This chapter describes what customers now expect from their key suppliers, while Chapter 7 explains how to analyse a customer to gain the level of understanding required. Chapter 8 goes on to show how to create worthwhile strategies that keep the customer interested.

Running alongside the development of those business strategies, however, there should also be relationship development strategies. While not enough on their own, suppliers can apply some useful tools and techniques to develop their relationships more quickly and more successfully.

## 4.1 The customer's point of view

### 4.1.1 What do customers want?

The kind of customer that is attractive to your company is probably seen as equally attractive to your competitors. They are likely to be the market leaders, the innovative companies who succeed and go on succeeding, year in and year out. Either they already have a very substantial business which is still growing, or they have great potential and are on a steep upward path. Such companies have plenty of choice in suppliers, and if your company is not giving them what they want, they will be welcomed with open arms by your competition. Having said that, most customers do not want the upheaval and cost of changing suppliers unless they have good reason to change.

Obviously, if customers are getting what they want from a relationship, then they will stay with it. However, suppliers often fail to recognize all the potential benefits of the relationship to the customer, so they overestimate the value of a few of elements of support they offer, and oversupply them too, while underestimating the importance of some of the other things they can do.

Some worthwhile initiatives might appear from seeing a broader list of benefits, such as that below, which was collated from the advantages cited by customers in our research:

- Trust – always behaving appropriately
- Leverage – something unique, and not always price
- Unique competitive advantage/customization – or else why bother?
- Cost reduction – without sacrificing value targets
- Simplicity – reducing their complexity
- Continuity – being around in the future as well as the present
- Supply chain integration – smoother, cheaper
- Global consistency – the same offer, anywhere
- Consultancy – calling on the supplier's expertise
- Strategic concentration of resources and investment – where worthwhile.

Above all, customers want suppliers they can trust and with whom they can build open, trusting relationships. Trust may be defined as: 'The expectation that a company will behave in a predictable and mutually acceptable way.' That works up to a point, but a customer expects more from a supplier with which it has substantial business and a close relationship than it does from one from which it buys a modest amount of commodity products. Indeed, the customer looks for different minimum levels of trustworthiness at different stages in the relationship, as Figure 4.1 shows.

**Figure 4.1**
Customer expectations of minimum levels or trust and relationship.

Most customers have thousands of suppliers, and if the bulk of them fulfil the terms of their contracts, that will be seen as quite adequate in transaction-focused relationships and is, indeed, the least that is expected in any trading relationship. Relationships would not reach a *cooperative* stage unless the customer believed in the supplier's competence, but even that is not enough for a key supplier at an *interdependent* stage of relationship. Key customers interpret trustworthiness differently at this level, and they look for a flexible response within the spirit of the relationship which is known as 'goodwill trust', when the customer expects that, however circumstances change, the supplier will endeavour to deliver what is best to meet new needs.

> Key customers expect a flexible response within the spirit of the relationship, not the letter of the contract.

Trust may be the first thing that customers want from a key supplier, but it is not the last thing, by any means. As David Heede, Director of Purchasing at Coors Brewers said, 'We want a key supplier who shares our vision and is a competitive weapon for us! We expect tangible, measurable, substantive evidence of (suppliers') short-term contribution toward our long term vision.'

> 'We want a key supplier who shares our vision and is a competitive weapon for us!'

In common with many other key customers, Heede looked for suppliers who anticipated his company's needs. He wanted proactive suppliers who would spot supply chain weaknesses, point them out and help come up with solutions. Some suppliers still say, 'We'll do anything the customer asks us to do', without realizing that the customer sees innovation in the supplier's offer as the supplier's job, not theirs. After all, the customer is not an expert in your business, so how can you expect them to know what to ask for? However, if you are an expert in their business, and also understand your own, then you should be able to suggest some new and relevant ideas to them.

> The customer sees innovation in the supplier's offer as the supplier's job, not theirs.

In the past, suppliers could just explain their products, negotiate price and fulfil the deal, but clearly that is nothing like enough now. Some are still trying to take the short cut to the sale but, without a far deeper understanding of the customer's business, they will not build the relationships they seek.

### 4.1.2 A deep understanding of the customer

Customers are aware that salespeople's expressions of interest in their business are mostly only skin deep. The perception is that they will collect just enough facts to sprinkle through their selling arguments, but that they do not make the effort to understand the customer's marketplace or its position and strategies in its marketplace. Whether that is because the salesperson does not have the time or the inclination or the intellectual capacity is immaterial: the customer perceives that the supplier is only interested in what it can extract from the relationship, without trying to add value to it, and responds accordingly.

> ## Case study insight
> ### A retailer's reaction to superficial approaches
> A major retailer clearly recognized the surface-deep approach of most of its suppliers. The purchasing director said, 'Last January they came in here in their droves, with their PowerPoint presentations and their flipcharts – I think they'd all been on the same course – but it was just the same as usual. They called it 'strategic planning' but it was all about how much more we were going to buy from them. They didn't bother with what we wanted, so we just ignored it all.'

Best practice suppliers realize the importance of understanding the customer and put real resource behind it. EDS, for example, has sector specialists that form part of the team that works with individual key customers. Other companies put resource into hiring market analysts who collect, interpret and distribute the information required by their key account managers. The understanding of the customer's world and the customer's business cannot be outsourced by the key account manager, but it can be made more accessible and easier to acquire.

As one purchasing director said, 'We want our key suppliers to help us realize our objectives. To do that, they have to understand our business, understand our marketplace and understand how we accumulate value: how we add value to our customers, and how we make money in our business.' This is a long way from 'Seven Steps to Closing the Sale', but it is the way forward in developing relationships with key customers.

We have heard a lot of talk about key account managers' 'value-added strategies', but even a cursory examination shows that these strategies add a lot more value to the supplier than to the customer. Not surprisingly, they

*Key account managers' 'value-added strategies' add a lot more value to the supplier than to the customer. Not surprisingly, they often fail.*

often fail, because the 'what's in it for me?' is missing for the customer – so why should they disturb what they already have in place? But if you understand how your customer adds value to their customers, you will see many more ways of really adding value to your customer than you did before.

IBM was one of the earliest adopters of key account management (KAM) and among the first to appreciate what best practice should look like. Every year, it tasked its global account managers with building on their in-depth understanding of their customers to identify or create at least one strategy for each customer that did *not* involve selling more IT equipment or services – as a purely added-value contribution to the customer. Not only did it demonstrate how well they knew their customers, it also showed that IBM would support them without expecting any direct return. Figure 4.2 illustrates the layers of understanding that suppliers need to consider when analysing a customer and its market.

**Figure 4.2**
Layers of understanding of the customer.

---

### Case study insight

#### IMI Cornelius: developing a relationship through aligning strategy

IMI Cornelius specializes in drinks dispense systems. When it first started working with Bass (later bought by Coors Brewers) it focused on providing excellently engineered equipment. As the company began to understand the customer and the beer business better, it realized that its equipment represented the brand at the point of sale and played a very important role in the consumer experience. The key account manager studied the beer market and consumer behaviour, and changed IMI Cornelius's mission for the customer from maximizing its own sales to supporting the customer in developing beer consumption. Together the two companies came up with some excellent ideas, including Arc – beer frozen at the point of pouring. The relationship survived and indeed thrived after the takeover by Coors, and the business grew substantially over five years.

To gain a deep understanding of the customer's business:

- collect and analyse all the information you have and all the information you can get about the customer and its marketplace,

- work out what that means in terms of its likely issues and strategies,

- sit down with the customer and see what is correct, what needs to be amended, and confirm what the analysis means in terms of its strategies,

- clarify what the customer expects of your company.

It is astonishing that something as obvious as analysing the customer's marketplace is still so neglected.

At Cranfield School of Management, we have shown a large number of key account managers how to approach this exercise, starting with the customer's defining reality – its marketplace – the importance of which is often overlooked. We have had many reports that such engagement in understanding the customer's business, even on its own, has helped immensely in developing their relationships, and developing them into territory they had never reached before. It is astonishing that something as obvious as analysing the customer's marketplace is still so neglected.

If your relationship with your customer is already close and *interdependent*, then you should have much of the information that you need, and you can go on to work to develop strategies for building the business you have together. If your relationship with your customer is at a more transactional stage, at a *basic* or *cooperative* level, then try 'putting yourself in the customer's shoes' and carry out a strategic analysis of the customer as if you were yourself in the customer's position. You will be able to understand not only the pressures that its people face, but also how they are likely to respond (see Chapter 7 on how to analyse a customer).

Customers generally do not explicitly tell suppliers which generic supplier management strategy has been selected for them, but that does not make it any less real.

In addition, suppliers should understand the customer's supplier management strategies (see Section 5.2), in order to understand how the customer sees them and whether they will want to develop a relationship. It should come as no surprise to learn that buyers operate strategies for working with suppliers that run parallel to those that selling companies use. That view governs the attention they get and the treatment they receive. Customers generally do not explicitly tell suppliers which generic supplier management strategy has been selected for them, but that does not make it any less real. Buyers are more inclined to 'let them work it out for themselves'. The problem is that many suppliers have clearly failed to work it out for themselves, maybe because they do not want to face up to that task and its implications.

Customers may apply different strategies to different products, and they may apply different strategies to the same products at different times. For example, their strategy may depend on the stage in the product's life cycle, which will affect the choice of suppliers. The relationship with you as a company will largely be managed by the prevailing strategy for your products, with some variation if they are buying a range of items from you.

KAM will not compensate for an inadequate marketing strategy and undifferentiated, commoditized offers, and applying it against all the indications that the customer is 'agog with indifference' will only result in misdirected, wasted resources. You will need to understand your customer's buying strategies as well as their business strategies.

*KAM will not compensate for an inadequate marketing strategy and undifferentiated, commoditised offers*

## 4.2 Developing relationships

### 4.2.1 Choosing the right relationship stage

Before you start to develop a relationship, you should first decide what stage of relationship you want to reach and believe is achievable with the customer. That choice will govern how you approach the relationship, even in the early stages, and how much your company invests in it. The *cooperative* stage should not be seen as an ultimate choice, but as a transition stage not to be prolonged unnecessarily.

The relationship you want to have with the customer should depend on the category into which the customer falls (see Section 2.3.1). What would be the point in aiming for an *interdependent* relationship with a customer you intend to manage for cash because of their relentless pressure on prices? Similarly, it would be impossible to apply strategic investment to a customer with whom the relationship was still at the *basic* level: the initiative would be hampered by the lack of contacts, limited understanding of the customer, and limited interest from the customer's side.

The matrix that categorizes customers by strategy, together with a version that overlays the portfolio with appropriate levels of relationship, is shown in Figure 4.3.

*What would be the point in aiming for an interdependent relationship with a customer you intend to manage for cash because of their relentless pressure on prices?*

Many people make the mistake of thinking that KAM means the development of close relationships with all selected customers. We would say that all of the customers in the portfolio are key accounts defined by the supplier's categorization criteria, but that they should be recognized as being different in nature and hence different in their treatment. That includes choosing the 'right' level of relationship to have, which will often *not* be *interdependent* or *integrated*. The matrix should drive the relationship stages targeted, although they do not fall exactly into the four boxes. However, it indicates that:

- *Basic* relationships are for:
  - 'streamline' customers (see Section 2.3.1) offered a 'manage for cash' treatment

**Figure 4.3** Matching relationship level with key customer strategies.

- declining 'status' customers
- 'star' customers with whom not much progress has yet been made.

- *Cooperative* relationships are for:
  - growing 'star' customers
  - 'status' customers where the relationship is being scaled down from *interdependent*.

- *Interdependent* relationships are for:
  - the majority of 'strategic' customers.

- *Integrated* relationships are for:
  - a few, exceptional 'strategic' customers.

---

### CHECKPOINT

#### Targeting relationship stages

- Have you categorized your customers?

- Have you matched your relationships appropriately with each customer's type?

---

It is not at all a good idea to give key account managers free rein to develop any of their customers as they see fit.

Taking into account the limited number of *interdependent* and *integrated* relationships that any supplier can handle (see Section 2.1.3), it is clearly important to consider very carefully how many of this kind of relationship can be sustained, and which companies will be targeted. It is not at all a good idea to give key account managers free rein to develop any of their customers as they see fit, because the company will be unable to support all of them. Indeed, the relationship level targeted should be included in the strategic account plan and formally approved.

### 4.2.2   Contact mapping

Of course, you need to understand the people in your customer's company and their positions in it, particularly those who affect your business. As early as you can in developing the relationship, build up a structured picture of them in a way that allows you to add more information as you find it. At the least, you will need a chart of the customer's formal organization so that you can see who reports to whom.

You can improve on this kind of chart in a number of ways. For example, consider building up a picture of the informal information-sharing networks that operate within the customer, so you can best decide how to spread the messages that you want transmitted inside the company. This will take some time, investigation and experience. Meanwhile, you can make better use of the organization chart by superimposing onto it two critical pieces of information for each person/position; first, how important are they to your business with the customer, and second, what is the status of your relationship with them currently? Figure 4.4 shows how this would look, together with scales for these two pieces of information, importance and relationship.

**Figure 4.4**   Customer organization chart overlaid with contact importance and relationship.

'Importance' here means relevance and influence in your business with the customer, not the individual's seniority within their own company. You can assign importance on a simple, intuitive scale of 0–5, or it may be more objectively evaluated by using criteria; like the extent of the position's involvement in activities relating to your area of interest, or the position's role in innovation, or the power of the position in making decisions on choosing between suppliers, etc.

Similarly, 'relationship' may be judged directly, or through drawing up a scale of thumbnail sketches of the relationship against each score. Avoid assessing the relationship in terms of how they feel about you personally: you should be assessing their relationship with your company, rather than you as an individual.

---

## CHECKPOINT

### Customer contacts

- Do you have an up-to-date copy of your customer's organization chart?

- Do you understand the relevance and importance of each person/position to your business?

- Do you know how each feels about your company?

- Have you looked at the overall picture and identified relationship gaps that need to be addressed?

---

## Case study insight

### The right relationships in the wrong places

One company reported that it had excellent, level 4 and 5 relationships in one of its key customers. However, when it added importance and relationship to the customer's organization chart, it became apparent that these relationships were mostly with people they worked with day-to-day, but that relationships with key decision makers were few and weak. At about the same time, they received the news that a director of their main competitor had been appointed as a non-executive director on the customer's Board. Their best relationships were in the wrong places, not with people who really mattered.

---

If this company had seen the gaps in its relationship sooner and more clearly, it might have been able to target senior people in the customer and itself achieve a closer rapport that might have pre-empted the competition winning a seat on the Board. It was now faced with accepting a position as an 'also-ran', or a very tough task to regain parity.

---

**CHECKPOINT**

**Are your relationships with the right people?**

- Are your strong relationships with people who are really important, or are they with nice, friendly, but less important people?

- Do you have any poor or weak relationships with people who are important?

- Are your relationships balanced across relevant areas of the company, or are there gaps in certain functions?

- Do you cover all levels in the customer or are you over-concentrated in one level? Are you missing certain levels like the Board, or the user level?

---

Visual representations of the situation are invaluable in making diagnoses and decisions, but you are likely to need software to help you coordinate and keep information up to date on all customer contacts as well. Make sure that you keep within the Data Protection Act if you are operating in the UK or in another country with similar legislation, and be careful if you are sharing information with subsidiaries in other countries that may not operate under the same restrictions. Very broadly, you should have no problems if you save information which relates to the post but not to the individual who holds it. Consider whether you would be comfortable if the customer demanded to see the information, and check your company's policy.

In large organizations there is constant change of personnel, as people enter and leave the company and, in many cases, people move on to new jobs internally every two years as well. Add to that the regular restructurings which seem to be a feature of corporate life, and you will see that updating your contact map needs to be a regular and frequent exercise.

> Updating your contact map needs to be a regular and frequent exercise.

In *interdependent* and *integrated* relationships, and also in *cooperative* relationships which are being managed towards *interdependence*, the links with customer contacts need to be shared out to the key account team and beyond, to ensure that each receives the attention he or she deserves. In order to manage the intercompany relationship, the key account manager needs a structured view of these interactions, such as that shown in Figure 4.5. This table is a simple way of capturing who (in your company) has links with whom (in the customer), and how good those relationships are. A similar scale can be used here as well as for the organization chart at the beginning of this section, reflecting the relationship between the individual in the customer and the supplier as a company. It also allows targets to be set for the individuals in your company to develop that relationship to a higher level, not just on a personal basis, but on behalf of the company.

Furthermore, the 'owner' of the relationship, or principal contact, can be identified by simply highlighting the relationship (e.g. with a blue box, as

| Supplier | Customer | | | | | |
|---|---|---|---|---|---|---|
| Staff | R Downly | W Brady | S Potter | V Bingley | D Plowright | T Trevor |
| N Marrer | 2 > 4 | | 4 > 5 | | 1 > 2 | |
| O Lilley | | 3 > 5 | | | | 2 > 4 |
| G Frome | | 1 > 2 | | 1 > 3 | | |
| H Dennis | | | | 2 > 3 | 3 > 4 | |

Relationship strength on scale of 0 to 5 (bold = target level)
Relationship 'owner' or principal contact denoted by ☐

**Figure 4.5**
Mapping team-based relationships.

in the example in Figure 4.5). It should tell anyone who wishes to talk to a contact in the customer, that it will be a good idea to have a word with the relationship 'owner' first, to understand how his or her approach might fit in with other activity and communication.

Just giving people a target does not necessarily help them understand how to develop a relationship, so most fall back on dinner and golf, which are not the only ways of doing it, nor even welcome in many cases today. Alternative strategies and ideas are needed, and discussed in the next section.

### 4.2.3 Relationship-building strategies

*If building relationships is at the core of the key account manager job, should it be left to the individual's intuition and luck?*

Asked about how his company's key account managers went about building relationships, one sales director said, 'I can't tell you. We just assume they know how to do it'. Well, often they don't. His attitude is common enough, if rather curious. How often in other parts of the company are people appointed to do a very specific job and then left to do it without training, guidance or even observation? If building relationships is at the core of the key account manager job, should it be left to the individual's intuition and luck? Or would their efforts stand a better – and earlier – chance of success if they were supported with structured approaches and visible processes?

*While people bonds are important, they are not an end in themselves.*

Relationships between complex companies are about much more than the chemistry between two people. The range and nature of the links is potentially large and varied. However, many key account managers still believe in the overriding importance of 'people bonds' to the exclusion of many other levers that they could and should operate, if they want to build robust relationships with customers. Professor Ivan Snehota (Håkansson and Snehota, 1995) identified three layers in intercompany relationships (see

**Figure 4.6**
Intercompany
relationship layers.

Figure 4.6). While people bonds are important, they are not an end in themselves, just as customer satisfaction is not an end in itself: it is an intermediary objective in delivering a sustainable stream of business. Your objective should be to develop such links with the people who can help put into place the other perhaps more robust and valuable elements of the relationship, which might involve better coordination through activity links, or investing in change through resource ties. This is likely to mean approaching people outside your normal sphere of operations who are therefore outside your 'comfort zone', but it is the route to lasting relationships.

The three layers identified by Snehota are:

- **Activity links**: Broadly, these are based around activities your company and your customer do together – like joint training, joint marketing campaigns, joint planning – which are often aimed at coordination of effort.

- **Resource ties**: These may be considered as investments – such as R&D projects, a jointly owned warehouse, or a new IT system used by both – which indicate and require a commitment between the two parties.

- **People bonds**: Only through interacting with people do any of the above get agreed and implemented, so people are the facilitators of all these other links, hence their importance.

It is easy to lose your way in relationship development. Everyone finds it more congenial to be welcomed by a friendly face in the buying company than to push forward to meet new people who speak unfamiliar languages, like finance and IT, who are not convinced that they want to meet suppliers anyway. However, you should focus firmly on your purpose, which is, after all, the development of the intercompany relationship, not a comfortable socializing.

Some key account managers believe that getting close to their contacts means meals and entertainment. This kind of approach has its place in developing relationships but it is often overemphasized. It is not the only way of developing relationships and, increasingly, not the most appropriate. Many customer staff, for example, those in the public sector and quite a few big companies, are not allowed to accept hospitality, and others simply do not have the time or inclination for it. They may work long days and have to fight to preserve their private space, so they do not really want it taken up by suppliers. Certainly, key account managers need to understand the customer's attitude to hospitality before offering it. Acceptance of hospitality from suppliers is often a cultural issue, which may stem from the national culture, the industry or sector, or the culture of that particular organization.

However, remember that the customer's staff are always representing the company that employs them. Very often, delivering a benefit to their area of the business is a better way of satisfying their objectives. In fact, delivering a business benefit might satisfy more than one individual's agenda, as well as having a more visible and enduring effect than any dinner or sporting event. Consider how you might add value in their business life: if you can save them hassle or make them business heroes, you will be building a strong relationship.

Of course, the intercompany relationship will necessarily be achieved through relationships with individuals. As Figure 4.7 suggests, both types of relationship have to be considered in determining strategies: the organizational level determines the overall nature, depth and opportunities

**Figure 4.7**
Combining organization and individual levels in relationship-building strategies.

of the relationship, but understanding and working at the individual level is crucial in facilitating it.

Suppliers talk a lot about 'added-value' strategies. However, the customer's view of what it perceives as adding value is somewhat different. They expect product support, training for their people about your products, providing accessible information about your products and services etc. as part of the package, and do not regard them as 'value-adding' services, even though they cost your company money to deliver. From the customer's point of view, these are all things that promote or support the sales of your product, which they see as adding value to your business at least as much as, or more than, to theirs. Such services may be useful, but they often see them as something they pay for in the price of the product. Consider the definition of value expressed in the following equation:

$$\text{Value} = \text{Perceived benefit} - \text{Perceived sacrifice (price/cost)}$$

The value calculated by this equation must be greater than 0 in order to gain a perception of added value in the customer's eyes. So, to build the relationship through adding value, you need to increase the customer's perception of the benefit received without increasing their price/cost.

---

### CHECKPOINT

**Do you add value to your customer?**

Which of the following or similar initiatives have you put into practice for your key customer in the last year?

- Help with solving glitches in their processes?

- Saving cost for their department?

- Providing useful information from your organization that is not readily available to them: market research data, for example?

- Lending them an expert to advise on something which is new to them?

- Supporting training for their staff to develop their skills (not training on your products)?

---

Added-value strategies are excellent relationship developers, which work really well when fitted to the needs of the company and the needs of the individual at work as well. In particular, those activities that involve interaction between people in your company and theirs, and have practical benefits, are very effective at building bridges that can come into play on other occasions as well.

### 4.2.4 *Building an interdependent relationship*

Most commonly, the aspirational level of relationship in key account management is *interdependent*, since *basic* relationships are not hard to achieve,

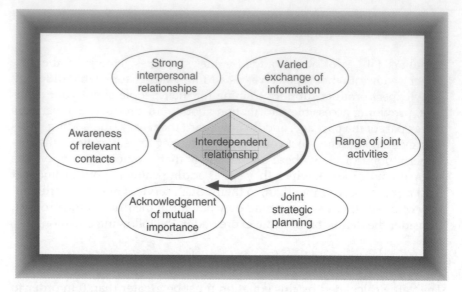

**Figure 4.8**
Features of
*interdependent*
relationships.

and the *cooperative* stage is best regarded as a transitional level. *Interdependent* relationships generally demonstrate the features shown in Figure 4.8. If you want to develop an *interdependent* relationship, try working on developing these features specifically. However, as Figure 4.8 suggests, there is, to some extent, an order of development: for example, you should map the people in the customer's organization and understand their positions before you spend too much time developing relationships. You may be using your time on people who are ultimately irrelevant. Similarly, you should facilitate an exchange of information that allows you to understand the customer very well before you embark on a joint strategic planning exercise, when you want to make a contribution through your knowledge of the customer's business, rather than exposing your ignorance of it. Table 4.1 contains some ideas on how to go about developing these features.

> More companies are adopting joint strategic planning as a regular part of the way they do business with their key accounts.

Ideally, strategic planning should be carried out jointly. Our original research showed that joint strategic planning (longer term than straightforward action planning) was found in only about a third of even the most important relationships (based on the top two or three in each case), so it was even more rare with key customers as a whole. However, best practice is spreading and more companies are adopting joint strategic planning as a regular part of the way they do business with their key accounts.

The relationship is the all-important medium that facilitates business growth, and deserves its own development strategies. Key account strategic plans should contain not only business strategies, but also statements of how the relationship itself will be developed.

A healthy medium is needed to support the interactions that will translate the agreed strategic intent into customized value propositions, and the interactions that will facilitate their delivery as part of regular operations. Everything will move forward faster and better when facilitated by a good intercompany relationship while if, on the other hand, the relationship is

**Table 4.1** Building relationships through developing specific features

| Relationship feature | Aim | Hints |
|---|---|---|
| Awareness of relevant contacts | All relevant contacts in the customer organization identified, mapped and researched | Increase quantity of contacts (number of people)<br><br>Increase quality of contact (contacts' importance to your company) (see Section 4.2.2) |
| Strong interpersonal relationship | Strong relationships with relevant contacts developed | Pair contact with designated member of staff (see Section 4.2.2)<br><br>Develop specific relationship strategies for each (see Section 4.2.3) |
| Varied exchange of information | Two-way sharing of a range range of information, sometimes confidential | Assess existing inventory of knowledge and gaps<br><br>Create a need to know and address requests to information holders |
| Range of joint activities | Joint participation in activities outside simple buying and selling, possibly joint marketing, IT projects, R&D projects, training, etc. | Develop list of value-adding options (see Section 4.2.3)<br><br>Propose those with most benefit for both parties |
| Joint strategic planning | Joint analysis of the market situation and formulation of a joint strategy for business development, annually at least | Identify worthwhile outcome of investment of time for senior people on both sides<br><br>Clarify process and schedule well in advance<br><br>Create some kind of innovation (see Chapter 7) |
| Acknowledgement of mutual importance | Explicit recognition by both sides of their importance to each other | Develop and manage individual and organizational trustworthiness<br><br>Encourage public expressions of relationship, at the right time |

poor, the process will be slow, difficult, expensive, fraught with misunder-standing, and likely to have a disappointing outcome.

## 4.3 Managing relationships

### 4.3.1 Multilevel relationships

Healthy, close relationships with customers should function at all levels in the supplier. Each participant should have a role assigned, even the most senior, and the operation of those roles should be coordinated by the key account manager. Indeed, that is what a large part of the job becomes at an *interdependent* level. Different levels have different roles to play:

● **Senior management** may only meet each other occasionally, but the links are there to confirm strategy, iron out any difficult issues, especially cross-boundary problems, and act as the last resort point of recourse.

● **Middle management** does the work of keeping the relationship moving forwards and bringing in a flow of new developments that make adding value changes for the customer.

● **Operations/transactions** keeps the wheels turning and ensures that delivery is as promised and hassle-free.

Furthermore, the key account manager is the person to monitor and adjust the balance in the relationship.

Mapping the links between people on the two sides of the relationship at different levels in both organizations can be very illuminating (Figure 4.9). Internal relationships can be added as well, if the resulting picture does not become too confusing. Figure 4.9 shows a network of relationships involving all levels and a variety of functions on both sides (the example shows abbreviated functions, but individual positions can be used instead). Provided that the key account manager has the internal relationships that allow him or her to gain and manage a full view of these interactions, then the picture should indicate a healthy, well-balanced relationship at the *interdependent* stage.

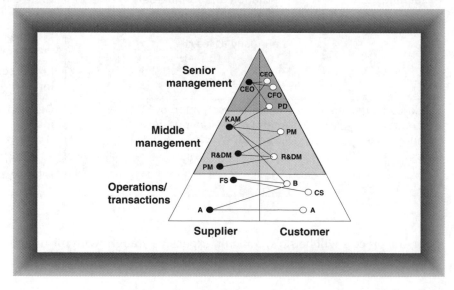

**Figure 4.9** Mapping relationship links with the customer at different levels of management.

Try charting the links between staff in your company and your customer, and compare that picture with those shown in Figure 4.9. It will help you to understand the contact map you currently have, and how you might

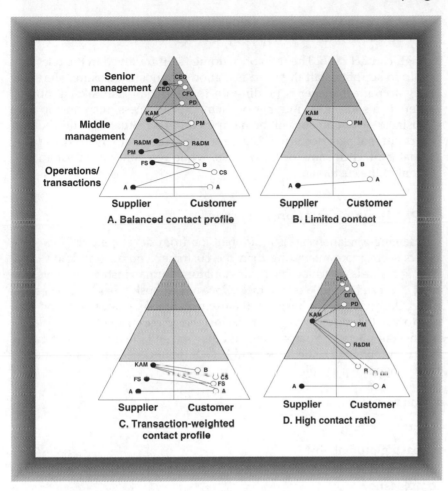

**Figure 4.10**
Mapping
relationship links at
different levels of
management.

change it to what you want. Is the relationship balanced as in the figure above or, if not, in what way is it skewed? Figure 4.10 shows four variants, but there may be others too.

A. **Balanced contact profile**: Indicates an *interdependent* relationship, if the key account manager is managing, briefing and coordinating the internal relationships as well. If not, it could indicate a *cooperative* relationship with insufficient coordination and control. There could be many more contacts than shown, but this kind of number is probably the least necessary for an *interdependent* relationship. Good coordination and management required.

B. **Limited contact**: Indicates a *basic* relationship, possibly a new one. To develop the relationship, appropriate contacts need to be identified on both sides and at all levels. People need to understand how the key account manager will run the relationship, what it is trying to achieve, what is their role in it, and what others will be doing as well.

C. **Transaction-weighted contact profile**: This also indicates a *basic* relationship, albeit an older one, in which more links have been established. However, links are all focused on people concerned with the short term and transactions. To develop this relationship, efforts need to be made to form links higher up the organization.

D. **High contact ratio**: The ratio of customer staff involved in the relationship to supplier staff involved is a good diagnostic measure. Here the key account manager is holding on to almost all the links, although there is a substantial number of them. Nevertheless, relationship and business development will be hampered in this situation, and the key account manager needs to delegate and encourage others to act as principal contact in some of these links, while retaining overall management of the customer.

### 4.3.2  Avoiding relationship traps

Maintaining a relationship is a different job from developing it. New customers seem more interesting than the customer you already know, and driving towards an achievable goal is a natural human instinct, so development is not so hard to keep on track. Once a relationship has become established, however big the business, the excitement may go out of it, and it is easy to take the customer for granted. However, these customers have plenty of other suppliers for comparison, and they are still the most important, so they are unlikely to settle for second best. Suppliers need to guard against three dangers in particular:

- Complacency
- Lapses in integrity
- Leaking profitability.

#### Complacency

Warning against complacency seems so obvious that it should not even be necessary to say it, like those announcements, 'Please take your baggage with you when leaving the plane'. Of course, you have no intention of being complacent. Nevertheless, companies often do take some of their oldest and best customers for granted and give them a poorer treatment than newer or more difficult and demanding customers. There is a danger that the individual key account manager will become casual in his or her dealings with the customer, but there is also a danger of institutional complacency which requires even more vigilance.

#### Lapses in integrity

Over a long period of time, one or other party in a relationship may want to change the original commitments and understanding on which the relationship was built. Indeed, as people move in and out of jobs, the original understanding may just get 'forgotten'. However, changing the parameters of a relationship without the full knowledge *and* consent of the other party will generally be seen as a lapse in integrity. Even if it is with the knowledge of the customer, then 'moving the goalposts' will be seen, not unreasonably, as a lack of integrity and result in a loss of trust if the customer is too enmeshed in the relationship to withdraw without great difficulty.

We have seen this pattern repeated many times over. Suppliers sometimes have to make tough decisions for the business, and *in extremis* they may have little choice. However, too often the decision to change the way customers are managed seems to be a more individual and personal choice, or one driven by non-customer-facing functions like finance or operations, which has been taken without a real understanding of the long-term damage that is wrought by such U-turns. The fact that the supplier has stayed within the letter of the contract is immaterial if it has reneged on the spirit of the relationship.

> The fact that the supplier has stayed within the letter of the contract is immaterial if it has reneged on the spirit of the relationship.

---

### Case study insight

#### Taking a customer for granted

One supplier had a long-term close relationship and steady business with one of its key customers. During a restructuring/cost-cutting exercise the decision was taken to reduce its resource from a full-time key account manager to just 10 per cent of her time. The supplier wrongly assumed that the business was 'theirs' in spite of the reduction in support. In fact, the relationship deteriorated to the point where the business was close to being lost.

To reclaim the business, the supplier had to reinstate the key account manager, reallocate her other customers, and dedicate a taskforce to retrieve the position. The relationship began to improve although the customer was not likely to forget the episode. In the end, the supplier had spent just as much on the relationship as it would have done anyway, if not more, had lost the trust of the customer and caused long-lasting damage to the relationship.

---

### Case study insight

#### 'Once bitten, twice shy'

Strongly sponsored by its sales director, a hi-tech company had developed a good key account programme and excellent relationships with clients. However, the sales director left the company and was replaced with a new sales director with a 'back to basics' philosophy. Service and support levels were reduced and a number of joint customer projects were dropped. When later on, the supplier wanted to reinstate KAM, customers were sceptical and unresponsive. They felt the support was part of the deal and that the supplier had gone back on its promise.

---

Opportunism is also seen by the customer as a breach of integrity. For example, customers in collaborative relationships expect that if a supplier receives an unexpected windfall that cuts its costs, like a fall in raw material prices, then the customer will be informed and some or all of the benefit will be

Failure to share the benefit of a cost saving is seen by the customer as a breach of trust.

passed on. Both research and experience show that failure to share the benefit of a cost saving is seen by the customer as a breach of trust. Presumably, suppliers' finance directors who refuse to realign prices do not share this view, or perhaps they do not realize that, in making such a decision, they are not acting with the integrity expected by the customer. Key account managers must take conscious and special care to manage their company's integrity as well as their own.

### Leaking profitability

In theory, profitability improves through the 'learning curve' effect as you work with a customer and get to understand the best way of dealing with their business. However, it can also decline over a period of time, through successive rounds of negotiations in which the customer squeezes down prices and wins new and incremental service concessions with significant costs attached (see Chapter 5). In fact, suppliers as well as customers are responsible for leaking the profits.

Suppliers make a lot of assumptions about customer profitability that have never been even tested in some companies, let alone properly monitored.

Suppliers make a lot of assumptions about customer profitability that have never been even tested in some companies, let alone properly monitored. One key account director investigated one of his company's top three accounts to test his assumptions, and found the result was 100 per cent different from his expectation. Where there is substantial business the stakes are too high to leave profitability to guesswork, so the first task must be to get genuine profitability measurement in place.

---

## CHECKPOINT
### Preventing profitability leakage

- Do you know what the real profitability of each key customer is, not just sales revenue or gross margin?

- Have you carried out a wide-ranging price and service review with the customer?

- Do you identify and clear out obsolete costs and anomalous prices from time to time?

---

## Summary

Too many companies think developing relationships alone will make a difference to the business. In fact, a good relationship is just the beginning, not an end in itself: some real benefit needs to materialize for the customer as well as the supplier. The relationship should be seen as the facilitator that allows the supplier to reach the people it needs to talk to and work with to deliver the business strategies and added value the customer seeks.

Conversely, some suppliers think that just doing business will develop relationships automatically. This is also a fallacy: there are many examples where companies have nothing going on between them that can be called anything other than straightforward trading although they have been trading for years, and they still have a very limited understanding or appreciation of each other.

Really, business and relationship development should go hand in hand, and a supplier that wants to achieve a closer relationship should consciously work on both simultaneously to reach the stage it desires more quickly and more certainly. In this chapter we have identified some of the major influences in relationship development, and discussed some practical approaches to managing and developing the relationship. In particular, we have highlighted the customer's view of relationships with suppliers, particularly the importance of the supplier's integrity and trustworthiness, to which suppliers could usefully give more explicit care and consideration.

# 5 The buyer perspective

As buying companies seek new routes to competitive advantage and value for their customers, they now look to key suppliers to help them. Naturally, customers are far more likely to act according to their own perceptions and aspirations than to any view or objective that selling companies might wish to impose on them. A buying company has its own set of strategic decision support tools to help it select the suppliers who are important to the fulfilment of its aspirations.

First, a selling company needs to understand whether it has the opportunity of being a key supplier. The chances are small if it is one of many competitors, or it is in a weak position relative to the customer, or it supplies a product or service which does not contribute to the customer's critical path. If analysis reveals that this is the selling company's situation with this customer, the supplier should look elsewhere for its own key relationships or possibly reposition itself through developing its offer. It should not waste money and effort on trying to develop a relationship that is unlikely to succeed and bear fruit.

At the same time, the supplier should decide what this customer can contribute to its own strategic objectives, using the methods described in the following chapters. These methods require an in-depth understanding of the customer's situation, needs and strategies and, indeed, successful key account managers are those who really know how their customers operate and why.

Generally speaking, only if buyer and seller strategies are complementary in terms of products, their approach to business and to the relationship between them will it be possible to develop the relationship beyond a fairly simple level towards an interdependent or integrated stage. However, if all these elements are in place and closer involvement is achieved, the flow of benefits to both parties can be very exciting.

At less-developed stages of the relationship the cost of nurturing the relationship can easily outweigh the benefits. The range and extent of cost savings increase on both sides as trust between the two parties grows and barriers are reduced. In some situations, reducing risk by working with a known partner can allow costs to be cut, for example by eliminating duplication of processes. In other situations, reduction of costs may increase risk, for example by moving to just-in-time supply and eliminating buffer stocks. Clearly, reduction of costs and reduction of risks are closely linked and need to be managed jointly from a foundation of a thorough understanding of the partner and its concerns.

Trust is a mediator through which most interactions pass and activities will be interpreted. Care should be taken to manage the partner's perceptions, as reserves of trust may be crucial in carrying a supplier through any difficult patches in performance or in the relationship. In the end, powerful customers still call the shots.

# Introduction

Books on selling and account management, and suppliers as well, often make the mistake of assuming that the customer is bound to fall in with a well-developed, well-presented plan. This is, of course, quite untrue. Customers have their own agendas, their own strategies and their own priorities. If, and only if, the selling company's plans fit the customer's plan, are they likely to succeed.

It follows that understanding the customer is fundamental to the selling company in adopting the right strategy and making acceptable offers. Yet suppliers generally devote remarkably little time and effort to gaining this crucial knowledge about their customers. In order to understand the customer's perspective fully, this chapter considers the buyer's standpoint and looks at the world and the supplier through the buyer's eyes, rather than viewing the customer from the buyer's standpoint.

We will look at the circumstances which provide fertile ground for close, cooperative relationships and at the circumstances which suggest that attempts at greater intimacy will fall on stony ground. However, even if intimacy is not an option, being very good at what you do still is.

## 5.1 The purchasing context

The companies in a modern supply chain are more closely connected together than ever before. The market environment of one becomes a factor in the market environment of the next. Pressures felt by one are passed on to the next. To understand its own business, each company needs to understand the business of the others to a far greater extent than it has in the past.

Within companies too, the aim is now cross-functional integration. Traditionally, buyers were quite remote from their own company's customer strategy and therefore operated to a different agenda. Suppliers responded to that agenda and sold on specification and price. Now that buyers are generally much more in tune with the concerns of their whole company, the key account manager can make more creative offers and business propositions to them. That kind of applied creativity can only come from a deeper and more extensive knowledge of the customer's business.

Even when a supplier is working with a deep understanding of the customer, this is still only one side of the equation: the receptiveness of the customer is also critical in achieving relationship success. Key account relationships do not generally exist at the higher levels discussed in Chapter 3 unless they are reciprocated. Selling companies are liable to delude themselves about the favourability of their position with the customer. In fact, close business relationships are constructed from two-way linkages wrought by frequent operational interactions, dedicated resources, shared assets, joint planning and other business-based bonds between buying and selling companies. Such linkages will not exist unless the buying company as well as the selling company chooses to participate actively in the relationship (McDonald and Woodburn, 1999).

There is a tendency for selling companies to view their relationships with buying companies in isolation as if buyers do not have relationships with other suppliers or with other kinds of organization. This is obviously not the case, and understanding the network of relationships within which the buying company operates can be very illuminating as a way of identifying what drives buyers to behave one way and not another.

An intelligent supplier achieves its objectives by helping the customer achieve theirs.

Figure 5.1 illustrates the different types of organization with which any company might have a relationship. As the buyer and supplier and, indeed, every other body represented in Figure 5.1 will each belong to a similar network, the business reality is exceedingly complex.

For suppliers competing in increasingly challenging business environments, understanding the purchasing context can provide valuable insight into buyer behaviour. Knowing, for example, what are the buyer's resources, motivations, pressures and sources of information can provide a supplier with a lucrative competitive edge. An intelligent supplier realizes that the best route to the achievement of its own objectives is by helping customers to

**Figure 5.1**   Business relationship network.

achieve their objectives. In summary, it is a simple three-step process:

1. Acquire an in-depth understanding of the customer environment and the customer drivers.

2. Discover or deduce the customer's objectives and strategic response in relation to suppliers.

3. Develop solutions to match the customer's strategy and needs.

Let us next examine the common customer drivers and the strategies customers adopt in relation to their suppliers. The actual processes by which companies deliver solutions are described later in Chapters 7 and 8.

### 5.1.1 Customer drivers

Often, the information held by a supplier about a buyer is either rudimentary and confined to contact details, purchase history with the company and sometimes wider purchasing activity, or it is more extensive but diffused around the company. However, the data do not attempt to identify the forces which are really driving the customer's business. These underlying influences are a combination of factors exclusive to the buying company, its business, its relationship network, and its environment. Some of the major forces that affect customers and, therefore, influence customer purchasing behaviour are as follows:

● Speed of change and flexibility

● Fast innovation and shorter product life cycles

- Emerging and collapsing routes to market
- Supply chain integration and customization
- Globalization
- Longer reach competition
- Geography – independent prices
- Downsizing, upsizing, merging
- Cost reduction
- Risk reduction.

Arguably, the business world is changing faster now than it ever has before: certainly it is more interconnected across the globe than ever before. Companies of every kind are fighting to deal with the new forces in order to manage this new speed of change. Managing and exploiting this escalating rate of change requires new creativity and competencies. Businesses need additional flexibility in order to respond in the timeframes available and they are seeking resources and allies to help them. Speed is of the essence in maximizing opportunities. Nimble competitors catch up very quickly, so 'windows' of profit-taking and competitive advantage are getting smaller all the time.

In the past, buying companies were reasonably confident about anticipating the future and were prepared to commit to assets which could be expected to provide a good return in the longer term. Nowadays, however, buying companies are less confident of the shape of the future, and so they prefer to secure their needs through supplier partners, rather than through wholly owned assets. Buyers are willing to trade off some of the margin they might have made themselves in order to maintain their flexibility and speed of response.

> Nowadays, buying companies are less confident of the shape of the future, and so they prefer to secure their needs through supplier partners, rather than through wholly owned assets.

One of the most important components of the rapid pace of change is faster innovation, which leads to faster product obsolescence and, hence, shorter product life cycles. As a result, companies which have developed a product or service innovation must capitalize on their lead very quickly before it is overtaken by the next development. This means that they need to get to market quickly, achieve wide penetration quickly and amortise the costs quickly. Traditional trial, production and launch processes do not work well enough at high speed, so companies are trying out all kinds of new formulas, such as concurrent engineering, modular design, electronic commerce and strategic alliances for every stage of the value chain. Suppliers who do not keep up with their customers will very soon be left behind.

> Turmoil at the product end is now amplified by upheaval in the marketing and distribution channel.

This turmoil at the product end is now amplified by upheaval in the marketing and distribution channel. Not very long ago, companies could concentrate on the development of new products and concepts and then simply release them through the value chain via well-understood processes. Today, with the arrival of electronic commerce, new routes to market are emerging while traditional routes are collapsing. Companies are no longer able to make standard assumptions about the most effective way of reaching their markets. They will be trialling new routes to market at the same time as they launch new products. Until electronic commerce has ceased to be a revolutionary force and a different pattern of doing business has established itself, and this will take some time, businesses will be multiplying their risk because they are venturing into the relatively unknown on two fronts simultaneously.

Some customers are making a late start on supply chain integration. Others are well advanced and have achieved smooth-running, robust processes, while others are only now discovering the pitfalls along with the benefits. Selling companies need to engage with the integration process and to work with the buying company in order to achieve the goals of the supply chain as a whole. Those who simply supply what they are asked for are likely to find themselves divorced from their original customer and managed by a primary supplier. However, closer collaboration is bound to demand customization rather than the provision of standardized offers, and suppliers need to be geared up to respond appropriately.

> Selling companies need to engage with the integration process and work with the buying company in order to achieve the goals of the supply chain as a whole.

Many blue-chip companies, and some smaller ones as well, now operate as global suppliers and/or in global markets. Nevertheless, almost all suppliers struggle to match the needs of customers who are involved in global markets. In fact, globalization is probably not as ubiquitous as we suggested in Chapter 1. It is a dominant factor in some markets, such as computer software and high-technology business-to-business products, which are driven by short product life cycles and a need to maximize sales in the least possible time. In other markets, particularly where services are consumed as they are produced, it is generally not so important.

Advances in information technology and telecommunications, which have culminated in the arrival of electronic commerce technology, have enabled customers to extend their reach to encompass the globe. Equally, competitors are lengthening their reach and are moving into yet more markets. Competitors who were previously confined to serving home markets by the costs of attracting customers overseas are joining the global arena, now that they can market from their base country and no longer need an expensive marketing infrastructure. This lowering of entry barriers opens the field to smaller companies as well, so that customers are not only facing an incursion of good competitors from elsewhere in the world, they are also facing an explosion in the range size and quality of competitors. As long as these new competitors can deliver, or hold out a reasonable expectation of delivery, prices will inevitably come under pressure.

In some markets the Internet acts as a 360-degree periscope on pricing. Buyers can surf the Web looking for best prices. Although they then return to the supplier they know, it will be with new targets for price decreases. Where the products they seek are made by well-known brands with global guarantees, the premium they will pay for using a familiar distributor will be minimal. Now that internal constraints have been removed, many selling companies inside the European Community are fighting a rearguard action on geography-independent pricing and may not succeed in maintaining differentials. Thus, suppliers and customers operating in high-cost areas

> Suppliers who are focused on maintaining their prices are likely to be abandoned.

such as Western Europe will have to work much better in order to maintain margins. The pressure will be felt all the way up the supply chain. Buying companies will seek to work with suppliers whose objective is to maintain margins on an equitable basis, while suppliers who are focused on maintaining their prices are likely to be abandoned.

Inevitably, the current turbulence will affect organizational structure. The rate of downsizing, upsizing and merging taking place has reached new highs as companies jostle to reposition themselves in growth markets and to escape from mature and declining markets. Second-tier companies are generally no longer viable and many have been subsumed into larger or more resourceful companies. The big and the bold are getting bigger and bolder still. The turbulence contains a mix of dangers and opportunities. Companies operating in the expectation of a takeover or acquisition are obviously limited in the commitments they can make and this presents difficulties for buyers as well as suppliers. A buyer in such a transitional situation needs a 'safe pair of hands', flexibility and understanding from its suppliers as it undergoes radical change. In the meantime, a supplier will want to protect the robustness of its buyer contact base in case some of its key contacts become casualties. Threats may appear from competitors who supply the other company in a takeover, while outsourcing opportunities may emerge from downsized companies. In short, uncertainty is increasing.

> Underlying all these customer drivers are the two most enduring ones: cost reduction and risk reduction.

Underlying all these customer drivers are the two most enduring ones: cost reduction and risk reduction. As the pressure to reduce costs features so strongly in customer purchasing behaviour, it is imperative that suppliers appreciate why customers pursue cost savings and what cost savings are potentially available. Suppliers also need to understand how customers perceive the risk in their relationship and how it might best be managed.

---

## Case study insight

### Understanding customers' needs

A public sector organization was merging several buying functions from very different parts of the organization. The buyers would have to move locations, deal with cultural issues, understand their new role and develop strategies to match. Meanwhile, if services to current users were not maintained, they would get off to a bad start with their customers. The supplier could have stood back until the situation became more settled. Instead, it aimed to increase support during the transition to gain commitment from the newly integrated buying function when it emerged from this period.

---

## CHECKPOINT

### Pressure on customers

Can you identify the main forces pressuring your key customers?

### 5.1.2  Cost reduction

While suppliers concentrate on customer value and profitability, the priority for buying companies is often cost reduction. Figure 5.2 shows the dramatic impact of cost savings on a customer's net profits. The authors were presenting to over 50 buying directors from some of the world's biggest multinational companies and most confirmed that cost reduction is indeed their number one priority. Indeed, in *Time* magazine, 1 August 2005, it was reported that most European corporations are doing spectacularly well, their profit growth being driven by cost-cutting.

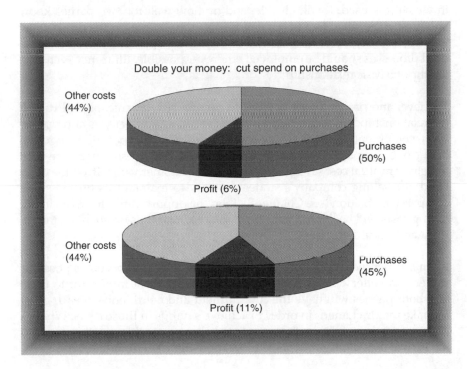

**Figure 5.2** Impact of cost savings on net profits.

This section examines the financial aspects of key account relationship management in terms of cost savings, which are not necessarily limited to the buying company. Some of the cost savings that are potentially available to companies when two links in the supply chain work closely together are as follows:

- Better information and reduced uncertainty
- Reduction of protective measures
- Elimination of duplicated processes
- Better flow of supplies
- Routinized transactions
- Tighter quality control
- Improved supply chain efficiency

- Reduced production costs

- Better, more cost-effective design of new products

- Cost sharing on research and development

- Lower sourcing/business development costs.

Undoubtedly, this list is not complete, nor will all of these savings be available in a single trading relationship. How much cost saving is available will clearly depend on the nature of the product or service and the environment in which it is used. It will also depend on how well the two parties know and trust each other. In a *basic* relationship (see Chapter 3) the parties may well enjoy a degree of familiarity, but very little trust and, therefore, standard processes should be employed wherever possible. Efficiency is characteristic of a *basic* relationship.

The level and nature of cost savings in *cooperative* relationships will vary. If the relationship has been singled out by the selling company as appropriate for development, then the selling company should be expecting to invest in it. The two companies will decide together how that investment can be used to deliver mutual cost savings and enhanced customer value. If, on the other hand, the selling company's strategy is only to maintain its business and competitive position (see Chapter 8), then the opportunities for reducing or saving costs will be limited, which will place constraints on enabling investment and underlying trust.

In an *interdependent* relationship, however, much more becomes possible. Buyer and seller will identify the cost elements most important to them and both parties will have the commitment and confidence in each other to make major changes in order to achieve savings in those costs. Where a high proportion of the cost savings listed above are achieved, this may signal arrival at the *integrated* stage of relationship development.

Better information and reduced uncertainty can save costs for buyers and sellers alike in all kinds of ways. Whether or not this is achieved through a better understanding of the market through making commitments, accurate demand forecasting can save substantial costs. Finance, staffing, use of plant and premises and marketing resources can all be optimized if requirements can accurately be predicted. Inputs can be bought at good rates rather than high, emergency prices. Strategies can be more useful, more effective and more likely to succeed. Shareholder expectations and share prices can be managed better. On both sides of the relationship, an openness and willingness to share information is important, both in itself and as an indicator of the closeness of the relationship.

> On both sides of the relationship, an openness and willingness to share information is important, both in itself and as an indicator of the closeness of the relationship.

When companies do not trust each other, they will install protective measures in order to prevent their trading partners from damaging their business. Vertical integration is one example of how buying companies protect themselves against unreliable or opportunistic suppliers. Upstream integration is designed to ensure continuity of supplies of a key input to core processes

(Ellram, 1991). For example, oil and chemical companies own mining operations which feed their refineries and plants. In fact, they may not always be the most efficient producers and they may be able to buy in at lower prices than the cost of their own production. However, since the companies must run their plant continuously in order to achieve competitive costs, they could not surrender their own sources of raw materials unless they had cast-iron and entirely credible guarantees from their suppliers that deliveries will be made on time.

Although vertical integration is clearly appropriate in certain sets of circumstances (Williamson, 1985), companies are now more inclined to question whether their funds are invested in strategically valuable assets or outmoded supply formats. There are many other examples of expensive protective measures for buying companies, including large buffer stockholdings, advance payments for shipments, legal fees and contract policing, quality checks on goods inwards, constant competitor monitoring and 'mystery shopping'. While buying companies may not be prepared to dismantle all barriers, substantial savings can be made even through partial reductions in protective measures.

> Substantial savings can be made even through partial reductions in protective measures.

The elimination of duplicated processes is an obvious candidate for cost savings. For example, the selling company counts goods out as they leave the factory and the supplier counts them in to confirm delivery in full. Quality is also checked by the producer and again by the receiver. Accounts departments in both companies are engaged endlessly in the reconciliation of purchase orders, delivery notes and invoice payments. These procedures cost money and cause delays, so many companies have gone part of the way to reducing the costs incurred in checking everything by operating spot checks. Some companies have gone one step further and reconfigured the whole process on the assumption that a check conducted by either party will be acceptable to the other.

This case is a good example of how the better flow of supplies and routinized transactions can affect efficiency and cost savings. Here, users receive their

## Case study insight

### Reducing procurement costs

The buying function of a major international company now only involves itself and its warehouses in purchases where it can add value to the process. Office supplies have been taken out of the goods received–store–internal requisition order sequence. Users manage their own budgets and orders direct, and their materials are delivered to their desks. The buying function sets up the supplier contract, receives a single monthly report which is automatically generated, and pays one monthly invoice for everything received. Substantial time and effort is saved by the buying company, while the supplier's costs balance out and prices remain competitive.

supplies the following day, whereas previously, availability varied from immediate delivery for a select few items to two to three days for most items. A transaction procedure was established, specifically tailored to the buying company's specification. It operated to a very regular and efficient routine because it was slimmed down exactly to the services required and omitted any 'frills'. Cutting out superfluous handling is one way of improving the flow of supplies. Other ways of streamlining processes include combined process engineering, joint forecasting and improved management gained from a better understanding of requirements, which is achieved through greater information sharing.

---

### Case study insight
#### Valued-added pricing

A multinational components company has developed a systematic approach to price negotiations with customers. Discussions focus on a matrix based around Porter's (1985) value chain, which identifies sources of cost. Together, the parties concerned identify which elements are valuable to the customer, and which are not, and derive an appropriate price from this resulting menu of tailored and standard elements.

---

Waste of material as reject product and waste of time in services are both regularly targeted sources of cost. However, reject product is a relatively minor part of the real cost of poor quality and, hence, the constant attention to tighter quality control is driven by the wider implications. For example, substantial amounts of time and money can be absorbed in handling and remedying complaints if a customer receives poor service or a defective product. Further, losing customers to the competition as a result of poor quality can result in substantial loss of earnings, with further repercussions if disappointed customers spread their disenchantment by word of mouth.

Today, after more than a decade of concentration on quality and the adoption of Japanese methods, quality standards have reached new highs: some companies are even committed to zero-defect production. However, quality is not cheap for suppliers. In addition, buying companies are always seeking to achieve tighter quality control at lower cost. In order to concentrate on the quality of their own processes, buyers want to be able to assume the quality of inputs. Suppliers who can meet buyers' stringent standards are saving costs for the buying companies, but they must equally control the costs for themselves.

These last three elements are major contributors to the improvement in supply chain efficiency overall, where the aim is the creation of a lean, mean, low-cost supply machine. Efficiency has been defined as 'doing things right' and effectiveness as 'doing the right things'. In fact, by working closely with a supplier, a buyer can significantly improve supply chain effectiveness as well as efficiency. Improvement of effectiveness in supply chain terms will mean identifying the critical pathways on both sides and ensuring that these processes in particular are seamless and robust.

Traditionally, suppliers would encourage customers to buy as much as possible from them and, if customers were using more of the product than was really necessary, so much the better. However, this kind of opportunistic behaviour generally meets with disapproval from buyers. Buyers expect trusted suppliers to point out over-specified products, unnecessary wastage or inefficient usage and to reduce production costs, even if it means lower revenue for the supplier. High production costs will make the buying company uncompetitive in the marketplace and, ultimately, the supplier will lose out as well. Suppliers (not necessarily the key account manager) should therefore have a high degree of technical understanding of their own products and be able to offer their expertise in order to support the customer's production function in various ways, including reducing the consumption of other inputs. To make gains beyond the normal levels, the buying company may have to give the supplier access to closely guarded production secrets, in the confidence that such critical information will not reach competitors.

> Buyers expect trusted suppliers to point out over-specified products, unnecessary wastage or inefficient usage.

However, information from the European Institute of Purchasing and Supply shows that, in many cases, as much as 90 per cent of the final unit cost of a product is determined before it reaches full production, most of which is committed in the design stage (Figure 5.3).

> The major opportunity for achieving low unit costs for the manufacturer lies in the design stage.

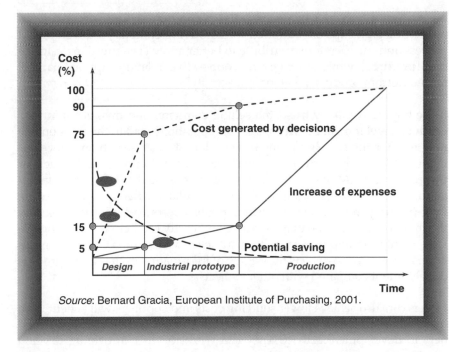

Source: Bernard Gracia, European Institute of Purchasing, 2001.

**Figure 5.3**
Progress of product development compared with commitment of final unit cost.

Thus, the major opportunity of achieving low unit costs for the manufacturer lies in the design stage. Research at Cranfield has shown a large difference between *cooperative* relationships and *interdependent* relationships

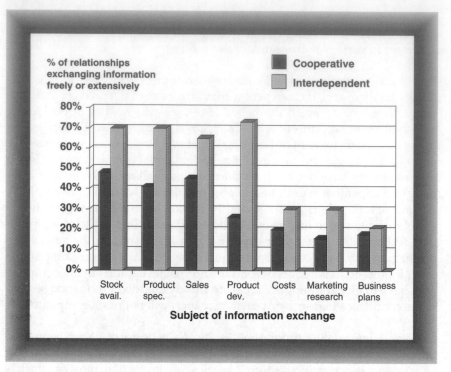

**Figure 5.4**
Topics for
information
exchange in KAM
relationships.

on this point (Figure 5.4): a substantial proportion of suppliers in *interdependent* relationships are admitted to the buying company's development process and can therefore contribute to better, more cost-effective design of new products, while suppliers in cooperative relationships are largely excluded from product development activity.

If the buying company trusts the selling company and involves it in new product development activities, this can potentially lead to the creation of a new role for the supplier in the buyer's long-term research and development (R&D) effort. Participation may mean contributing expertise and/or project funding. Much mutual benefit can be gained from such collaboration, including cost sharing on R&D, particularly where programmes are long-running and expensive. Further, pooling resources in order to secure the input of experts who may be scarce and costly can help to avoid the pitfalls of entering into projects with insufficient vision and directional guidance. Figure 5.4 also depicts the degree of information exchange on product development compared with other subjects.

Buyers can also achieve lower sourcing costs and suppliers will benefit from lower business development costs through involving trusted trading partners in development activity. They can work together in helping develop specifications and sourcing criteria and, if the supplier can then fulfil the need, the buying company may decide to look no further. If the buyer believes that the selling company is a good source for the product required and will not make opportunistic profits, then the working processes and widespread familiarity which already exist represent a real bonus: the buyer can avoid the effort, delays and costs involved in evaluating alternatives.

The public sector seems reluctant to take this pragmatic approach and generally insists on compulsory competitive tendering, which not only incurs huge bid costs for suppliers, but also means that buyers ultimately carry the costs of implementing the process through higher prices. In the private sector the supplier's unique expertise and competence may prove so invaluable to the buyer that, even where the selling company itself may not represent an attractive source for the product or service required, the partnership may grow to the point where the supplier takes on the sourcing and ongoing management of the supply as a primary contractor managing smaller, secondary contractors. This arrangement is increasingly common as buying companies seek to reduce their supplier base.

Clearly, close relationships between buying and selling companies have the potential for saving a substantial amount of cost for both sides. However, both sides will have to invest significantly in order to secure these cost savings, in relationship building, communication and committing time to joint projects, and also in new facilities, equipment, staff or whatever is needed for implementation. Expenditure on the less tangible activities, such as relationship building, is as real as expenditure on tangibles, though often the systems applied to accounting for it are very poor or non-existent.

> Both sides will have to invest significantly in order to secure these cost savings.

It is important for business success that expectations are set correctly and that the timescales used for evaluation are of a suitable length. In *basic* or *cooperative* relationships, both sides realize that exit is quite easy and either company will look for a quick return on any investment it makes because it cannot be sure that the relationship will last. Obviously, many cost-saving opportunities are barred if only those with rapid payback are acceptable. Therefore, the value of cost savings which can be made at these relationship stages is limited and may not even exceed the costs of running the relationship. In contrast, in *interdependent* or *integrated* relationships there is an expectation of durability and trustworthiness which lowers the perceived risk and allows longer term investments to be considered.

> Many cost-saving opportunities are barred if only those with rapid payback are acceptable.

In effect, reducing risks leads to lower costs and, indeed, risks and costs are closely linked. Sensible companies and, in particular, companies in their buying capacity are extremely concerned about risk. Risk reduction is therefore worthy of a separate discussion and this follows in the next section.

---

### CHECKPOINT

#### Cost-saving opportunities

Can you identify any strategies that could achieve cost savings benefiting both a key customer and your own organization?

### 5.1.3 Risk reduction

Reduction of risk is one of the major drivers that cause companies to seek closer relationships and encompasses the following:

- A reduction of uncertainty generally
- Protection against pressures from the business environment
- Protection against opportunism by powerful trading partners
- Protection against losing the business altogether.

If buyers or sellers were to articulate the main reason why they strive so hard to make closer relationships work, it would be because they seek the security of retaining trading partners who will be critical to their long-term business future.

The value of risk reduction to both parties can easily be overlooked in the day-to-day management of the relationship. It is therefore a worthwhile exercise for companies to understand what risks their partner perceives and to deconstruct them to see how they might be diminished and/or be seen to be diminished. The model developed by the International Marketing and Purchasing (IMP) Group (see Figure 5.5) provides a useful framework from which to view sources of risk.

Business risks derive from two dimensions: external to the relationship (environment in the IMP model) and internal to the relationship (atmosphere of relationship in the IMP model). External risks originate in the marketplace or the wider environment, but have an impact on the market, for example government legislation. A wide range of external factors potentially have implications for both parties, such as new technology (for example substituting for current products), economic recession (downturn in demand), competitor activity (downturn in demand and pressure on prices) and many more.

Buyers perceive plenty of internal risks as well. The buying company's first concern is always opportunism on the part of selling companies (Williamson, 1985). Will suppliers pass on any lower costs to the buyer? Will they hold the buyer to ransom for higher prices if they have the advantage? Will they respect confidential information? Will they provide continuity of supply? Buying companies can and do protect themselves against such behaviour in all sorts of ways, such as broadening their supplier base, playing one supplier off against another and insisting on contracts being fully specified to every last detail. However, these 'protective' measures cost buyers money and flexibility, and tend to reduce their leverage with suppliers. Nor do buying companies which carry such 'sandbags' stand up well today against leaner competitors who have taken calculated risks in order to work with suppliers and who have opted for speed and adaptability rather than security and safety.

'Protective' measures cost buyers money and flexibility.

Assuming the supplier is indeed ethical, honest, committed and currently competent, the buyer's second concern is the long-term orientation and

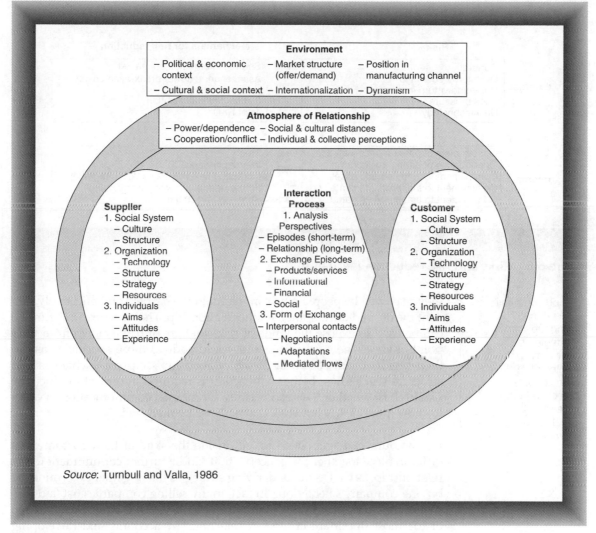

**Figure 5.5**  The IMP model.

capability of the selling company. Does the supplier represent the best available partner? After all, an honest fool is not necessarily more valuable as an ally than a talented knave. The buying company is likely to be looking for a partner who is at the leading edge of current products and practice and looks certain to stay there. If they have to make investments in assets dedicated to a particular supplier's products or systems, buyers want to be sure that they are making prudent purchases. They do not want to be obliged to write off the costs of such equipment and systems in the event that they need to change their supplier in order to stay ahead. Figure 5.6 shows some examples of risks and the ways in which they can be tackled.

There will be people inside the buying company, particularly those who are not normally in contact with the selling company, who are uncomfortable about lowering their protective barriers against suppliers. Unfortunately,

> The buyer's second concern is the long-term orientation and capability of the selling company.

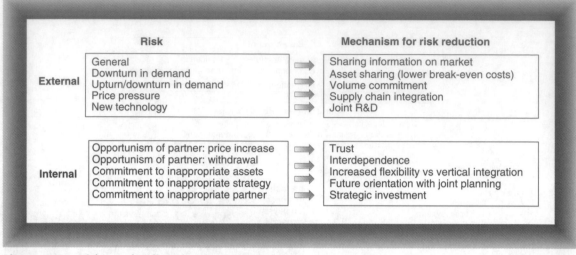

**Figure 5.6** Risks and risk reduction mechanisms.

Selling companies believe that compatibility of strategies is necessary to the fulfilment of their own corporate objectives and, indeed to the development of an intimate relationship.

they may well be people who can maintain the barriers and effectively prevent the desired development of the relationship. The structure in Figure 5.6 can be used to expose the kinds of risks that are of real concern from their point of view. The mechanisms that could address those specific areas can then be identified. An audit of the relationship's current exchanges and structure will show whether new action is required in order to reduce the risk itself or whether the need is really for internal communication in order to show more clearly how risk is already being managed.

Key account managers need to 'get inside the skin' of their customers in order to piece together the concerns that kindle further commitment to the relationship, as well as the underlying strategies that together determine the buying company's behaviour. In fact, many selling companies list 'a desire to partner' (with acceptance of the risks involved) and 'strategic fit' as two of the most important criteria in selecting key accounts and developing close relationships with them. They believe that compatibility of strategies is necessary to the fulfilment of their own corporate objectives and, indeed, to the development of an intimate relationship.

## 5.2 Buying company strategies

### 5.2.1 Strategy independence

It should come as no surprise to learn that buyers operate strategies for working with suppliers which run parallel to those that selling companies use. The most successful buying companies, and particularly those focused on achieving drastic reductions in their supplier base, develop specific strategies for their key suppliers individually. However, many buying companies take a more generic approach and work to simple strategies such as 'cut supplier numbers', 'reduce prices by 10 per cent all round' or 'use ISO 9000 suppliers only'. Even if these generic strategies are not entirely and explicitly exposed to suppliers, they are very real and suppliers need to understand them.

Selling companies are rarely good at acknowledging and responding to the customer's strategy. At one level, selling companies know that their customers have some kind of strategy and yet, at another, they are capable of ignoring it completely and developing their own strategy to be applied to the key account, quite independently of the customer's strategy. Not surprisingly, customer buy-in is poor and the exercise tends to get swept to one side.

> Selling companies are rarely good at acknowledging and responding to the customer's strategy.

When selling companies do not understand what causes their customers to respond to them in the way that they do, they have little chance of developing an appropriate strategy, in other words one that is likely to succeed. Ideally, strategic planning should be carried out jointly, but research has shown that this is still not the norm (McDonald and Woodburn, 1999). Joint strategic planning was found in only approximately one-third of even the most important relationships (the top two or three in each case) and it is presumably even more rare at the next level down.

> An appropriate strategy is one which is likely to succeed.

### 5.2.2 Strategy direction matrix

If the selling company's relationship with the customer is not close enough for joint planning, then the next best approach is to carry out a strategic analysis from the customer's point of view and to deduce an appropriate strategy on the basis of the findings. To do this, selling companies may find it helpful to employ the strategy direction tool commonly used by buyers to determine how they should manage their suppliers (Figure 5.7). This is the equivalent of the selling company strategic direction matrix shown earlier in Figure 2.5.

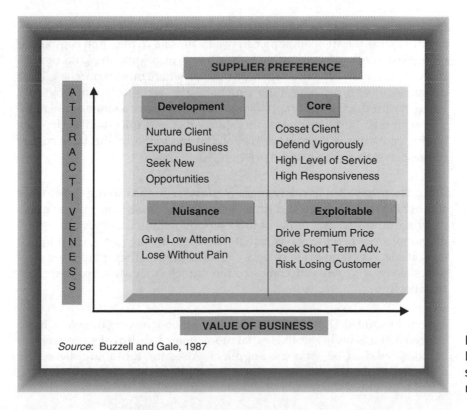

*Source*: Buzzell and Gale, 1987

**Figure 5.7**
Buying company's strategy direction matrix.

The horizontal axis 'Supplier preference' is self-explanatory. The quantity purchased will obviously be the most important factor, but others may also be taken into account, such as stability of demand, product quality and competitive position in the marketplace. The vertical axis 'Attractiveness' is a proxy for market risk and refers to the supply position. Market risk will include factors such as the number and quality of suppliers, capacity to cope with demand, market turbulence and price stability. Stability and plenty of choice for the buying company will give a low market risk assessment. Unpredictable fluctuations and few suppliers to choose from will result in a high market risk assessment. Each buying company will define the criteria by which it wants to measure its purchasing power and the market risk for itself, largely depending on the sector in which it operates.

If the buying company has low purchasing power in a low-risk market situation (bottom left box), then it will simply seek efficiency and a transactional relationship. The purchase will not be deemed sufficiently important to warrant further engagement with the supplier and the buyer will not be in a strong bargaining position anyway.

If, on the other hand, the product market is high risk, then there is a chance that supplies could be interrupted (top left box). The buying company is not in a strong enough position to apply leverage and protect itself. Buyers in this situation may react by increasing buffer stocks, seeking a substitute product or finding a more reliable source.

In situations of high purchasing power and a low-risk market (bottom right box), the buying company can use its muscle to play one competitor off against another in order to secure a better price or some kind of additional value. However, in a high-risk market, where buyers purchase large quantities and, thus, have high purchasing power (top right box) and where the product is important to them, they may seek a strategic relationship with their supplier in order to reduce risk and uncertainty. Here the buying company is more likely to look at the value or the total cost of acquisition rather than just the price.

The authors have spent many years working with the buying directors of some of the world's biggest companies. On many occasions, buying directors have admitted that many of their suppliers think that they are 'strategic' suppliers, when the reality is that they are in the low-price, commodity, exploitable, leverage-price category. Consequently, they play their suppliers along and, when it comes to the crunch, they drive prices down relentlessly.

Indeed, looking at Figure 5.8 (provided by a global buying director), it can be seen that it is highly unlikely that more than a handful of suppliers will be considered to be strategic suppliers. Also, for those suppliers who really want to be considered as strategic suppliers, the same global buying director provided the set of criteria shown in Figure 5.9.

**Figure 5.8** Supplier relationships as a source of business advantage.

**Figure 5.9** Strategic supplier criteria.

Buying companies, like selling companies, have a limited capacity for intimacy.

Of the four options in Figure 5.7, only in the top right box is a high-involvement relationship with the supplier likely to take root. Buying companies, like selling companies, have a limited capacity for intimacy and they cannot squander it on situations and suppliers that are not important. It therefore follows that, if the supplier's product/service falls into one of the other boxes of the matrix, however important that customer is to the supplier, the selling company is unlikely to succeed in developing a close relationship.

A need for strategic product development should not be mistaken for a need for relationship development.

This conclusion suggests that the selling company should not waste its resources on such a relationship. Investment would be better employed in becoming super-efficient in order to operate effectively in either of the two boxes on the bottom than in developing a different offer which is designed to fall into the top right box of the matrix. If the matrix indicates a need for strategic product development, it should not be mistaken for a need for relationship development. Key account management (KAM) will not compensate for an inadequate offer and misapplication will only result in misdirected, wasted resources.

### 5.2.3 Supply chain integration

Determination of strategy should be a collective process.

Supply chain management and integration strategies, which are often accompanied by supplier base reduction, have had a major impact on many selling companies in recent years. New electronic commerce capabilities will drive this trend forward and few companies are likely to be unaffected. Figure 5.10 shows the development of supply chain management from the baseline of traditional management to current advanced practice in which companies are operating cross-boundary integration.

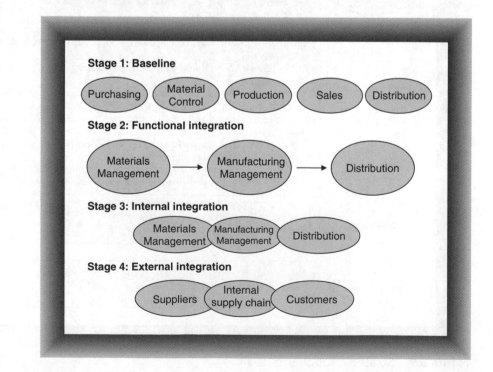

**Figure 5.10** Development of supply chain management.

Figure 5.10 charts the change from a traditional manufacturing approach, which keeps the supplier on the doorstep, to one in which the supplier has become part of an extended enterprise. The boundary between one company and the next in the chain is breached and may even be dissolved. Processes and strategies must be integrated. As the organizations are so closely linked, they cannot operate to different strategies successfully and, therefore, determination of strategy should be a collective process, not a process owned by an individual member of the chain.

The roles played by the supplier, its customer and other members of the extended enterprise are clearly different from the role played in the other configurations. Some companies are very uncomfortable with the loss of distinction between 'us' and 'them'. Other companies, such as Amazon, the Internet bookseller, can operate the model with equanimity. It is undoubtedly easier to start a company in a new mode than convert an existing one, which will have innumerable functions and processes orientated in a different way. However, the arrival of electronic business in force, which we are now witnessing, will oblige many companies to adapt to cross-boundary activity. The contrast between single-company, boundary-confined thinking and extended-enterprise, cross-boundary thinking is shown in Table 5.1.

> The arrival of electronic business in force will oblige many companies to adapt to cross-boundary activity.

| Single company thinking | Extended enterprise thinking |
|---|---|
| Focus on the customer | Focus on the ultimate consumer |
| Increase own profits | Increase profits for all |
| Consider own costs only | Consider total costs |
| Spread the business around | Team with the best |
| Guard ideas, information and resources | Share ideas, information and resources |
| Improve internal process efficiency | Improve joint process efficiency |

**Table 5.1**
Single company thinking versus extended enterprise thinking

The external context in which buyer–seller relationships exist is becoming increasingly extensive and complex. Change drivers include the rapid pace of change, the refinement of processes, market maturity, heightened customer power and the globalization of business. At the same time, the internal, organizational context is also changing, removing traditional delineations of remit and responsibility. Conditions are more conducive to 'partnering' between suppliers and customers and, hence, the nature of marketing has altered. Marketers are moving away from a traditional transaction focus towards a customer focus. Thus, there is a pressing need to find ways to describe relationships as a basis from which to understand them better and build them stronger – and this has led to the ascendancy of KAM.

Supply chain integration is probably the strategic development that is most critical for suppliers. A selling company that is not selected as a dependable

A selling company which is not selected as a dependable ally in a newly integrated core supply chain is likely to end up as a secondary supplier.

ally in a newly integrated core supply chain is likely to end up as a secondary supplier, dealing with the original customer through an intermediary. Being separated from the customer limits the supplier's access to information and restricts its ability to demonstrate added value. The supplier becomes much more vulnerable to the agenda of the intermediary.

Most opportunities for cost reduction and value enhancement are currently seen to lie at the interface between members of the supply chain. Much has therefore been written about this subject and it cannot be adequately covered here. Clearly though, understanding the position and strategy of neighbouring members in its supply chain is fundamental to the buying company's strategy and the management of the relationship between itself and its upstream suppliers and its own downstream customers.

### 5.2.4 Matching strategies

In many cases suppliers have found the new partnering philosophy to be little more than skin deep.

The climate and culture of purchasing has changed in recent years and supply chain partnerships have become more acceptable and, indeed, popular. Even so, in many cases suppliers have found the new partnering philosophy to be little more than skin deep. Customers have promised a partnership approach with a focus on added value and mutual benefit and then have forced prices to the floor anyway, resulting in the sorry state of customer profitability described in Chapter 6.

Of course, buying companies are not absolutely bound by the strategic direction indicators discussed here: they can choose to adopt different approaches and behaviour. However, buyers will readily revert to type if that strategy is not founded on sound logic and sense, so selling companies should beware of a customer promising a strategy which is out of line with that indicated by analysis.

The customer's propensity to partner must be a criterion for admission to a supplier's KAM programme.

Companies naturally seek to work with other companies whose strategies and goals match theirs. If the selling company has adopted a strategy of developing high-involvement partnerships with key customers, then it will look for buying companies whose strategies mirror its own and who will reciprocate. The customer's propensity to partner must be a criterion for admission to a supplier's KAM programme. Some companies have managed to be fairly ruthless in wielding that criterion and have excluded any customer who, however huge, operates a price fighter strategy and plays competitors off against one another. Key account managers are often horrified at the thought of excluding this type of customer but, of course, there is no obligation to tell the customer of the decision.

KAM programmes restricted to customers who offer genuine opportunities for mutual and committed relationships have shown excellent growth in revenues and margins, even astronomical in some cases. Pressure from key account managers and buyers to include other types of large customer is often considerable, but the temptation should be resisted. As emphasized elsewhere in this book, a company's capacity for close business relationships is limited and expansion of the customer base will inevitably detract from the focus on the most important customers. Inclusion of other, less-suitable customers will add plenty of cost and probably not much growth. Of course, these customers are still very important to the selling company. They probably represent a large part of its current cash income, but they should be managed in a different way, with a focus on efficient transactions.

---

### Case study insight
#### Managing intimacy (Hewlett Packard)

Hewlett Packard started their global account programme in 1993 with 26 global key accounts. By 1996 it had grown 10-fold to 250. The following year, Hewlett Packard cut the number back to 95.

---

### 5.2.5  Supplier delusions

A relationship is intrinsically reciprocal: you cannot be married to some-one unless they are married to you. Only the reciprocated elements of a relationship are relevant and real. If there is a mismatch of perceptions, the relationship is defined only by the elements that are matched. Figure 5.11 illustrates this point: the genuine extent of the relationship is represented by a square, which defines an equal and shared perception. Anything out-side the square is delusion.

> Only the reciprocated elements of a relationship are relevant and real.

Determining what stage of development a relationship has reached depends on the views of both of the parties involved. Research has shown,

> Beware the pitfalls of supplier delusion.

*Source*: Adapted from Millman and Wilson, 1994.

**Figure 5.11**
Buyer and supplier perceptions of relationships.

perhaps not surprisingly, that key account managers tend to overestimate the stage relationship by approximately one development stage (McDonald and Woodburn, 1999). From the buyer's perspective, the two parties are not as close as the supplier probably imagines. Selling companies need to be aware of this phenomenon if they are to avoid engaging in inappropriate behaviour and embarking on premature strategies.

### 5.2.6 *Trust*

Trust plays a major role in buyer behaviour.

Trust, or confidence in a partner's reliability and integrity, is one of the most important elements in high-involvement relationships. A significant body of research supports the notion that trust plays a major role in buyer behaviour. Buying companies rated 'integrity/honesty' as one of the two most important attributes of a good key account manager (equal with 'product knowledge') (McDonald *et al.*, 1996). Interestingly, when selling companies were similarly questioned, they selected completely different attributes and scarcely rated integrity at all. This difference in opinion suggests that selling companies might be wise to re-evaluate their priorities if they want to align themselves more closely with their customers.

Trust can be regarded as a mediator through which many of the interactions between buyer and seller pass. Interactions potentially increase the level of trust but, as in a game of snakes and ladders, they also have the potential to damage it. Suppliers would do well to manage interactions with a view to how the buyer might perceive them and whether they build or destroy trust. Activities such as improving performance, sharing more information, improving communications and even admitting mistakes should all help to build trust if they are handled sensitively. In addition, trust will, according to the degree to which it pre-exists, either add to or detract from the perceived value of these activities.

Achieving a high degree of trust has numerous positive outcomes. There will be more readily offered cooperation between the two sides, less uncertainty when sensitive information is shared, more commitment to the relationship and a lower probability that one or other will exit. Trust can also bridge a patch in the relationship where something is going wrong. However, if the problem persists for too long, then it will eat away at the 'reserves' of trust and, eventually, relationship breakdown will occur. In effect, a dynamic balance exists in the relationship between past experience of performance and behaviour and current perception of performance and behaviour, which is buffered by trust.

Trust is certainly more than an abstract concept in buyer–seller relationships. Lack of trust has significant cost implications for buying and selling companies at both the strategic and tactical levels. At the strategic level, there are many initiatives that a customer could undertake jointly with a supplier to their mutual benefit. However, if the supplier is not trusted sufficiently, the customer may pursue the opportunity alone or with a more appropriate and trusted partner.

At a tactical level, the existence of trust can open up a range of processes for the examination of cost-cutting opportunities. For example, a selling company undertakes an internal environmental audit. Meanwhile, a buying company looking to do business with the selling company requires assurance that the supplier complies with certain environmental standards and proceeds to conduct its own audit of the supplier. Obviously this duplicate auditing adds extra cost. Much of the cost could be avoided if the buying company trusted the selling company to carry out the audit objectively and if the selling company trusted the buying company to respond sensibly to the audit's results.

A retailer formalizes the degree of trust it places in its numerous suppliers. On the arrival of deliveries, the retailer may quality check 100 per cent, 10 per cent or 1 per cent of the goods. Suppliers are effectively penalized for being 'untrustworthy' by being charged for the cost of checking deliveries at the level deemed appropriate. In a very few cases of trusted suppliers, 0 per cent of the goods are checked (saves handling costs) and the retailer invoices itself (saves 'paperwork').

It is not by accident, or course, that these costs are widely incurred. Naturally, many companies feel a need to guard themselves against the opportunism of other companies. Indeed, in innumerable cases companies have been shown to be right in dealing cautiously with other profit-seeking entities. So, although there has been a cultural shift over the last five years towards closer relationships with trading partners, the shift has not been universal. Many companies have not bought into the idea and, even where they have in theory, they may not have done so in practice.

In contrast, where trust exists between two companies, a considerable range of cost savings become available, as shown in Section 5.1.2. As a further incentive, greater profits may be achieved through tackling opportunities together.

Companies should therefore adopt a policy of scepticism, but stop short of cynicism. Treating all-comers with universal suspicion is, ultimately, rather limiting. Trustworthy partners do exist, either because they have

Companies should therefore adopt a policy of scepticism, but stop short of cynicism.

## Case study insight

### Defining 'trust'

Customer managers in a commercial banking organization were asked to predict whether their key customer relationships would survive another two years at least. The results were analysed against a number of relationship parameters. The research concluded that holding a favourable 'balance of power' or the previous 'duration of the relationship' did not affect expectations of the continuation of relations, whereas 'trust' was strongly linked to expected relationship life (Perrien et al., 1999).

enshrined ethical principles or because they see it as being in their long-term interest to behave in a trustworthy manner. It is important that companies first choose their strategic trading partners carefully and then work concertedly to develop a productive, mutually beneficial relationship with them. They can continue to work with other companies more cautiously.

## 5.3 Balance of power

It is abundantly clear to practitioners of KAM that, although the balance of power between a supplier and a customer might not affect the duration of a relationship, it certainly makes a huge difference to its nature. However, to date, little academic attention has been given to studying the role of control and influence in trading relationships, perhaps because it is not an easy subject to research.

> Power is linked to the perceived degree of dependency on the partner.

Power is obviously linked to the perceived degree of dependency on the partner. In fact, the one is the reverse of the other. Dependency increases as the size of the business with the trading partner increases and as its share of the company's turnover grows. Dependency also increases if loss of the business would damage either company's reputation and trigger the defection of other partners, or if finding a substitute would be difficult. For a selling company with high fixed costs, the consequences of losing a major customer can be devastating, but where most costs are variable the effects are more manageable.

Table 5.2 outlines the sources of power in a buyer–seller relationship as identified by a group of practitioners from blue-chip companies. Whether the company is buying or selling, most of the sources of power are potentially mirror images of each other. What differs is the list of them possessed by each organization in a given relationship at a given point in time. For example, the balance of power may favour a selling company over a small buying company in need of its advanced technological support.

Suppliers can be just as powerful as buyers, although that is not the everyday perception of their key account managers, who usually feel that buyers have the upper hand.

Power may be thought of in terms of the overall 'quantity' of power, as well as the balance of it in a relationship. The framework shown in Table 5.2 can be used to audit the power position in a particular relationship. First, identify the actual sources of power for each side using Table 5.2 as a preliminary checklist. Then give each source of power a score that represents its relevance and strength in the relationship and total scores afterwards. This exercise will help to clarify the nature of the power that may be leveraged. It will also indicate the direction and degree of any imbalance in an objective way.

Regardless of the relative power positions, companies with the balance of power in their favour can still choose how they exercise their advantage. Power can be used constructively or destructively. For example, a buying

**Table 5.2**   Sources of power

| Nature of source | Buyers' sources of power | Sellers' sources of power |
|---|---|---|
| Size/importance | Big<br>Consolidation: bigger<br>Globalization: even bigger<br>Share of total supplier business | Criticality to buyer<br>Capacity to meet demand<br>Share of purchases |
| Competitor options | Supply excess<br>Commodity markets<br>Globalization: cherry-pick suppliers<br>Globalization: pick currency and prices | Supply shortage<br>Key differentiation<br>Access to innovation<br>Patents and monopolies<br>Brand/demand pull<br>Erect barriers to new competitors |
| Buying/selling skills | Access to information<br>Leverage market knowledge<br>Higher expectations<br>Competent buyers | Access to information<br>Leverage market knowledge<br>Easy to work with<br>Competent key account managers |
| New strategies | Supply chain management<br>Supplier rationalization<br>Globalization<br>E-commerce | Recognized relevant expertise<br>Track record and reputation<br>Global competence<br>Flexible |
| Threat of exit | Low cost of switching for customer<br>High cost of switching for supplier<br>Effect of loss on supplier cost base | High cost of switching for customer<br>Low cost of switching for supplier<br>Limited availability of alternatives |
| Leverage of contacts | Within supplier<br>Within markets/ability to damage reputation<br>Within regulatory bodies | Within customer<br>Within markets<br>Within regulatory bodies |

company in a very powerful position could demand very low prices and stand a good chance of obtaining them. However, the selling company's profits may be depressed to the point where it cannot invest in innovation which would ultimately benefit its customer, or it might go out of business. Alternatively, the customer could decide that its long-term interests lie more in imposing specific strategies or higher standards of practice on the supplier because it would make the supplier a better trading partner, to the benefit of both companies.

So, while the balance of power is clearly important in determining the nature of a relationship, it does not provide sufficient explanation on its own. Linking the balance of power with the concepts of common interest/ mutual benefit does, however, offer further insight into relationships

(Krapfel et al., 1991). Common interest may be defined as the compatibility between the goals of the companies that are trading together. Companies that approach the business between them in the same manner and share the same aims and objectives are said to have a high degree of common interest. A good example is to be found where both supplier and buyer are dedicated to the same industry sector and have evolved similar responses to the environmental forces at work in that sector. Figure 5.12 plots the balance of power against the degree of common interest and summarizes the different situations to be found in each of the six sets of circumstances shown.

**Power balance**

| | Favours seller | Balanced | Favours buyer |
|---|---|---|---|
| **High** | High level of communication, not really open. Promises mutual benefit, actually win/lose | Cooperative, open, trusting, info sharing, Long-term horizons | Useful info offered by seller. Sends signals of cooperation |
| **Low** | Directive communication, more threats than promises | Info exchanged as necessary not high volume | Seller may not even signal cooperation |

*Common interest* (vertical axis label)

**Figure 5.12**
Balance of power versus common interest.

The research behind the development of this matrix showed that, in situations of a low degree of common interest (bottom three boxes), the volume of communication is generally not high, and information is only exchanged as necessary. The volume of communication is much higher where a high degree of common interest exists. However, this volume does not necessarily indicate information sharing: a large part of it may be directive, more like a one-way 'lecture' than a two-way 'conversation'. Chapter 3 highlighted the important roles that communication and information exchange play in key account relationships. Clearly, the quality and nature of each as well as the quantity need to be taken into consideration in understanding the relationship.

The matrix suggests that the only situation in which a collaborative, cooperative relationship will exist is where the two parties have the same amount of power and a high degree of common interest. In fact, even where the balance of power lies in favour of one of them, a collaborative relationship could exist if the company with the upper hand chooses to behave in a cooperative manner. Nevertheless, the weaker side should always be wary of the possibility that a policy of cooperation which is not backed up by necessity is liable to change. For example, a selling company might agree to investment in equipment dedicated to a powerful customer, on the understanding that the price of the product will yield a margin sufficient to give a return on the investment in, say, two years. In a relationship based on balanced power and mutual necessity, the agreement might safely be quite flexible and relatively informal. In a relationship based on the benevolence or enlightenment of a powerful partner, a sound contract might be wise protection against the chance of a change in the partner's policy.

> The only situation in which a collaborative, cooperative relationship will exist is where the two parties have the same amount of power and a high degree of common interest.

## Case study insight

### Identifying the balance of power (NHS Supplies)

NHS Supplies divided its contracts into eight major product groups. The organization held meetings with its most important suppliers in each group in order to promote dialogue with them. The organization noticed that, although the meetings had the same agenda and were held in the same kind of environment, each meeting had a very different atmosphere in terms of the suppliers' expressed willingness to participate and cooperate with NHS Supplies. The turnout at some meetings was almost 100 per cent while for others it was relatively low. Afterwards, the organization mapped the balance of power between itself and each group against the evident degree of common interest. The predictions matched the actual responsiveness of the suppliers and the degree of cooperation offered.

## Summary

The most important point to be made in this chapter is that suppliers need to understand where they currently sit in the buying company's classification matrix of its suppliers. Some suppliers will be seen by the customer as truly strategic and will want an interdependent or integrated relationship with them by dint of their crucial importance to their organization's success. Such suppliers, however, are few in number and if a supplier is merely one of many who can offer similar products or services, success is likely to accrue to the supplier with the lowest prices. In such cases, the supplier should either seek to get its own costs down, or strive to develop a business model that adds value to its selected customer's operation.

# 6 Key account profitability

## Fast track

Marketing as a discipline has failed during the past 50 years by concentrating on promotion rather than on developing world-class marketing strategies. The result is that in most companies, marketing has been relegated to running promotional campaigns and designing T-shirts and does not deserve a place at the high table, that is, the board of directors.

The result of this sad lack of marketing leadership is the demise of many of our erstwhile famous organizations. Most of the highest earning Return on Investment plcs during the decade up to 1990 have gone into liquidation or were acquired in desperate circumstances, whilst many of the leading companies in different sectors up to the year 2000 also got into financial difficulties or were acquired.

All of this happened against a background of three major challenges that industry was facing during this period and still faces – market maturity, globalization and customer power.

The most dramatic challenge has been the massive shift of power to customers away from suppliers. Today, customers are destroying old make/sell business models, whilst technology has empowered customers to have more information about their suppliers than they have about them. Meanwhile, a new wave of business metrics and new pressures from institutional shareholders to report meaningful facts about corporate performance, combined with demands from other stakeholders for exemplary corporate behaviour, have resulted in a need for strategies other than downsizing and cost-cutting as a route to increased profitability.

Never before has the need for real marketing professionalism in relation to key account management been greater.

This raises the question of what marketing is. It is a function, just like finance, with its own professional institute and body of knowledge. The challenge is to understand the needs of customers, then to formulate strategies for meeting these needs in a way that enables the company to create long-term net free cash flows which, having taken account of the associated risks, represent a financial return over and above the cost of capital, thus creating shareholder value. This strategic imperative is quantitatively measurable using the body of existing marketing knowledge and CEOs must demand of their chief marketing officers that their strategic forecasts for their key account performances are subjected to the same rigorous due diligence as other initiatives, such as acquisitions.

Some key accounts will inevitably reduce shareholder value, but providing these are managed to increase net free cash flows and to reduce risk, this is acceptable. Overall, as long as the aggregate of the net forecast value from all key accounts is positive, having taken account of the risks and the cost of capital tied up in servicing them, then it is possible to prove to the Board and to shareholders that the key account performance is creating shareholder value continuously.

## Introduction

Marketing accountability has become one of the burning issues facing boards of directors today. Given the increasing power of a small number of major customers in many sectors, key account profitability has risen to the top of the agenda as part of this movement towards marketing due diligence, which is why a whole chapter has been devoted to this topic.

This chapter puts key account profitability within the context of marketing accountability and goes on to explain a state-of-the-art method for proving to the Board that the key account programme as a whole is creating shareholder value added.

## 6.1  Sustainable competitive advantage and key accounts

Marketing has a central role in creating sustainable competitive advantage. In fact, the overall purpose of strategic marketing is the creation of sustainable competitive advantage.

Typically, stock exchanges scatter the shares of companies in a graph according to return and according to their own estimates of risk. The diagonal line (the line of best fit) is known as the beta. Figure 6.1 shows a typical array from any stock exchange of the relationship between risk and return. Any firm on the line will normally be making industry-average returns for its shareholders – in other words, making returns equal to the weighted average cost of capital (WACC). Firms making consistent returns

**Figure 6.1**
Financial risk and return.

greater than the WACC are creating shareholder wealth, known generally as shareholder value added, economic value added, positive net present value, super profits, sustainable competitive advantage and so on.

Figure 6.2 shows diagrammatically how sustainable competitive advantage can be achieved. This shows that, when an organization has state-of-the-art operations, has its cash flows firmly under control and, more importantly, when its offers are sufficiently differentiated by being matched to the specific needs of market segments, these all combine to create positive net free cash flows (positive net present value, having taken account of the risks inherent in future strategies, the true value of money and the cost of capital) or shareholder value added.

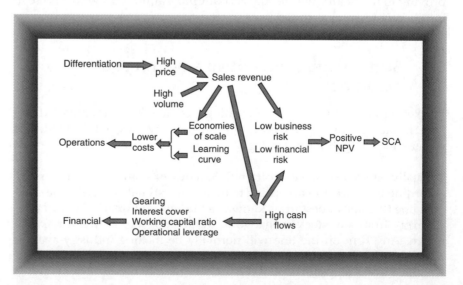

**Figure 6.2**
The route to sustainable competitive advantage (SCA).

Modern finance is based on four principles:

- Cash flow (the basis of value)
- The true value of money
- The opportunity cost of capital (other investments of a similar risk)
- The concept of net present value (the sum of the net cash flows discounted by the opportunity cost of capital).

Also, it is well known that, whilst accountants do not measure intangible assets, the discrepancy between market and book values shows that investors do. Hence, expenditures to develop marketing assets make sense if the sum of the discounted cash flow they generate is positive.

A little thought will indicate that every single corporate activity, whether it be R&D, IT, purchasing or logistics, is ultimately reflected in the relative value put on a firm's offer by its customers. The marketing function is central to this, as every one of the four (or five, six or seven Ps) can only be improved by the whole organization focusing its attention on its customers.

The crux of the matter is failure to align marketing with the fundamental shareholder value objective. Marketing objective setting is, in practice, murky or, at worst, downright wrong. Increasing sales volume, the most widely cited marketing objective, can easily be achieved by sacrificing profitability, for instance. Increasing profit, another commonly cited marketing objective can be also attained in the short term by relinquishing investments for future growth.

Perhaps more worrying than comments about lack of alignment between marketing strategies and corporate objectives are charges of poor marketing professionalism. There is widespread evidence from research that very few marketing professionals actually understand or know how to use the widely available strategic analysis tools that would help them to dovetail their plans with what is going on in the wider marketplace, and elsewhere in their organizations.

There are numerous tried and tested tools that can be of immediate value in improving marketing's contribution to the main board agenda. For example:

- Financial rigour in appraising marketing objectives would be a useful start. Financial managers have used tools such as shareholder value added for at least 10 years now to support investment appraisal and resource allocation. However these methods are mainly applied to capital projects and mergers and acquisitions. Although discounted cash flow is occasionally used to calculate brand valuations, it is not widely used to support marketing decision making. Now frequently referred to as NPV (net present value), it is still in widespread use by accountants for capital projects.

- Marketing planning methods should be more strategic. Unfortunately, the annual budget cycle has a stranglehold over marketing objective setting. Studies of the marketing planning processes reveal that less than 20 per cent of marketing professionals use strategic objective-setting methods. Objectives are predominantly short term and have little connection with wider corporate plans for growing shareholder value.

- Resource allocation to support customer projects needs to be aligned with business growth. Yet there is a widespread disconnect between customer-related objectives, and corporate cost-cutting objectives. Symptoms of this disconnect can be observed in the exceedingly poor service provided by the majority of call centres, and the inadequate customer response from many Internet business ventures, which are very often set up as corporate cost-cutting ventures. Again the treatment is conceptually easy. Surprisingly few marketing plans adequately assess their resource implications (especially not cross-functionally).

- Customer profitability is also known to be a key driver of shareholder value, according to academic studies. Again the state of marketing practice is poor. Remarkably few organizations use this vital tool.

- Customer retention analysis and root-cause customer defection analysis are widely written about, yet our research at Cranfield shows that few companies bother to measure them (Figure 6.3).

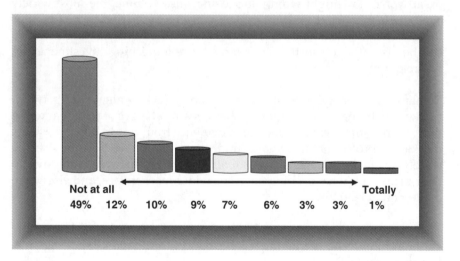

**Figure 6.3**
Customer retention by segment (answers to a Cranfield questionnaire using an audience response system to guarantee anonymity. The question was 'We measure customer retention by segment').

The low value that marketing places on measurement is brought home by looking at what marketing spends today on market research – about 700 million euros annually in each of the major Western European economies. Compare this with the amount *one* oil company recently spent on a new financial information system – 700 million euros – the same figure that each Western European market spends on marketing information.

It is in response to the challenges outlined above that the authors have developed a process for auditing the main elements of marketing investments and for linking these investments to shareholder wealth. We have named this process 'marketing due diligence' in order to indicate that marketing should be treated in exactly the same way as, for example, an organization's financial audit, with the board, through their marketers, held accountable for the investments made in building shareholder value. This process has been developed in this book to cover investments made in key accounts and will be described in detail later in this chapter.

The purpose of a financial audit, which is a legal requirement, is to ensure financial due diligence and, whilst the ENRON scandal demonstrates that it does not always work as it should, in the main, the financial audit process has served the business community well. It is clear, however, that the time has come for a similar process of due diligence to be initiated for marketing processes and this includes key account management (KAM).

The time has come for a due diligence process to cover marketing.

As we have already indicated, in capital markets success is measured in terms of shareholder value added, having taken account of the risks associated with the proposed strategies, the time value of money and the cost of capital. This is totally different from what is commonly referred to as 'profit'. The problem with this approach is that it is backward looking. Later in this chapter we will show how to calculate shareholder added value for the future.

The following simple calculation shows the principle of shareholder value added:

| | |
|---|---|
| Operating profit after tax | £2000 |
| Capital employed | £15 000 |
| Cost of capital | 10% |
| Operating profit after tax | £2000 |
| Less cost of capital | £1500 (15 000 × 10%) |
| Economic profit | £500 |

Figure 6.4 illustrates how intangible assets have become the major proportion of an organization's assets. Brand Finance estimate that for the FTSE top 350 and the Fortune 300 companies, about 75 per cent of their value is in intangibles. Indeed, the recent takeover of Gillette by Procter and Gamble showed that they bought £27 billion of intangible assets out of the total price of £31 billion. Thus, £4 billion of their purchase was for tangible assets (Table 6.1).

There are four main types of marketing asset:

- **Marketing knowledge** (skills, systems and information)
- **Brands** (strong brands often earn premium prices and can be enduring case generators)
- **Customer loyalty** (loyal customers buy more, are cheaper to serve, are less price sensitive and refer new customers)
- **Strategic relationships** (channel partners provide access to new products and markets).

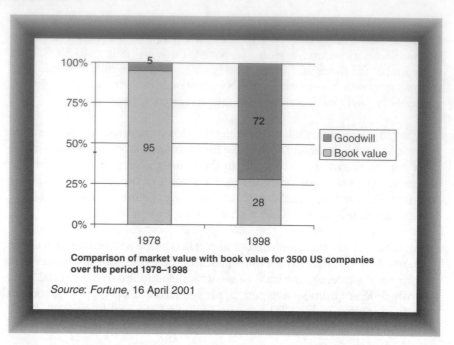

**Figure 6.4**
Intangibles are the key driver of shareholder value.

Comparison of market value with book value for 3500 US companies over the period 1978–1998

*Source: Fortune*, 16 April 2001

**Table 6.1**
Intangible assets acquired by Procter and Gamble when they bought Gillette for a total price of £31 billion

| | |
|---|---|
| Gillette brand | £4.0 billion |
| Duracell brand | £2.5 billion |
| Oral B | £2.0 billion |
| Braun | £1.5 billion |
| Retail and supplier network | £10.0 billion |
| Gillette innovative capability | £7.0 billion |
| **Total** | **£27.0 billion** |

*Source*: Haigh, 2005

It will be seen from this that customers are a significant part of these intangible assets and it is to this aspect of value that the remainder of this chapter is devoted, because just as certain markets can either create or destroy shareholder value, so can major customers. Later in this chapter, we will give a 'step-by-step process for valuing key accounts.

## 6.2 Customer retention and profitability

It has been suggested that it costs up to five times as much to win a new customer as it does to retain an existing customer.

It has been suggested by international consultants Bain and Company that it costs up to five times as much to win a new customer as it does to retain an existing customer. Despite this finding, many organizations have traditionally focused their marketing activity on acquiring new customers rather than retaining existing customers. The costs of capturing market share are not always easy to gauge, but there are many companies who now regret earlier strategies based upon the blind pursuit of sales volume. While strong evidence exists to suggest a link between market share and profitability there is equally strong evidence to show that it is the quality of the market share that counts. In other words, does our customer base comprise, in the main, long-established, loyal customers or is there a high degree of customer turnover or 'churn'? If the latter is the case, then the chances are that we are not as profitable as we might be.

Bain and Company have suggested that even a relatively small improvement in the customer retention rate (measured as a percentage of retained business from one defined period to another) can have a marked impact upon profitability. They have found that, on average, an improvement of five percentage points in customer retention can lead to profit improvements of between 25 and 85 per cent in the NPV of the future flow of earnings.

So why should a retained customer be more profitable than a new one? According to Reichheld and Sasser (1990), there are several reasons. First, the costs of acquiring new business may be significant and, thus, it may take time, even years, to turn a new customer into a profitable customer. Second, the more satisfied customers are with the relationship, the more likely they are to place a larger proportion of their total purchase with us, even to the extent of single sourcing. Third, as the relationship develops, there is greater mutual understanding and collaboration which serves to reduce costs. Retained customers become easier to sell to and economies of scale produce lower operating costs. These customers are also more willing to integrate their IT systems (for example, their planning, scheduling and ordering systems) with ours, leading to further cost reductions. Fourth, satisfied customers are more likely to refer others to us, which promotes profit generation as the cost of acquiring these new customers is dramatically reduced. Finally, loyal customers are often less price sensitive and less inclined to switch suppliers because of price rises.

These factors collectively suggest that retained customers generate considerable more profit then new ones. Figure 6.5 summarizes this connection between customer retention and profitability.

## Case study insight

### Customer retention in the car industry

A study of the North American car industry found that a satisfied customer is likely to stay with the same supplier for a further 12 years after the first satisfactory purchase and during that period will buy four more cars of the same make. It is estimated that, to a car manufacturer, this level of customer retention is worth $400 million in new car sales annually.

There is a direct linkage between the customer retention rate and the average customer lifetime, meaning the lifetime of a customer relationship. For example, if the customer retention rate is 90 per cent per annum (meaning that we lose 10 per cent of our existing customer base each year), then the

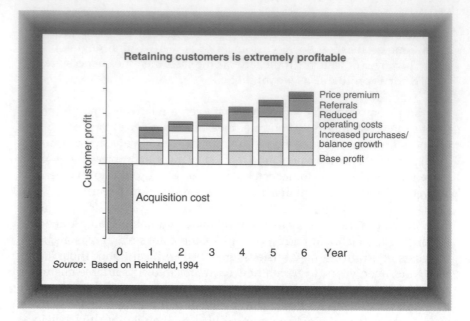

**Figure 6.5**
Customer profit
contribution over
time.

average customer lifetime will be 10 years. If, on the other hand, we manage to improve the retention rate to 95 per cent per annum (meaning that we lose 5 per cent of our customers each year), then the average customer lifetime will be 20 years. In other words, a doubling of the average customer lifetime is achieved for a relatively small improvement in the retention rate. Figure 6.6 illustrates the relationship between the retention rate and customer lifetime.

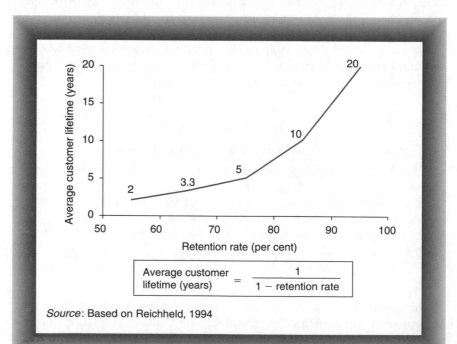

**Figure 6.6**
Impact of customer
retention rate on
customer lifetime.

An important statistic that is not always measured is the lifetime value of a customer. Put very simply this is a measure of the financial worth to the organization of a retained customer. If customers are loyal and continue to spend money with us into the future, then clearly their lifetime value is greater than that of a customer who buys only once or twice from us and then switches to another brand or supplier.

If customers are loyal and continue to spend money with us into the future, then clearly their lifetime value is greater than that of a customer who buys only once or twice from us and then switches to another brand or supplier.

Measuring the lifetime value of a customer requires an estimation of the likely cash flow to be provided by that customer if he or she achieves an average loyalty level. In other words, if a typical account lasts for 10 years, then we need to calculate the NPV of the profits that would flow from that customer over 10 years. We are now in a position to calculate the impact that increasing the retention rate of customers will have upon profitability and also what the effect of extending the customer lifetime by a given amount will be. This information provides a sound basis for marketing investment decision making, indicating how much it is worth spending for either improving the retention rate or extending the life of a customer relationship. The key question is who to retain and who to invest in.

Let us revisit the hierarchy of key relationships model (Figure 6.7). The development of profitable key accounts begins with the development of the key account relationship. Having qualified 'prospective' key accounts and selected certain accounts for investment strategies, the next step is to implement the marketing planning process.

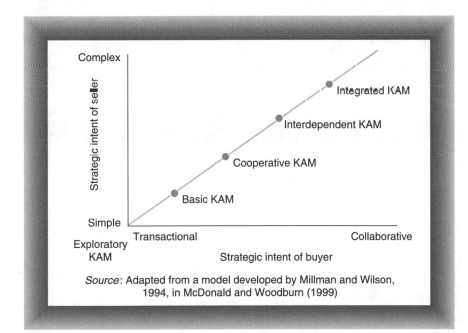

*Source*: Adapted from a model developed by Millman and Wilson, 1994, in McDonald and Woodburn (1999)

**Figure 6.7**
The relationship development model.

For many companies, the closing of a sale is regarded as the culmination of the marketing process.

Once a sale has been made, then we have a *basic* customer. For many companies, the closing of a sale is regarded as the culmination of the marketing process. However, smart marketers realize that this is only the beginning of a process of building customer loyalty leading to potentially lucrative, long-lasting customer relationships.

To convert the customer into a *cooperative* client requires that we establish a pattern of repeat buying by making it easy for the customers to do business with us. However, being a *cooperative* client does not necessarily signal commitment. For example, banks have regular customers who might be termed *cooperative* clients. However, many of those customers may express high levels of dissatisfaction with the service they receive and, if it were possible to move accounts easily, would defect to another bank. What is required is for us to develop such an effective customer-oriented approach that these *cooperative* customers become *interdependent* customers, meaning they are pleased with the service they receive. In fact, if they are really impressed with the quality of the relationship, they may become *integrated* customers who are moved to tell others about their satisfaction with our offer. Given the power of word of mouth, this type of advocacy can be worth more than any amount of advertising.

> The *integrated* customer relationship reaches the ultimate rung on the ladder of customer loyalty.

The *integrated* customer relationship reaches the ultimate rung on the ladder of customer loyalty. It marks the achievement of a mutually rewarding relationship where neither party intends to leave the other. Increasingly, the idea of 'partnership' is being accepted as a desirable goal of business relationships. This is particularly the case in industrial marketing and business-to-business marketing.

The relationship development model, while a simple idea, can provide a practical framework around which to build specific customer-retention strategies. The first of these strategies concerns financial risk and business risk, as represented in Figure 6.8. The top left quadrant in the matrix

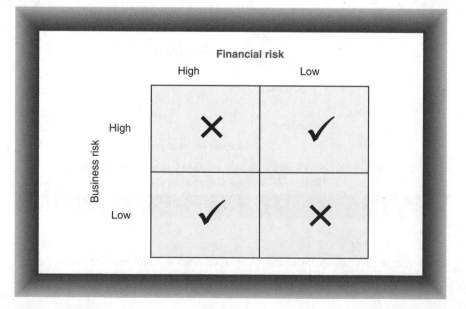

**Figure 6.8**
Financial risk versus business risk.

denotes high financial risk combined with high business risk, an often lethal combination. Experience and logic dictates that where the business risk is high, financial risk should be low and vice versa.

---

### Case study insight

#### High risk in the airline market

Consider the late Sir Freddie Laker's Sky Train venture in the 1980s. With a very high financial gearing, given the high cost of entering the airline business, he entered the most competitive market in the world – the London–North Atlantic route. Furthermore, his strategy against the mighty global airlines was one of low price, which, given Laker's high break-even point, became unsustainable in the long run against special price promotions mounted by the top airlines to counteract the impact of Sky Train.

---

### Case study insight

#### Low risk in the airline market

Turning now to the top right quadrant (low financial risk/high business risk), compare this situation with Richard Branson's market debut with Virgin Airlines. He entered the market with very few planes and low financial gearing, initially leasing his aircraft. Like Sir Freddie Laker, he also entered the lucrative North Atlantic route, but his strategy was one of differentiation, something he has very successfully sustained ever since. There is no doubt that Virgin's service is fundamentally different from that of other airlines, particularly Virgin Upper Class, which the younger travellers find particularly appealing. Virgin Airlines continues to go from strength to strength.

---

A similar impact was experienced in the UK housing market of the late 1980s and early 1990s. As homeowners borrowed more and more money against the hope that property values would continue to rise, millions of people were left with negative equity when house prices plunged dramatically.

Now consider the bottom right quadrant (low financial risk/low business risk). Any organization in this delightful position would be ill-advised to hoard the cash! For many years, Marks & Spencer adopted this type of strategy until the company cleverly invested in higher business risk ventures and repositioned itself in the top right quadrant. On the other hand, in situations of low business risk, it seems sensible to opt if necessary, for a higher financial risk (bottom left). A low business risk, high financial risk position would describe organizations such as Olympia and York before the property market fell through the floor in the late 1980s.

Having briefly examined the concept of business and financial risk, we can now begin to appreciate why some businesses do better than others over extended periods of time. The world's stock exchanges as represented by the line of best fit shown in Figure 6.1 earlier in this chapter shows financial return plotted against financial risk. Successful organizations produce either the same return for a lower perceived risk or a higher return for the same risk or both. Being north-west of the line of best fit year after year is the mark of organizations whose shares continuously outperform the sectors to which they belong. Taking the cost of capital and using this as a discount rate against future earnings to produce a positive NPV is indicative of super profits or sustainable competitive advantage.

This is not to be mistaken for producing super profits in one single year, which can be achieved relatively easily by cutting costs, limiting capital expenditure or even by selling off some of the company's assets. The trouble with short-term strategies such as these is that financial markets today are much too sophisticated to be taken in by this, so it is a common phenomenon to see the capital value of the shares fall after an increase in a single year's profits and an increased dividend.

The following two examples illustrate the tenuous nature of the future profitability of many organizations. Table 6.2 shows the performance of a fictitious company which appears to be excelling on virtually every business dimension. Table 6.3, however, shows the same company's performance compared with the market as a whole. Here the performance figures reveal severe underperformance, indicating that the company is heading for disaster when market growth slows down.

**Table 6.2**
Example of market growth performance: InterTech's five-year performance

| Performance (£ million) | Base year | 1 | 2 | 3 | 4 | 5 |
|---|---|---|---|---|---|---|
| Sales revenue | £254 | £293 | £318 | £387 | £431 | £454 |
| Cost of goods sold | £135 | £152 | £167 | £201 | £224 | £236 |
| Gross contribution | £119 | £141 | £151 | £186 | £207 | £218 |
| Manufacturing overhead | £48 | £58 | £63 | £82 | £90 | £95 |
| Marketing and sales | £18 | £23 | £24 | £26 | £27 | £28 |
| Research and development | £22 | £23 | £23 | £25 | £24 | £24 |
| Net profit | £16 | £22 | £26 | £37 | £50 | £55 |
| Return on sales (%) | 6.3% | 7.5% | 8.2% | 9.6% | 11.6% | 12.2% |
| Assets | £141 | £162 | £167 | £194 | £205 | £206 |
| Assets (% of sales) | 56% | 55% | 53% | 50% | 48% | 45% |
| Return on assets (%) | 11.3% | 13.5% | 15.6% | 19.1% | 24.4% | 26.7% |

| Performance (£ million) | Base year (%) | 1 (%) | 2 (%) | 3 (%) | 4 (%) | 5 (%) |
|---|---|---|---|---|---|---|
| Market growth | 18.3 | 23.4 | 17.6 | 34.4 | 24.0 | 17.9 |
| InterTech sales growth | 12.8 | 17.4 | 11.2 | 27.1 | 16.5 | 10.9 |
| Market share | 20.3 | 19.1 | 18.4 | 17.1 | 16.3 | 14.9 |
| Customer retention | 88.2 | 87.1 | 85.0 | 82.2 | 80.9 | 80.0 |
| New customers | 11.7 | 12.9 | 14.9 | 24.1 | 22.5 | 29.2 |
| Dissatisfied customers | 13.6 | 14.3 | 16.1 | 17.3 | 18.9 | 19.6 |
| Relative product quality | +10.0 | +8.0 | +5.0 | +3.0 | +1.0 | +0.0 |
| Relative service quality | +0.0 | +0.0 | −20.0 | −3.0 | −5.0 | −8.0 |
| Relative new product sales | +8.0 | +8.0 | +7.0 | +5.0 | +1.0 | −4.0 |

**Table 6.3**
Example of market-based performance: InterTech's five-year market-based performance

Table 6.4 is taken from Hugh Davidson's book, *Even More Offensive Marketing*, and is reproduced here with his kind permission. The table shows two companies making the same return on sales on the same turnover, but even a cursory glance at the two sets of figures clearly shows that Dissembler plc is heading for disaster. Financial institutions around the world are rarely fooled by so-called 'successful' annual results.

The Cranfield/*Financial Times* research report into KAM (McDonald and Woodburn, 1999) concluded that there is much supplier delusion about the stage of development customer relationships have reached and that much of the profitability of key accounts is leaked away through the provision of levels of service which are not justified by the revenue.

This is perfectly in order if it is done deliberately as an investment strategy in key accounts selected as having the best potential over, say, a three-year planning horizon. However, where there is no such proactive strategy, money is being lost without justification.

Let us examine Figure 6.9. The line of best fit indicates a perfect match between the strategic intent of both the supplying and buying companies. In Figures 6.10 and 6.11, however, we see an obvious mismatch and it is likely that both companies are losing money unnecessarily. This judgement of the situation of course presupposes that supplying organizations have systems that can measure *attributable* costs, that is to say those costs which are directly related to a particular account. Alas, our database at Cranfield shows that a very substantial majority of Western European companies do not measure attributable costs. Figure 6.12 – from a Cranfield database of over 500 leading European companies over a five-year period – illustrates this point. The figure shows the spread of answers to the

Supplier delusion about relationships leads to profitability leaking away through unjustified levels of customer service.

**Table 6.4**  Quality of profits

| % | Virtuous plc (%) | Dissembler plc (%) |
|---|---|---|
| Sales revenue | 100 | 100 |
| Cost of goods sold | 43 | 61 |
| Profit margin | 57 | 39 |
| Advertising | 11 | 3 |
| R&D | 5 | – |
| Capital investment | 7 | 2 |
| Investment ratio | 23 | 5 |
| Operating expenses | 20 | 20 |
| Operating profit | 14 | 14 |
| Key trends | Past five year revenue growth 10% pa Heavy advertising investment in new/improved products Premium priced products,new plant, so low cost of goods sold | Flat revenue, declining volume No recent product innovation, little advertising Discounted pricing, so high cost of goods sold |
| The make-up of 14% operating profits Factor | | |
| Profit on existing products over three years old | 21 | 15 |
| Losses on products recently launched or in development | (7) | (1) |
| Total operating profits | 14 | 14 |

Note: This table is similar to a profit and loss with one important exception – depreciation, a standard item in any profit and loss has been replaced by capital investment, which does not appear in profit and loss statements. In the long term, capital investment levels determine depreciation costs. Capital investment as a percentage of sales is an investment ratio often ignored by marketers, and it has been included in this table to emphasize its importance (Reichheld and Sasser, 1990).

*Source*: Davidson, 1998

question: 'How well do you know the real profitability of your top 10 accounts, having taken into account attributable costs' (1 = not at all, 9 = totally).

Yet suppliers still persist in using operating systems that spread the overheads across the customer base according to turnover, in effect penalizing customers who are easy to serve and rewarding customers who are difficult and costly to serve.

Unless there is a 'square', there is a mismatch between either the SDMU (Supplier Decision-Making Unit) or the BDMU (Buyer Decision Making Unit) Where there is a 'square' there is a perfect match

**Figure 6.9**
A match between buyers and sellers.

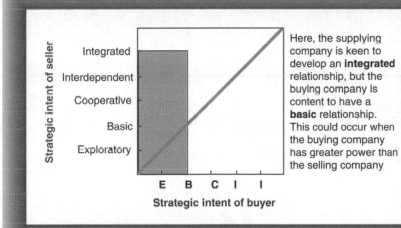

Here, the supplying company is keen to develop an **integrated** relationship, but the buying company is content to have a **basic** relationship. This could occur when the buying company has greater power than the selling company

**Figure 6.10**
Mismatch between buyer (*basic*) and seller (*integrated*).

Here, the buyer company is keen to develop an **interdependent** relationship, but the supplying company is content to have a **basic** relationship. This could occur when the selling company has greater power than the buying company

**Figure 6.11**
Mismatch between buyer (*inter-dependent*) and seller (*basic*).

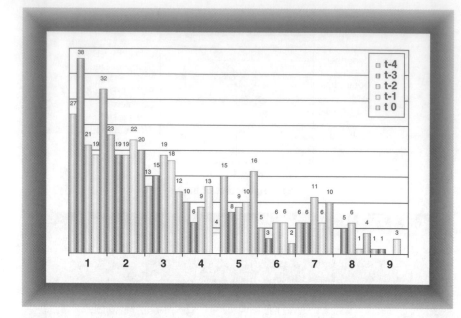

**Figure 6.12**
Cranfield survey on key account profitability.

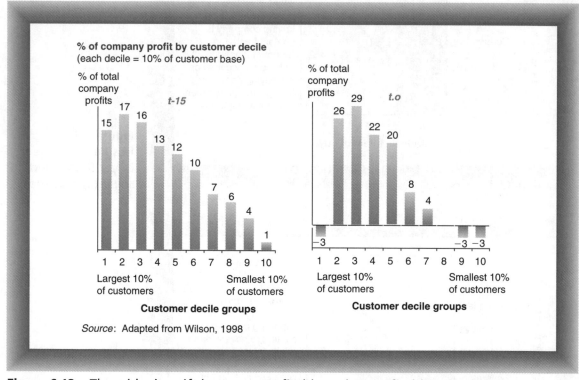

Source: Adapted from Wilson, 1998

**Figure 6.13**   The widening rift between profitable and unprofitable customers.

Figure 6.13 shows the current profitability of the top 10 per cent of customers of a major European print company as compared with 15 years ago. This comparative example is taken from Charles Wilson's excellent book, *Profitable Customers: How to Identify, Develop and Keep Them* (Wilson, 1998), and confirms the Cranfield research finding highlighted in Figure 6.12 that most companies today fail to keep a prudent check on key account profitability. This disturbing trend must be of particular concern to chief executives and also to financial directors. To understand and measure key account profitability is to direct/define the destiny of your customer relationships and, thus, your business future!

---

### CHECKPOINT

#### Partner level relationships

- Are you able to measure the real profitability of your key accounts?
- How has the level of profitability changed over the past three years?

---

## 6.3 The impact on business of this lack of customer focus

On top of all the pressures referred to earlier, a new wave of business metrics such as shareholder added value and balanced scorecards, together with pressure from institutional shareholders to report meaningful facts about corporate performance rather than the traditional, high-level financial reporting that appears every year in corporate accounts, are forcing business leaders to re-examine tired corporate behaviours such as cost-cutting, mergers and downsizing as a route to profitability.

Finally, business leaders are under intense pressure to deliver against stakeholder expectations; customers are demanding greater levels of customization, access, service and value; shareholders are expecting to see continuous growth in earnings per share and in the capital value of shares; and pressure groups are demanding exemplary corporate citizenship.

The result is that, at long last, the world has genuinely moved from *caveat emptor* to *caveat vendor*. No longer can we continue to hammer into the soggy brains of erstwhile supine customers the messages that *we* want them to receive. No, the world has changed forever and 'marketing' (in the sense that the world contains the word 'market') must now be taken seriously.

> At long last the world has genuinely moved from *caveat emptor* to *caveat vendor*.

Some evidence of the results of a lack of a robust strategy towards markets follows.

What better place to start than with *In Search of Excellence: Lessons from America's Best-Run Companies* (Peters and Waterman, 1982)? According to Richard Pascale, of Tom Peters' original 43 excellent companies, 14 were still excellent five years later and only six were still excellent eight years later! (Pascale, 1990).

**Table 6.5**
Performance of
selected companies
1979–1989

| Year | Company[a] | Market value (£m) | Return on investment[b] | Subsequent performance |
|------|-----------|-------------------|------------------------|------------------------|
| 1979 | MFI | 57 | 50 | Collapsed |
| 1980 | Lasmo | 134 | 97 | Still profitable |
| 1981 | Bejam | 79 | 34 | Acquired |
| 1982 | Racal | 940 | 36 | Still profitable |
| 1983 | Polly Peck | 128 | 79 | Collapsed |
| 1984 | Atlantic Computers | 151 | 36 | Collapsed |
| 1985 | BSR | 197 | 32 | Still profitable |
| 1986 | Jaguar | 819 | 60 | Acquired |
| 1987 | Amstrad | 987 | 89 | Still profitable |
| 1988 | Body Shop | 225 | 89 | Still profitable |
| 1989 | Blue Arrow | 653 | 135 | Collapsed |

[a] Where a company has been top for more than one year, the next best company has been chosen in the subsequent year, e.g. Polly Peck was related top 1983, 1984 and 1985.
[b] Pre-tax profit as a percentage of investment capital.
*Source*: Professor Peter Doyle, Warwick University

Table 6.5 shows clearly that many of Britain's best-performing companies during the decade up to 1990 subsequently collapsed and Table 6.6 shows a selection of leading companies in different sectors during the decade up to 2000 and what happened to them.

Table 6.7 shows the retention rate of a real company by segment. Other unpublished research from the Cranfield University School of Management research club that looks at marketing measurement shows that, almost 16 years after the famous Reicheld and Sasser (1990) article, very few companies have learned the lesson about retaining profitable customers.

To summarize this section, we conclude that short-termism – in the sense of maximizing profits in a single fiscal period to the detriment of long-term profitability – is a 'disease' of management rather than of the financial investment community, who fully understand that the two are not mutually exclusive. Indeed, it has always been those companies such as Procter and Gamble, 3M, General Electric and Tesco which grow their short-term profits annually, whilst investing in a long-term profitable future, that have been continuously successful financially for many years.

**Table 6.6**  Performance of sector leaders 1990–2000

| Year | Company[a] | Market value (£m)[b] | Return on investment (%)[c] | Subsequent performance |
|------|-----------|----------------------|------------------------------|------------------------|
| 1990 | Maxwell Communications plc | 1.0 | 5 | Collapsed |
| 1991 | Imperial Chemical Industries plc | 8.6 | 13 | Collapsed |
| 1992 | Wellcome plc | 8.3 | 40 | Acquired |
| 1993 | ASDA Group | 1.6 | 7 | Acquired |
| 1994 | TSB Group plc | 3.7 | 20 | Acquired |
| 1995 | British Telecommunications plc | 22.2 | 17 | Not profitable |
| 1996 | British Steel plc | 3.3 | 19 | Collapsed |
| 1997 | British Airways plc | 6.1 | 7 | Not profitable |
| 1998 | National Westminster Bank plc | 19.6 | 14 | Acquired |
| 1999 | Marconi plc | 29.8 | 22 | Acquired |
| 2000 | Marks & Spencer plc | 5.3 | 7 | Not profitable |

[a] Each company was a FTSE100 when selected.
[b] Market values as of 31 December of each year.
[c] Pre-tax profit as a percentage of equity and long-term debt.

**Table 6.7**  Retention of customers by segment

| | Total market | Segment | | | | | |
|---|---|---|---|---|---|---|---|
| | | 1 | 2 | 3 | 4 | 5 | 6 |
| Percentage of market represented by segment | 100.0 | 14.8 | 9.5 | 27.1 | 18.8 | 18.8 | 11.0 |
| Percentage of all profits in total market produced by segment | 100.0 | 7.1 | 4.9 | 14.7 | 21.8 | 28.5 | 23.0 |
| Ratio of profit produced by segment to weight of segment in total population | 1.00 | 0.48 | 0.52 | 0.54 | 1.16 | 1.52 | 2.09 |
| Defection rate | 23% | 20% | 17% | **15%** | 28% | 30% | **35%** |

## 6.4 How to measure risk and return and how to estimate whether key accounts are creating or destroying shareholder value

First, it is necessary to understand the concept of net free cash flow in relation to key accounts. This is the total sales revenue generated from a customer, less all the costs that are incurred in servicing that account. As already stated, overhead costs include a proportion of overhead costs in relation to their use in servicing the account. Activity-based costing (ABC) can be used to determine how much this should be.

Knowing key account profitability in terms of net free cash flow:

- assists in deciding whether to keep the customer and on what terms,
- helps in strategic decisions about the allocation of scarce company resources and
- enables informed decisions to be taken in negotiations and in pricing.

A basic profitability model is shown in Figure 6.14.

Related to these calculations, the following kinds of questions need to be discussed:

- How much does the customer buy in a year?
- What is the direct cost of those goods?
- Are the products standard or bespoke?
- Is it steady work, or seasonal peaks?
- How many orders do they place in a year? By what mechanism? How many of these are 'emergency' orders? Are they small quantities or large?
- How many times do sales people have to visit them?
- Do you have to maintain stock for them, or do you make to order?
- How many delivery sites are there? Where? What delivery terms?
- How many invoices do you raise to them? How many credit notes?
- Do they pay promptly? What are your credit control costs? How much does it cost you to finance their debts?
- How much after-sales service do they need?
- What is likely to change in the future?

It is worth remembering that in the early stages of dealing with a major customer, cash flows may be negative whilst a position of strength is established, so it is important to calculate cash flows over a planning period of at least three years.

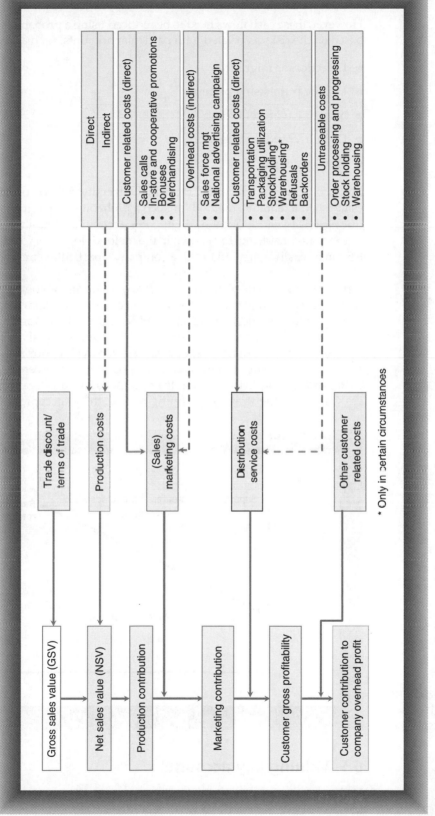

**Figure 6.14**  A basic profitability model.

However, these cash flows need to be reduced using a probability assessment based on the risks associated with particular accounts, such as the risk of:

● Defection or migration

● Volatile purchasing patterns

● Negative word of mouth

● Default, fraud, or litigation

● Slow payment.

Professor Lynette Ryals of Cranfield University School of Management, established a tentative method for such a probabilistic quantification of risks during a five-year doctoral study into key account profitability (Ryals, 2002). The factors considered and shown in the methodology that follows in Section 6.5 can be easily amended to suit a company's particular circumstances.

First, however, Figure 6.15 shows that key accounts can be positioned on a risk/return graph in the same way that companies or markets can. Those below the line are destroying shareholder value; those above are creating shareholder value. The reality, of course, is that there will always be some key accounts that are not creating shareholder value, but as long as these are managed appropriately (i.e. trying to increase revenue and reduce costs) and as long as the aggregate of key accounts are creating shareholders value over the strategic planning period, this is acceptable.

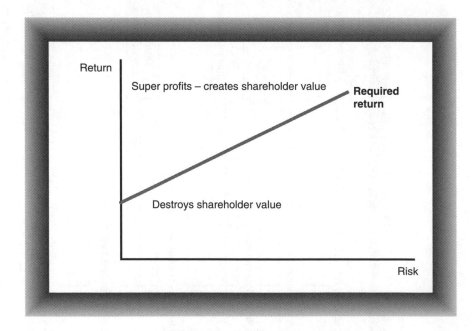

**Figure 6.15**
How organizations build value from key accounts.

## 6.5  Valuing key accounts

In this section we provide a step-by-step method for calculating whether key accounts create or destroy shareholder value.

### 6.5.1 Background/facts

- Risk and return are positively correlated, that is, as risk increases, investors expect a higher return.

- Risk is measured by the volatility in returns, that is, the likelihood of making a very good return or losing money. This can be described as the quality of returns.

- All assets are defined as having future value to the organization. Hence assets to be valued include not only tangible assets like plant and machinery, but intangible assets, such as key accounts.

- The present value of future cash flows is one of the most acceptable methods to value assets including key accounts.

- The present value is increased by:
  - increasing the future cash flows,
  - making the future cash flows 'happen' earlier and
  - reducing the risk in these cash flows, that is, improving the certainty of these cash flows, and, hence, reducing the required rate of return.

### 6.5.2 Suggested approach

- Identify your key accounts. It is helpful if they can be classified on a vertical axis (a kind of thermometer) according to their attractiveness to your company. 'Attractiveness' usually means the potential of each for growth in your profits over a period of between three and five years (Figure 6.16).

- Based on your current experience and a planning horizon that you are confident with, make a projection of future net free cash in-flows from your key customers. It is normal to select a period such as three or five years.

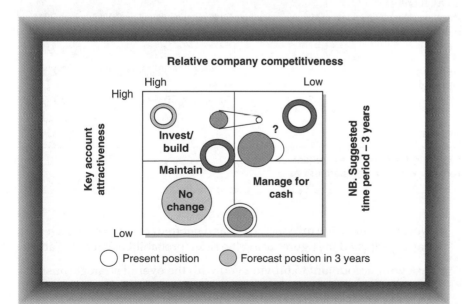

**Figure 6.16**
Portfolio analysis – directional policy matrix.

- These calculations will consist of three parts:
  - revenue forecasts for each year,
  - cost forecasts for each year and
  - net free cash flow for each key customer for each year.

- Identify the key factors that are likely to either increase or decrease these future cash flows. These factors are risks.

- These risks are likely to be assessed according to the factors shown on the relationship risk scorecard shown in Table 6.8 (used here with the kind permission of Professor Lynette Ryals of Cranfield University School of Management).

**Table 6.8**   Relationship risk factors

| Relationship risk factors | Minimum value | Maximum value | Assigned probability |
|---|---|---|---|
| **Overall relationship with the company** | | | |
| 1. Number of relationships with other business units | 0 | 3 | 0 = 40%, 1 = 60%, 2 = 80%, >2 = 90% |
| 2. Number of business lines within this business unit | 3 | 10 | 1 = 40%, 2 = 50%, 3 = 60%, 4 = 70%, 5–10 = 80%, >10 = 90% |
| 3. Longevity of relationship (years) | 0.5 | 16 | <3 = 40%, 3 = 60%, 4 = 70%, 5 = 80%, >5 = 90% |
| **Account relationship** | | | |
| 4. Company's relationship with broker[a] | 1 | 5 | 1 = 40%, 2 = 60%, 3 = 70%, 5 = 80%, 5 = 90% |
| 5. Quality and warmth of company/client relationship[a] | 1 | 5 | 1 = 40%, 2 = 60%, 3 = 70%, 4 = 80%, 5 = 90% |
| 6. Number of relationship contacts company has at client | 2 | 8 | 1 = 50%, 2 = 60%, 3 = 80%, >3 = 90% |
| 7. Number of relationship contacts client has at company | 3 | 10 | 1 = 50%, 2 = 60%, 3 = 80%, >3 = 90% |
| **Understanding of client** | | | |
| 8. How good was our understanding of their company[a] | 1 | 5 | 1 = 40%, 2 = 60%, 3 = 70%, 4 = 80%, 5 = 90% |
| 9. How good was our understanding of their industry[a] | 1 | 5 | 1 = 40%, 2 = 60%, 3 = 70%, 4 = 80%, 5 = 90% |

[a] 1 = very poor, 2 = poor, 3 = fair, 4 = good, 5 = excellent.
*Source*: Ryals (2002). Reproduced with her kind permission.

- Now recalculate the revenues, costs and net free cash flows for each year, having adjusted the figures using the risks (probabilities) from the above.

- Ask your accountant to provide you with the overall strategic business unit (SBU) cost of capital and capital used in the SBU. This will not consist only of tangible assets.

- Deduct the proportional cost of capital from the free cash flow for each key customer for each year.

- An aggregate positive NPV indicates that you are creating shareholder value – that is, achieving overall returns greater than the weighted average cost of capital, having taken into account the risk associated with future cash flows.

---

### CHECKPOINT

#### Partner level relationships

- Are you able to measure the real profitability of your key accounts?

- How has the level of profitability changed over the past three years?

---

## Summary

Marketing accountability is one of the biggest challenges facing all organizations today and a major component of this is key account profitability. Major customers are assets, just like buildings and cash. This chapter has positioned key account profitability firmly within the context of marketing accountability and has spelled out a state-of-the-art methodology for calculating whether the key account programme creates or destroys shareholder value.

# 7 Key account analysis

Correct market definition and market segmentation are essential prerequisites of successful key account management. A market is the aggregation of all goods and services that can satisfy a particular need or set of needs. Drawing a map of how goods and services flow through the value chain helps a key account manager understand the customer's business, as well as revealing ways in which you may be able to add value as a supplier.

Market segmentation is the process of breaking a market down into smaller groups of customers who share the same or similar needs. It is important at two distinct levels. First, key accounts in one segment may have different needs from those in another segment. Second, understanding how your customer's market is segmented provides much potential for helping them to succeed.

The total process of preplanning prior to producing a strategic plan for your customer is shown in the following diagram.

Steps 1, 2 and 3 should, ideally, be completed centrally to avoid duplication of effort by key account managers. Step 3 is about understanding in depth the forces that are being brought to bear on competitors in an industry. These are: customers, supplies, substitutes, potential entrants and, of course, industry competitors. A PEST analysis (political, economic, sociological, technological) is also an extremely useful way of understanding more about the customer's trading environment.

Each key account manager can now use this information to delve further into each customer's specific business processes. This includes understanding the customer's objectives and strategies, their financial ratios, how their business processes work, their buying processes, their sales history and their dealings with competitors.

One extremely useful vehicle for summarizing much of this is the traditional SWOT analysis (strengths, weaknesses, opportunities and threats), completed as if it were the customers themselves completing it.

All the CSFs (critical success factors) for the customer can now be sorted into those categories that merely help them to avoid disadvantage and, crucially, those that can create advantage for them, for clearly it is this latter group that will encourage a key customer to prefer dealing with you rather than with one of your competitors. You now have everything you need to approach the customer with your proposals for how you can help them increase sales, reduce costs, avoid costs or add value in other ways. They are usually so impressed that they are prepared to give you additional confidential information. You are now ready to prepare a strategic plan for the customers.

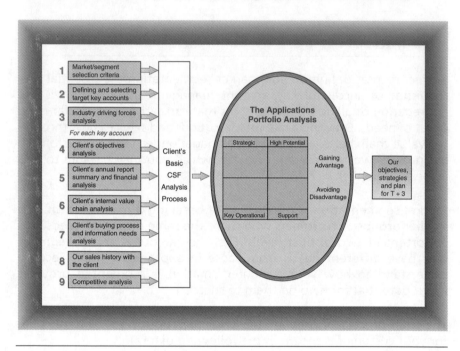

# Introduction

One of the objectives of this chapter is to place key account management (KAM) in the context of market segmentation, for it is creative market segmentation which is universally recognized as the key to sustainable competitive advantage. Another is to spell out how to understand in depth the environment in which key accounts operate. Finally, it explains in detail how to understand how key accounts run their business as a route to revealing ways in which you can help them to increase sales, avoid costs, reduce costs or add value.

# 7.1  Market segmentation and key account management

## 7.1.1  Understanding markets

Most organizations' different market segments will contain a number of key accounts. Before proceeding to analyse the needs of key accounts and set objectives and strategies for them, it is necessary to ensure that you have the clearest understanding of how your own market works, what the key segments are and where you can exert the most influence on decisions about what is bought and from whom. It is equally important to understand your customers' segmentation and how their market works. This is essential knowledge, for it will provide the backcloth against which plans for key accounts are evaluated and eventually controlled. Indeed, it would be fair to say that an appreciation of market segmentation is an essential criterion for effective KAM. Before explaining a little more about market segmentation, however, here are some introductory comments by way of background.

'The good thing about being mediocre is you are always at your best.' Someone once said this about corporate life. Imagine getting your sales-force up at five every morning to go out and kill for 'We are really mediocre!' Everyone has heard of Alexander the Great. Had he been mediocre, he certainly would not be in our history books. So what makes any of us think that making mediocre offers to our customers is ever going to have anything but mediocre results?

Taking this theme a stage further, we can ask ourselves what sort of company would make a commodity out of bread, fertilizer, glass, chlorine, potatoes, mobile phones, etc.? By way of an answer, ask whether anyone can 'taste' the difference between Castrol GTX or any other manufacturer's oil, or between Alfa Laval Steel, SKF Bearings, Intel Microprocessors and so on. Yet these great companies, dealing with low differentiation products in mainly mature markets, are perennially successful. So, what is the secret of success?

A review of the work of a number of gurus, such as Sir Michael Perry ex-chairman of Unilever, Tom Peters and Phillip Kotler, reveals a striking similarity between what they consider to be the key elements of world-class marketing.

1. A profound understanding of the market

2. Market segmentation and selection

3. Powerful differentiation, positioning and branding

4. Effective marketing planning processes

5. Long-term integrated marketing strategies.

> It is intensely irritating when the questioners know so little about their markets.

While this is not the complete list, it is interesting to note the order of the elements listed here. We find it remarkable that, even in the new millennium, so many companies are changing their brand strategies without really understanding their market and how it is segmented or their competitive position. Indeed, 'What shall we do with our brand?' is one of the most recurrent questions and, while it is easy to understand why it is asked, branding being the glamorous part of marketing, it is intensely irritating when the questioners know so little about their markets.

Let us explain what we mean. We frequently run workshops for the Boards of strategic business units. Before we start the workshop, we ask the directors to write a list, in order of priority, of their key target markets. Often they write down their products, such as pensions or mainframe computers. Rarely is there any sensible grasp of the meaning of the word 'market'. So, they fail the first test. The second part of the exercise is to write down their sources of differential advantages against each key target market listed. When these senior people fail such an elementary test, it is clear that their organization is either in or heading towards trouble.

> A segment is a group of customers with the same or similar needs. Companies still persist in confusing sectors with segments.

We recently came across one insurance company which prided itself on its market segmentation. On questioning, however, its segments turned out to be sectors, which explained why it had little or no differentiation and was competing mainly on price. Indeed, this is one of the most commonly observed misconceptions about market segmentation. Everyone knows that a segment is a group of customers with the same or similar needs and that there are many different purchase combinations within and across sectors, yet companies still persist in confusing sectors with segments.

Perhaps the most frequent mistake however is a priori segmentation, which is largely the result of the vast amount of prescriptive literature on the subject of segmentation. All books state that there are several bases for segmentation, such as demographics, socioeconomics, geography, usage, psychographics, geo-demographics, lifestyle and so on, and the literature is replete with proponents of one or more of these. However, this is to miss the point completely, for in any market there is only one correct segmentation. One hundred per cent of goods and services are 'made', distributed, influenced and used and the purchase combinations that result are a fact not a figment of someone's imagination. The task is to understand the market structure, how it works and what the actual segments are at different junctions in the market.

This brings us to the starting point in market segmentation – market definition and market structure. Correct market definition is crucial for measuring market share and market growth, identifying relevant competitors and, of course, the formulating of marketing strategies in order to deliver differential advantage.

The general rule for defining a 'market' is that it should be described in terms of a customer need in a way that covers the aggregation of all the alternative products or services which customers regard as being capable of satisfying that same need. For example, we would regard the in-company caterer as only one option when it comes to satisfying lunchtime hunger. That need could also be satisfied at external restaurants, public houses, fast food outlets and sandwich bars. The emphasis in the definition is therefore clearly on the word 'need'.

Figure 7.1 is an example of a complete 'market map', showing how goods move from originators through to final users, with volumes, values and market shares all adding up in a manner not unlike a balance sheet. However, few companies give sufficient intellectual thought to market definition – witness Gestetner, who thought it was in the duplicator market, and IBM, who thought it was in the mainframe market. Hence few can draw anything approaching an accurate market map and have little chance of doing any kind of sensible segmentation at the key influence points of junctions along the market map.

### 7.1.2  Market segmentation

At each of these key junctions, segmentation is not only possible, but necessary. It is here that the process becomes quite complicated, for the trick is to make an exhaustive list of all the different purchase combinations that take place at each junction. This entails listing what is bought (to include applications, features, where, when and how products or services are bought), together with the associated descriptors (who buys what). This will often produce somewhere between 30 and 50 different purchase combinations, or what we term micro segments. A micro segment is one of a large number of different purchase combinations that take place in a market. However,

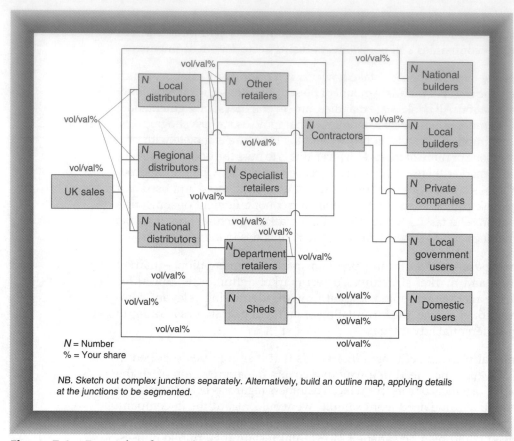

**Figure 7.1** Example of a market map including the number of each customer type.

the reality is that these micro segments do indeed represent what actually happens in the market.

The next step is to specify the benefits that each of these micro segments seek by buying what they buy in the way they do. This is crucial. It is often here that external market research is necessary.

It is now simply a question of using one of the many software packages available to cluster micro segments with similar requirements; clusters are given a dimension of size by adding the volumes or values represented by each micro segment. It is our experience that most markets can be broken down into 10 or fewer segments. The only remaining task is to ensure that our offers meet the requirements of each segment and that we, as suppliers, are organized to sell, deliver and support the appropriate value propositions.

Faced with a plethora of options for segmentation, as illustrated in Figure 7.2, it is not difficult to understand why most organizations take an overly simplistic approach to segmentation and end up with little or no differential advantage.

One thing is abundantly clear from our detailed segmentation work: price is rarely the prime motivator in the way people buy. The following case history will illustrate the point.

**Cooking appliances**
Is it a single market or several separate markets?

| | |
|---|---|
| Volume | (units) |
| Value | |
| Domestic/commercial | |
| Fuels | (gas, electricity, coal, oil, etc.) |
| Cooking methods | (heat, radiation, convection) |
| Cooking function | (surface heating, baking, roasting, charcoal, etc.) |
| Design | (free standing, built-in, combination) |
| Prices | |
| Product features | |
| OEM/replacement | |
| Geography | |
| Channels | (direct, shops, wholesalers, mail order) |
| Why bought | |
| Others | (promotional response, lifestyle, demographics) |
| Usage | |

**Figure 7.2**
Determining the presence of market segments.

## Case study insight

### How ICI used market segmentation to its advantage

ICI Fertilizers went through a severe loss-making period during the late 1980s as the market matured and foreign competitors entered the market with cheap imports. Prices and margins fell to disastrous levels. However, the company had the perspicacity to go through the segmentation process described here and discovered seven relatively distinct segments of farmers, only one of which was price sensitive. This segment represented only 10 per cent of the market, not 100 per cent, as had been previously thought. One segment was highly technological in its approach, while another was more influenced by the appearance of crops. Yet another was loyal to merchants. Yet another was loyal to brands. Each segment was given a name and the needs of each were researched in depth. Products were developed and offers made to match the precise needs of the individual segments, while the company and its processes were reorganized in order to ensure that the appropriate value could be delivered. ICI Fertilizers became an extremely profitable company in an industry whose own governing body had officially designated fertilizer as a commodity!

Hopefully, this heartening story of creative segmentation leading to sustained profitability in a mature and generally unprofitable industry will encourage readers to rethink their approach to segmentation. The market segmentation process described here is summarized in Figure 7.3.

Price is rarely the prime motivator in the way people buy.

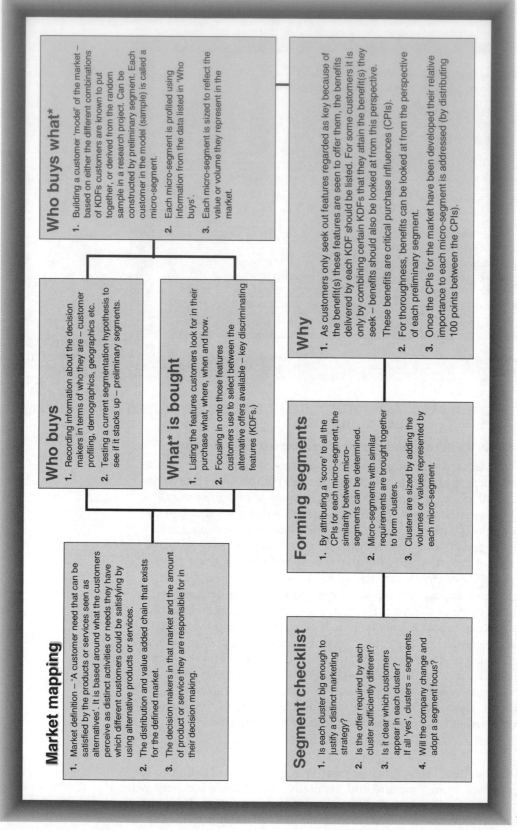

**Figure 7.3** Market segmentation process.

### 7.1.3 Why market segmentation is vital in key account planning

In today's highly competitive world, few companies can afford to compete only on price, for the product has not yet been sold that someone cannot sell cheaper – apart from which, in many markets it is rarely the cheapest product that succeeds anyway. What this means is that we have to find some way of differentiating ourselves from the competition, and the answer lies in market segmentation.

The truth is that very few companies can afford to be 'all things to all people'. The main aim of market segmentation as part of the marketing planning process is to enable a business concern to target its effort at the most promising opportunities. However, what is an opportunity for firm A is not necessarily an opportunity for firm B. So a firm needs to develop a typology of the customers or segment it prefers, for this can be an instrument of great productivity in the marketplace.

The whole point of market segmentation is that a firm must either:

- define its markets broadly enough to ensure that its costs for key activities are competitive or
- define its markets in such a way that it can develop specialized skills in serving them to overcome a relative cost disadvantage.

Both strategies have to be related to a firm's distinctive competence and to that of its competitors.

To summarize, the objectives of market segmentation are as follows:

- To help determine marketing direction through the analysis and understanding of trends and buyer behaviour.
- To help determine realistic and obtainable marketing and sales objectives.
- To help improve decision making by forcing managers to consider the available options in depth.

A clear and comprehensive understanding of their market, how it works, how it breaks down into natural segments and the specific nature of the unique value sought by each of these segments will obviously give key account managers a significant advantage in building long-term relationships with their customers within these segments.

---

### CHECKPOINT

#### Market segmentation

- Has your organization developed a segmentation that meets the criteria described in this section?
- How many segments are there in your market?

## 7.2 Key account analysis

We saw the basis on which key accounts should be defined and selected in Chapter 2. This was summarized diagrammatically in Figure 2.4. Another version of the portfolio is shown here in Figure 7.4.

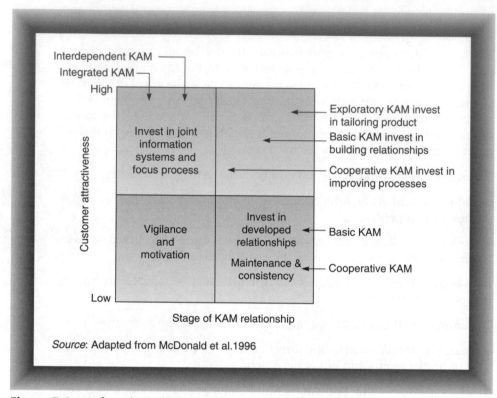

**Figure 7.4** A four-box directional policy matrix.

We now provide a set of specific and detailed procedures for key account analysis prior to producing a strategic marketing plan for each key account selected as being worthy of focused attention by the key account team. An overview of the total process, which we have called the business partnership process, is given in Figure 7.5.

Step 1 in Figure 7.5 has just been described and step 2 was dealt with in Chapter 2.

### 7.2.1 Industry driving forces and PEST analysis (step 3)

Step 3 is known as Porter's industry five-forces analysis. It is taken from Porter's book *Competitive Strategy* (Porter, 1980) and has been of enormous value to generations of managers since its first publication. It is shown in summary form as Figure 7.6.

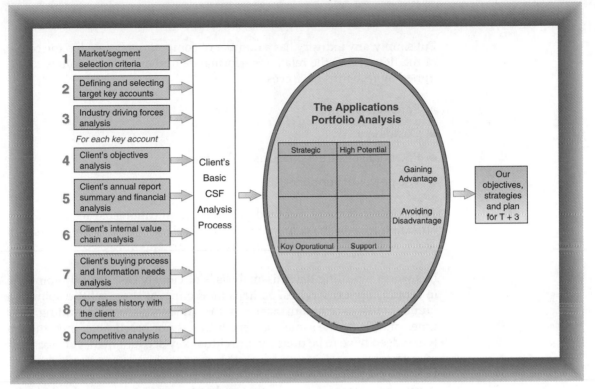

**Figure 7.5** Business partnership process.

**Figure 7.6** Forces driving industry competition.

Put simply, any industry has a number of competitors (located in the centre of the figure) and the relative performance of these competitors is determined by recognizable forces:

- Potential entrants
- Customers
- Potential substitute products and services
- The power of suppliers.

The words in Figure 7.6 aptly describe the implications of each of the four outside forces on the competitors and it is clear that all competitors in a sector or industry will be affected by these driving forces.

It is worth repeating that this analysis is obviously best done by someone in central support services, perhaps marketing, as there is little point in a number of key account managers in the same industry all spending their time conducting the same analysis. If this is not practicable, then the job will indeed have to be done by individual key account managers for their own sectors.

It must be stressed, however, that such an analysis is a prerequisite to the individual account analysis described later in this chapter, as it provides key account managers with a deep analysis of their customers' industry and how it works and affects their performance.

In Tables 7.1 and 7.2 there are checklists of areas that should be investigated as part of the process of understanding your customers' business environment. This is analysed in greater detail in Table 7.3. The first section is about the business and economic environment in which your customer operates (PEST). The second part is about understanding your customer's market. The third part is about understanding your customer's internal operations (Table 7.4). The second and third parts (the customer's market and their operations) should be carried out by each key account manager for specific customers.

The next section of this chapter expands on how the information and data should be used. It is fully appreciated that this long list is an ideal and you will be unable to find some of it. Nevertheless, by knowing what you need to know you can continuously search for answers.

### Operations and resources

- **Marketing objectives**: Are the marketing objectives clearly stated and consistent with marketing and corporate objectives?
- **Marketing strategy**: What is the strategy for achieving the stated objectives? Are sufficient resources available to achieve these objectives? Are the available resources sufficient and optimally allocated across elements of the marketing mix?

- **Structure**: Are the marketing responsibilities and authorities clearly structured along functional, product, end-user and territorial lines?

- **Information system**: Is the marketing intelligence system producing accurate, sufficient and timely information about developments in the marketplace?

  Is information gathered being used effectively in making marketing decisions?

- **Planning system**: Is the marketing planning system well conceived and effective?

- **Control system**: Do control mechanisms and procedures exist within the group to ensure planned objectives are achieved (e.g. meeting overall objectives etc.)?

**Table 7.1** External audit

| *Business and economic environment* | *Competition* |
|---|---|
| ● Economic | ● Major competitors |
| ● Political/fiscal/legal | ● Size |
| ● Social/cultural | ● Market shares/coverage |
| ● Technological | ● Market standing/reputation |
| ● Intracompany | ● Production capabilities |
| | ● Distribution policies |
| *The market* | ● Marketing methods |
| ● Total market, size, growth and trends (value/volume) | ● Extent of diversification |
| ● Market characteristics, development and trends | ● Personnel issues |
| ● Products | ● International links |
| ● Prices | ● Profitability |
| ● Physical distribution | ● Key strengths and weaknesses |
| ● Channels | |
| ● Customer/consumers | |
| ● Communication | |
| ● Industry practices | |

**Table 7.2** Internal audit

| *Marketing operational variables* | *Marketing mix variables* |
|---|---|
| ● Own company | ● Product management |
| ● Sales (total, by geographical location, industrial type, by customer, by product) | ● Price |
| | ● Distribution |
| ● Market shares | ● Promotion |
| ● Profit margins/costs | |
| ● Marketing procedures | |
| ● Marketing organization | |
| ● Marketing information/research | |

**Table 7.3** PEST analysis and market factors – external (opportunities and threats)

| | | |
|---|---|---|
| **Business and economic environment** | | |
| Economic | Inflation, unemployment, energy, price, volatility, materials availability, etc. | As they affect the customer business |
| Political/ fiscal/legal | Nationalization, union legislation, human rights legislation, taxation, duty increases, regulatory constraints (e.g. labelling, product quality, packaging, trade practices, advertising, pricing, etc.) | As they affect the customer business |
| Social/cultural | Education, immigration, emigration, religion, environment, population distribution and dynamics (e.g. age distribution, regional distribution, etc.), changes in consumer lifestyle, etc. | As they affect the customer business |
| Technological | Aspects of product and/or production technology which could profoundly affect the economics of the industry (e.g. new technology, the Internet, cost savings, materials components, equipment, machinery, methods and systems, availability of substitutes, etc.) | As they affect the customer business |
| Intracompany | Capital investment, closures, strikes, etc. | As they affect the customer business |
| **The market** | | |
| Total market | Size, growth, and trends (value, volume). *Customers/consumers:* changing demographics, psychographics and purchasing behaviour | |
| Market characteristics, developments and trends | *Products:* principal products bought; end-use of products; product characteristics (weights, measures, sizes, physical characteristics packaging, accessories, associated products, etc.) | |
| | *Prices:* price levels and range; terms and conditions of sale; normal trade practices; official regulations; etc. | |
| | *Physical distribution:* principal method of physical distribution | |
| | *Channels:* principal channels: purchasing patterns (e.g. types of product bought; prices paid, etc.); purchasing ability; geographical location; stocks; turnover; profits; needs; tastes; attitudes; decision makers, bases of purchasing decision; etc. | |
| | *Communication:* principal methods of communication, e.g. the Internet, sales force, advertising, direct response, exhibitions, public relations, etc. | |
| | *Industry practices:* e.g. trade associations, government bodies, historical attitudes, interim comparisons, etc. | |
| Competition | *Industry structure:* make-up of companies in the industry, major market standing/reputation; extent of excess capacity; production capability; distribution capability; marketing methods; competitive arrangements; extent of diversification into other areas by major companies in the industry; new entrants; mergers; acquisitions; bankruptcies; significant aspects; international links; key strengths and weaknesses | |
| | *Industry profitability:* financial and non-financial barriers to entry; industry profitability and the relative performance of individual companies; structure of operating costs; investment; effect on return on investment of changes in price; volume; cost of investment; source of industry profits, etc. | |

**Table 7.4**
Internal factors
(strengths and
weaknesses)

| *Sales (total, by geographical location, by industrial type, by customer by product)* | |
|---|---|
| Market shares<br>Profit margins<br>Marketing procedures<br><br>● Market research<br>● Product development<br>● Product range<br>● Product quality<br>● Unit of sale<br>● Stock levels<br>● Distribution<br>● Dealer support<br>● Pricing, discounts, credit<br>● Packaging | Marketing organization<br>Sales/marketing control data<br>Marketing mix variables:<br><br>● Samples<br>● Exhibitions<br>● Selling<br>● Sales aids<br>● Point of sale<br>● Advertising<br>● Sales promotion<br>● Public relations<br>● After-sales service<br>● Training |

● **Functional efficiency**: Are internal communications within the group effective?

● **Interfunctional efficiency**: Are there any problems between marketing and other corporate functions? Is the question of centralized versus decentralized marketing an issue in the company?

● **Profitability analysis**: Is the profitability performance monitored by product, served markets, etc. to assess where the best profits and biggest costs of the operations are located?

● **Cost-effectiveness analysis**: Do any current marketing activities seem to have excess costs? Are these valid or could they be reduced?

It should also be stressed here that steps 4–9 in Figure 7.5 are all concerned with the analysis/diagnosis stage, which must be completed by each key account manager before preparing a strategic plan for each key account.

The remainder of this chapter explains how the data and information collected by the key account manager should be used.

### 7.2.2  Key account analysis preplanning

Before it is possible to plan for key accounts, a detailed analysis of each key account must be undertaken by each individual key account manager and their team, somewhat in the manner of conducting a marketing audit. First, however, steps 1, 2 and 3 in Figure 7.5 should be completed. The reason steps 1 to 3 are separate from the next six steps is that it is recommended that if you have a marketing department, these first three steps should be carried out by them, otherwise individual key account managers may consume their valuable time by repeating analysis already completed elsewhere.

### Step 4 (Figure 7.5): Client's objectives analysis

The exercise given in Figure 7.7 should be completed for each key account being targeted. It can be seen that the intention is to take the industry driving forces analysis and apply it specifically to any individual account in order to understand better what advantages and disadvantages it has. The main reason for doing this is to help you to understand ways in which your products or services may enable the customer to exploit advantages and minimize disadvantages.

**Figure 7.7**   Objectives analysis exercise (industry driving forces).

It is not the intention to complete this document as if it were a proforma. Each heading is intended merely to act as a trigger for some powerful conclusions about your customer's competitive situation. This information will be used along with the further information to be gathered in steps 5–9.

### Step 5 (Figure 7.5): Client's annual report summary and financial analysis

Figure 7.8 enables a summary to be made of the analysis referred to in the previous section and of a careful reading and analysis of a customer's published annual report. Even if there is not a formal report published for the shareholders (say, for example, if your customer is a subsidiary or division of a larger company), the directors do nonetheless tend to produce internal reports and newsletters that can be used instead.

| 1. Major achievements | |
| 2. Major problems/issues | |
| 3. Objectives | |
| 4. Strategies | |
| 5. Conclusions/opportunities | |

**Figure 7.8**
Annual report summary.

Such documents can be a major source of information on what your customer believes to be the major issues facing them, their achievements and their objectives and strategies – in other words, their hopes for the future.

It is always possible to extract valuable information which can be used in helping you understand how your organization might be of assistance. This information can now be put alongside the information gleaned from the previous objectives analysis summary.

Figure 7.9 focuses on the financial affairs of your customer and concerns information which can also be obtained from annual reports and other published sources. At first sight, this might appear to be some way removed from the reality of selling goods and services to a major account. However, a little thought will reveal that most organizations today are acutely aware of their financial performance indicators:

- Current ratios
- Net profit margins
- Return on assets
- Debtor control
- Asset turnover.

Most organizations today are acutely aware of their financial performance indicators.

The purpose of the analysis contained in Figure 7.9 is to help you focus on the financial issues faced by your customer and to encourage you to explore whether any of your products and services could improve any of these ratios.

It will be obvious that any supplier who has taken the trouble to work out what impact its products and services have on the customer's bottom line will be preferred to a potential supplier who focuses only on product features.

| Financial ratio indicator | Formula | Source | | | | | Company standing | Industry standing | Does it appear as though improvement is needed? | |
|---|---|---|---|---|---|---|---|---|---|---|
| | | Annual report | | | | | | | Yes | No |
| Current ratio | Current assets Current liabilities | | | | | | | | | |
| Net profit margin | Net profit Net sales | | | | | | | | | |
| Return on assets | Net profit Total assets | | | | | | | | | |
| Collection period | Debtors less bad debt Average day's sales | | | | | | | | | |
| Stock turnover | Cost of goods sold Stock | | | | | | | | | |
| | | | | | | | | | | |

| Description of indicators | Current ratio | Measures the liquidity of a company – does it have enough money to pay the bills? |
|---|---|---|
| | Net profit margin | Measures the overall profitability of a company by showing the percentage of sales retained as profit after taxes have been paid. If this ratio is acceptable, there probably is no need to calculate the gross profit or operating profit margins |
| | Return on assets | Evaluates how effectively a company is managed by comparing the profitability of a company and its investments |
| | Collection period | Measures the activity of debtors. A prolonged collection period means that a company's funds are financing customers and not contributing to the cash flow of the company |
| | Stock turnover | Evaluates how fast funds are flowing through cost of goods sold to produce profit. If stock turns over faster, it is not in the plant as long before it is saleable as a product. |

**Figure 7.9**  Financial analysis.

### Step 6 (Figure 7.5): Client's internal value chain analysis

Figure 7.10 illustrates an organization's internal value chain as popularized by Professor Michael Porter in his book *Competitive Strategies* (Porter, 1980). It is assumed that readers are familiar with this concept. The value chain is introduced here as an invaluable tool in understanding how a major

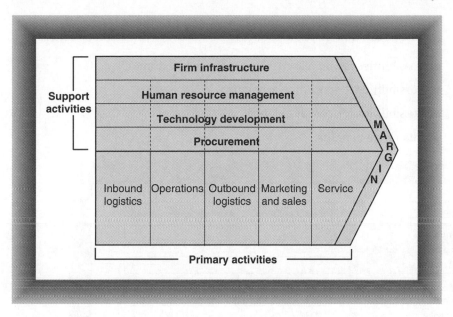

**Figure 7.10**
The value chain.

account actually functions. The bottom level shows bought-in goods or services entering the organization, passing through operations and then moving out to their markets through distribution, marketing and sales and service. Sitting above these core processes are organizational support activities such as human resource management, procurement and so on.

Figure 7.11 is a very simple illustration of some of these issues and how they could be improved, thus representing sources of differentiation in the value chain. All information emanating from this analysis can be usefully

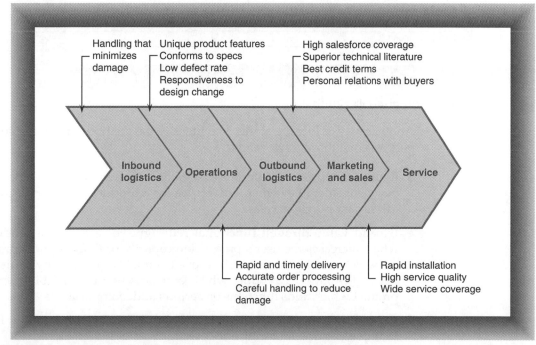

**Figure 7.11** Sources of differentiation in the value chain.

summarized using a format similar to that shown in Figure 7.12. From this, it will be seen that there are four general headings of customer benefits:

- Possibilities for increased revenue for the customer
- Possibilities for cost displacement
- Possibilities for cost avoidance
- Intangible benefits.

| Tangible benefits | Product solution | Analysis and comment |
|---|---|---|
| **Increased revenue** | | |
| Increased sales volume | | |
| Enhanced product line | | |
| | | |
| **Cost displacement** | | |
| Reduced labour costs | | |
| Reduced equipment costs | | |
| Reduced maintenance costs | | |
| Lowered stock costs | | |
| Reduced energy costs | | |
| | | |
| **Cost avoidance** | | |
| Reduced new personnel requirement | | |
| Eliminate planned new equipment | | |
| | | |
| **Intangible benefits** | | |
| Customer goodwill | | |
| Improved decision making | | |

**Figure 7.12**  Value chain analysis summary.

Another way of looking at this is to identify the methods of gaining competitive edge through value in use:

- **Reduce the life cycle/Alter the cost mix**: Customers are often willing to pay a considerable higher initial price for a product with significantly lower post-purchase costs.

- **Expand value through functional redesign**: For example, a product which increases the user's production capacity or throughput, a product which enables the user to improve the quality or reliability of his or her end-product, a product which enhances end-use flexibility or a product which adds functions or permits added applications.

- **Expand incremental value by developing associated intangibles**: For example, service, financing and 'prestige'.

---

## Case study insight
### Value chain analysis for a packaging company

An international chemical company undertook this investigation process using a novel method. They organized a two-day event for eight very senior people from different functions in a large packaging company. These executives included marketing people, a health and safety executive, an environmental specialist, a logistics manager, a manufacturing manager and a couple of directors! These executives were matched by equivalent managers and directors from the supplying company. An independent consultant was asked to chair the two-day event.

The purpose of the event, which was held in a neutral location, was to investigate ways in which the several goods and services of the supplying company were received, used and perceived by the customer. This inquiry was obviously only possible because of the good relationships already enjoyed by the supplier.

While it took a few hours for the independent moderator to break down the natural barriers to honest and open communication, the event had a major impact on the processes and attitudes of the supplier. For example, at one stage the customers were asked to go into a syndicate room and write down all the things they did not like or found inadequate in the supplying company. The sheer size of the list and the contents so shocked the supplier that it immediately agreed to set up a number of functional and cross-functional working groups comprising executives from both sides in order to study how cost-effective improvements could be made.

All issues were investigated openly and honestly, ranging from the strategic issues faced by the customer in its industry, to very tactical issues concerned with processes. The end-result was a dramatically improved relationship, which led to substantial benefits to both sides.

---

It is not suggested that this is the only way to discover the kind of detailed information outlined in Figure 7.12. In many cases, much patience is required over considerable periods of time and the effectiveness and efficiency with which this investigative task can be carried out will be a function of how good and deep the existing relationships are. Nonetheless, it is difficult to see how improvements can be made without a thorough understanding of the customer's systems and processes.

The list of possibilities for improvement for the supplier is now growing quite considerably. However, there are still more aspects of the business which need to be analysed.

### Step 7 (Figure 7.5): The customer's buying process
Figure 7.13 outlines the buying process for goods and services. In the remainder of this section it will be assumed that you are selling a product, although the same process applies equally well to services.

Selling to an organization can be a complex process because it is possible for a number of different people to become involved at the customer end. Although theoretically only one of these is the buyer, in practice he or she might not be allowed to make a decision to purchase until others with technical expertise or hierarchical responsibility have given their approval.

Customer Analysis Form  Customer _____
Salesperson _____  Address _____
Products _____  Telephone number _____
Date of analysis _____  Buy class: new buy _____ straight rebuy _____ modified rebuy _____
Date of reviews _____

| Member of Decision-Making Unit (DMU) | Production | Sales & Marketing | Research & Development | Finance & Accounts | Purchasing | Data Processing | Other |
|---|---|---|---|---|---|---|---|
| Buy Phase  Name | | | | | | | |
| 1 Recognizes need or problem and works out general solution | | | | | | | |
| 2 Works out characteristics and quantity of what is needed | | | | | | | |
| 3 Prepares detailed specification | | | | | | | |
| 4 Searches for and locates potential sources of supply | | | | | | | |
| 5 Analyses and evaluates tenders, plans, products | | | | | | | |
| 6 Selects supplier | | | | | | | |
| 7 Places order | | | | | | | |
| 8 Checks and tests products | | | | | | | |

Factors for consideration
1 price
2 performance
3 availability
4 back-up service
5 reliability of supplier
6 other users' experience
7 guarantees and warranties
8 payment terms, credit or discount
9 other, e.g. past purchases, prestige, image, etc.

Adapted from Robinson et al., 1967.

**Figure 7.13** Buying process for goods and services.

The personal authority of the buyer will to a large extent be governed by the following factors:

- **The cost of the product**: The higher the cost, the higher up in the organization will the purchasing decision be made (Table 7.5). (Please note that, although the level of expenditure figures will have increased substantially during the past 22 years, this table is included because it is indicative of a hierarchy of purchasing authority.)

- **The 'newness' of the product**: The relative novelty of the product will pose an element of commercial risk for an organization. A new and untried proposition will require support at a senior management level, whereas a routine, non-risky service can be handled at a lower level.

- **The complexity of the product**: The more complex the product offered, the more technical the implications which have to be understood within the client company. Several specialist managers might be required to give their approval before the transaction can be completed.

All those involved in the buying decision are known as the decision-making unit (DMU) and it is important for the key account manager to identify the DMU in all current and prospective customer companies. Table 7.6 provides some research findings which demonstrate how rarely salespeople reach all component members of the DMU.

All those involved in the buying decision are known as the decision-making unit (DMU).

| Level of expenditure | Level at which decision is taken | | | |
|---|---|---|---|---|
| | Board (collective) | Individual director | Departmental manager | Lower management or clerical |
| Over £50 000 | 88% | 11% | 2% | – |
| Up to £50 000 | 70% | 25% | 4% | Less than 0.5% |
| Up to £5000 | 29% | 55% | 14% | 2% |
| Up to £2500 | 18% | 54% | 24% | 4% |
| Up to £500 | 4% | 31% | 52% | 14% |

*Source*: 'How British Industry Buys', a survey conducted by Cranfield School of Management for the *Financial Times*, January 1984.

**Table 7.5**
Responsibility for financial expenditure

| Number of employees | Average number of buying influences (DMU) | Average number of contacts made by salesperson |
|---|---|---|
| 0–200 | 3.42 | 1.72 |
| 201–400 | 4.85 | 1.75 |
| 401–1000 | 5.81 | 1.90 |
| 41 000 plus | 6.50 | 1.65 |

**Table 7.6**
Buying influences by company size

A useful way of working out who would be involved in the decision-making processes in a company is to consider the sales transaction from the buyer's point of view. It has been recognized that the process can be split into a number of distinct steps known as 'buy phases'. These buy phases will be followed in most cases, particularly for major purchases. It will be obvious that at stages beyond the *cooperative* KAM stage, the incumbent supplier will have an inside track and, hence, an advantage, throughout the process. In many cases, customers do not even bother to put their proposed purchase requirements out to tender, preferring to deal with their current trusted partner.

Buy phases relate to the stages through which organizations go when making major purchases. The phases can be listed as follows: (This section of the text owes much to the original research conducted by the Marketing Science Institute in the USA under the guidance of Patrick J Robinson.)

1. **Problem identification**: A problem is identified or anticipated and a general solution worked out. For example, the marketing department finds that it has inadequate information about sales records and costs. It needs better information made available on the computer.

2. **Problem definition**: The problem is examined in more detail in order to grasp the dimensions and, hence, the nature of the ultimate choice of solution. Taking our earlier example of the international chemical company further, investigation shows that the supplier's original software system was not devised with the customer's current marketing planning requirements in mind. A new system is required which can also provide the option for the inclusion of other new data.

3. **Solution specification**: The various technical requirements are listed and a sum of money is allocated to cover the cost of investing in new software.

4. **Search**: A search is made for potential suppliers, in this case those with the capability of devising a 'tailor-made' system to meet the above requirements.

5. **Assessment**: Proposals from interested suppliers are assessed and evaluated.

6. **Selection**: A supplier is selected and final details are probably negotiated prior to the next step.

7. **Agreement**: A contract/agreement is signed.

8. **Monitoring**: The service is monitored in terms of meeting installation deadlines and performance claims.

If we happened to be running a computer programming service to industry, we could deduce from the buying process that the DMU at this company might well contain the following people: a marketing planner, a sales director, a sales office manager, the company computer specialist, the company accountant, the company secretary and perhaps even the managing director, depending on the nature of the contract and the buyer. Sometimes the buyer might be one of those already listed and not exist as a separate role.

We could also speculate with some certainty that each of these people would need to be satisfied about different aspects of the efficiency of our service and we would need to plan accordingly. For now, it is enough to recognize that, when selling to an organization, the person with the title of buyer is often unable to make important decisions on their own. Although he or she can be a useful cog in the company's purchasing machine, he or she is often not a free agent.

> The person with the title of buyer is often unable to make important decisions on their own.

There are also many pressures on the buyer. We know from our own experience – when we purchase something for the home, for example – how difficult it can sometimes be. Even if we are only buying a carpet, we have to agree whether or not it should be plain or patterned, what colour, what price, what quality and so on. Even seemingly straightforward considerations like these are clouded by issues such as whether the neighbours or relatives will think we are copying them or whether we are being too chic or too outrageous. The buying decision makers in a typical company are faced with a greater multitude of pressures coming from two directions: from outside the company and from inside the company.

External pressures can be many and various and may involve important issues such as the following:

- **The economic situation**: What will be the cost of borrowing? Are interest rates likely to rise or fall? Is it a good time to invest in a new service now? Is the market decline really over or should we wait for more signals of recovery?

- **Political considerations**: How will government fiscal policy affect our business or that of our customers? Will proposed legislation have an impact on either us or our markets?

- **Technology**: How are we as a company keeping up with technological developments? How does this new proposal rate on a technological scale? Is it too near the frontiers of existing knowledge? How long will it be before a whole new phase of technology supersedes this investment?

- **Environmental considerations**: Will this new service be advantageous to us in terms of energy conservation or pollution control? Does it present any increase in hazards to our workforce? Will we need more room to expand? Is such room available?

- **The business climate**: How do our profit levels compare with those of companies in general and those in our type of business in particular? Are there material cost increases in the pipeline which could reduce our profits? Is the cost of labour increasing?

Any one of these external issues could put pressure on the buying decision maker – and this is only half the picture. There are also many internal pressures on the buyer:

- **Confused information**: It is often difficult to obtain the correct information to support a buying decision. Either the information does not exist or it has not been communicated accurately from the specialist department. Sometimes it is not presented in a convenient form and leads to confusion and misunderstanding.

- **Internal politics**: The relative status of individuals or departments can sometimes hinder the buying process. Personal rivalries or vested interests can create difficulties about priorities or standards. The 'politics' might entail non-essential people being involved in the decision-making process, thereby elongating the communication chain and slowing down decision making.

- **Organizational**: How the company is organized can affect the efficiency of its buying process. It is essential for everyone within the company to be aware of their role and level of authority if they are to perform effectively.

Finally, there are a number of personal pressures on the buyer. Buyers can be pressurized by a number of personal matters, some real, others imagined. They might be unsure about their role and how their colleagues accept their judgement. They might lack experience in the buying role and be unsure of how to conduct themselves. They might prefer a quiet life and therefore be against change, preferring to continue transactions with tried and tested suppliers – even if it can be clearly demonstrated that there are advantages in changing them. They might be naturally shy and not enjoy first meetings. They might find it difficult to learn new information about technical developments or the special features of your particular service.

All of these pressures, both external and internal, have a profound bearing on the behaviour of the buyer and, if the account manager is to relate to the buyer, he or she must try to understand them.

By way of summarizing this section on business-to-business selling, it can be demonstrated that the successful account manager needs to be aware of all these things when approaching a buyer acting on behalf of an organization. All of the following elements need to be known and understood.

- The relative influence of the buyer in the context of the particular product or service being offered.

- What constitutes the DMU in the buying company.

- How the buying process works.

- The pressures on the buying decision maker.

With this information, the account manager is in a better position to plan his or her work and to adopt appropriate conduct when face-to-face with the buying decision maker(s). Exactly how this information should be used will be covered later in the chapter.

---

### CHECKPOINT

**Buying pressures**

Can you compile a list of pressures that are particular to the procurement function in one of your key accounts?

---

Some explanation is needed of the 'buy classes' shown in Figure 7.13. Whether the account manager is selling to an individual or to an organization, the decision-making processes of the prospects can be divided into what are termed 'buy classes'. There are three types of buy class:

> There are three types of buy class: new buy, straight rebuy and modified rebuy.

- **New buy**: In effect, all the foregoing discussion has focused on the new buy category. It is here that those people who make up the DMU are fully exercised as the buy phases unfold. In the new buy class, the needs of all decision makers must be met and influenced by the key account manager. Not surprisingly, this takes time and so it is not unusual for a lengthy period to elapse between the initial discussion and contract closure.

- **Straight rebuy**: Once the key account manager has had the opportunity to demonstrate how the service can help the customer, further purchases of the service do not generally require such a rigorous examination of all of the buy phases. In fact, should the customer merely want a repeat purchase of the same service, then their only questions are likely to be: Has the price been held to the same level as before? Will the standard of the service be unchanged? Can it be provided at a specific time? Such issues can generally be resolved by negotiation with the buyer.

- **Modified rebuy**: Sometimes a modification of the product or service might be necessary. It might be that the supplier wants to update the product or service and provide better performance by using different methods or equipment. Alternatively, it could be the customer who calls for some form of modification from the original purchase. Whatever the origin, all or some of the buy phases will have to be re-examined and again the key account manager will have to meet with and persuade and satisfy the relevant members of the DMU.

There are often advantages for an account manager in trying to change a straight rebuy into a modified rebuy. They are twofold:

- A modified rebuy reactivates and strengthens the relationship with the various members of the customer's DMU.

- The more closely a supplier can match its service to the customer's needs (and remember this matching only comes about as a result of a mutual learning, as communication and trust develop between the

> There are often advantages for an account manager in trying to change a straight rebuy into a modified rebuy.

supplier and the customer), the more committed the customer becomes to the product or service.

The higher the commitment the customer has to the particular product for service and the supplier, the more difficult it becomes for competitors to break in.

If you are not reaching the key decision maker then all your efforts could well be in vain.

The higher the commitment the customer has to the particular product or service and the supplier, the more difficult it becomes for competitors to break in.

Finally, the 'decision maker' in Figure 7.13 needs to be identified. Recognizing that there is a DMU is an important first step for the account manager but, having done this, it is essential to identify who actually has the power to authorize the purchase. No matter how persuasive the arguments for buying your products, if you are not reaching the key decision maker, then all your efforts could well be in vain. Identifying this person is too important to be left to chance and yet many account managers fail to meet with them. Sometimes they just have not done enough research about the company to obtain an accurate picture of its character and key concerns. It is important that the account manager research the company sufficiently in order to obtain a thorough understanding of its operations, personnel and priorities.

Alternatively, many account managers prefer to continue liaising with their original contacts in the client company, the ones with whom they feel comfortable and have come to regard as friends, rather than to extend their network to include more influential client representatives. Because many purchase decision makers will hold senior positions, the thought of meeting them somehow seems a daunting prospect, particularly to complacent or ill-prepared account managers.

Yet many of these fears are groundless. There is no evidence that senior executives set out to be deliberately obstructive or use meetings to expose the account manager's possible inadequacies. In fact, quite the opposite appears to be true.

Certainly, the decision makers will be busy people and so will want discussion to be to the point and relevant. At the same time, they will be trying to get the best deal for the company and it is only natural that they should.

### Step 8 (Figure 7.5): Your sales history with the client
Figure 7.14 is a very simple analysis of your sales over a designated period of time working with the customer. The purpose is merely to summarize your business history, share and prospects with this customer.

### Step 9 (Figure 7.5): Competitive comparison and competitor strategy
Figure 7.15 shows one of a number of possible ways of establishing how well you are meeting the customer's needs in comparison with your competitors. It is obviously better if this is done using evidence obtained from independent market research, but providing the analysis suggested in this chapter is carried out thoroughly and with diligence, it should be possible to complete this part of the analysis internally with sufficient accuracy.

| Your sales history with the client | | | | | |
|---|---|---|---|---|---|
| Products | | T-2 | T-1 | T-0 | Trend |
| Customer volume (Total) | | | | | |
| YOUR volume | | | | | |
| YOUR share volume | | | | | |
| YOUR share value | | | | | |
| Sales analysis | | | | | |
| Products | | T-2 | T-1 | T-0 | Trend |
| | Val | | | | |
| | Vol | | | | |
| | % | | | | |
| | Val | | | | |
| | Vol | | | | |
| | % | | | | |
| | Val | | | | |
| | Vol | | | | |
| | % | | | | |
| | Val | | | | |
| | Vol | | | | |
| | % | | | | |
| | Val | | | | |
| | Vol | | | | |
| | % | | | | |
| Comments | | | | | |

**Figure 7.14**  Sales analysis and history.

Some people prefer to carry out this analysis using a more traditional SWOT (strengths, weaknesses, opportunities and threats) format as given in Figure 7.16. The main point, of course, is that any organization hoping to get and keep business with a major account needs to provide superior customer value and this can only be achieved by comparisons with the best that competitors have to offer.

## 7.3   Next steps

The painstaking key account analysis is now complete and a number of customer critical success factors will have been accumulated, together with specific ways in which your products or services and processes can help.

Figure 7.17 shows an applications portfolio, which is a useful way of categorizing your business solutions and approaches to your client prior to

| Competitive comparison | Importance rating | You | Competitor 1 2 3 | Implications |
|---|---|---|---|---|
| Product quality | | | | |
| Product range | | | | |
| Availability | | | | |
| Delivery | | | | |
| Price/discounts | | | | |
| Terms | | | | |
| Sales support | | | | |
| Promotion support | | | | |
| Other | | | | |
| | | | | |

Importance rating
(by customer)
A – very important (essential)
B – important (desirable)
C – low importance

Rating
(customer view)
1 – consistently/fully meets needs
2 – meets needs inconsistently
3 – fails to meet needs

| Competitors' strategy | |
|---|---|
| Competitor | Strategy |
| 1. | |
| 2. | |
| 3. | |

**Figure 7.15** Competitive comparison and competitor strategy.

producing a strategic marketing plan for your customer, which will be explained in the next chapter.

The applications portfolio comprises four quadrants. The quadrants at the bottom left and right are labelled avoiding disadvantage. While the meaning of this label might be self-evident, it is nonetheless worth providing an example of this category. Take, for instance, a bank considering buying automatic teller machines (ATMs) for use by customers outside bank opening hours. Not having ATMs would clearly place the bank at a disadvantage. However, having them does not give the bank any advantage either. The majority of commercial transactions fall into this category.

The bottom left quadrant represents key operational activities, such as basic accounting, manufacturing and distribution systems. The bottom right quadrant might include activities such as producing overhead slides for internal presentations. In contrast, the top two quadrants represent a real opportunity for differentiating your organization's offering by creating advantage for the customer. The top right quadrant might be beta testing a product, service or process prior to making a major investment in launching it for the customer.

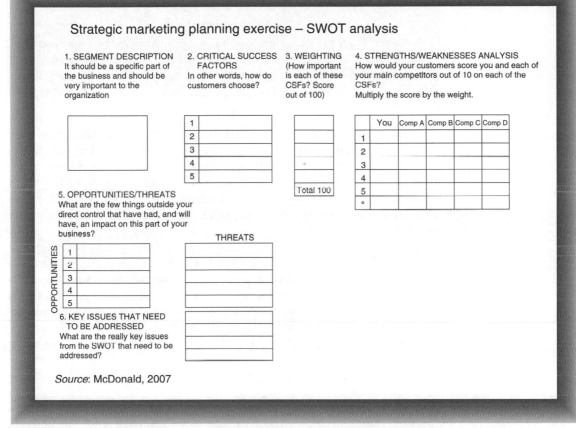

**Figure 7.16**  Strategic marketing planning exercise – SWOT analysis.

Strategic marketing planning exercise – SWOT analysis

1. SEGMENT DESCRIPTION
It should be a specific part of the business and should be very important to the organization

2. CRITICAL SUCCESS FACTORS
In other words, how do customers choose?

3. WEIGHTING
(How important is each of these CSFs? Score out of 100)

4. STRENGTHS/WEAKNESSES ANALYSIS
How would your customers score you and each of your main competitors out of 10 on each of the CSFs?
Multiply the score by the weight.

Total 100

5. OPPORTUNITIES/THREATS
What are the few things outside your direct control that have had, and will have, an impact on this part of your business?

THREATS

OPPORTUNITIES

6. KEY ISSUES THAT NEED TO BE ADDRESSED
What are the really key issues from the SWOT that need to be addressed?

*Source*: McDonald, 2007

| | You | Comp A | Comp B | Comp C | Comp D |
|---|---|---|---|---|---|
| 1 | | | | | |
| 2 | | | | | |
| 3 | | | | | |
| 4 | | | | | |
| 5 | | | | | |

|  | Strategic | High potential |
|---|---|---|
| **Creating advantage** | Applications which are critical to achieving future business strategy | Applications which may be critical in achieving future business strategy |
| **Avoiding disadvantage** | Applications upon which the organization currently depends for success | Applications which are valuable but not critical to success |
|  | Key operational | Support |

**Figure 7.17**  The applications portfolio.

The reality of commercial life is that most of what any organization does falls into the avoiding disadvantage category. However, leading companies adopt a proactive business approach. They work hard at developing products, services and processes designed to deliver advantage for their major accounts, for it is clear that creative, customer-focused suppliers will always be preferred over those who merely offer 'me too' products and trade only on price.

The KAM Best Practice Research Club at Cranfield has strong evidence to suggest that, once such an audit on a key account has been completed, if it is presented formally to senior managers in the account, the response is extremely favourable and, further, that additional confidential information is likely to be provided by the customer to enable the supplier to prepare a strategic marketing plan. This is the main topic addressed in Chapter 8.

## Summary

Research at Cranfield (McDonald and Woodburn, 1999) has shown that organizations that invest resources in detailed analysis of the needs and processes of their key accounts fare much better in building long-term profitable relationships. We have termed this stage pre-planning. Armed with a detailed knowledge of your customer's business, it is more likely that you can discover ways of helping them create advantages in their marketplace.

# 8 Planning for key accounts

## Fast track

Marketing planning is a logical sequence of events leading to the setting of marketing objectives and the formulation of plans for achieving them. The sequence is:

1. Mission statement

2. Set corporate objectives

3. Conduct marketing object

4. Conduct SWOT (strengths, weaknesses, opportunities and threats) analyses

5. Make assumptions

6. Set marketing objectives and strategies

7. Estimate expected results

8. Identify alternative plans and mixes

9. Set the budget

10. Establish first-year implementation programmes

The plan itself contains:

1. Mission statement

2. Financial summary

3. Market overview

4. SWOT analyses

5. Portfolio summary

6. Assumptions

7. Marketing objectives and strategies

8. Forecasts and budgets

All companies need to have a longer term (strategic) marketing view as well as a short-term (tactical) marketing operation. Often the most potent short-term tactic is the use of the salesforce. These can combine as shown in the matrix below.

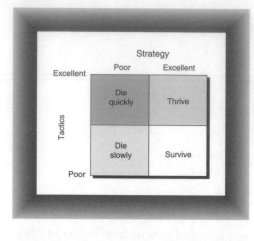

From this it can be seen that being good at implementation of the wrong strategy can lead to a very quick death!

Exactly the same philosophy must be applied to planning for key accounts, as sophisticated customers will only build integrated relationships with suppliers who understand this business and can help them to increase sales, reduce costs, avoid costs and create value for them on a continuous basis. As this involves committing resources to such suppliers, they insist on well-researched strategic plans which are agreed jointly.

Even in cases where suppliers do not enjoy integrated relationships, it is still essential to prepare strategic plans designed to capture the inherent value planned for customers.

In this chapter a template is provided for preparing a strategic plan for a key account. Finally, a format used by customers for preparing strategies for their key suppliers is provided.

## Introduction

The purpose of this chapter is threefold: to explain the key elements of marketing planning, to position key account planning within this context and to provide a step-by-step approach to putting together a strategic plan for a key account. These themes are set out in three sections. The first section describes the nature of marketing planning and outlines the main steps involved in the marketing planning process. The second section locates key account planning within this process and explains its fundamental characteristics. The third section provides a step-by-step process for completing a strategic plan for a key account.

No matter where a key account is positioned in the relationship development model (RDM) (Figure 8.1), if a supplier has aspirations for building a relationship with a customer over time, then some kind of plan setting out a strategy for how this is to be achieved will be necessary. The problem with this is that most organizations are not very good at or even very knowledgeable about planning. Thus, this chapter will also explain how to prepare a strategic plan for a key account. However, key account planning must be placed firmly in the context of strategic marketing planning, otherwise it will not be effective.

> The problem with this is that most organizations are not very good at planning.

> Key account planning must be placed firmly in the context of strategic marketing planning, otherwise it will not be effective.

## 8.1 Strategic marketing planning

Marketing planning contributes to business success both by providing a detailed analysis of opportunities for meeting customer needs and by promoting a professional approach to making available those products or services that deliver the benefits customers are seeking to well-defined market segments.

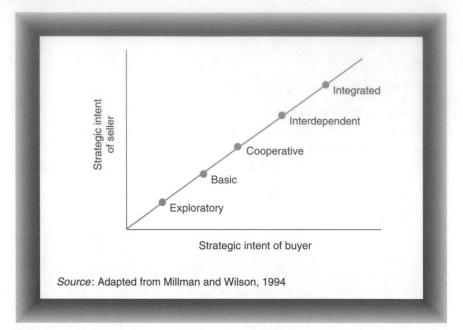

**Figure 8.1**
The relationship
development
model.

Marketing planning should not be confused with budgets and forecasts. Marketing planning is specifically concerned with identifying what and to whom sales need be made in the longer term to give revenue budgets any chance of succeeding.

> There is no such thing as a 'market' – only people with needs and money.

There is no such thing as a 'market' – only people with needs and money. An organization must offer something to prospective customers that will make them want to buy from it rather than from any other supplier. Nowadays, markets are generally over-supplied and customers have a wide choice. So, if an organization is to persuade people to part with their money, it has to understand their needs in depth and to develop specific 'offers' with a differential advantage over competitors' offers. These offers are not just physical products or services, they are to do with the totality of the relationship between supplier and customer and include the organization's reputation, brand name, accessibility, service levels and so on.

In the less complex environments of the 1960s and 1970s, which were characterized by growth and the easy marketability of products and services, a 'production' orientation was possible, largely because demand seemed limitless. During the late 1980s, when demand was less buoyant, financial husbandry began its ascendancy. Indeed, it seemed to work for a while: profits continued to rise as costs and productivity increased. Alas, the ratio-driven, cost-cutting, margin-management mentality persisted. Every product had to make a prescribed margin over what it cost to produce it, otherwise prices were raised or it was taken off the market. Too little attention was paid to the number of times products were turned over, so low margin products were sacrificed. However, overheads either remained or were rationalized as organizations drove themselves towards fewer, more profitable products. Eventually 'anorexia industrialosa' (an excessive desire to be leaner and fitter, leading to emaciation and death) set in.

Companies went bankrupt at an unprecedented rate and even the innovative approaches developed in the 1990s (total quality management, balanced scorecards, business process re-engineering, relationship marketing, knowledge management, customer relationship management and so on) were unable to halt the rot that had set in.

Indeed, as described in Chapter 6, over a 20-year period up to 2000, most of Britain's highest return on investment public limited companies either disappeared, downsized or got into severe financial difficulties. Nor was the contagion confirmed to Britain. According to Richard Pascale, author of *Managing on the Edge: How Successful Companies Use Conflict to Stay Ahead* (Pascale, 1990), only six of the 43 excellent companies named in Tom Peters and Robert Waterman's *In Search of Excellence: Lessons from America's Best-Run Companies* (Peters and Waterman, 1982) would have been considered excellent a mere eight years later.

It became increasingly clear that, sooner or later, corporations were going to have to turn their attention to addressing their markets and their customers instead of tinkering with their own internal processes, and this is where strategic marketing planning comes into its own.

There is now a substantial body of evidence to show that requisite marketing planning not only results in greater profitability and stability over time, but it also helps to reduce the friction and operational difficulties which arise within organizations.

Marketing planning is a logical sequence of activities leading to the setting of marketing objective and the formulating of plans for achieving them. It is a management process which is conceptually very simple. As a planning system, it is a way of identifying options, of making them explicit, of formulating marketing objectives which are consistent with the organization's overall objectives and of scheduling and costing out the activities most likely to achieve the objectives.

> Marketing planning is a logical sequence of activities leading to the setting of marketing objective and the formulating of plans for achieving them.

Marketing planning is a managerial process, from which there are two outputs:

- The **strategic marketing plan**, which covers a period of between three and five years.

- The **tactical marketing plan**, which is the scheduling and costing out of the specific actions necessary to achieve the first year's objectives in the strategic marketing plan.

The process itself and the output of the process are shown Figure 8.2.

The marketing planning process begins with an identification of the organization's mission and financial objectives, which serves to confirm the

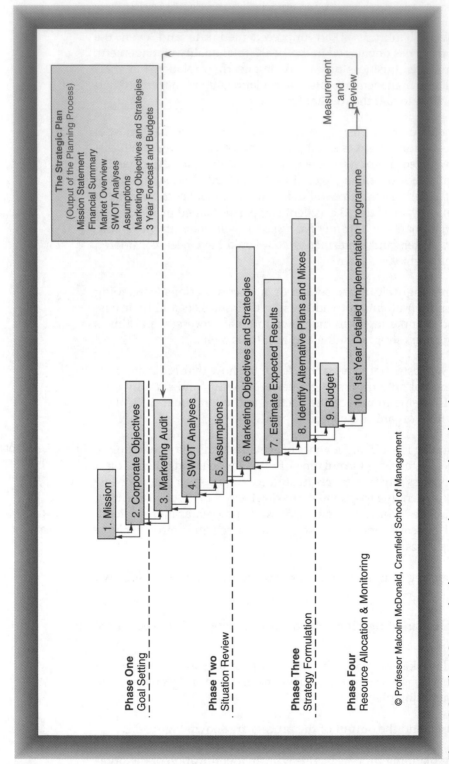

**The Strategic Plan**
(Output of the Planning Process)
Mission Statement
Financial Summary
Market Overview
SWOT Analyses
Assumptions
Marketing Objectives and Strategies
3 Year Forecast and Budgets

Measurement and Review

1. Mission

2. Corporate Objectives

3. Marketing Audit

4. SWOT Analyses

5. Assumptions

6. Marketing Objectives and Strategies

7. Estimate Expected Results

8. Identify Alternative Plans and Mixes

9. Budget

10. 1st Year Detailed Implementation Programme

**Phase One**
Goal Setting

**Phase Two**
Situation Review

**Phase Three**
Strategy Formulation

**Phase Four**
Resource Allocation & Monitoring

© Professor Malcolm McDonald, Cranfield School of Management

**Figure 8.2**   The 10 steps in the strategic marketing planning process.

organization's purpose and outline its aspirations. The next phase embodies a comprehensive situation review or marketing audit in order to establish inherent problems and potential. This involves summaries in the form of SWOT (strengths, weaknesses, opportunities and threats) analyses for main products/markets, leading to the making of assumptions and the setting of draft marketing objectives and strategies for a three- to five-year period. At this stage, other functional managers get involved in order to ensure that the organization is capable of resourcing marketing's requirements.

Alternative plans and budgets are then finalized and, eventually, tactical marketing plans prepared. Company headquarters will often consolidate both the strategic plans and the tactical plans into business or corporate plans. At the start of the organization's fiscal year, the tactical marketing plan is implemented and monitored via the management information system, until the whole process begins again in the next fiscal cycle.

This strategic and operational planning system can be represented as a circle (Figure 8.3), which obviates the question about whether the process is top-down or bottom-up for, clearly, it is continuous.

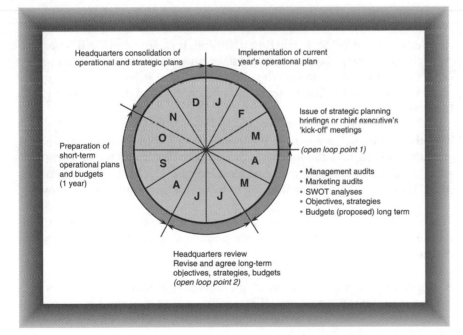

**Figure 8.3**
Strategic and operational planning.

The contents of a strategic marketing plan are listed in Table 8.1. The plan can be made as formal or informal as necessary according to the particular circumstances. The main point is that it should combine thoroughness with creativity.

Over 20 scholarly research studies have identified hostile corporate cultures and financially driven systems and procedures as the main barriers to

**Table 8.1**
Contents of a strategic marketing plan

1 A mission or purpose statement

2 A financial summary

3 A market overview
   ● What the market is
   ● How it works
   ● What the key segments are

4 A SWOT on each segment
   ● What value does each require?
   ● What value can we create to persuade customers to buy from us?

5 A portfolio summary of the SWOT
   ● This classifies segments according to our relative strengths and the potential of each for growth in profits over the next three years

6 Assumptions

7 Marketing objectives and strategies
   ● Prioritized in accordance with the portfolio summary

8 A budget
   ● For three years

implementing effective marketing planning. It is clear that until organizations learn to grasp the nettle of customer orientation, financial husbandry will dominate corporate life, despite the fact that it has caused so many casualties during the last 25 years and will continue to do so well into 2007 and beyond.

Another endemic problem in business is the depth of ignorance about what marketing actually is. This is graphically illustrated by the comment of one managing director, who announced aggressively at a public seminar that 'There is no time for marketing in my company until sales improve!'

How can any organization achieve customer focus while it continues to organize itself around what it makes rather than around its customers or its markets?.

The simple truth is that, while it is the marketing people who work out the value required by customers, it is the whole company which delivers this value.

Companies that persist in organizing themselves around tribes such as personnel, accountants, engineers, IT specialists, salespeople and so on, cannot by their very nature achieve this integrated delivery of customer value.

Such groups will never subjugate their own tribal goals to the broader aims of customer satisfaction and retention. In addition, how can any organization achieve customer focus while it continues to organize itself around what it makes rather than around its customers or its markets? Many corporate cultures are, in the main, hostile to the marketing ethic. Directors who got their job as a result of professional behaviour considered appropriate in the 1960s, 1970s, 1980s and 1990s do not know how to respond to increased competition and static or declining markets. Their natural reaction is to resort to traditional measures, one of which is to cut costs without addressing the fundamental issue of growth. However, crucially, growth requires customers who want to buy things from us rather than from our competitors.

It also takes intellect, confidence and courage to take a strategic rather than a purely tactical approach. Unsuccessful organizations do not bother with strategic marketing planning at all; instead, they rely on sales forecasts and associated budgets. It is a bit like steering from the wake all right in calm, clear waters, but not so sensible in busy and choppy waters!

The problem with this route is that many salespeople sell the products they find easiest to sell (usually at a maximum discount) to those customers who treat them nicest. Thus, by developing short-term budgets first and then extrapolating them, companies only succeed in extrapolating their own inadequacies.

Preoccupation with short-term forecasts is typical of those companies that confuse this approach with strategic marketing planning. Such companies are being left behind by companies led by directors with a pioneering spirit anchored in practical expertise. These business frontiers men and women lead the effort in understanding their markets and customers, for they know that it is only by creating superior customer value that their companies will be able to survive and thrive.

Transforming 'vision' into reality is where strategic marketing planning comes in, enabling a number of plans or models to be developed which spell out quantitatively and qualitatively the value that each employee must create in order to achieve collective prosperity.

The authors' research has shown that in peering into the murky depths of organizational behaviour in relation to marketing planning, confusion reigns supreme, and nowhere more so than over the terminology of marketing.

This brings us to one of the most fundamental points in this chapter – an understanding of the difference between strategy and tactics and the association with the relevant adjectives 'effective' and 'efficient'. This point is illustrated by the matrix in Figure 8.4, in which the horizontal axis represents strategy as a continuum from ineffective to effective and the vertical axis represents tactics on a continuum from inefficient to efficient. Those firms with an effective strategy (top right) continue to thrive. Those with an effective strategy but inefficient tactics (bottom right) have merely survived. Those firms to the left of the matrix are destined to die, as too much emphasis is placed on tactics, so avoiding the underlying strategic issues surrounding changing market needs. Any organization doing the wrong things more efficiently (top left) is destined to die more quickly than their less efficient counterparts. It is a bit like making a stupid manager work harder, thus doubling the chaos and probably offending twice as many customers!

**Figure 8.4**
The impact of effectiveness and efficiency on success.

As we have already said, companies led by chief executives with a proactive orientation that stretches beyond the end of the current fiscal year have begun to show results visibly better than the old reactive companies with only a short-term vision.

---

### Case study insight

#### Preventing a potential case of anorexia industrialosa

One Scandinavian capital goods manufacturer was devoting its energies to stock control, headcount reduction, cash flow and the like. The problem, however, was of falling demand. Had it not been pointed out to the Board that this underlying marketing issue had to be addressed, it is easy to imagine how anorexia industrialosa could have resulted (an excessive desire to be leaner and fitter, leading to emaciation and, eventually, death).

---

Figure 8.5 shows the old style of company in which very little attention is paid to strategy by any level of management. It will be seen that lower levels of management do not get involved at all, while the directors spend most of their time on operational/tactical issues. Figure 8.6, on the other hand, is a representation of those companies that recognize the importance of strategy and who manage to involve all levels of management in strategy formulation.

The rule, then, is simple:

● Develop the strategic plan first. This entails greater emphasis on scanning the external environment, the early identification of forces emanating from it, and developing appropriate strategic responses, involving all levels of management in the process.

**Figure 8.5**
Tactical orientation.

**Figure 8.6**
Strategic orientation.

● A strategic plan should cover a period of between three and five years, and only when this has been developed and agreed should the one-year operational marketing plan be developed. Never write the one-year plan first and extrapolate it.

The emphasis throughout this chapter is on the preparation of a strategic key account plan. The format for an operational or tactical plan is exactly the same, except for the amount of detail.

---

## CHECKPOINT

### Strategic focus

Do you think that your company places sufficient emphasis on strategy?

---

## 8.2 Key account planning

Key account planning must take place at the same time as or even before draft plans are prepared for a strategic business unit. The following health sector case study illustrates why this is necessary.

> ### Case study insight
>
> **Key account planning in a medical supplies company**
>
> It will be seen from Figure 8.7 that there are four 'markets' within hospitals to be served:
>
> - Medical
> - Administration
> - Catering
> - Energy.
>
> The supplies company will service a number of hospital groups or key accounts, referred to here as A, B, C, D, etc. Each of these hospital groups may well have its own key account manager who has to plan for the group. Thus, for example, the key account manager for hospital A has to prepare a draft plan across all four markets and this would clearly be a key input to the planning process shown in Figure 8.2.

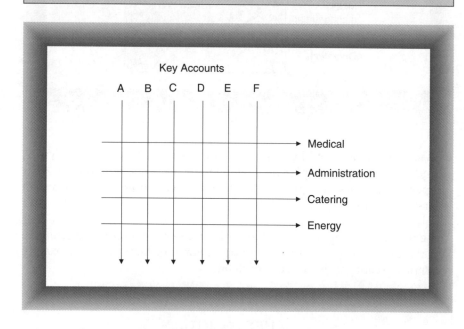

**Figure 8.7**
Hospital groups
and key account
managers.

### 8.2.1 The position of key account planning in strategic marketing planning

All planning should start with the market where the customers are. Indeed, in anything other than small organizations it is clearly absurd to think that any kind of meaningful planning can take place without the committed inputs of those who operate most directly with customers.

Figure 8.8 shows a hierarchy of planning with key account planning at the base. Every principle outlined in this chapter applies right down to the individual key account. Thus, the planning process shown in Figure 8.2 would be first applied to key accounts.

**Figure 8.8**
The planning hierarchy.

From this point onwards in this chapter the discussion of strategic and tactical planning will focus on key accounts.

### 8.2.2  Guidelines for setting key account objectives and strategies

The first point to be made is that all key accounts are not the same. This adage applies at two levels. First, it is obvious that all organizations will have preferred markets and preferred segments within these markets. Figure 8.9 shows the current and projected revenues from different segments within a single market.

Clearly, any organization without a distinct policy towards each of these market segments is unlikely to be able to make a success of key account management (KAM). On the understanding that your organization has a clear and well-communicated policy for each of its target markets, we can now turn our attention to setting objectives and strategies for key accounts within each segment.

Let us take another look at the key account portfolio matrix shown in Figure 8.10. Taking each quadrant in turn, it is possible to work out sensible objectives and strategies for each key account. Accounts meeting the

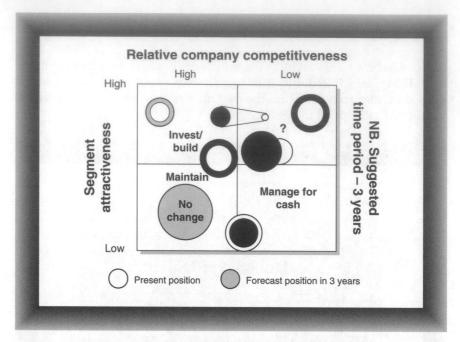

**Figure 8.9**
Prioritizing and
selecting segments.

**Figure 8.10**
Portfolio analysis
matrix.

profile of the bottom left quadrant are likely to continue to deliver excellent revenues for some considerable time, even though they may be in static or declining markets. Good relationships are already enjoyed and should be preserved. Retention strategies are therefore advisable, incorporating prudence, vigilance and motivation. More importantly, as the supplying company will be seeking a good return on previous investment, any further financial input here should be of the maintenance kind.

In this way, it should be possible to free up cash and resources for investing in key accounts with greater growth potential.

The quadrant to the top left (high potential/high strengths) represents accounts with the highest potential for growth in sales and profits. These warrant a quite aggressive investment approach, providing it is justified by returns. Net present value (NPV) calculations may be used as a basis for evaluating these returns, having taken account of the additional risks involved. Any investment here will probably be directed towards developing joint information systems and collaborative relationships.

Accounts situated in the quadrant to the top right (high potential/low strength) pose a problem, for few organizations have sufficient resources for investing in building better relationships with all of them. To determine which ones justify investment, net revenue streams should be forecast for each account for, say, three years and discounted to take account of the high risks involved. Having made these calculations and having selected the promising accounts, under no circumstances should financial accounting measures such as NPV be used to control them within the budget year. To do so would be a bit like pulling up a new plant every few weeks to see if it had grown! The achievement of objectives should instead be monitored using measures such as sales volume, value, 'share of wallet' and the quality of the relationship, enabling selected accounts to be moved gradually towards partnerships and, in some cases, towards integrated relationships. Only then will it become more appropriate to measure profitability as a control procedure.

> To do so would be a bit like pulling up a new plant every few weeks to see whether it had grown!

Accounts which the company cannot afford to invest in should be managed in a similar way to those residing in the bottom right quadrant. Accounts found in this quadrant (low potential/low strength) should not occupy too much of a company's time. Some of these accounts can be handed over to distributors, while others can be handled by an organization's sales personnel, providing all transactions are profitable and deliver net free cash flow.

First, consider the problem of aiming for OTIF (on time in full) delivery. It is well known that, as shown in Figure 8.11, as delivery service levels increase, so the cost of holding inventory grows exponentially.

It is worth expanding on this point, because so many suppliers have ridiculous mission statements that include a desire 'to delight customers'. Let us explain why such statements are ridiculous and are guaranteed to lose your company lots of money. It is easy to understand if you consider Figure 8.12. Let us assume that a research survey had shown that, in a given period, orders ranged from 500 to 10 000, with an average of 3000. Holding 3000 in stock would only provide a 50 per cent level of availability – clearly unacceptable. If one standard deviation was 100, putting 3100 into stock would provide an 85 per cent level of service (approximately). Two standard deviations would provide a service level of well over 90 per cent. Three standard deviations would provide a service level well into the high nineties, which would clearly be very acceptable. The only problem with this is

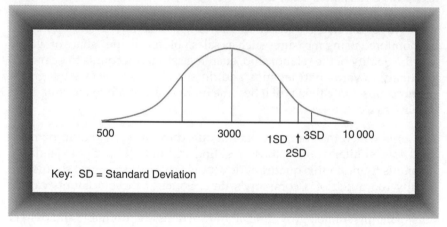

**Figure 8.11**
Delivery service
levels vs cost of
holding inventory.

**Figure 8.12**
Results of a survey
of orders over a
defined period.

that, for each small increase in service levels, large amounts of additional inventory have to be held, hence the big increase in the cost of inventory for high levels of service shown in Figure 8.11.

The answer, of course, is to select those segments that deserve very high levels of service. The same applies to key accounts.

The authors were involved recently in running a sales conference for a global company in the roller bearing business. The managing director announced at the beginning of the conference that in the forthcoming year, debtor days had to be reduced from 65 to 45. This objective depressed the salesforce considerably because there was a recession at the time and customers were taking extra credit. We solved the problem by asking the salesforce to categorize their customers according to sales potential for the forthcoming year – the vertical axis in Figure 8.13 – and according to whether their customers loved them or hated them – the horizontal axis (the lines in the matrix represent customers).

**Figure 8.13**
Short-term (one-year) customer classification.

We then advised them to offer 35 days credit to customers in box 1 (being nice to them, as well, of course), to offer 45 days credit to customers in box 2 (being even nicer to them, of course) and to offer 65 days credit to those in box 3, (being mega nice to them as well). Finally, for customers in box 4, we advised them to ask for cash on acceptance of their order and to insist that they collected their orders personally!

It is clear that this story is a very exaggerated version of what actually happened. Nonetheless, it gives more than a clue that not all customers are created equal and throws into sharp relief the stupidity of those companies that set out 'to delight' their customers. The reality, of course, is that some kind of customer classification system is essential before setting objectives and strategies for them.

It is now appropriate to return to the issue of what kind of objectives and strategies to set for key accounts that fall into the bottom right hand quadrant of Figure 8.10. Sometimes, there are very big key accounts in this box – customers who do little other than drive suppliers' prices down and who do not want to build close relationships with any supplier. Nonetheless, their size ensures that they have to be in the key account programme.

For such companies, net free cash flow must be the prime objective. It makes sense to try to secure such accounts, by lowest prices if necessary in order to secure the high volume of sales, preferably via a two- or three-year contract. Thereafter, service should be kept to the minimum, orders should, if possible, be made via the Internet or a call centre and personal calls should be kept to a minimum in order to save costs. If such a customer insists on lots of free services, this pressure should be refused, remembering that the objective is to maximize net free cash flow.

Figures 8.14 and 8.15 indicate the implications of high fixed costs/low variable costs versus low fixed costs/high variant costs. Even local traders, such as builders, instinctively understand this bit of traditional accounting

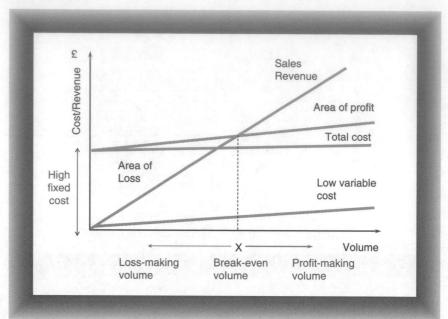

**Figure 8.14**
Breakdown chart with high fixed costs.

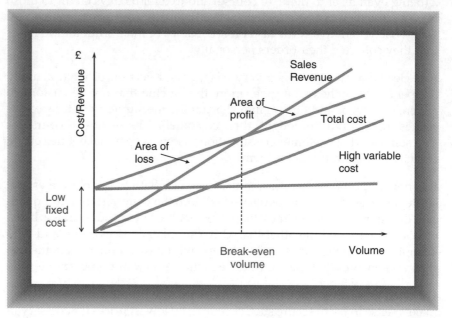

**Figure 8.15**
Breakdown chart with low fixed costs.

theory. In a high fixed cost situation, for example where variable costs are low, once revenue passes the breakdown point, profitability is very high. In a low fixed cost situation where variable costs are high, once revenue passes the breakdown point, profitability is much lower. This is why builders employ their own workpeople such as carpenters and buy their own diggers and so on in times when the construction market is buoyant (i.e. high fixed costs). When the construction market is difficult, however, they hire in workpeople and equipment as necessary (i.e. low fixed costs).

The point is that, with customers in the bottom right quadrant of Figure 8.10 every effort should be made to reduce the fixed costs, as this is the best way of maximizing net free cash flows.

Having explained all this, it should be clear that strategic plans should be prepared for all accounts in the bottom left and top left quadrants of Figure 8.10, selectively for those in the top right quadrant, and not at all for customers in the bottom right quadrant, when short-term forecasts, budgets and action plans will suffice.

All other company functions and activities should be consistent with the goals set for key accounts according to the general categorization given in Figure 8.10. This rule includes the appointment of key account managers to key accounts. For example, some key account managers will be extremely good at managing accounts in the *exploratory*, *basic* and *cooperative* KAM stages where their excellent selling and negotiating skills are essential, whereas others will be better suited to the more complex business and managerial issues surrounding *interdependent* and *integrated* relationships. The implications for key account managers are examined in Chapter 9.

## 8.3  Developing a strategic marketing plan for key accounts

We repeat here what we said in Chapter 1 about the need for a strategic plan as well as a tactical, short-term plan. We said that the good thing about not having a strategy is that failure comes as a complete surprise and is not preceded by a long period of worry and depression.

It is worth mentioning that preparing a strategic plan for a key account is an intellectually demanding task that cannot be accomplished merely by completing proformas. The authors have worked with many major organizations and the plans that emanate from them are rarely of the high quality that they need to be for the plans to have any chance of becoming reality. Accordingly, the authors have developed the criteria listed in Table 8.2 for evaluating the quality of strategic plans for key accounts. We should like to stress that only plans that fall close to the left hand side of the chart have any chance of achieving their objectives.

Earlier in the chapter, we outlined the contents of a strategic marketing plan in Table 8.1. We now provide an annotated set of proformas for completing a strategic plan for a key account.

**Summary**

Strategic plans for key accounts are essential, but these must be positioned clearly within the organization's strategic marketing planning process. Where possible, key account strategic plans need to be agreed and signed off with the functional managers within the organization who will be delivering the promises to the customer. Ideally, they should also be agreed with the customer

**Table 8.2** KAM plan evaluation guidelines

| Plan element | Reference sections | Level 1 | Level 2 | Level 3 | Level 4 | Level 5 |
|---|---|---|---|---|---|---|
| Overall Business issues Presentation | Executive summary | Excellent understanding of KAM Complete, coherent Addresses key issues Appropriate emphasis Focused and clear Creative | Good understanding of KAM Mostly complete, some visible coherence. Addresses key issues Clear | Acceptable understanding of KAM Essential components No significant contradictions or omissions | Weak understanding of KAM Significantly incomplete or incoherent | Little or no understanding of KAM Incomplete and/or includes major contradictions |
| Analyses, esp. market map | Section A, outline Section B, customer Appendices | Comprehensive & effective use of tools Valid conclusions drawn Deep understanding of customer | Significant & effective use of tools Illustrates main points of customer situation | Some use of tools Elucidates key issues facing customer | Little use of tools Does not draw valid conclusions | Little or no use of tools No collusions, poor customer understandings |
| Objectives | Section C, your plans | Realistic Joined up with customer situation, customer and supplier strategies | Realistic Connects current situation and supplier strategies | Statement building from current situation | Unclear or not well connected to situation | Not stated, or just sales targets |
| Strategy | Section C, your plans | Clearly stated Targeted Added value for customer Feasible, clear resource requirement Consistent with objectives | Clearly stated Targeted Added value for customer Feasible, clear resource requirement Consistent with objectives | Clearly stated Targeted Added value for customer | Strategy simply stated | Strategy not stated, and/or stated strategies are outcomes or actions |
| Action | Section C, your plans | 12 month development 3 year major action Matched with strategy Thorough measurement framework | 12 month development 3 year major action Matched with strategy Focused measurement framework | 12 month development Limited measurement framework | Short-term action Measurement is just sales targets | Short-term action No control mechanism |

# ExCo
# Key Account Plan

## Notes

Customer:
Customer relationship manager:
Dates: – completed/submitted:
     – approved:
     – last modified:

# Index

# Executive summary

| Main elements | Potential for profit | |
|---|---|---|
| **Account attractiveness score** <br> To be scored against ExCo criteria | | |
| | **Last year** | **This year +3** |
| **ExCo relative business strength** <br> Score against customer's criteria vs best competitor | | |
| **ExCo generic strategy for customer** <br> Manage for cash, proactive maintenance, selective investment/development, strategic investment | | |
| **Equivalent customer strategy for ExCo** <br> Efficiency, leverage, security, strategic | | |
| **Intercompany relationship** <br> Basic, Co-operative, Interdependent, Integrated | | |
| **Forecast business** <br> State whether forecast given in terms of volume, GM, contribution | | |

## A.   Current position

## B.   The customer's business

## C. ExCo objectives and strategies

| Business with customer | LY | TY | TY + 1 | TY + 2 | TY + 3 |
|---|---|---|---|---|---|
| Total revenue | | | | | |
| Rev change vs previous year | | | | | |
| Gross margin | | | | | |
| GM% | | | | | |
| Customer wallet | | | | | |
| Share of customer wallet | | | | | |

## D. Action and review

# A. Current position

## A.1 ExCo account team

| Name | Title/Function | Role |
|---|---|---|
| | | Examples: |
| | | Overall account manager |
| | | Customer operations |
| | | Market analysis |
| | | Quality issues |
| | | |
| | | |
| | | |

## A.2 Principal customer contacts/relationships (see Worksheet 1 for organogram/contact map)

| Name | Title/Function | Role in relationship with ExCo | Level of relationship with ExCo | Level of importance to ExCo |
|---|---|---|---|---|
| | | Examples: Principal contact | 0–5, see Appendix 1.4 | 0–5, see Appendix 1.4 |
| | | Buyer | | |
| | | Marketing | | |
| | | | | |
| | | | | |
| | | | | |
| | | | | |
| | | | | |
| **Stage of intercompany relationship overall** | | | See Appendix 1.3 | |

Comments, e.g. on power structure and importance of contacts

## A.3 Customer history with ExCo
Sales history

| Sales by product/ product group | LY-2 | | | | | | LY-1 | | | | | | LY | | | | | |
|---|---|---|---|---|---|---|---|---|---|---|---|---|---|---|---|---|---|---|
| | ExCo sales | Sales inc/ dec | ExCo GM | | | | ExCo sales | Sales inc/ dec | ExCo GM | | | | ExCo sales | Sales inc/ dec | ExCo GM | | | |
| | £m | % | £m | % | £m | % | £m | % | £m | % | £m | % | £m | % | £m | % | £m | % |
| | | | | | | | | | | | | | | | | | | |
| | | | | | | | | | | | | | | | | | | |
| | | | | | | | | | | | | | | | | | | |
| | | | | | | | | | | | | | | | | | | |
| | | | | | | | | | | | | | | | | | | |
| ExCo total | | | | | | | | | | | | | | | | | | |
| Size of customer wallet | * | | | | | | | | | | | | | | | | | |
| Share of customer wallet | ExCo ÷ total | | | | | | | | | | | | | | | | | |
| Definition of wallet | Scope of wallet: content and limits (what is included, what is excluded) | | | | | | | | | | | | | | | | | |

*Customer's spend on the category of goods/services currently/potentially supplied by ExCo

# Background to trading history

| Customer's supplier management strategy | See Appendix 1.2 |
|---|---|

Explain events influencing these results

## A.4 Current issues

Recent sales history: to (month).............................................

| Sales by product/ product group | LYTD | | | | TYTD | | | |
|---|---|---|---|---|---|---|---|---|
| | ExCo sales | Sales inc/ dec | ExCo GM | | ExCo sales | Sales inc/ dec | ExCo GM | |
| | £m | % | £m | % | £m | % | £m | % |
| | | | | | | | | |
| | | | | | | | | |
| | | | | | | | | |
| | | | | | | | | |
| | | | | | | | | |
| ExCo total | | | | | | | | |

Note significant issues and the date when this section was last revised

# B. The customer's business

## B.1 Market position
### Outline of the customer's business: definition and scope
What do they do and where? What markets are they in?

## B.2 Role/participation in marketplaces
Summarize and draw conclusions from the market map

## B.3 Market/business environment
Summarize important points

## B.4 Key external issues for customer
Note key opportunities and threats for the customer

## B.5 Competitive position

Draw conclusions on position relative to competition and value to the customer

## B.6 Customer objectives
### Customer's mission statement and goals

Where your customer wants to take their business (beware website verbiage)
Examples: aspirations, status, image and range of activity.
Either: as stated by the customer itself, or as far as you know it (but state which).

### Customer's quantified objectives

Your customer's specific corporate objectives, quantified and time-bound. I.e. WHAT exactly do they want to achieve in the foreseeable future? If you cannot obtain quantified information, give your understanding qualitatively.

## B.7 Customer strategies

List the major strategies they are pursuing/intend to pursue: i.e. HOW exactly do they intend to achieve the above objectives?

# C. ExCo objectives and strategies

## C.1 Customer critical success factors
(see Worksheet 7)

| Critical success factor | Importance weighting | ExCo rating | ExCo score | Best competitor rating* | Best competitor score |
|---|---|---|---|---|---|
| | | | | Identify best competitor | |
| | | | | | |
| | | | | | |
| | | | | | |
| | | | | | |
| | | | | | |
| | | | | | |
| | | | | | |
| Total | 100 | | | | |

## C.2 Key external issues for ExCo
Note key opportunities and threats for ExCo with the customer

## C.3 Competitive position

# C.4 ExCo objectives
## Business/financial

| Purchases by product/ product group | LY | TY | | | | TY + 1 | | | | TY + 2 | | | | TY + 3 | | | |
|---|---|---|---|---|---|---|---|---|---|---|---|---|---|---|---|---|---|
| | ExCo sales | ExCo sales | Sales inc/ dec | ExCo GM | ExCo GM | ExCo sales | Sales inc/ dec | ExCo GM | ExCo GM | ExCo GM | ExCo GM | ExCo | ExCo GM | ExCo sales | Sales inc/ dec | ExCo GM | ExCo GM |
| | £m | £m | % | £m | % | £m | % | £m | % | £m | % | £m | % | £m | % | £m | % |
| Existing business | | | | | | | | | | | | | | | | | |
| | | | | | | | | | | | | | | | | | |
| | | | | | | | | | | | | | | | | | |
| Total existing | | | | | | | | | | | | | | | | | |
| New business | Business not received as at date of completing plan | | | | | | | | | | | | | | | | |
| | | | | | | | | | | | | | | | | | |
| Total new | | | | | | | | | | | | | | | | | |
| Overall total | | | | | | | | | | | | | | | | | |
| Customer wallet | | | | | | | | | | | | | | | | | |
| Share of customer wallet | | | | | | | | | | | | | | | | | |

# Other objectives
E.g. relationships, image, product range, range of activity

| Objective | Measurement | LY | TY | TY + 1 | TY + 2 | TY + 3 |
|---|---|---|---|---|---|---|
| Intercompany relationship | Target stage: | | | | | |
| | | | | | | |
| | | | | | | |

# C.5 ExCo business strategies
Planned business strategies

| ExCo strategy | TY+1 | | | | TY+2 | | | | TY+3 | | | |
|---|---|---|---|---|---|---|---|---|---|---|---|---|
| | Sales | GM | Reso-urce | Net | Sales | GM | Reso-urce | Net | Sales | GM | Reso-urce | Net |
| | | | | | | | | | | | | |
| | | | | | | | | | | | | |
| | | | | | | | | | | | | |
| | | | | | | | | | | | | |
| | | | | | | | | | | | | |
| ExCo's customer management strategy overall | | | | | | | | | | | | |

Comment on issues, barriers, alliances, feasibility

# C.6 ExCo relationship strategies
Additional to business strategies

| Relationship development strategy | Target contact name(s) & role(s) |
|---|---|
| | |
| | |
| | |
| | |
| | |

Targeted relationship levels (by date) – – – – – – – – – –

| ExCo staff | Customer staff | | | | | | |
|---|---|---|---|---|---|---|---|
| | Name 1 | Name 2 | Name 3 | Name 4 | | | |
| Name A | 2 > 4 | | | 1 > 3 | | | |
| Name B | | | 1 > 2 | | | | |
| Name C | | | | | | | |
| Name D | | | | | | | |

# C.7 Risks (external) & dependencies (internal)

What external events could prevent your strategy being fulfilled (risks)?
On what internal events (or lack of them) does your strategy depend
for it fulfilment (dependencies)?

| Strategy | Risk/ dependency | Chance of occurrence | Nature of impact | Potential difference from objectives | | |
|---|---|---|---|---|---|---|
| | | | | TY + 1 | TY + 2 | TY + 3 |
| | | | | | | |
| | | | | | | |
| | | | | | | |
| | | | | | | |
| | | | | | | |

# D. Action and review

## D.1 Key action plan

| Key actions | ExCo owner of action | Other depart-ments involved | Resource demand | Progress measure | Metric target | Due date | Date completed |
|---|---|---|---|---|---|---|---|
| Identify ExCo strategy here | | | | | | | |
| Action to fulfil specific strategy | | | | | | | |
| | | | | | | | |
| | | | | | | | |
| Identify ExCo strategy here | | | | | | | |
| | | | | | | | |
| | | | | | | | |
| | | | | | | | |
| Identify ExCo strategy here | | | | | | | |
| | | | | | | | |
| | | | | | | | |
| | | | | | | | |
| Identify ExCo strategy here | | | | | | | |
| | | | | | | | |
| | | | | | | | |
| | | | | | | | |

# D.2 Review

Make copies of this page for the other review periods.

| | |
|---|---|
| **People involved** | |
| **Review due date** | |
| **Actual date completed** | |

| Element | Progress measure | | Corrective action | 'Owner' of corrective action | Date for further review |
|---|---|---|---|---|---|
| | **Target metric** | **Actual metric** | | | |
| **Objectives** | | | | | |
| | | | | | |
| | | | | | |
| | | | | | |

| Strategy | Key action | | | | | |
|---|---|---|---|---|---|---|
| | | | | | | |
| | | | | | | |
| | | | | | | |
| | | | | | | |
| | | | | | | |

| Risks/dependencies | | | | | |
|---|---|---|---|---|---|
| | | | | | |
| | | | | | |
| | | | | | |

# 9 Processes – making key account management work

## Fast track

Today, the delivery of superior customer value is as much about a company's business processes as it is about the core product or service, and yet implementation gets nothing like as much attention as it needs. If something has to be done more than once, and almost everything does recur, then there should be a process for doing it. A process can even be mapped for relationship development and, indeed, relationships might develop a lot faster if such a process were followed.

A process may be defined as 'A continuous and systematic series of actions performed in a definite manner directed to some end'. It should represent the most effective and efficient route to converting inputs into outputs. Suppliers' processes are generally designed to deliver to many customers in a standardized, replicable manner, which is good for costs but often not good for key accounts. Start by 'auditing' your processes to see which perform well for key accounts and which, from their point of view, are too slow, inflexible, unreliable, opaque, uninformative, uncosted and unsuitable for integration with the customer's processes.

While, at first sight, you may think that there are only a limited number of processes which impact on key customers, on closer examination you will see that there are far more. They can be divided into:

- **strategic** processes that involve senior management, to which key account managers contribute,

- **strategy realization** processes that add value to the supplier and customer through realizing the agreed strategy, with which the key account manager spends most of his or her time,

- **operational/transactional** processes concerned with the delivery of what has been promised.

The key account manager plays a different role in each and has different levels of 'ownership' of the process. For example, key account managers need to understand operational processes and be alerted to deviations from expectations, but should not be part of the daily machinery or they will never do anything else.

Each process should be broken down into its component steps, and the role of the key account manager and others identified at each stage. This exercise demonstrates how the process works, and also builds up a picture of what their job should be.

Senior management is responsible for a number of processes in successful key account management, and if they are not aware of that at the outset, the requirement and the means to fulfil them should be identified for them at an early stage. The key account manager's role is mostly provision of information to these processes, so he or she needs to be aware of them, how they work, and what should be contributed. The strategic processes include:

- Selecting attractiveness criteria and key customers
- Managing the customer portfolio
- Considering implications of customer strategies
- Incorporating account plans in business planning
- Allocating/prioritizing resources
- Assessing and managing risk to the company
- Sponsoring key customers
- Coordinating across boundaries
- Enabling organizational learning.

Key account managers have another set of processes with which to work. 'Developing' occurs frequently in this list, because their job is to add value to both organizations by managing change:

- Analysing key accounts, developing strategy and planning
- Developing relationships with customers
- Developing business, capturing opportunities
- Selling and negotiating
- Pricing
- Developing new products
- Customizing products and service
- Managing the product mix
- Developing marketing programmes
- Developing the supply chain
- Developing transaction handling
- Providing customer training

- Developing internal relationships
- Providing information.

Below is a simplified list of operational processes, which run day in, day out. Key account managers, whether they like it or not, are held responsible by the customer for the delivery of what they have promised, so they need a process of two-way communication with operations by which they can brief operations with information they get from the customer, and operations can brief them as appropriate, about good and poor performance.

- Selling
- Processing orders
- Manufacturing/operations
- Servicing customers
- Delivering to customers
- Collecting payment.

A good deal of sales activity belongs at this operational/transactional level, and may be carried out by the field salesforce or telesales, rather than the key account manager.

Measurement should be fit for purpose: it does not come free. Measurement is closely related to processes and is often about processes, so it fits alongside them at the three layers of the company identified earlier:

- **Strategy:** Measurement of profit to support making the right strategic decisions.

- **Strategy realization:** Measurement of value and progress to support the alignment of implementation with strategy, including the 'amount' of key account management (KAM) invested in the customer.

- **Operational/transactional:** Measurement of cost and performance to support improvements in efficiency and productivity.

Key customers in different categories, treated to different strategies, should clearly be measured differently. Performance objectives should reflect these different expectations.

# Introduction

Today, the delivery of superior customer value is as much about a company's business processes as it is about the core product or service. Because many markets and products are mature and opportunities for differentiation are few, suppliers have to look further for means of differentiating themselves. Indeed, great implementation offers real competitive advantage, while good implementation is a minimum requirement at key account level.

> Implementation, rather than structure and strategy, is most often at the root of organizations' problems.
>
> (Bonoma, 1985)

It may be the least 'sexy' part of key account management, but it is arguably the most important. Key customers overwhelmingly prefer suppliers that are 'easy to do business with', and that means the on-going management of the business at least as much, if not more than, the deal-making process. Implementation gets nothing like as much attention as it needs.

Key account managers need to realize that they cannot do the whole job on their own, or even just with the team. Once that is admitted, it becomes clear that they must work with and through other parts of the company, and then their job becomes one of finding out how to get their plans implemented. This chapter focuses particularly on the idea that engaging a process is the best way to get things done, and that if key account managers embrace the processes in their organizations and work with them rather than against them, then the chances of success with customers, and repeated success, is much greater.

## 9.1  The role of processes in implementing key account management

### 9.1.1  The importance of processes

Over the last few years, the fields of supply chain management and procurement have upgraded their whole approach to their role in the organization. They have taken on new tools and techniques, developed new processes, and educated people to use them and do a really professional job. These disciplines have now made companies billions of pounds, and they have rightly taken a seat at the boardroom table on the back of those achievements.

Customer management is due, if not overdue, for the same kind of makeover. Indeed, it is essential if it is to have any chance of standing up to the fully analysed, carefully prepared and operationalized demands of the customer's procurement and supply chain management. It will involve learning much more about how the supplier operates and what its capabilities are, learning more techniques like process mapping, project management, activity-based costing, bid development, etc. to work with customers in a far less superficial way than in the past. Instead of being on the outside of the company's processes, key account managers need to get to grips with them and understand:

● How the process works

● How it interfaces with other processes

● What costs money to change or has negative onward effects

● How to go about getting modifications and who to talk to.

Without this understanding, key account managers cannot represent the customer's needs in the supplier's process design and specification; and if they do not, who will? When customer input is missing, companies can make decisions that make sense in their own terms of reference, but are potentially very damaging to customers.

However good the relationship with a customer, ultimately, a supplier is judged by what it delivers, and quite rightly too. Key account managers cannot abdicate responsibility for current operations, even though they are not directly responsible. Customers are clear that, if the key account manager effectively makes a promise to them, as part of whatever deal is struck, then it is the key account manager who is responsible for its fulfilment. In that case, you would want to be sure that your promise can be delivered

*Key account managers cannot abdicate responsibility for current operations.*

and that a robust way of doing it exists, or will exist within the timeframe agreed. Some companies and key account managers have tried to separate the two, but unsuccessfully, as far as customers are concerned.

Chapter 11 discusses ways of organizing key account management and trying to minimize the 'silos' or independently operating divisions in a company that prevent a joined-up delivery to the customer. With all the goodwill in the world, companies will still operate in silos and, more than sometimes, goodwill is not enough to cross the boundaries. Far better is a defined and robust process.

---

### Case study insight

**The customer's take on responsibility for operational issues**

'We realize now that the previous key account manager must have done a lot of fixing for us. The new one doesn't see that as his role, so now we're seeing all the warts. We have said we aren't happy, but he just doesn't seem to take it in. *He* wants to talk about new services, and *we* want to know when they're going to sort out what they've already got.' (Supply chain director, multinational company)

---

> As companies get more complex on both sides, the need for transparent and trackable processes becomes more important, not less.

As companies get more complex on both sides, the need for transparent and trackable processes becomes more important, not less. You should be considering not only how you persuade and motivate people to support the key customer, but also how you can develop or modify a process that can deliver what is required with greater certainty, and over a longer period.

### 9.1.2   *The nature of processes*

We are really concerned with processes that relate to key accounts. However, these might turn out, on closer examination, to be quite a large proportion of the company's processes. Manufacturing processes, for example, might seem quite remote from key accounts, but they can block the creation of customized products, so they are highly relevant. In making the kind of commitments that will drive business with key customers forward, you are likely to encounter more processes than you ever thought existed in your company. They need to work well, and in a way that satisfies key customers, and you need to engage with them. Understanding them is the first step.

> A process (is) 'A continuous and systematic series of actions performed in a definite manner directed to some end'.

A process may be defined as 'A continuous and systematic series of actions performed in a definite manner directed to some end'. Processes may be seen as a way of converting inputs into outputs, where the inputs and outputs can be of many kinds, from very tangible physical materials to intangibles that may or may not even be captured in a physical form. 'Process' therefore contains the ideas of:

- Purpose
- Definition

- Inputs
- Linked steps
- Action
- Outputs
- Performance.

Whether you are trying to follow a process or develop a new one, you can use this as a checklist to systematically collect the information you need to understand how it works or should work. Figure 9.1 represents a process as a joined-up series of steps with inputs to and outputs from each. Process mapping is a well-developed technique, with commercially available software to support it, but you can get a long way by just drawing a series of boxes and linking them up (Practical tip: use one large self-stick note for each step, and then you can move them as you learn more about the sequence, without having to start again!).

**Figure 9.1**   A process as a series of steps.

In some cases, a process might not currently exist and might need to be created, such as a process for relationship development. If an activity is genuinely one-off and will not be repeated, then developing and specifying a process may not be worthwhile but, in fact, many activities described as unique are not. Other people in the organization may be doing the same thing as another 'one-off', and could achieve their objectives faster, with less pain and more success, through following a specified process that someone else has trialled and tested.

Key customers have high expectations. From our research, we have identified what is required of a supplier's processes to meet their expectations and to meet the supplier's needs. Processes need to be:

- **Flexible**: Responsive to the customer's needs and open to customization.
- **Fast**: Performance to agreed timing is generally what is required but, when speed is important, the process needs to be able to shift up a gear to meet that need.

- **'Integratable'**: Aligned and able to integrate with customers' processes, based on the same or a complementary framework to ensure a smooth 'handshake'.

- **Robust**: Reliable delivery to expectation every time, not fragile or likely to collapse under pressure or change.

- **Transparent**: Able to answer questions like 'What is happening now? What progress has been made?'

- **Informative**: To yield accurate, accessible, manageable performance measurement.

- **Costed**: Suppliers (possibly customers too) should have an understanding of where the costs are so the cost/saving impact of changes can be discussed.

> For key customers, some kind of differentiation is obligatory.

You may feel that your company's processes do not perform well for key customers and, indeed, often they do not. They have been set up with different objectives in mind, for example, handling a large number of smaller customers as efficiently as possible, or reducing inventory costs, or reducing debtor days. Generally, they aim for more standardization, whereas for key customers, some kind of differentiation is obligatory, and that differentiation may lie in how effectively the supplier operates its processes in delivering to the customer.

You may need to start a debate about the suitability of your company's processes for key accounts. If you begin with an 'audit' such as that shown in Figure 9.2, which assesses your processes against their expectations, you can quickly gather the views from around the company. Start by identifying the

| Process attribute | Process | | | | | | Average score by attribute |
|---|---|---|---|---|---|---|---|
| | A .......... | B .......... | C .......... | D .......... | E .......... | F .......... | |
| Flexible | | | | | | | |
| Fast | | | | | | | |
| Integratable | | | | | | | |
| Robust | | | | | | | |
| Transparent | | | | | | | |
| Informative | | | | | | | |
| Costed | | | | | | | |
| **Average score by process** | | | | | | | |

**Figure 9.2**  Audit framework for supplier processes.

relevant processes (see Section 9.2) and then score each against the process attributes on a scale of 0–10. It could be interesting to see intuitive assessments gained by completing the grey boxes in the table first, and then comparing them with views gained more systematically.

Completing such an audit will help suppliers to:

- discuss where views are different, and why, which should reveal misunderstandings and gaps in understanding

- identify which processes seem satisfactory and which are not, and start to address those most in need of attention

- identify in what way poorly performing processes are failing key customers, in order to clarify change objectives.

An audit of company processes clearly must start with identifying the processes concerned. The model of an organization in terms of layers of activity, as in Figure 9.3, provides a useful framework, since processes (and people) will be largely attached to each layer. Look for processes relevant to key account management in each of these layers.

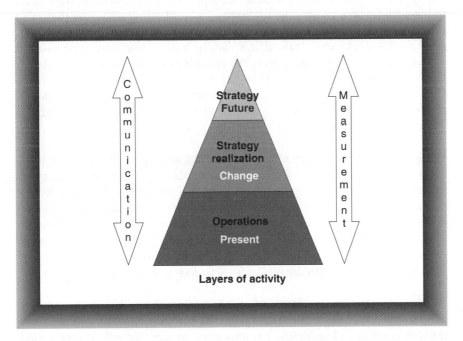

**Figure 9.3**
Layers of activity
and processes.

At the top level, the Board's activities focus on strategy and managing the future. As key account management has a major impact on strategy, there are processes that the Board will need to implement to ensure that key account managers can do their jobs (see Section 9.2). The next layer, which includes key account managers, consists of value-adding activities to realize or fulfil the strategy, involving change. The operational level is very much to do with current delivery, and is generally the responsibility of people other than the key account manager, although he or she has an essential degree of involvement here too. Two processes, communication and measurement, stand out because they are important from top to bottom of the organization (see Sections 9.2 and 9.3).

---

### CHECKPOINT

**Are your company's processes friendly to key customers?**

Has your company:

● Mapped the processes that most concern key customers?

● Audited their performance against key customer's expectations and your company's needs in managing them?

---

### 9.1.3  The key account manager's role in processes

*There is a grave danger of becoming sucked into being integral to the daily activity and fire-fighting, and only having time left to fulfil a minor part of the role.*

Key account managers play different roles in the processes that belong to each of these levels. Most of their time will be taken up with activities in the value-adding layer, working to change current situations, but they also have major contributions to make to strategic layer processes and to operational activities as well. Indeed, it is very important that they have a sound understanding of how the operational processes work in order to clarify for themselves and for everyone else what they do and do not do at this level. Otherwise, there is a grave danger of becoming sucked into being integral to the daily activity and fire-fighting, and only having time left to fulfil a minor part of the role.

While the strategic processes 'belong' to senior managers, key account managers make important contributions to them, particularly in providing information. Consider carefully how you play this part, since that will have a major influence on the outcomes. For example, if your strategic account plan is late and incomplete, you cannot be surprised if you do not get backing for it. If you do not brief your executive sponsor clearly, he or she may not understand the issues fully and may say something inappropriate to the customer. You need to engage with the higher level processes as well as your own.

To identify how the key account manager should be involved with each process, start with breaking it down into its component steps and mapping the sequence, as in Figure 9.4. It is important to identify who is responsible for each step. For some steps it will be the key account manager, in others it will be someone else. Even when the main responsibility lies elsewhere, the key account manager may have a role to play that should be specified and accepted by all.

This exercise can expose serious gaps and misunderstandings, which can then be addressed. Figure 9.5 converts this diagram into a form that collects additional useful information. Where the picture shows frequent

**Figure 9.4**
The key account manager's role by process component.

| Specification | Step 1 | Step 2 | Step 3 | Step 4 | Step 5 | Step 6 |
|---|---|---|---|---|---|---|
| Process component | | | | | | |
| Person mainly responsible | | | | | | |
| Key account manager's role | | | | | | |
| Other's role: who and what | | | | | | |
| Inputs to process component | | | | | | |
| Outputs from process component | | | | | | |
| Flexibility | | | | | | |
| Linkages with other processes | | | | | | |
| Performance metrics | | | | | | |
| Cost | | | | | | |

**Figure 9.5**  Process data capture proforma.

interactions with particular people or functions, it suggests that these people should be part of the account team (see Section 10.2). Through completing a series of these maps, key account managers will build up for themselves and their colleagues a very clear view of their job, and how they interact with others in the company.

Companies that have carried out this exercise have been impressed by:

- The scope and variety of the key account manager's job
- The competencies required to carry out the responsibilities
- The quantity of activity that depends on the key account manager.

Indeed, the exercise provides valuable input to a discussion on whether the key account manager can carry out the substantial workload which normally appears in this investigation. Check your results against Dr Sue Holt's findings (Holt, 2003), that good key account managers typically spend their time as follows:

- 30 per cent interacting with the customer
- 60 per cent internal activity
- 10 per cent account planning.

---

**CHECKPOINT**

**Do you know how your company's key account managers spend their time?**

- Internal vs external activity?
- What kind of internal activity?
- Do you know the balance between short-term and longer term activity?

---

The following sections describe the individual processes with which key account managers are normally concerned, but there will undoubtedly be more than can be mentioned here.

## 9.2    Key account management implementation processes

### 9.2.1    Strategic processes

The supplier's Board has an important role to play in key processes that crucially address how key accounts as a group are managed in the company. There is a very great difference between suppliers where the Board has recognized what it has to do, has developed the processes for which it is responsible and is operating them, and one in which the Board has pushed all activity down to the key account manager level and is, basically, 'sitting on its hands'. The former will be reaping the rewards of its efforts, the latter will probably be losing key accounts and key account managers as well.

Some key account managers are ambivalent about having their Boards involved with customer management in any way, but excluding them is unwise and passes up invaluable support. Key account managers need the Board to leverage its authority from time to time in order to achieve certain goals. This authority is better operated through a proper process, which is recognized by all and which delivers the right decisions because of the Board's on-going involvement with key customers. Figure 9.6 shows the main processes attached to senior management.

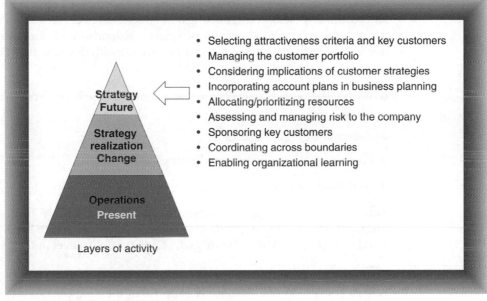

**Figure 9.6** Strategic processes in key account management.

### Strategic process: Selecting attractiveness criteria and key customers

The criteria for evaluating the attractiveness of key customers need to be identified and agreed at the most senior level, since they have serious implications for the company and for individuals within it, and can be quite controversial in their implications. These criteria (see Chapter 2) determine which customers are candidates for receiving special resource and which are not. A multi-step process should be adopted.

1. Agree the criteria (senior management) to reflect the company's strategy and their interpretation of it.

2. Roll the criteria out to key account managers and others in the company with customer knowledge to score the customers.

3. Collect the customers' views of the supplier.

4. Build a portfolio view of the candidates for key customer status.

5. Review the portfolio (senior management), confirm and communicate the selection.

The implications are too important to allow the selection and categorization to be subjected to bias and personal opinion. Take care to obtain objective evidence and the corroboration of third parties wherever possible.

Selection and deselection decisions should not be taken lightly, hastily or on short-term evidence.

In addition, the original process of selection needs to include a proper process for adding key customers to the portfolio, and also for removing others, or a portfolio can quickly get out of control. Selection and deselection decisions are not easily reversed, so they should not be taken lightly, hastily or on short-term evidence.

## Strategic process: Managing the customer portfolio

Like a fund manager, someone should be overseeing the performance of the key customer portfolio and making adjustments as necessary. Even where a person has this role, a process of review, response and communication needs to be in place. If there is no single person with this role, then it is even more important that processes exist to:

● enable the performance of these customers to be brought into a single view,

● determine and agree action,

● communicate with concerned parties and

● implement action.

This is a tough area for companies without a central KAM unit, and the tougher it is, the more important it will be to establish a robust process that is at least sponsored, if not managed, at a very senior level in the company.

## Strategic process: Considering implications of customer strategies

Unless there is a distinct process for conveying customers' strategy to senior managers, it does not happen.

Key customers do not realistically expect that their suppliers' strategies are entirely driven by their needs, even if they would like it, but they do expect that staff at senior levels will at least know what they are doing and why. However, unless there is a distinct process for conveying customers' strategy to senior managers, it does not happen. Some Boards are out and about in the marketplace and have excellent 'antennae' for sensing customer strategies, and others are very introspective, and will have no such understanding unless it is systematically fed to them. We have observed several processes for this purpose, but you need to decide which one or, better, which combination of them will be most effective in your company. The processes include:

● Monthly reports featuring customer strategy submitted to the Board and discussed as an agenda item.

● Regular presentations of key customer strategies by the key account manager at Board meetings (e.g. two or three per meeting).

● Quarterly or annual forum for presenting key customers and discussing strategic implications.

● Annual/quarterly meetings between the customer's senior management and the executive sponsor (see below).

In developing your process, consider how to use the Board's limited time to best advantage, balancing information input with the time required for it to make a response or decision and communicate it, or you may end up with a one-way reporting process that has no apparent outcome.

**Strategic process: Incorporating account plans in business planning**
In most companies the business planning cycle is already a tortuous series of strategy documents and forecasts whose origins may lie in a supplier's regional organization, production department, finance function or elsewhere. Without a defined step in the business planning process which asks for input from key account plans, they will not make any contribution, and key account managers will feel they have wasted the time they spent on planning. Unless the plans are specifically linked into the process, they will not fulfil the vital function that is an invaluable part of the reason for having key customers at all – their ability to guide the supplier successfully through changing market conditions in partnership with leading customers.

Generally speaking, business plans developed by internal departments will rely heavily on trends mechanically extrapolated from the past. This approach assumes that the future will look like the past, which is a very dangerous assumption these days. Unless strategic key account plans are incorporated into the process, the company could easily find itself under-financed, or geared up to produce the wrong items in the wrong place, or failing to invest in innovation for new markets, or suffering a host of other unintended consequences of a failure to institutionalize these plans.

**Strategic process: Allocating/prioritizing resources**
The amount a supplier is prepared to invest in a customer marks the critical difference between key accounts and other customers. A company should keep careful control of its resources and which customers receive them, and that demands a proper process of approval at the right level in the company. Some companies still allow significant amounts of resource to be won through key account managers using their powers of influence and persuasion to elicit resources from department managers and budget holders, which cannot be the right way to manage a company if, indeed, it can be called management at all.

---

### Case study insight

#### Investing in R&D with customers in the hi-tech sector

For an innovative hi-tech supplier, co-developing R&D projects with customers was an ideal way of creating new products and the markets for them simultaneously. However, on reviewing the results of its new product development after several years, it realized that it had invested a good deal of time and effort in projects that had been very successful technically, but had failed to yield the commercial returns expected. On further examination, it found that quite a high proportion of these projects had been driven by exciting ideas from rather small companies that did not have the capacity to commercialize the new products when they had been created. From then on, it decided that only key accounts should be offered R&D projects, and introduced a process of approval that ensured enforcement.

The process should include the following steps, at least:

1. Agree resource available to the key account portfolio.

2. Key account managers submit strategic account plans including requests for specified resources.

3. Approval to commit resources in principle agreed (or not) in line with total budget.

4. At appropriate time, detailed business case submitted for final approval.

5. Approval to spend resource given (or not) in line with forecast outcomes and budget available.

---

## Case study insight

### Controlling resources in a global manufacturing company

A new global accounts director reviewed the plans and performance of all key accounts in his first week after appointment. He was disappointed with both. Performance was mediocre and key account managers were acting ad hoc, not using the plans or keeping them up to date. He immediately insisted that all plans be rewritten, including the case for any resource. He made it clear that he would allocate his entire budget based on the business cases in the plans, and therefore that any late requests would not and could not be approved. Some key account managers responded, some continued in the same way – until they discovered that, indeed, they could not get any resources from ad hoc requests. Key account planning and performance both improved significantly.

---

**Strategic process: Assessing and managing risk to the company**

Low risk is inexorably related to low returns. While making every sensible effort to reduce exposure to risk, all business activities and all customers involve some residual degree of risk. Companies need to decide on the exposure to risk they are prepared to accept, and then manage towards that level. However, companies talk about risk but rarely measure it and generally do not have a process for managing it. As with everything else discussed in this chapter, you can assume that if there is no process to manage something, it is not being managed.

> You can assume that if there is no process to manage something, it is not being managed.

The process of balancing risk in the portfolio can be included within the overall management of the portfolio discussed above. In addition, though, there needs to be a process for:

● Assessing the riskiness of individual customers relative to other customers and reassessing it regularly

● Supplying the data to the portfolio manager or management process

● Analysing the position and deciding on what action should be taken, if any

● Communicating decisions

● Monitoring their fulfilment.

Many companies only assess the financial stability of their customers in order to establish their ability to pay their bills. There are many more risks involved in KAM which should be properly and objectively evaluated on a regular basis.

### Strategic process: Sponsoring key customers

Executive sponsorship of key customers is a great idea that needs careful execution. Board members should each be allocated a manageable number of key accounts, somewhere between one and three, in which they will take an on-going interest and meet a few times per year, somewhere between annually and quarterly. The sponsor gives the key customer a defined route to the supplier's boardroom and a point of final escalation if absolutely needed, which demonstrates to the customer its importance to the supplier. It gives the Board contact with the most important part of its marketplace, and provides support to the key account manager.

Again, executive sponsorship needs a process to make it work properly, one that includes the following elements:

- Matching directors with appropriate key accounts
- Reviewing customer strategy with the key account manager
- Defining and agreeing the role of the executive sponsor and key account manager
- Briefing the executive sponsor on specific aims or occasions
- Providing access on demand to the account plan and current issues.

---

### Case study insight

#### The Siemens approach to executive sponsorship

Siemens saw that its top management needed to be more involved with its key accounts in order to open doors in the customers and to gain support internally, so the company introduced TERP, its Top Executive Relationship Process, which included an overall plan for TERP meetings and pre-meeting briefings; plus protocols and actions. In Siemens' words, the programme was designed to:

- 'Orchestrate/align the TOP management of Siemens to the TOP management of our customer
- Executive support of account plan projects – key projects and cross selling
- Consistent process of executive meetings and actions (standardized)
- Easy to use systematic information management from executive engagement
  - cross account team portals
  - cross customer
  - cross units.'

The initiative resulted in accelerated growth in Siemens' top accounts and was an important part of a hugely successful KAM programme.

### Strategic process: Coordinating across boundaries

Key account managers have to work across boundaries, but they normally have to fall back on goodwill and good corporate citizenship to achieve their objectives. At times, that is not enough. Key account managers may encounter internal functional boundaries, and global account managers have to tackle extra barriers from national boundaries in order to coordinate the collection of information and commitment to deals they are trying to negotiate across numerous countries. If each occasion has to be approached as a new occurrence, key account manager talent will wear out very quickly.

These issues are fairly predictable in their nature, if not in detail, so it is quite possible for companies to establish a process to deal with them, although it is not really possible to generalize this process here as much as the others described previously. Several processes are involved: for example, cross-boundary information collection; cross-boundary proposition development and approval; and conflict resolution, on occasion. These processes need to be fitted to each company's structure and managed proactively by senior managers in the interests of the company as a whole, rather than narrow functional or strategic business unit (SBU) interests.

### Strategic process: Enabling organizational learning

Key account managers develop brilliant ideas, execute fantastic projects, win difficult bids and achieve fabulous results – but not all in the same place at the same time. Imagine how much better the results could be if all of this could be brought together. Sadly, this wonderful experience often stays where it was gained, and is inaccessible to the rest of the company. People are wasting time and resources and failing where others have succeeded, when they could have learned from internal best practice, because there is no process through which their experience can be logged and retrieved when needed.

> People are wasting time and resources and failing where others have succeeded, when they could have learned from internal best practice.

---

## Case study insight

### IMI promoting sharing globally and across diverse engineering businesses

IMI plc has an extensive list of blue-chip customers across a range of industries and geographies. Key account management is an IMI competency that has supported the delivery of higher added value solutions to this group.

Over the past five years IMI's CEO and senior executive sponsorship of KAM has been active, and high levels of investment have supported skill and behaviour changes. The 'IMI KAM Academy' is coordinated centrally and drives and supports continuous improvements in key account activities and processes across each of IMI's five 'platform' business areas.

The Academy initiates and organizes extensive training activities for key account and line managers. It provides best practice tools and techniques covering areas such as account planning and relationship mapping. There is also a market intelligence service that key account managers from across the globe call on for insights tailored to their needs. In addition, the Academy also coordinates activities to deliver creative concept generation and innovation. An extensive 'best practice' outside network of agencies, consultants and councils, including Cranfield University, is used across these areas.

Before a process can be developed, companies must first decide the best way for them to share knowledge. Consider using some or all of:

- Best practice forums
- Communities of interest
- Prepared case studies
- Access to documents like account plans
- Dedicated websites.

When the mix of media has been agreed, a process should be developed to keep sharing live, easy to access and supplied with fresh material. Incentives may be offered for contributing material and for using the system.

> A process should be developed to keep sharing live, easy to access and supplied with fresh material.

### 9.2.2   Strategy realization key account management processes

The majority of the key account manager's time should be spent on the strategy realization processes in Figure 9.7, or how key account management adds value to the organization and to the customer. These are the ones in which he or she plays pole position in managing the inputs to the process, coordinating and driving progress, and managing the outputs from the process.

The word 'developing' appears frequently in the list, which is indicative of the role. Key account managers should be focused on what they are doing to develop and change the relationship with the customer, what value they are adding to the customer's business, and what value they are adding to their own business. That should cover 90 per cent of their time, with no more than 10 per cent, and ideally less, devoted to fire-fighting and problem-solving.

**Strategy realization process: Analysing key accounts, developing strategy and planning**
The key account manager is responsible for most of this process, which explains why Sue Holt found that it took 10 per cent of the key account manager's time (Holt, 2003). The planning process, time-consuming though it is, should not be 'outsourced' to another team member. Only intimate knowledge of the plan and the rationale behind it can give the key account

> The planning process, time-consuming though it is, should not be 'outsourced' to another team member.

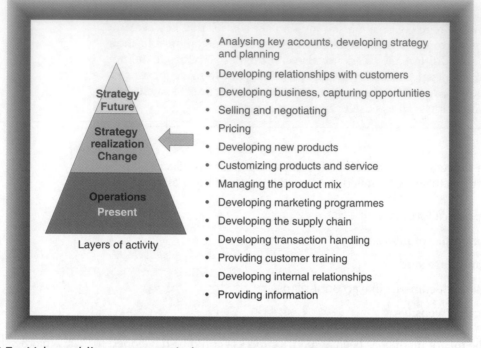

- Analysing key accounts, developing strategy and planning
- Developing relationships with customers
- Developing business, capturing opportunities
- Selling and negotiating
- Pricing
- Developing new products
- Customizing products and service
- Managing the product mix
- Developing marketing programmes
- Developing the supply chain
- Developing transaction handling
- Providing customer training
- Developing internal relationships
- Providing information

Strategy Future

Strategy realization Change

Operations Present

Layers of activity

**Figure 9.7** Value-adding processes in key account management.

manager sufficient confidence to discuss it in detail with customers. However, the key account manager can and should work with a team in order to gain a broader range of contributions to improve the quality of the plan.

The key account manager manages this process from start to finish:

- **Setting up**: Identifying, training and briefing the team
- **Analysis and strategy setting**: Development workshops and information gathering
- **Planning**: Producing the plan and planning communication
- **Roll-out**: Get approval, assemble implementation team and communicate
- **Measure and monitor**: Set up and run measurement, review and response.

### Strategy realization process: Developing relationships with customers

One key account director, when asked if there was a process for relationship development in his company, replied that he did not think so, because people 'just know' how to develop relationships. In fact, he was quite dissatisfied with the state of his company's relationships, and perhaps he should have considered whether a lack of process might be responsible for the situation. Many people know how to develop personal relationships, but not necessarily intercompany relationships, and even the best key account managers would be helped by seeing relationship development as a process.

It fits our definition of a process at the beginning of this chapter just as well as many others. Indeed, seeing relationship development as a process, as in Figure 9.8, has a number of advantages:

- Missing out steps is less likely to happen
- Seeing the whole process helps planning, which generally improves speed and certainty
- Other people can see how they can help
- Progress can be monitored
- Progress can be compared with other relationships.

**Figure 9.8**   Relationship development as a process.

### Strategy realization process: Developing business, capturing opportunities

Some companies, particularly those involved in markets characterized by very large, infrequent bids, are brilliant at business development. They may track opportunities from the moment that they first appear until they are finally won, several years later. There is now plenty of good software available to help the process, so the quality of approach should be improving. The trouble is that if everyone is upgrading their game you need to find more ways of being out ahead. Successful companies seem to be better at some of the steps in the process that their competitors may not even recognize (Figure 9.9).

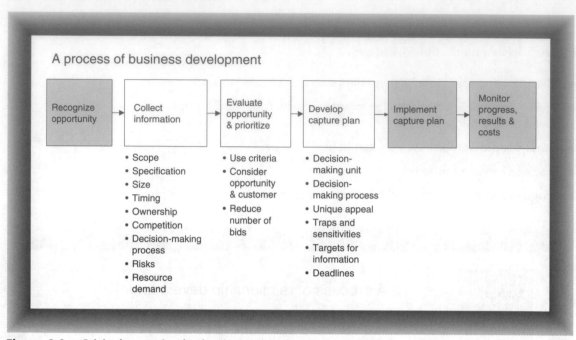

**Figure 9.9**   Critical steps in the business development process.

- They collect more information at an early stage so they can fully understand and qualify the opportunity.

- They evaluate and select opportunities objectively according to strategic criteria, and say 'no bid' more often.

- They use formal capture planning – how they will win the business, rather than how they will execute the business – to develop their approach.

### Strategy realization process: Selling and negotiating

Selling means managing the sales cycle through to the face-to-face negotiation, but plenty has been written elsewhere about the selling process that does not need to be repeated here. Increasingly, negotiation is conducted remotely, as in reverse e-auctions, which are still new to some sectors while they are diminishing in importance in others. In a reverse e-auction, the customer declares the specification of what it wants to buy, prequalifies a shortlist of suppliers, all of which it considers acceptable. Suppliers then bid for the business through a website over a period of, say, two hours, offering lower prices to beat the competition. Often, prices from other suppliers are visible, albeit anonymously, until the last phase of the auction, which gives the customer the option of selecting the lowest price, or not. It is a brutal process!

Customers have cut the prices they pay dramatically in some cases, which has whetted their appetite to buy more through this route, although some have gained very low prices but suffered poor delivery and are moderating their activity. Nevertheless, suppliers must realize that they are very much at risk of losing their volume or losing their margin in reverse e-auctions if they sell a commodity product.

The customer's procurement department normally runs an e-auction, and they are very clear about the whole process from the issuing of invitations to prequalify to participate in the auction, through to the actual auction itself. You must respond with an equally clear process of preparation and response: a great deal of work needs to be completed before the auction begins.

1. Analyse the customer's expressed needs and implicit wants.

2. Propose a specification that plays to your strengths and challenges competition.

3. Establish the buying process and criteria.

4. Carry out a detailed analysis of costs.

5. Build a cost and pricing model to enable testing of prices and terms.

6. Build a model to test results of winning or losing the business.

7. Respond to and pass the qualification process.

8. Decide on the e-auction team, who does what, who approves the final offer on the day or decides to drop out.

9. Agree pricing floors with appropriate people (e.g. finance).

10. Participate in the auction.

The reverse auction process will probably strip out costs for features or services that the customer does not require, so suppliers that bundle costs together are ill-prepared to participate in e-auctions. Winning prices and terms are very finely tuned and negotiators must be able to work with full cost transparency internally.

> Winning prices and terms are very finely tuned and negotiators must be able to work with full cost transparency internally.

In very big deals the selling process for a key customer is normally carried out by the key account manager, with or without a team. Often, this really amounts to a licence to sell to the customer's sites, rather than a guaranteed volume of business. In many markets, thereafter, orders are facilitated on the ground by the field salesforce in each division or locality, not by the key account manager personally. This is a very different selling process, which still needs to be managed by the key account manager, usually without any direct authority (see Chapters 10 and 11). The key account manager needs to build and participate appropriately in a process of:

- communicating information to the salesforce

- supporting their selling process

- monitoring performance

- tracking the customer's response

- recognizing achievements.

From what we have seen, it is not easy to build a robust process in this kind of very common situation, although it is absolutely necessary. It is hard, time-consuming labour to make it work, and any process available to help should be used. If the key account manager does not succeed, the salesforce will be selling other things to other customers, and the volume from centrally negotiated deals may never materialize.

### Strategy realization process: Pricing

Key customers do not accept standard pricing, and they have enough buying power to put plenty of pressure on prices. They will also be constantly trying out customized products and customized service offerings in order to gain advantage in the marketplace and optimize what they pay for. The volume of pricing exercises is bound to be high and getting higher. Intelligent suppliers have worked to achieve a good understanding of their own cost base, so that they can respond quickly and appropriately with prices.

---

### Case study insight

**Fast, consultative pricing in a global services supplier**

In order to establish costs and prices, a global supplier needed to consult numerous national SBUs and service experts every time a global or multinational customer asked for prices. The process involved several iterations and took longer than big customers were prepared to wait. It had to change its process from the safe, sequential one it had always used to one with simultaneous consultation at several stages. It introduced brightly coloured, fast-track covers for critical pricing documents, moved them to the top of any recipient's task list, and enforced the discipline. They executed 6–8 iterations in half the time it had taken before – not every time – but whenever it was really necessary.

---

Pricing for key customers demands a very transparent process: mistakes can cost a supplier dear.

Pricing for key customers demands a very transparent process: mistakes can cost a supplier dear. It needs to be absolutely clear who provides input, who needs to be informed, who has final approval, what degree of variance is allowable, and when the customer can be approached. Key account managers should play a pivotal role in pricing. They should know what other costs are affected in the customer's business, how the terms can be made more attractive without reducing margins, on what basis the customer will assess a price, what they are likely to pay, and so on.

Suppliers should look at their short-term volume-based incentive schemes and ask themselves who created this conflict of interest and why.

However, in many companies key account managers are largely excluded from pricing decisions, except as a source of specific information, because they are not sufficiently trusted. To some extent, this mistrust may arise from a feeling that they are not financially competent, but often it is because their objectivity and commitment to acting in the company's interests rather than their own is questioned. Suppliers should look at their short-term volume-based incentive schemes and ask themselves who created this conflict of interest and why.

**Strategy realization process:**

- Developing new products;
- Customizing products and service;
- Managing the product mix;
- Developing marketing programmes;
- Developing the supply chain;
- Developing transaction handling;
- Providing customer training.

These processes address very different aspects of the customer's business, and it is through these processes that the supplier will fulfil most of the added value it can offer to the customer, which makes them extremely important. As processes, however, they can be considered together, since they will generally consist of a project carried out by the supplier's experts, possibly working alongside customer staff. The key account manager will be involved in the coordination and communication during the project, but particularly at the beginning and the end. Figure 9.10 shows the outline of a typical process for such a project, with the key account manager's role highlighted. Step 4 is deceptive, as the bulk of the work lies in this box, so it may need to be split into greater detail in practice.

Where key account managers have an understanding of supply chain issues, marketing, product development, etc., they are more likely to spot opportunities like this, and are better able to support the project and ensure that it stays on track to deliver to the customer's needs than if they do not. They should not fulfil the role of project manager, generally, as the project and the project team should be driven by the subject expert, leaving the key account manager free to take a more detached view and liaise with the customer.

**Strategy realisation process: Developing internal relationships**

The same process and techniques can be applied to developing internal relationships as have been suggested for developing external relationships. Indeed, finding your way round a large organization, even if it is your own employer, absolutely requires as systematic an approach as you would apply to a customer.

**Strategy realisation process: Providing information**

A substantial part of the key account manager's job will be about providing information, from and to the customer, from and to people internally. The information will be of all kinds, about strategic account plans, project progress, performance figures, customer positioning, personalities, current issues, etc. So it is not possible to chart a single generic process to provide this disparate collection of information. Wherever it is required regularly, the key account manager should think about developing processes for sourcing and delivering it to its destination in a suitable form in order to

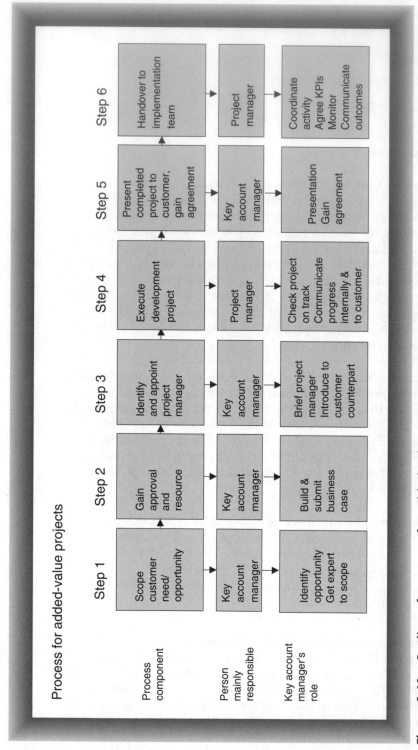

**Figure 9.10** Outline of a process for added-value customer projects.

avoid a lot of sweat, tears and late nights. If a process has been mapped, it will be possible to clarify the sources of data and the role of other people in providing the information, and hence to delegate some of the work.

This list of processes forms a major part of the key account manager's activity:

- plus his or her contribution to the strategic processes in Section 9.2.1
- plus his or her role in operational processes in Section 9.2.3
- plus communication, in Section 9.2.4
- plus monitoring and measurement in Section 9.3.

Key account managers have a big job, and they should use all the processes they can.

### 9.2.3 Operational processes

Operational processes are those that run the day-to-day activity of a company, that actually deliver what the customer has bought. Key account managers need to be involved with them, to the extent that is required to ensure that promises are fulfilled. They must therefore understand the company's operational capabilities; what it can and cannot do, and what is and is not expensive to do. The kinds of processes that we class as operational or transactional are shown in Figure 9.11, and include the regular sales process and transaction and payment handling, as well as production and physical delivery.

**Figure 9.11** Operational processes.

Unfortunately, key account managers easily get sucked into fire-fighting and problem-solving in this area. Operational people will be more than happy to allow you to take on the role of liaising with the customer and bearing bad news when necessary, and you quickly become a part of the regular mechanism. You are then in danger of being an overpaid customer service executive, and finding yourself with no time or energy to fulfil your own, proper role. Ultimately, the key account manager does take responsibility and communicate with the customer when things are seriously wrong: the issue is balance.

You need to agree with the operational team how you can best work together, so that you supply them with what they need, when they need it, and then let them get on with the job, including talking to the customer. There have been some fabulous relationships built up between suppliers' order processing people and customers' purchasing and supply chain people, which have saved both sides a great deal of trouble. If operational people have been properly briefed and consulted, then they should be trusted to do their job, and to find solutions to issues when required. Figure 9.5 might be a useful way of working out what they need from you, and what you need from them.

---

### CHECKPOINT

Are both key account managers and operations clear about what decisions each can make:

● Without needing to inform the other?

● Informing the other, but after the decision is taken?

● Needing to consult with the other before a decision is taken?

---

Lines of communication must be open, but they must also be used with discipline, in order to have manageable workloads and sensible working practices. One operations director said, 'You can easily tell the difference between a good key account manager and a bad one: when things go pear-shaped, the good one will bring us the bad news and tell us it's going to happen beforehand, but you won't find the bad one anywhere.' Figure 9.12

**Figure 9.12**
Lines of
communication.

illustrates the view of Graham Booth, supply chain director of Tesco, when he said, quite simply, 'It's not my job to work out what we should offer to customers, that's what marketing and sales does. My job, once I know what it is, is to make it happen.' Obviously, operations cannot make 'it' happen if they do not know what 'it' is, and the link between operations and sales/marketing/key account management is notoriously poor.

Links between the customer and sales and marketing should be good, and links between the customer and operations and logistics should also be good but links between sales and marketing, and operations and logistics, are often poor. So it could be that while the customer has a full view of what it was offered to match what it received, when nobody in the supplier has a complete picture! This is surely an exposed and perilous position to be in. Key account managers need to strengthen their internal relationships with operations and agree some protocols and processes through which they can work together.

> The link between operations and marketing/sales/key account management is notoriously poor.

---

### Case study insight

#### A wasted opportunity in the automotive sector

In companies supplying the automotive industry, contracts are negotiated around each car model, and are agreed quite some time before production actually begins. The key account manager's involvement peaks at contract negotiation, and their attention has normally moved on by the time the goods are actually delivered. As a result, probably, they have virtually no contact with operations and the people do not even recognize each other. The operations manager said, 'I deal with this customer every day, and I think I know a lot about them. But I wouldn't even know who the key account manager is, so I don't pass any of it on. I don't know how or where to call.'

---

In summary, getting the balance right here is both important and difficult. Key account managers should find it worthwhile to invoke some processes and to start by mapping them to clarify who does what, under what circumstances.

### 9.2.4  *The process of communication*

We do not plan to deal with interpersonal communication here, but we do want to make a plea for communication to be considered as a process and dealt with much more systematically than it normally is. As relationships develop, a large part of the key account manager's job becomes communication. Think of all the people with whom you need to communicate inside your own organization, as well as inside the customer organization. If they are not kept fully informed, they cannot make the decisions appropriate to the customer that will allow them to do their jobs properly, and good communication is essential to effective team working. However, communication is often an afterthought, whereas with some forethought, a lot of activities would work much better.

| What you want to say is crucial to how and where you say it. |
| :--- |

Start by deciding your purpose, why you are communicating. What you want to say is crucial to how and where you say it. What kind of action do you want as an outcome? Do you want someone to give you information? Or do you want to give them information, so that they will do … what? Do you want a response? What kind of response? Do recipients know how to make contact, and are you ready to receive it?

Figure 9.13 shows some of the reasons you may be communicating; and the first step is to decide which.

**Figure 9.13**
Reasons to
communicate.

| The communicator must take responsibility for directing the audience's attention to the right place and making the meaning readily accessible. |
| :--- |

Material sent out is often overloaded and unfocused, so that recipients do not know which part is for them, and may easily miss it. The communicator must take responsibility for directing the audience's attention to the right place and making the meaning readily accessible. Sending out a communication is only the beginning of the process. A communication cannot be considered as effective unless it:

● reaches the intended recipient,

● is absorbed by the intended recipient,

● is understood,

● produces the desired response, and

● is retained (though not always).

These are rather obvious requirements, but if they were taken seriously, plenty of communications would turn out very different. Communication does not achieve these objectives if it is misdirected, incomplete, impenetrable or confusing. It might just as well not have been sent if it does not produce the desired response.

The advertising industry has clearly given a great deal of thought to communication, and we can learn from it. It particularly recognizes the importance of the audience. Just like consumer audiences, business audiences are of different sizes and profiles, speak different languages (finance or logistics or marketing), belong to different cultures that interpret messages differently, and are best accessed via different media. However, business communication often treats them as if they were all identical, which is simply not so. The audience, and the need to communicate, drives the message and the communication of the message, as shown in Figure 9.14.

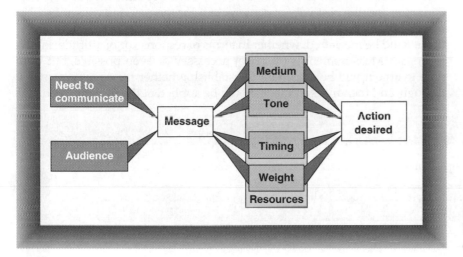

**Figure 9.14** Planning communication.

In deciding the most effective way to convey your message, you need to think about:

● **The medium**: Choose email, telephone, videoconference, face-to-face meeting, presentation, special event and so on. Which is most suitable for the audience and most suitable for the message? Use multiple media to reinforce messages.

● **Tone/style**: The audience and the message determine whether the tone should be informative, financial, motivational, humorous or serious, and so on.

● **Timing**: At what point in the year should the message be sent? Calendar year, financial year, or sales seasons? Should it be timed before, during or after an event, and by how much? Does it need to link with other events or communications?

● **Weight**: Should the message be flagged as very important? How much space should it get? Should it be 'showcased'? Should it be repeated? How often?

These are the elements that begin to take up resources, which may be money in business to consumer terms, but are more likely to be time in business to business. Having no budget at all for communication to or about key customers can be a barrier, but relatively small sums could be used very effectively.

Of course, not all communication requires detailed planning, but certainly strategic account plans, major programmes, initiatives and projects involve a great many people in both the customer and the supplier. Planning them would improve timeliness greatly, and prevent many problems from ever arising. Figure 9.15 gives a planning framework to use based on Figure 9.14. Start by writing all the audiences involved, internally and externally, in the first column, and then complete each row with the specific message for each audience, and the best way of conveying it for them. Clearly identify what response is expected, and consider how the effectiveness of the communication should be measured, whether in terms of response or of attitude, knowledge, etc. Measurement is often not necessary or even possible, but from time to time it will be important to establish whether messages are getting through, and then measurement should be applied at the receiving end.

Need to communicate ...................................................................................

| Audience | Message | Tone | Media | Timing | Weight | Desired action | Metrics/ KPIs |
|----------|---------|------|-------|--------|--------|----------------|---------------|
|          |         |      |       |        |        |                |               |
|          |         |      |       |        |        |                |               |
|          |         |      |       |        |        |                |               |
|          |         |      |       |        |        |                |               |
|          |         |      |       |        |        |                |               |
|          |         |      |       |        |        |                |               |
|          |         |      |       |        |        |                |               |

**Figure 9.15** Developing a communication plan.

*Key account managers struggle with the fundamental requirements of communication.*

We have assumed so far that people have basic communication skills but, in reality, key account managers struggle with the fundamental requirements of communication, especially expressing themselves in writing in an appropriate manner and length for business. The strategic account plan is a core item of communication but, sadly, many of those that we have seen fail to communicate clearly or accurately. They veer from the extreme of terseness to the other extreme of verbosity, and fail to do even the essential job of explaining the account in the absence of the key account manager.

## 9.3 Performance measurement and monitoring

### 9.3.1 Measuring key account management

Management craves measurement, and not without good reason. Unfortunately, most measurement is unimaginative, and relates only to financial outcomes. Financial results represent the goals that businesses are striving to achieve, but as measurements to manage with they have a huge flaw. Financial results are 'lag' measurements: they represent outcomes and, by definition, it is too late to do anything about outcomes. They are the product of what has already happened. The clock cannot be wound back to make different inputs and get a different result, so financial measurements can only be observed and, hopefully, used to provide learning and improvement.

> Financial results are 'lag' measurements: they represent outcomes and, by definition, it is too late to do anything about outcomes.

So, measurements that inform, diagnose and track progress need to be found, albeit without losing sight of the fundamental need to measure the financial yield from activities. There is as much danger from measuring too much as there is in measuring too little. Obviously, too little measurement can mean that misleading assumptions and wrong decisions are made; too much, and important information can be lost in a storm of figures. Measurements cost time and money, so they should not be collected unless there is a clear understanding of who wants to know and what they will do differently when they do know. 'Who cares?' is a very good question to ask.

> 'Who cares?' is a very good question to ask.

---

**CHECKPOINT**

For each of the measurements your company collects, is it clear:

● What purpose it represents?

● Who wants to receive it?

● Who reviews it?

● Who has the authority to respond to it?

---

Companies should aim to establish a set of measurements for any part of their business, not just key account management, that are:

● necessary – likely to provoke a response,

● sufficient – enough and no more,

● purposeful – matched to desired outcomes,

● monitored and reviewed, and

● acted upon.

The purposes of measurement in KAM can be aligned with the three levels of the company described at the beginning of the chapter (Figure 9.16). At the top level, the Board will want to know quantitatively what KAM is contributing to its strategic objectives, to enable them to 'steer the ship'. At the next level, questions will be asked about how KAM adds value to the company, which measurement should aim to answer. At the operational/transactional level, major choices have already been made, but decisions are still required about the best and most cost-effective way to run activities.

**Figure 9.16**
Purposes of
measurement and
measurements.

Different purposes
drive different
measurements, so
before specifying and
setting up your
measurement set,
you should identify
your purpose.

Different purposes drive different measurements, so before specifying and setting up your measurement set you should identify your purpose. You should be seeking to have a 'necessary and sufficient' set of measurements for KAM at each level in the company, to enable appropriate decision making from top to bottom. Indeed, two further purposes of measurement – gaining visibility and learning and improvement – are relevant to all levels in the company.

● **Making the right decisions**: Measurement allows objective assessment of strategies and enables senior management to make evidence-based decisions. Measurements should be aligned with the Board's profit focus.

● **Aligning implementation with strategy**: These measurements are designed to track the alignment of changes: of implementation against strategy; of progress against plan; and of supplier and customer. They can encourage motivation and pinpoint underlying problems. Measurements should focus on the value that KAM adds to the business.

● **Improving efficiency and productivity**: Measurement allows objective monitoring and highlights opportunities for performance improvement. Measurements will relate to cost and the key performance indicators (KPIs) used to monitor activity.

● **Gaining visibility**: Measurement is a more powerful communication vehicle than words. It can show the value of KAM and improve multi-function cooperation in a way that anecdotal and qualitative evidence does not.

● **Learning and improvement**: Measurement defines problems and solutions so that organizations can gain a better understanding of situations and outcomes, from which they can learn and change their behaviour.

### 9.3.2   The three levels of key account management metrics

At each level of activity in the company, suppliers should have metrics that provide the people managing at each of those levels with information about KAM, so that they can manage what they are doing and align it with KAM objectives.

#### Strategy and key account management measurements

The Board develops strategy to address its ultimate concern, which is profit. If KAM is to register with the Board and gain its understanding and support, it needs to identify and report measurements that are profit-related. Boards take a long-term view in order to respond to demands for increased shareholder value, but they are also sensitive to City and investor reactions in the short term. In fact, more customer measurements like the following might enable them to manage investor expectations better.

- **Opportunity**: The Board needs to set corporate objectives in the light of the opportunity available to it. Key customers represent a major opportunity that should be reported to the Board and monitored. The size and nature of the opportunity should be detailed in the strategic account plans.

- **Risk**: The Board is responsible for the company's stability, so risk is a major issue. Customer riskiness can be quantified in comparative terms and monitored independently of the customer asset value. Risk should be measured and applied as a probability in forecasting customer asset value.

- **Customer asset value**: Customer lifetime value is the net present value of individual customers and of the key customer portfolio as a whole over the lifetime of the relationship. Lifetimes are difficult to assess, so a fixed term can be adopted, say three or five years, or longer, according to the business. The Board should see how much these customers are worth as assets, and should monitor the growth of their value.

- **Return on Investment (RoI)**: This measurement can be driven out of the strategic account plans for individual customers, provided that they forecast several years ahead, and include the costs of the resource required to achieve the forecast. The Board can then make decisions on where to invest, like any other investment decision.

#### Strategy realization and key account management measurements

The KAM function needs measurements to help it manage its effectiveness, which should be judged against expectations of the value it is designed to add to the business, and the progress that it is making towards adding that value. KAM is a medium to long-term strategy that should nevertheless be able to demonstrate success as it makes that journey. Each of the measures below should be monitored at the level of individual accounts, and at the overall portfolio level. However, if there is no person or process for managing key customers as a portfolio, even if the measurements are collected and aggregated, it will not be possible to take appropriate action.

- **Customer attractiveness**: The measurement of customer attractiveness is described in Chapter 2. It needs to be monitored to ensure that the company's strategy is correctly aligned with the customer's attractiveness. It would be good if the sum total of customer attractiveness of the portfolio increased, and cause for concern and action if it declines.

- **Customer profitability**: Customer profitability is a crucial measure, discussed in Chapter 6. The company should be able to measure it, and the key account manager should manage it. The overall profitability of the key customer portfolio is an indispensable measurement.

- **Risk measurement**: Absolute measurement of risk is difficult, but by considering the sources of risk in customers in the supplier's sector, and assessing customers against each of these, a composite risk measurement can be calculated and used to compare key customers against each other. If the risk is quantified, it is much more likely that it will be managed.

- **Customer satisfaction**: This is an obvious measurement, but it needs to be measured properly, addressing the views of decision makers in the customer on their issues, not on standardized operational KPIs. Best conducted by a third party, depth is more important than frequency.

- **Relationship**: Companies measure relationship in a number of ways, taking into account the number of contact points, quality of the relationship, and importance/relevance of the contact. Again, it is advisable to use a third party to avoid bias: several research companies offer an established approach. Relationship is an appropriate measurement of the facilitation element of KAM, which should be regarded as a 'lead', or advance, input indicator rather than a 'lag' or outcome indicator.

- **Business extension**: There will be accounts in which growth and business extension is not expected, but where it is, it should be measured. Measuring volume or even margin is not sufficient, as they can rise or fall from swings in the customer's own business and do not indicate the success or otherwise of KAM. Business extension is defined as business gained from new products or lines of business taken by the customer, or any sales to new parts of the customer's business.

- **Customer retention**: Again, measuring volume or margin alone does not demonstrate whether a key customer is retained or not: business can continue even when a customer has been effectively lost to a competitor. The measure for customer retention should be based on share of wallet or relevant spend, defining a retained customer as one where the share is the same or better, and counting the customer as lost if share is declining.

### Operations and key account management measurements

As the customer, not surprisingly, retains its interest in the quality of what it receives and the service that goes with it, so must the key account manager. However, operational measurements will be collected by other functions, and it is the key account manager's responsibility to be aware of them and to review them, rather than to collect them him or herself. The measurements below are some of the most important, but it is by no means an exhaustive list. These are the KPIs on which both suppliers and customers tend to focus but, as we have seen, they tell only a part of the story, and are not sufficient on their own.

- **Cost/price**: The key account manager can have a major impact on costs through the deals negotiated with the customer. Obviously, costs need to be monitored to make sure they are not getting too high, but cost reduction also needs to be monitored for impact on the customer.

- **Revenue/volume**: This is a standard measurement, which is regarded as being of paramount importance in terms of operational management and outcomes, but it has limitations, as discussed above.

- **Service levels**: Service levels are crucial to customers, so they measure them closely themselves. The supplier's measurements should be carefully aligned with the customer's (e.g. delivery to time should be measured as arrival at the customer's premises, rather than departure from the supplier).

- **Failure rates**: Breakdown rates are important to identify as they represent the real pressure points which the key account manager needs to understand.

Operational metrics can be benchmarked against a previous period or against the service level agreement with the customer. In the case of key customers, the service level agreement embodies their expectations, so the latter is the right benchmark to use.

Suppliers need to consider who takes ownership and responsibility for operational performance. Customers are clear about this: while they understand how companies work, they also see the key account manager as the

---

### Case study insight

#### False economies

A key account manager negotiated a major contract with one of the biggest hospital trusts in the UK. It was a tough and complex deal that kept the customer's inventory costs to a minimum through just-in-time delivery, in effect, daily. Orders would be placed by an agreed time the previous day, when the hospital was clear about the next day's demand.

A few months into the contract, the supplier's regional distribution manager decided to restructure delivery routes and frequency to cut costs, and reduced deliveries to the trust's area to twice per week. Hospitals had to change their workflow planning processes to cope with the change, and the trust was, understandably, furious.

person the supplier has put in place to represent it, and that person must, almost by definition, carry the ultimate responsibility for performance. However, it seems that the key account manager carries this responsibility without any authority: in most suppliers the operations managers have sole authority for performance. While the best work closely with key account managers, others see them as peripheral to their activity and communication and consultation is poor. These issues must be resolved, and developing a process that specifies how the two interact and what is required of each is probably the best way to do it.

### Summary of key account management measurements

Suppliers often have plenty of measurement of operations and finance, but are short of measurements of value and change, and good diagnostics. Table 9.1 summarizes the balanced view of measurement of KAM that we have suggested above. Use it to check what you have in place and what is missing, to ensure that you have adequate measurement through the different levels of activity, rather than too much at one level and not enough at another.

**Table 9.1** Summary of measurements for key account management

| Company level | Strategy | Strategy realization | Operations |
|---|---|---|---|
| Who cares | Directors<br>Shareholders | Key account managers<br>Functional heads | Operations line managers<br>Buyers<br>Key account managers |
| Focus | Profit | Value and progress | Performance |
| Measurements | Return on Investment<br>Customer asset value<br>Risk<br>Opportunity | Customer attractiveness<br>Customer profitability<br>Risk measurement<br>Customer satisfaction<br>Business extension<br>Customer retention<br>Key account portfolio contribution growth | Cost/price<br>Revenue/volume<br>Service levels<br>Failure rates |
| Benchmarks | Performance against business plan<br>Growth in shareholder value | Customer expectation<br>Portfolio contribution plan | Performance against previous period<br>Performance against agreement |
| Length of view | Long term<br>Short term | Medium term | Short term |

Every measurement needs a benchmark, something to compare with it. For example, 95 per cent of orders delivered complete might be excellent in a fast-moving sector with continuous new product introductions and short life cycles, where the norm is 85 per cent, but it may be poor in a more established business which generally achieves 99 per cent. Benchmarks are important in clarifying expectations, and should be chosen with care.

### 9.3.3 Measuring input

Suppliers naturally pursue the outcomes of KAM, and tend to focus their energies and attention on what it produces. However, in order to assess the outcomes, an understanding of the inputs is needed. Obviously, a supplier would want to see greater outcomes from greater inputs and, conversely, should expect lesser outcomes from lesser inputs. It is therefore important to find a way of measuring how much 'key account management' the customer actually receives.

Table 9.2 shows a scheme that measures KAM input to a specific customer on a points system, which at least quantifies the view of what the customer is receiving, and enables it to be compared with other customers. If the supplier were able to value the input in currency, so much the better. That provides the information needed to make a sound input to decisions about investing in the customer – or not investing, as the case may be.

Such a measurement scheme implies that KAM is not either 'on' or 'off' but, in practice, is likely to be applied in varying amounts. It is easy to assume that a customer is receiving KAM when, in fact, they are not. There might be all kinds of reasons why delivery is not living up to what was planned, but without some such measurement scheme, the customer's response, or lack of it, is in danger of being misjudged.

### 9.3.4 Performance monitoring

Needless to say, it is not logical to expect the same level of performance from every key account, especially when they receive different degrees of KAM. Indeed, the supplier should expect a different kind of performance from customers, according to where they have been placed in the key account selection matrix described in Chapter 2. Customers will have been effectively categorized according to whether revenue growth is expected, leading to greater profits, or whether profits will be achieved through maintaining or improving profitability by cost reduction, as illustrated in Figure 9.17.

Suppliers probably do not want a *streamline*, 'manage for cash' customer to grow, and they do not expect that a *status*, 'maintain proactively' customer can grow, or they would be more attractive than they are. They should be looking for cost reduction and monitoring profitability in these customers, whereas they should be targeting far higher growth rates from *star*, 'invest for growth' customers, but not cost reduction at this stage. A healthy balance might be expected for *strategic* customers.

Expectations need to be reflected in the performance monitoring system. The critical metrics for the customer should be identified, and results judged by those. Certainly, it is entirely inappropriate to judge all key customers (and key account managers) on the same metric, or the same change in that metric. Targeting everyone on, say, 10 per cent growth, is a

**Table 9.2**  Measuring key account management input

| Indicator | Score | | | |
|---|---|---|---|---|
| | 0 | 1 | 2 | 3 |
| Designated key account manager | Key account manager's time: <10% | 10–50% | 50–100% | 100% |
| KAM team | Non-existent | Exists but ad hoc, reactive, unclear membership | Proactive, internally focused | Externally focused, formal ways of operating, clear membership |
| Relationship governance in place | Ad hoc | Unconscious, asymmetrical | Conscious, asymmetrical Medium: meets customer | Formally defined, joint |
| Executive sponsorship (Board or equivalent) | None | Low participation (e.g. once per year) | 2/3 times a year, calls for reports on issues, responds on request | High: meets customer regularly, knows account issues, actively promotes, solves problems, accepts brief |
| Customized offer | Standard offer only | Minor adjustments, superficial | Major adjustments, not exclusive | Major adjustments, exclusive |
| Organization-wide awareness of status | Nobody knows | Everyone in sales and customer service knows | Everyone in supplier division/country knows | Everyone in supplier division/country knows plus top to bottom in customer division |
| Joint three-year strategic plan | Budget and annual review | Annual review, action plan and budget | Annual review, joint input to one-year action plan and budget | Analysis of customer and strategy, validated and jointly developed, agreed strategies for three years, predicted outputs and measures |
| Extra resource allocation | Standard | Ad hoc | Defined but short term | Regular and frequent resource input, valued by customer |
| Evaluation of results | | | | |
| Level of KAM input | None[a] | Low | Medium | High |
| Score | 0–4 | 5–11 | 12–18 | 19–24 |

[a] A customer not being subject to KAM may score on one or two parameters, but cannot be considered to be receiving real KAM.

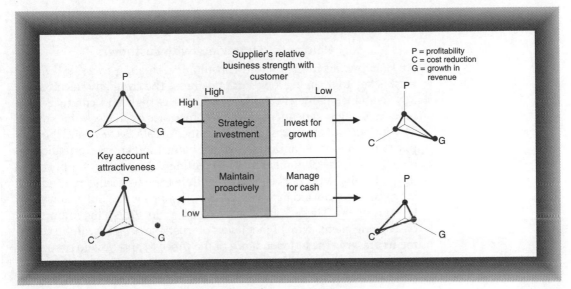

**Figure 9.17**    Financial expectations from key accounts.

nonsense. Performance monitoring should reflect the spread of metrics shown in Section 9.3.2. The supplier will then be monitoring:

- at the strategic level, the results/yield from the customer,
- at the strategy realization level, the progress towards change that will pay off in the medium term, and
- at the operational level, current fulfilment of customer expectations.

The strategic account plan charts what is expected and sets out the measurements that indicate that progress is on track. Using this set of metrics is the most effective way of demonstrating the specific commitment of inputs, activity and outputs to the supplier's senior management, to the key account manager, and to the customer. The strategic account plan can effectively become a contract between all three parties, and then performance should be measured against the particular contract, not standard metrics applied to all customers. If, indeed, strategic plans did become contracts, we suspect there would be an immediate improvement in their quality and the attention they would command in the business.

Some suppliers have earned considerable success with customers, and even turned round deteriorating situations, by installing a shared measurement framework with customers. Such frameworks make everyone concentrate on what they really want and expect from a relationship, and remove ambiguity and different interpretations, which is invaluable whether there is good or bad performance. If performance is good, the customer has to acknowledge and give credit for it. If performance is poor, less time and energy is wasted on arguing about what has happened, because it is clearly inadequate, and more time is spent on the action that needs to be taken.

> ## Case study insight
> ### Halcrow's 360° review with customers
>
> At Halcrow, an infrastructure consultancy, creating *client lock-in* and trust is key to retaining long-term business. The company selects a few key relationships where the level of trust is high and conducts 360° reviews using independent research companies or an electronic survey. This instrument measures the performance of *both the client* and the supplier against each organization's stated values and key performance criteria. It helps the customer focus on creating value in their supply chain through being a better client, while building the whole team. Feedback is typically conducted in face-to-face workshops with joint action plans taken forward. The lessons Halcrow learned included: the importance of selecting clients with higher levels of trust; the need for careful coaching to preserve the independence of the process; and how to prepare to build real honesty and trust.

Performance monitoring generally has two purposes:

1. To establish whether plans are on track in order to take action if necessary

2. To reward contributors to good performance.

The more important purpose is the first, to make sure that intentions are being kept and expectations will be fulfilled. To complete the process, there should be a recognized and active system of 'review and respond', rather than an inert 'review and report' approach. Limits of deviation from the plan can be put into place in advance. When these limits are reached, action is triggered to counter the danger of passively observing a slight trend that becomes a major gap after a few months.

> Suppliers should think very seriously about what they reward and what reaction the reward system might provoke.

The second purpose can actually frustrate the first, which is obviously contrary to what it is supposed to achieve. Rewards encourage people to sabotage metrics and conceal poor performance, as well as spurring them on to new efforts. Suppliers should think very seriously about what they reward and what reaction the reward system might provoke. There are many examples where reward systems have shaped the business and the marketplace to the point where it is permanently distorted from its natural shape; for example, in financial services, mobile phones, most of the public sector and many more.

## Summary

If something has to be done more than once, there should be a process for doing it. As one disillusioned company said, two years after its introduction of KAM, 'We've discovered, the hard way, that it's all about process in the end.' Indeed, process is the way that companies get things done, so that should not come as a surprise. When people like key account managers touch on a great many activities in the company, they can only achieve their objectives by allowing processes to fulfil the tasks. Key customers expect robust and consistent performance across the board, and that can only be managed by good processes.

This chapter is a plea to key account managers to engage actively and positively with their company's processes, because unless they do, they will fail. If the process is rigid and unresponsive, then clarify and discuss the issues with whoever is responsible for it, rather than working round it, so that next time it will work in a more appropriate way. If there is no process at all, and one is needed, then find out where it belongs in the organization and work with those people to come up with a robust solution.

Key account managers who try to do everything themselves will be very limited in what they can achieve – and very tired. In fact, good or excellent processes are fundamental to the success of KAM, and to the success of individual key account managers. If the organization does not make them responsive to the needs of key customers, key account managers will find that they have very little room to manoeuvre in what they can offer, and will be constantly frustrated, fighting 'with one hand tied behind their backs'. If they are good, competent key account managers, they are likely to leave and find an organization that has better processes.

However, if a supplier gets its processes right for key customers, the chances are they will work well for other customers too, and the whole business will benefit. Market-leading customers can teach suppliers a lot, as long as they are able to learn.

**Implementation is the graveyard of strategy**

# 10 The role and requirements of key account managers

In order to determine the role of key account managers, suppliers first need to ask themselves what they intend the role of key account management (KAM) itself to be. That should decide what its 'agents', the key account managers, have to do. The objectives for KAM and the route to achieving them should be worked out in some detail.

Normally, the prime driver will be the marketplace and leading customers in it, so the company should have a view on how KAM will work from their point of view. Specifying the role that KAM plays in the supplier's strategy is of the greatest importance, and one often underestimated or misunderstood. Initially, KAM is about making reciprocated commitments to customers, but that quickly needs to be followed by fulfilment of those commitments, so companies should anticipate the issues in operations and adapt. In fact, they will find that adaptation means changing the organization and culture, as well as plans and processes.

The question then arises of 'who does what?' Obviously, key account managers are responsible for a great deal of the activity, but the company is also responsible for supporting them, by providing resources, communicating organization-wide, tackling barriers and making decisions that are beyond the remit of the individual.

The scope of the KAM initiative will highlight the breadth of the key account manager's role. At the simplest level, the key account manager has two roles: *implementation* of a business strategy with the customer, and *facilitation* of that implementation through building the relationship. The relationship is not an end in itself, but should be employed to create and implement strategies that will develop business with the customer. These two roles go hand-in-hand: success requires both.

Exactly how the key account manager plays these roles depends on the nature of the customer and the overall strategy allotted to it. *Streamline* customers allocated a 'manage for cash' strategy should receive different treatment from *strategic* or *star* customers, so the key account manager's role must be adjusted accordingly. The first require a tough negotiator who will need to manage costs and operations rigorously, while the latter require someone to create a vision of the future and work to make it happen.

The key account team, however, can take on part of the role. The team can apply its expertise to fulfil some elements, though some, like team leadership, cannot be separated from the key account manager. Unfortunately, key account managers' experience of team-working is often very limited, and they make poor team leaders unless they receive proper training and support for this part of their role. To make matters worse, the members of the account team normally do not report directly to the key account manager, but still remain within their function or region. Nevertheless, the key account team should be an on-going group of people committed to the same objectives for the customer's business, not a project team or other transient group of people. Important customers expect team support and increasingly are getting it from suppliers.

Generally, there are two key account teams that exist simultaneously: the head office, cross-functional team, which is concerned with current delivery of commitments to the customer and also with how to adapt and develop new value; and the regional sales team, which supports customer strategic business units (SBUs) in the field and applies the deals agreed centrally.

Such a broad role demands a wide range of competencies and attributes. Regrettably, in many cases, suppliers have automatically appointed senior salespeople to the role without considering the competencies needed, and then found later that a substantial proportion of them do not have and are unable to acquire them. Indeed, 'selling' is a comparatively minor part of the role, and not one that should be used exclusively for determining the right people for the job.

To make appropriate appointments, suppliers should ideally start by establishing an 'inventory' of their key customers categorized into four types according to the strategy selected for them. Clearly, customers should be managed by a key account manager who is suited to applying the strategy selected for each of them, i.e. an 'entrepreneur', 'business manager', 'customer manager' or 'tactician'. Once the supplier has assembled its customer inventory, it can see how many of each of four types of key account manager are needed.

Different competencies and attributes are demanded by each of these roles, although they also have some in common. Competencies are defined as behaviours required to achieve high levels of performance, whereas attributes are more about the way people think and the values they hold, though they also affect behaviour. Attributes are harder to learn and to change. The competencies and attributes that relate to each of the four roles have been worked out, so that individuals can be profiled and matched to the role they would perform best. Such an approach can be used as a foundation for a conversation with the key account manager to discuss how he or she can develop to achieve personal and organizational objectives, now and in the future.

# Introduction

Suppliers often ask us 'Are our key account managers the right people for the job?' At first glance, this might appear to be a reasonable question. A second glance suggests that, before it can be answered, the questions 'What is the job? What do you want them to do?' should be asked. Indeed, even more important is the question, 'What do you want key account management to do for your organization?'

> What do you want key account management to do for your organization?

Obviously, companies have different views of what key account management (KAM) can and should deliver. These expectations will drive the investment they make in the initiative; the scope of the change they envisage; the remit they give to key account managers and therefore the quality and capabilities of the key account managers they employ to fill the role.

For example, if KAM is expected to manage customers who are going global, then globally competent, culturally versatile people are required to do the job. If it needs to deliver profitability in an increasingly competitive, mature marketplace, then the company is likely to need people with a strong focus on operations. If it intends to develop and disseminate innovations through its key customers, then it will need people with vision and passion to drive that through.

Clearly, the company should identify its corporate strategy and then consider how its strategy for key accounts will be aligned to and deliver it. After all, if its key customers do not deliver a substantial part of the corporate strategy, the strategy probably will not succeed at all; because it is unlikely that the smaller, follower accounts can do it on their own.

Rather often, suppliers start KAM with incompatible objectives that have in-built limitations. They tend to underestimate the scope of the key account manager's role and the level of competencies required to succeed, and hence they make unsuitable appointments, mostly of senior salespeople, and later discover that some of them are not able to do the demanding job that KAM requires.

## 10.1   Roles

### 10.1.1   The role of key account management

KAM is building close relationships ... that add superior value to the customer's business as well as to the supplier's business.

The first step in determining the role of the key account manager must be to define the role of KAM itself in the organization. Describing KAM as 'building close relationships between supplier and customer organizations that add superior value to the customer's business as well as to the supplier's' immediately suggests a role in building bridges, defining strategies and delivering them as well. Our research discovered a variety of objectives in developing relationships with key customers:

● Visibility of key account needs

● Shared customer understanding internally

● Proactive strategies

● Prioritization of resources and investment

● Global coordination

● Increased margins even in very competitive areas

● Profitability

● Growth

● Greater (not guaranteed) security.

When SAP analysed the background for its global account management initiative in 1999, it was very clear about what it wanted the programme to deal with, which contributed to the undoubted success of the programme.

Companies often start out thinking that KAM is just another way of approaching customers that can be left to the salesforce. As you will now realize, it has to be much more than that if it is to succeed (see Chapter 11). In fact, it should take an important position in corporate strategy, and therefore impacts internally on the organization, culture and operations; and externally on the marketplace, as illustrated in Figure 10.1, which shows four major areas of a company's concerns and activity, highlighting the parts that are core to KAM.

**Figure 10.1**
The role of key account management internally and externally.

KAM is generally activated in response to a marketplace with key customers at the heart of it. Sometimes the stimulus is a negative event like a large contract that the supplier loses, or expects but fails to win. Most often, major customers demand KAM, rather than suppliers adopting it proactively. The supplier responds by building its strategy and encapsulating it in its plans. The strategy and plans should identify support needed from the organization and culture, which will particularly relate to key account managers and how they do the job. In addition, the strategy should highlight developments needed in the operations side of the business, which will concern the processes that actually deliver commitments to key customers (the focus of Chapter 9).

The role of KAM as identified by a group of practitioners from blue-chip companies is shown in Table 10.1, divided into three of these four areas. These three represent those that drive activity, while the fourth, organization and culture, should support the activity. If this table captures the elements that make up the role of KAM, then it can be divided again into what part the organization should take on, and what part key account managers play. Suppliers should make up their own list, or start with this and add to and subtract from it.

Before it can define the 'job', each company has to work out for itself what it wants KAM to achieve and how it expects it to operate. Consider these lists and check which ones are most important and relevant for your organization.

**Table 10.1** The role of key account management

| Strategy: Delivering the organization's strategy | Marketplace: Working with key customers | Operations: Effective KAM implementation |
| --- | --- | --- |
| Realizing the strategy and vision | Working together with customers *who want to work with your company* | Offering a single point of contact, internally and externally |
| Providing market insight and reflecting market changes through leading customers | Developing relationship-led business (not product selling) | Orchestrating cross-functionally, cross-boundary |
| Identifying and creating new markets | Enabling joint development | Aligning strategy and plans with operations |
| Defining and achieving value-add for customer and supplier | Leveraging suppliers' range of capabilities and broader portfolio of products into customer | Implementing transactional cost reductions |
| Providing a route to innovation | Planning and forecasting | Developing effective processes |
| Integrating route-to-market strategy with marketing and product development | Providing suppliers' credibility with customers | Enabling contact review and control |
| Managing a major 'source of risk' | Managing resources | Providing tailored reporting |

> ## CHECKPOINT
> ### Defining the role of key account management
>
> Has your company:
>
> - Identified the role of KAM in its strategy?
> - Identified how it expects KAM to work with key customers?
> - Specified how KAM will engage with operational processes to deliver its promises?

### 10.1.2 The role of the organization

Some companies seem to have the idea that they will train key account managers to develop relationships with key customers, and then leave them alone with whatever issues arise, using their powers of influence and persuasion to deal with them. It is a curious approach, and one destined to deliver frustration and fury to key account managers, the rest of the company and, worst of all, to key customers. In so doing, senior managers are abdicating their responsibility and, along with it, any hope of success.

Consider the customer pressures and implications for suppliers outlined by Lisa Napolitano, CEO of SAMA (the Strategic Account Management Association in the US), to which we have added the kind of responses suppliers need to make to stay in business, shown in Figure 10.2. Even the most

**Figure 10.2** Purchasing trends and supplier responses.

talented key account managers would not be able to deal with these issues alone. They should understand the position and they should be part of creating the solutions, but they do not have a remit to take the critical decisions. The supplier organization must play its role. Only senior management can commit the whole business to customer-driven change or push lower costs through the business and introduce more flexible approaches, like replacing people through outsourcing. Of course, key account managers should have a deep understanding of the customer's value chain, but they will still need the help of technical experts to analyse it and identify how the company can add value to it.

The organization's role in KAM can be broken down into a number of crucial activities (Table 10.2). Without this kind of engagement, key account managers are set up to fail. The worst ones will revert to their old ways and the best ones will simply migrate to a company that is really prepared to back the initiative, and maybe the customers will do that too. People will tolerate a start-up period during which the company finds its way and works out what is needed to support the programme, but after that period of grace has expired, key account managers are thoroughly demotivated if the company does not seem to be matching its own effort with what it is asking of them.

**Table 10.2** The role of the organization in key account management

| Activity | Expectation |
|---|---|
| Determines and **communicates** strategy | High-profile commitment from senior management, enterprise-wide communication |
| Tackles cultural and organizational **barriers** | Removes barriers, develops appropriate culture, polices alignment, rewards collaboration, rejects bad citizenship, mobilizes resources across 'silos' |
| Provides **resources** | Provides sufficient resource, makes it accessible and usable, exposes talent pool (e.g. account team, training, development, research, technical expertise, marketing intelligence, etc.) |
| **Supports** key account managers | Trusts, understands their role, gives visible support, gives authority, promotes their credentials internally and externally |
| Promotes **sharing** | Of proof of capability, cases, key account plans, ideas, information, knowledge, resources |
| Makes specific **decisions** | Like resource allocation, approved sources, appointments, marketing responses to competition |
| Develops the **brand** | Provides pull-through from market, develops positioning and competitor understanding |
| **Monitors** results | Identifies measurements, is objective, makes valid comparisons, requires business cases |

> ## CHECKPOINT
> ### Is your organization playing its part in KAM?
>
> ● Is your company performing all of the parts of its role in the KAM pro-
> gramme? (Use the list in Table 10.2 as a checklist.)
>
> ● Where fulfilment is incomplete, have you identified what areas are
> missing?

### 10.1.3  The role of the key account manager

There are numerous ways in which the role of the key account manager
can be expressed. Put very simply, the key account manager has two roles:

● **Implementation**: This means deciding what should happen in an account
and making sure it is delivered. Implementation demands appropriate
strategies and plans, which depend on a deep understanding of the
customer, so all of that can be seen as part of effective implementation.

● **Facilitation**: This involves developing the relationships that will enable
the business strategy. It goes beyond the relationship with the key point
of contact in the customer, and requires relationships with other functions in the customer, cross-functional relationships in the supplier and
possibly relationships with external associates too.

The key account manager must maintain a balance between these two
roles, remembering that building relationships is pointless without a business purpose, but equally that business strategies are unlikely to be realized unless the right network of relationships is in place.

> Building relationships
> is pointless without a
> business purpose.

Not surprisingly, both the supplier and the customer have views on the
role that the key account manager should play, which are more or less
aligned for a large amount of the role, even though they may be expressed
in slightly different ways by each side, as Figure 10.3 suggests.

**Implementation roles**

● Expert in the customer

● Value developer

● Point of accountability.

These roles do not seem to be very well clarified and expressed in many supplier organizations, especially that of **'expert in the customer'** and **'value
developer'**, although they are core to the job. Key account managers are
often woefully lacking in their understanding of the customer's business
and marketplace, which is why we spend a good deal of our time showing
them how to gain this understanding. Without it, they cannot be considered

> Key account
> managers are often
> woefully lacking in
> their understanding
> of the customer's
> business and
> marketplace.

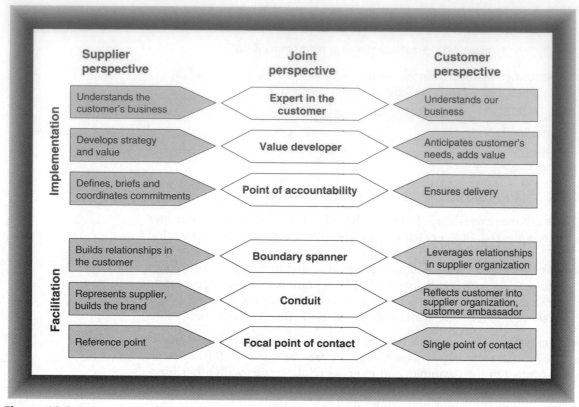

**Figure 10.3** Corresponding perspectives on the role of the key account manager.

as much of an expert in the customer, nor do they stand much chance of knowing how to add value to the customer, not just as a one-off, but in a continuing stream of added value initiatives.

> The key account manager … has very often not been given the authority to match either the supplier's or the customer's interpretations of accountability.

Both sides seem to be much clearer about what they expect from their **'point of accountability'**. The customer means that whatever the key account manager has promised, he or she is accountable for delivering: not necessarily in person, but by whatever route it takes. The supplier means that the key account manager will deliver the revenue, gross margin or contribution targeted. Both are tough for the key account manager, who very often has not been given the authority to match either the supplier's or the customer's interpretations of accountability.

### Facilitation roles

- Boundary spanner
- Conduit
- Focal point of contact.

> Probably the most disputed role is that of 'boundary spanner'.

Probably the most disputed role is that of **'boundary spanner'**. Consider a very common situation, in which KAM is introduced into part of a supplier's business on the expectation that it will produce growth. Closer examination shows that the business is mature and the market is not growing, as in a majority of European markets, so the best opportunity for growth resides in the key customer divisions or SBUs with which the supplier does not currently deal. That means spanning boundaries within the customer organization, obviously, and it may also mean spanning boundaries within the supplier organization.

At the least, there will be a substantial job of coordination to be done, especially between two large, complex organizations. Finding all the information and solving all the issues requires goodwill in parts of the supplier on the other side of organizational boundaries but, unfortunately, goodwill is not always there. It may be because that part of the company feels that it owns the targeted customer division and is not prepared to give it up, or even share it, even if little has been achieved so far. Again, that division may not see the new business as worthwhile and does not want to use its limited resources to support it, even though it may be an unavoidable part of the offer to the customer.

In any event, the role of boundary spanner is fundamental to KAM and therefore to the key account manager. If there are no boundaries to span, a simpler, cheaper form of account management can be applied. KAM, by definition, should be boundary-spanning.

> Key account management, by definition, should be boundary-spanning.

The role of '**conduit**' for information and communication is fairly obvious, though it really goes deeper and means more than the supplier generally anticipates. The customer expects that its strategy will be made known at the highest level in the supplier organization, so that the supplier will give consideration to it in developing its own strategy. The customer also expects to be informed of any changes in the supplier that will have an impact on its business before they become public, such as mergers and acquisitions, key personnel moves, supply chain issues, adverse publicity, etc. Generally, the supplier is seeing the role of 'conduit' more in terms of receiving information about the customer's activities, and gives little consideration to the reverse flow and how it should be managed, never mind encouraged and facilitated.

## Case study insight

### Seeing communication from the customer's perspective

One supplier caught up in the effects of the 9/11 attack said, 'We didn't call our customers that day or the one after, because we didn't know what was going on. We didn't have any information, as we saw it, and we didn't know what to say. In retrospect, that was a bad idea, and they were frustrated and angry at our silence. Even though we didn't know much, we could have answered a few concerns; for example, we did know that some activities should not be affected because they were driven from somewhere else completely. But by not contacting them, we were effectively placing the obligation on them to call us. We should have just called and told them what we did and didn't know and how we would update them as the situation emerged.'

> ## CHECKPOINT
> ### Does your company have two-way communication with customers?
>
> - Does your company have a clear, recognizable process for listening to customers at a senior level?
>
> - Does your company have predefined processes in place that would operate when particular types of event occur?

There is wide agreement that the key account manager should act as a '**focal point of contact**'. Unfortunately, this is often called a 'single point of contact', which is not what anyone really means: it implies that the key account manager is the only point of contact, which is not desirable except in some *basic* relationships. The supplier wants robust, reciprocated relationships involving at least several people on both sides, and the customer also wants to know that its business merits support from a team of people, so a single, one-to-one relationship is not the real intention. In addition, as Dr Sue Holt identified in her research (Holt, 2003), the key account manager acts as:

- **A 'single' point of contact** – accepting responsibility for and prepared to be the channel for handling any customer issue

- **An 'escalation' point of contact** – able to take on any contentious issue and work out a solution, with access to the Board if necessary

- **A 'similar' point of contact** – reflecting the seniority of the key people in the customer in terms of his or her own authority

- **A 'strategic' point of contact** – developing the supplier's strategy for the customer and aligning it with the corporate strategy and the customer's strategy.

As if all this were not challenging enough, the supplier has a few more roles it requires of its key account managers.

### Internal roles

- **Resource manager**: To make the business case for resource use, apply resource in line with strategies, and control and optimize usage.

- **Risk manager**: To understand the risks in the customer, communicate them to his or her own organization, and minimize and manage them.

- **Team leader**: To lead and enable the account team to bring value to the customer and supplier.

### Customer-facing roles

- **Salesperson**: To manage the sales cycle, build deals, present propositions and negotiate.

- **Competition monitor**: To identify competitors and understand their role in the customer's business, and the customer's attitude and perception of them.

- **Lever for full range of capabilities**: To understand the full range of the supplier's capabilities, how they are relevant to the customer, and facilitate their application in the customer.

If you think this looks like a tall order by now, you are right. However, not all customer relationships warrant the full range of roles, or not at full strength. Simple relationships and stripped-down strategies do not require the key account manager to play all these roles. For example, if the customer does not justify an account team, the key account manager does not have to be a team leader. If, on the other hand, the strategy is very demanding, and an account team does exist, members may be able to take up some of the roles required (e.g. competition monitor). The role required of the key account manager and the team is related to the relationship and strategy for the customer, which will also determine the competencies needed, as Figure 10.4 shows.

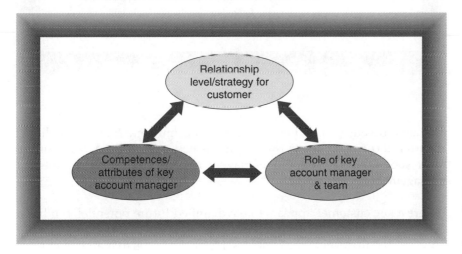

**Figure 10.4**
Link between customer relationship, roles and competencies.

If the relationship with the customer is not very developed, but it is an attractive customer which the supplier wishes to develop, then a key account manager with an entrepreneurial approach is required (Figure 10.5). Suppliers often call this role a 'hunter', though that implies a search-and-find approach. Normally, the customer has already been found and identified as a key account with potential, and the real need is for an **entrepreneur** who can open doors up to the most senior level, who can hold an appropriate conversation at any level, and who also knows what compelling things to say when the opportunity arises.

If a strategic relationship has already been built with a key customer, then the key account manager has to work closely with it to develop and deliver a variety of business strategies. This role is called **'business**

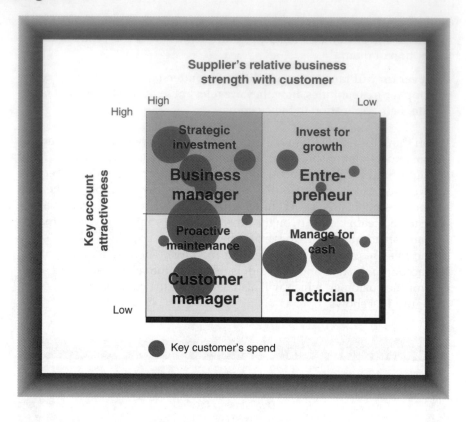

**Figure 10.5**
Linking roles to the key account strategy matrix.

**manager**' because it requires activities and competencies not very different from those of someone running a business unit. Indeed, some of the most successful key account managers have a general or commercial management background.

Where a key customer appears to have limited future potential, but has a very positive view of the supplier, the key account manager is generally not expected to develop the business. He or she needs to maintain current business proactively, keeping costs in control without stripping away too much value, and keeping a healthy flow of profitable revenue. This role needs a strong operational focus. It suits many people who do not want or would be unlikely to penetrate higher and wider into the customer, but who can manage relationships very well, so this role is called the '**customer manager**' (though all of these roles are, of course, managing customers in one way or another).

Some customers are designated as key accounts because they bring a lot of business, but apply relentless pressure on prices and are not interested in added-value strategies (unless they are free) or strategic development. Suppliers should take a 'manage for cash' approach to them, so the people in charge of this kind of customer also need a strong operational focus in order to strip out excess costs, while they apply tough negotiating skills to counter the customer's assault. The business should be kept as simple as possible, because anything else will eat up resource which will not be repaid, so this role requires a skilful **tactician** who can cope with these gorillas.

If a healthy portfolio should have some customers in every quadrant, suppliers will need a portfolio of different types of people to manage these customers and to play these different roles. 'Key account manager' is not a single role – there are at least four separate roles. It should not be assumed that any particular role is superior to another: each has its part to play in earning the company's current or future profits. However, objectives, targets, resources, metrics and number of customers per key account manager should be different for each customer type and key account manager role. Companies struggle to manage such flexibility.

> Objectives, targets, resources, metrics and number of customers per key account manager should be different for each customer type and key account manager role.

Every role has its value and its challenges. A 'business manager' with a one-to-one relationship often has less business under management than a 'tactician' handling a small portfolio of customers, but it is usually more complex. A tactician's margins may be very thin, which makes this role crucial to the supplier to make sure it does not slip into a loss-making situation. 'Customer managers' should also be able to handle a small portfolio of customers, and they are vital in maintaining a good quality cash flow from their customers. These customers are probably paying a substantial amount of the salaries of everyone in the company. The volume of business the 'entrepreneur' manages may be relatively small, by definition, but without their efforts to develop the customers of the future, the company will not be sustainable. Each role carries different parameters, expectations and competency needs, and all are important to the supplier.

## 10.2  Key account management teams

### 10.2.1  The role of the key account team

Teams get better results than individuals in situations like key customer management, which require the combination of multiple skills, experience and judgements. Indeed, the team can play a very beneficial role in providing through its team members some of the competencies that the key account manager may not have: financial analysis for example, or supply chain understanding.

> Teams get better results than individuals in situations like key customer management.

However, we should first clarify what we mean by a team, before we can talk about key account teams. The defining characteristics of a team is that it has a shared objective and consists of more than one person.

> A team is a group of two or more people who must interact cooperatively and adaptively in pursuit of shared, valued objectives.
>
> (Canon-Bowers *et al.*, 1993)

> Teams are a set of interdependent individuals bound by a collective aim.
>
> (Glassop, 2002)

Not only have key account managers no experience of leading a team, they have no experience of even being on a team!

A key account team is therefore *not* a supplier's collection of key account managers, who are working with different customers and hence with different objectives. Indeed, although suppliers frequently talk about 'the sales team', these definitions show that such a bunch of fiercely competing individuals is not a team at all. This leads to a major issue when key account managers are supposed to lead teams (see Section 10.2.3). Not only have key account managers no experience of leading a team, they have no experience of even being on a team! Teamwork is not part of the average sales environment.

Key account teams are on-going groups of people with a consistent membership, working together around a particular customer or a very small number of customers. Normally, most of the members give a significant part of their time to the team, but not all of it. They are called 'virtual teams' as they continue to report to their head of function, and only indirectly to the key account manager. In addition, if they are spread out geographically, they may rarely be in the same place at the same time.

A key account team is also not a collection of people who just come together to deliver a specific project.

So a key account team is also *not* a collection of people who just come together to deliver a specific project and then break up and go their separate ways, even though they had a shared objective for the project at the time. The composition of project teams changes, as the next project for the customer will involve different people possibly from a different pool.

---

## CHECKPOINT

### Does your company operate key account teams?

Try this litmus test: Imagine all the staff in your company are in one big room together, and someone in a corner shouts, 'Key account team for Customer X, come and stand over here!' Would a specific number of people identify themselves, collect at that point and recognize each other as fellow team members?

---

As we said in Chapter 3, an *interdependent* relationship is probably the most common aspirational level for strategic key accounts, and this naturally implies the existence of team working. *Basic* relationships may or may not require team support, depending on the size, spread and complexity of the customer. In an *interdependent* relationship the key account manager has to manage the relationship through and with others, as Figure 10.6 suggests, because there is more to do than he or she can achieve alone.

The team has the same high-level roles as the key account manager (i.e. implementation and facilitation). The operational part of the team may take the major share of responsibility for ensuring the efficient implementation of commitments, but everyone takes on the role of building more links with the customer, to make the relationship itself more robust and to support facilitation.

**Figure 10.6**
A model of an *interdependent* relationship.

Those people who are regularly involved in dealing with the customer should become part of the key account team. Where the customer interacts frequently, as in customer service or accounts, for example, suppliers should consider directing contact through designated department members who understand the contract with that customer and know how to deal with that customer's issues. These people then also become part of the key account team.

Allocating specific people to customers is often resisted because departmental and call centre managers assume that designating staff to key customers in this way reduces efficiency (i.e. allotting part of their time to a specific customers or customers, but generally not all of it), and that the 'next in the queue' approach is a more efficient use of staff time. In fact, companies are increasingly realizing that dealing with an issue 'right first time' is more efficient still, and that is best done by someone with an ongoing appreciation of the customer's issues.

---

### Case study insight

#### Cutting costs through key account teams

Xerox carried out a major exercise to assess the profitability of its key customers. The company had already allocated all or some of the time of specified staff to manage activity with key customers where there was a substantial amount of interaction with the customers. The profitability exercise picked up these costs and compared them with situations where customers were dealt with on the traditional 'first come first served' basis. Xerox found that it saved up to 6 per cent of sales, administration and general costs by working with customer-designated staff.

Key customers expect to have a team working on their business.

Key customers expect to have a team working on their business. While they want to know who is their focal point of contact, they want more than the efforts and expertise of just one person applied to their business. Key customers expect excellent performance without having to explain themselves over and over again to different members of the supplier's organization, and they expect consistent performance as well.

Consistency can only be achieved by people with experience of working together, who have learned about the customer and the value proposition for it and know how to implement it. Research in the airline industry, while admittedly in a different environment, shows what teams can achieve compared with collections of people just assembled for an immediate purpose.

---

## Case study insight

### Findings from the airline industry

Researchers studying the effectiveness of flying teams found that:

- Seventy-three per cent of all incidents occur on a crew's first time of flying together.

- Fatigued crews made far fewer errors than did crews of rested pilots who had not flown together before.

- The experience crews gained working together as teams more than overcame the debilitating affects of individual fatigue.

*Source*: Hackman, 2002

---

### 10.2.2 The nature of the team

Teams can work much more successfully if the organization formalizes their role and membership. Given that the members do not report direct to the key account manager, without some formalization the whole idea can get lost. The organization needs to make members' role on the team clear to them, and also to the rest of the company, especially to the head of the function to which they belong. Otherwise, a situation that is hard enough to manage, even in theory, can become impossibly difficult.

If the team has formal recognition, members will be prepared to invest more into it, and the organization should then see some of the outcomes associated with team working:

- More favourable employee attitudes
- More comprehensive pool of knowledge
- Enhanced productivity
- Improvements in product/service quality

---

**Case study insight**

**Key account team development in a
European manufacturing company**

A supplier set up pan-European key account teams to manage its key customers, especially those whose business crossed national boundaries. A year later it conducted a survey of the teams, with the following findings:

● A third of the teams had made progress and were working quite well, but had improvements to make.

● Another third of the teams were working to a rather limited extent, but not well.

● The last third were not working, and the members contacted had forgotten that they were supposed to be on a team at all!

---

● Improved overall organizational effectiveness

● Delivering superior value.

Along with formal recognition, team members should have roles assigned to them, so they know what they are responsible for and what they are expected to contribute. One may take responsibility for reporting on customer performance, for example; another may track and capture personnel changes in the customer and contact details; another may collect and analyse market information, and so on. Given the complex situations in which theses teams operate, it is important to remove as much ambiguity as is reasonably possible.

Key account teams have a different make-up according to the nature of the customer and the supplier, and what they are trying to achieve. They often split into two in suppliers:

● The cross-functional, head office team

● The geographically based sales and/or support team.

These teams normally exist simultaneously, but for practical reasons, such as opportunities to get together, they tend to be managed separately by the key account manager. These two types of team interface with another type of team, their equivalents in the customer. The key account manager plays a pivotal role in linking the teams and overseeing their interactions with the customer's teams, as Figure 10.7 shows.

### The cross-functional team
The nature and operations of the cross-functional team depends a great deal on the supplier's set-up. The team has two aims: the smooth running

**Figure 10.7**
Cross-functional and sales teams in key account management.

of current business, and the development of new initiatives, which may be customizations or innovations that are part of the strategy for the customer. Often, there will be a core team of people from functions that are regularly involved with the customer, and they will coordinate projects to which other parts of the company are contributing.

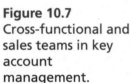

Where team working is not a mainstay of the company culture, key account managers have a tough job on their hands.

At first sight, these teams would be expected to have a better chance of meeting each other and bonding together than the geographical sales team, as they are more likely to be concentrated in one place. However, each member has a different technical expertise and a different background related to that expertise, and they have their line manager's demands on their time to consider as well, so getting them to work as a team is still rather challenging. The culture of the company makes a big difference: some have embraced the view that 'One of the values emerging as a requirement for business success in the new and demanding environment is teamwork over individualism. In fact, the team approach must become a management philosophy' (Deeter-Schmelz and Ramsey, 1995), and some have not. Where team working is not a mainstay of the company culture, key account managers have a tough job on their hands.

### The geographical sales or support team
Normally, the appointment of a key account manager does not remove the need for local sales and support teams to work with the customer, although the customer's central purchasing function may decide that it only wants operational interaction, not sales interaction. Without the local sales team, the customer's SBUs would feel isolated and neglected.

However, the role of the salesperson changes, and this creates an issue. In the new role, they should be:

- promoting and implementing the deal agreed at head office level,
- keeping the customer informed of developments specific to them, and
- removing barriers to ordering and fulfilment.

As salespeople, this is not what they mostly want to do. They are 'programmed' to make deals and sell products, both by themselves and by their managers so, if the deal has already been done, the other tasks tend to fail to capture their enthusiasm. As a result, the attention that key customers receive at local level often falls off dramatically, and to the detriment of the business, as local salespeople focus their energies on 'their' customers. This produces a major and on-going contentious area for many suppliers, both with the customer which is suffering from such intransigent pockets of poor service, and with the local SBU.

Sales-driven bonus schemes for salespeople are often to blame, but companies have a blinkered belief in sales incentivization, in spite of all the evidence of the negative behaviours that they induce, and are loathe to change them. If local salespeople make more money for themselves by selling to their local customers than they do by spending time with key customers, that is what they will do. If the local SBU is similarly targeted and bonused at SBU level and therefore at senior management level, this behaviour will be driven from the top and reinforced to an insurmountable degree.

> The attention that key customers receive at local level often falls off dramatically as local salespeople focus their energies on 'their' customers.

Companies have tried to get around the problem by making sure that sales and profit from the local operations of key customers are credited to local SBUs, in recognition of the fact that the business needs local service and support, and it has worked well in some companies, but is still uphill work in others. If, however big the customer is globally, it is relatively unimportant in a particular territory, then gaining the level of service committed by head office is a relentless task for the key account manager.

---

## CHECKPOINT

### Securing support from the local team

- Does your company have a clear policy on who is incentivized for what in selling to and servicing key customers at local level?

- Is that policy aligned with:
  - the global deal for the key customer?
  - local SBU objectives?
  - local salespeople's targets and preferences?
  - key account manager targets?

---

This ambivalence in implementing centrally agreed deals is one of the most common and the most intransigent issues that key customers and key account managers face in KAM. The problem is largely self-induced by the supplier, but it strikes at the notion of territory and ownership that is ingrained in many companies. As a result, many suppliers fail to decide and enforce a clear policy that would resolve it. They suffer the consequences as a company, and the key account manager most of all.

### The customer's teams

A large relationship is likely to need a team of people on the customer side as well. As Figure 10.6 suggests, customer teams often mirror the supplier teams, with the make-up of the cross-functional team being appropriate to each business and the relationship goals. Fewer people are probably involved than on the supplier side, but they still constitute a team and the key account manager should see them as such.

If the people on the customer side act as a team, the key account manager should consider:

- What are the team's goals and priorities
- Who makes decisions, and how they are made
- Who communicates with whom and how
- Who influences whom and how
- How team effort can best be engaged and leveraged.

Indeed, if you have developed the skills of leading 'virtual' teams (people who do not report directly to you) in your own business, then perhaps you can use those skills to lead teams of people one step further removed, in the customer's business. With a more proactive, politically sensitive approach, inclusive of your key contact, of course, you could achieve a great deal through leading the customer's teams as well as your own.

### 10.2.3  Leading the team

Leadership is a big subject, which we can only touch on here, although it is an essential part of the key account manager's role. Some companies, disappointed with the performance of their key account managers as leaders, have speculated on whether someone else could be appointed to carry out that part of the role. Ultimately, abdicating team leadership does not seem to be a viable option. Although team leadership may be a specific competency to learn, leadership positions are given to staff to signify seniority and authority. Giving the job to someone else could only send the wrong messages about the quality and position of the key account manager to the customer and, equally important, internally. The key account manager has to be the leader, and must learn how to lead in this environment.

The team leader needs to consult, to listen and also, ultimately, to make decisions.

In a sales environment, leadership is interpreted as 'winning'. Here, 'winning', whether as an individual or even as a team, is not the goal. Indeed, it is likely to lead to inappropriate behaviour on a personal or team level where key customer support and teams are concerned. Leaders should set appropriate goals and help the team to achieve them, by showing the way forward and helping to remove obstacles, rather than achieving the goals themselves. As key account managers have very limited direct authority, they are rarely able to give orders to a team member, so they will have to adopt an appealing and appropriate approach, which may be supportive or participative, according to the maturity of the person. The team leader needs to consult, to listen and also, ultimately, to make decisions.

In fact, leadership that encourages team participation is generally associated with greater team member satisfaction, although it is not always associated with higher productivity. Nevertheless, it fits with the matrix mentality and is probably more successful in complex and changing situations where more than straightforward productivity is required, and team members need to be empowered to make decisions and responses to the customer.

Key account managers should consider what makes teams successful in the quest to lead one. Research has identified eight factors of specific importance in KAM teams, as shown in Figure 10.8. The list of these success factors in Table 10.3 explains how team members interpret each of them, and hence what the key account manager needs to clarify for them. Team members also need to contribute to the development of the customer strategy. It will be a better, more rounded strategy that is more likely to be implemented if the team understands it and accepts it.

*Source*: Holt, 2003

**Figure 10.8**   Success factors for key account teams.

**Table 10.3**
Interpretation of success factors for key account teams

| Success factor | Team member's interpretation |
|---|---|
| Defined organization | Who is doing what? |
| Defined team roles and goals | What am I doing, what am I trying to achieve? |
| Good communication channels | How do I find out what is going on? |
| Exchange of ideas and knowledge | How can we pool our expertise? |
| Senior management support | Is the rest of the organization behind us? |
| Local empowerment | What decisions and action can I take? |
| Customer understanding | How can I get to know the customer? |
| Trust | You can rely on me, can I rely on you? |

'Virtual' teams may rarely get to meet. With modern communication technology, this may not matter very much most of the time. However, in our experience, a team must get together physically from time to time, in order to gain any real team feeling and synergy. Members need to meet at the outset and then at least once per year, ideally more. It is important that everyone is included, especially in the inaugural meeting. People who are left out at the beginning never really seem to become properly recognized and integrated.

*Not nearly enough conscious thought and effort is given to communication.*

Good communication is crucial, and the leader must consider how good and effective communication will take place, and when. In fact, communication is one of the key account manager's core roles, and he or she needs to think about it systematically and implement it efficiently and effectively (see Section 9.2.4). Not nearly enough conscious thought and effort is given to communication, and many team failures lie at the door of poor communication.

In summary, the average key account manager has minimal understanding of how teams work and less of what to do about it. When they get a poor response to their poor leadership, they tend to blame team members and lapse into trying to do everything themselves, which is inefficient and unsustainable. Leadership is a competency which should be learned.

## 10.3 Requirements of key account managers

### 10.3.1 *Matching roles and requirements*

Suppliers asking, 'Have we got the right people?' should really start with the question, 'Have we got the right customers?' or, better still, 'How many of each type of customer do we have?' Start with taking a systematic 'inventory' of your customers and constructing a portfolio view of them, as described in Chapter 2. The portfolio shows how many of each kind of customer your company has, and therefore how many of each kind of key account manager you need.

You may not use exactly the same ratios as the example shown in Figure 10.9 and, indeed, you would want to check out the results with real customers in mind to make sure that it makes sense on the ground, but you should apply some such differential ratio of key account managers to customers in order to optimize your resources.

**Figure 10.9**
Example of how to allocate key account managers to customers.

Smaller companies with less business per customer may not feel they can afford a 1:1 ratio even for their *strategic* customers, but they should still ensure that they have done the analysis and apply a higher ratio than they do for, say, *status* customers. Most suppliers' portfolio analyses will show that they need considerably more business managers than tacticians, though they probably have many more tacticians than business managers, currently.

> Most suppliers' portfolio analyses will show that they need considerably more business managers than tacticians.

Rather than make assumptions about the nature of their people, companies would do well to apply a systematic profiling approach such as KAMScope© (a competency and attribute framework for KAM developed by the author specifically for this purpose). This is a detailed 360° review of competencies and attributes (see Section 10.3.2) modelled against the requirements of the four key account manager roles. KAMScope enables key account managers and line managers to focus on the role to which they aspire and identify specifically the competencies that they need to develop to fulfil that role. It leads to a clarity of conversation that is hard to achieve without some such foundation for it.

Suppliers should be matching key account managers with customers according to their ability to play the role required, but traditionally they have been allocated according to:

● Geographical location

● Product expertise

- Industry expertise

- Historical relationship with the customer

- Variety or mix.

Geographical location
and product expertise
are becoming
increasingly irrelevant.

Although the key account manager's competency set is taken into consideration intuitively, in practice, these other factors normally outweigh it in making allocations. However, geographical location and product expertise are becoming increasingly irrelevant, and an existing relationship with the customer might or might not be a good thing. The fallacy of variety or mix is demonstrated in this case study.

---

### Case study insight

#### Encouraging schizophrenia in the pharmaceutical industry

A pharmaceutical manufacturer described its key customer segments as divided into:

- 'visionaries' – whose strategy looked at the industry in 5–10 years' time

- 'strategists' – who considered developments on a 2–5 year timeframe

- 'operations' – who 'couldn't see beyond breakfast'.

Based on this clear segmentation, we presumed that the supplier had identified those of their key account managers who had vision and matched them with the visionaries; those who took a strategic view and matched them with the strategists; and matched the tactical ones with the 'operations' customers. In fact, they had given all their key account managers a mix, for the sake of 'variety'.

---

Giving key account managers a mix of customers has two outcomes:

- either key account managers worked according to their preferred style, which would always be inappropriate for some of their customers

- or they tried to change their style every time they dealt with a different customer, several times per day, which would be stressful and probably impossible.

Not surprisingly, the key account managers were finding it difficult to cope.

Whether companies use KAMScope or something else, line managers should find a way of making the role clear to key account managers, and also how they are expected to fulfil it. That means being clear and consistent about it themselves, without falling into the trap of standardizing. With key customers, standardization does not give consistency: indeed, it is inconsistent with joined-up thinking about the customer.

Where the supplier has different kinds of key customers it should have different expectations of their requirements, responses and performance, which should begin to demand different roles from the key account manager. It should also begin to challenge instinctive and cherished ideas about the role. Most sales directors would insist that key account managers should have a sales background. However, we have asked several groups to analyse the role in detail, and they have consistently agreed that only 5–10 per cent of the role is selling (i.e. managing the sales cycle and bid closure).

Only 5–10 per cent of the role is selling.

Table 10.4 shows the breakdown of time that one group of practitioners from different sectors thought ideal – which was certainly not how their key account managers were spending their time currently! In fact, they agreed that there were three activities which should take up more time than selling:

- Developing relationships (internal and external)

- Operational implementation

- Developing knowledge and strategy.

| Activity | Share of time |
|---|---|
| Developing relationships | 20% |
| Implementing deal operationally | 15% |
| Developing industry knowledge, strategy and planning | 10% |
| Selling | 5–10% |
| Ensuring internal alignment for deal commercially | 5–10% |
| Understanding of internal capability | 5% |
| Solving internal day-to-day problems | 5% |
| Promoting brand/business | 5% |
| Reporting/providing information | 5% |
| Training and education | 5% |
| Managing the team | 5% |
| Other | 10% |
| Total | 100% |

**Table 10.4** Practitioners' view of the ideal breakdown of key account managers' time

In other words, the selling part of the role is less important than any of these, and not much more important than several others. Needless to say, selling is not a part of the role that customers value, as research has confirmed.

So the big question is, 'Why do suppliers insist on appointing salespeople to the role of key account manager, when their background fits only a small part of the role? And why are they so reluctant to appoint people with other backgrounds, which may equip them to fulfil a larger part of the role?'

The big question is, 'Why do suppliers insist on appointing salespeople to the role of key account manager, when their background fits only a small part of the role?

Either group will need support and development to take on their roles fully, but training non-salespeople to sell might actually be easier than training salespeople to understand the operation of other internal functions, strategy, finance, marketing, etc.

### 10.3.2 Competencies and attributes

Clearly, key account managers need a wide range of capabilities, which may be seen as 'competencies' and 'attributes'.

- **Competency** is normally defined as the behaviours that employees must have, or must acquire, to input into a situation in order to achieve high levels of performance. Competencies represent what people can do. They can be developed in various ways; by work experience, observation of others, and through training delivered in a number of ways. They can be assessed through the demonstration of task completion, the production of evidence of different kinds and through observation of the key account manager's activity in the workplace. Generally speaking, everyone is more comfortable with developing and talking about competencies than with attributes.

- **Attributes** are individual qualities that differ from competencies in the difficulty of acquisition or change. Attributes represent what people are like, which has an impact on how they do things. They relate more to the underlying values and beliefs that influence the way people think, the way they do things and the way they deal with other people. Attributes are more difficult to develop than competencies. Acquisition depends more on the desire of the individual to make such a change personally, rather than the more externalized acquisition of a competency.

The availability of courses gives a clue as to whether a characteristic is a competency or an attribute. There are plenty of courses to be found for competencies, because they are much more teachable than attributes. 'Selling' is a competency, for example, as is 'financial awareness and analysis': there are plenty of courses in both to be found. In contrast, 'integrity' and 'vision' are attributes, both frequently requested by key customers, but few courses, if any, are offered because they do not respond to that kind of intervention.

---

### Case study insight

#### The importance of attributes as well as competencies in the hi-tech industry

The customer, a huge global corporation, had already rejected one global account manager, so the supplier, also a huge global company, was careful to select a highly competent person to put forward to succeed the previous incumbent. Unfortunately, this global account manager was also rejected after a few months. In spite of his many undisputed competencies, the customer did not appreciate his approach to the relationship. Every time something went wrong, he produced some minor clause in the contract, buried item of information, or obscure communication that 'proved' that he was not at fault. The customer called him 'Mr Teflon', because nothing stuck to him! His competencies did not outweigh this almost legalistic approach and refusal to accept responsibility or ever be 'in the wrong', which were driven by his underlying values and beliefs. (The next global account manager was a great success and stayed in the post for five years.)

Each of the four roles in Section 10.3 (i.e. business manager, entrepreneur, customer manager, tactician) can be described as a set of competencies and attributes. There are a few that are specific to a particular role, but many of them are the same, as you would expect. The latter can be called the core competencies and attributes, as shown in Figure 10.10. In fact, the area of core competencies and attributes is probably even greater than that shown but, in some roles, although the competency is needed to some extent, it is not required to the same degree as in other roles.

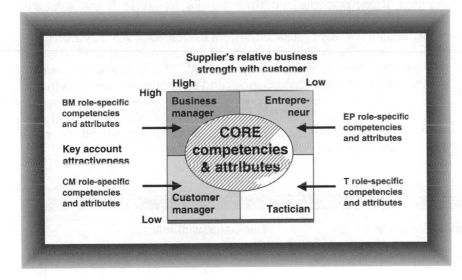

**Figure 10.10**
Roles and core competencies and attributes.

The business manager and the entrepreneur have a lot in common. They both need a wide range of competencies and attributes developed to a high degree. This comes as a surprise to many people who see the entrepreneur as a foot-in-the-door encyclopaedia salesman or 'hunter'. While there are, indeed, particular characteristics of robustness and persistence that this role requires, winning over a customer big enough to become a key account is a complex and highly skilled job, that needs as much understanding of the customer and what it would value as the business manager has, achieved from a disadvantageous position on the outside, rather than the inside. However, the level of competencies and attributes required by the customer manager and tactician is lower by a significant amount, as their jobs are less complex. These positions can usually be filled from the supplier's existing pool of account managers.

Finding enough business managers and entrepreneurs will always be difficult – these people have a lot to offer and are in great demand. There is not one 'killer' competency that marks out business managers and entrepreneurs, because that concept is too simple to reflect a job that has so many facets. People who can play these roles should be recognized against a range of competencies and attributes specifically selected to reflect the requirements of key account managers.

KAMScope is based on a set of competencies and attributes assembled from research interviews with key account managers, line managers and customers in a diverse range of companies and sectors; other research studies; competency profiles collected from a number of blue-chip companies; numerous key account manager development projects with national, regional and global companies; and practitioner workgroups exploring this area.

Key account managers and their organizations receive from KAMScope a reflection of the key account manager's and others' views of his or her existing level of competencies and attributes (Figure 10.11). It also compares their profiles with a model of their current role (business manager, entrepreneur, customer manager, tactician) and the role to which they aspire. The models incorporate the importance of each competency and attribute to the role, and the level of performance required. The key account manager receives a view of which competencies and attributes are already sufficient for the role he or she currently performs, and which need development to reach the level required for that role. Output also shows what would need to be developed to fulfil the role he or she would like in the future, which may or may not be different from the current position.

**Figure 10.11**   Examples of KAMScope© feedback.

Any such approach which specifically describes expectations of key account managers will be valuable in shedding light on this area, where there is a shortage of clarity at the moment. The real value for both key account manager and employer lies in the conversation that follows any form of profiling.

## Summary

The role of key account management itself should drive the definition of the role of the key account manager. What is required of the people will be determined by what the organization wants and expects to achieve, but suppliers generally need to do more to clarify their objectives and strategies, and also their responsibilities to support their key account managers.

Key account managers have a very demanding role to play, and finding the people to play it is not easy. Organizations can, however, deploy their resources more effectively by:

- Operating account teams which can provide some of the competencies that are needed to manage the customer relationship, rather than expecting the key account manager to fulfil it all.

- Identifying the relationship required for each customer and hence which of four roles the key account manager needs to play, and making sure that those with the widest competency range are allocated to customers who need them.

Suppliers need to operate some intelligent talent management to ensure that they have the people to fulfil these roles, both through identifying the competencies and attributes they already have, and then through putting in place programmes to develop what else is needed.

# 11 Organizing for key account management

## Fast track

Key account management (KAM) is essentially a boundary-crossing initiative. Many of the benefits accrue from crossing boundaries, whether they are internal ones or those in the customer's organization.

- More interesting and powerful propositions with hard-to-match competitive advantage can be achieved by integrating offers from different parts of the supplier organization.

- Substantial growth can be won by developing business with new parts of the customer's organization.

Companies need a clear organizational structure, understandably, especially as they become bigger and more complex, but the structure should be used positively to enact the company's strategy, not to frustrate it. Any structure has its advantages and disadvantages, which can be offset by a genuine will to work across the structure, whatever it may be. Unfortunately, structures and their boundaries are often reinforced by a culture of ownership and defence of a territorial power base, which is not helpful in KAM. Suppliers need to be aware of how the structure can operate to produce 'blind spots', such as an inability to aggregate customer information that will obscure the identity of potential key customers; the ways in which they are organized; and how they make their decisions.

The supplier's structure is not the only consideration in deciding how to organize for KAM. Obviously, the customer's structure must be taken into account as well. For example, whether the supplier is a global or local organization, and whether its customer is global or local, produces a number of different forms of KAM.

In a traditional, country-based organization, the key account manager and hence the customer is several layers away from the top of the company, so communicating their strategies and gaining attention for their needs at a high level is very difficult, and not what key customers expect if they have been invited to participate in a strategic relationship. This form of organization also makes the management of key customers as a portfolio more or less impossible. In fact, if there is no clear process which brings them together in the same framework and authorizes the same person or people to make decisions about them, then portfolio management is not happening.

The ultimate form of organization for KAM is a central unit which has its own resources, with a director of key accounts who reports direct to the main Board rather than a national or divisional Board. Key account managers in a central unit should have the authority to make central or global deals, albeit in consultation and with a defined approval process. In all forms of organization, however, the local company or region will have to support and service the deal on the ground, so it is always important that they back it. Successful suppliers employ various mechanisms to deal with this tricky issue.

In fact, it is the company's targets that are often responsible for many of the conflicts that arise between different parts of the organization. Suppliers that can properly align their targets will avoid many of the problems frequently encountered in KAM, just by resolving that single issue.

## Introduction

Restructuring is a favourite occupation of organizations, although it is hard to understand why in terms of business logic. Every few years – indeed, as little as two years in many companies – staff are thrown into a melting pot from which they emerge confused and demoralized, after a prolonged period of distraction and resentment which generally means that attention to customers has suffered, along with a substantial number of other business activities. Competitors may only have to reduce their number of restructurings in order to achieve an advantage over the rivals who cannot resist constantly reshuffling the pieces on the board. In many cases, they still have the same pieces on the board when they finish as they did when they started.

Normally, the driver behind all this activity is the appointment of new directors or other pressures on the Board. Restructuring is easy for Boards to do, though painful for the participants. A Board that is genuinely concerned to improve its customer focus and performance should understand that key customers dislike frequent changes in their interface with their suppliers or in the smooth running of the support teams and activities that underpin their relationship with the supplier. Restructuring generally means that any information the organization may have about its performance is dislocated from previous periods, so that whether or not the organization is increasing or decreasing its effectiveness is obscured.

Suppliers should therefore consider very carefully the impact on customers before they change their structure for any purpose. Incremental

Suppliers should consider very carefully the impact on customers before they change their structure.

and therefore constant changes are inadvisable, which means that some deep thought should be put into deciding the best possible structure rather than compromising on short-term options. The Board should consider whether the new structure delivers significant benefit to customers, as well as to its costs, because the change in itself means that anything less will be decidedly unpopular. They should also consider what they believe to be the proper structure, get there quickly, and stay there for a good while.

Willingness to work across boundaries is at least as important, if not more so, than any formal structure.

Having said all that, we need to accept that no structure is perfect and that all involve issues which need to be solved – but by an alternative route to another restructuring. Fostering a willingness to work across boundaries for the good of the customer and the supplier is at least as important, if not more so, than any formal structure.

## 11.1 Drivers of organizational structure

### 11.1.1 Crossing boundaries

Key account management (KAM) is an intrinsically cross-boundary activity. If, in your company, KAM does not cross boundaries, you are probably wasting money on an approach that has been prevented from giving you the return you imagined you would get from it. As Figure 11.1 shows, KAM and key account managers are obliged to cross:

● Internal, functional boundaries

● 'External' boundaries like the supplier's divisions or country management structures, which might be considered internal as they belong to the same organization

● Genuinely external boundaries in the customer's organization, which may be its own divisional or geographical structure.

**Figure 11.1**
Boundaries limiting key account management success.

**Internal functional boundaries inside the supplier strategic business unit (SBU)**

We established in Chapter 4 that customers enter a key relationship in the reasonable expectation that they will get something different from the supplier's standard offer. New, added value for leading customers is likely to require the support of several other functions. These functions may be involved on an on-going basis, if they have regular and frequent input (see Section 10.2 on key account teams), or on a project basis. In order to engage successfully with other functions in the supplier, the key account manager needs to have an acknowledged and accepted role that allows him or her to assemble the resources needed to implement the plan for the customer.

Too often, key account managers are left to beg, borrow or steal the resource they need, which they may have been allocated in theory, but for which, in practice, they have to battle with functional heads who see the resource as part of their 'territory'. Some companies, although they believe they are implementing KAM, have failed to tackle the issues of the ownership of resource that is determined by structure, and, as a consequence, key account managers are left with little hope of delivering what they know the customer wants and feels it has been promised. In that case, KAM can not deliver and the company should withdraw promises of innovative approaches and revert to a sound, standard, less expensive sales structure.

> Too often, key account managers are left to beg, borrow or steal the resource they need.

**Inter-SBU boundaries in the supplier organization**

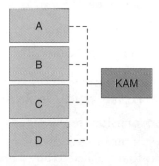

Large suppliers often have several SBUs, determined either by product or by geography, selling to large customers, with the sales effort organized independently by each division effectively operating as separate companies. Customers deal with suppliers according to their differentiation and strategic importance to their business (see Chapter 5), and if each individual division is offering products/services that are seen as undifferentiated by the customers, which can easily happen, each division is then addressed with a 'leverage the volume' strategy from the customer which leads to price competition and hence margin erosion.

However, although the supplier may have strong, comparable competition in each of its divisions, taken separately, together they might be able to offer a combination of goods and services that no other competitor can offer. Suddenly, not only does it achieve differentiation, but its aggregated sales means that it is much more important to the supplier and worthy of its attention.

Similarly, a supplier that competes on a country-by-country basis will probably find a strong body of competitors in each country. If, however, it makes a pan-region offer to its key customer, the majority of these competitors will be excluded automatically from competing on the same basis because they do not have establishments in the same range of countries.

Increasingly, integrated offers actually create a supplier's differentiation.

Increasingly, for key customers, which are likely to be expanding their own businesses and want suppliers which can expand with them, integrated offers are interesting and actually create a supplier's differentiation. However, integration needs to be real, not just 'lip service', which means that suppliers must work hard to coordinate across their internal boundaries to ensure that a seamless offer is delivered in reality.

Suppliers may feel that the customers' divisions are just as obstructive as theirs, and they may be right, but that does not prevent customers being scathing about supplier 'silos'. In our research, customers clearly stated that they saw supplier's internal boundaries as:

- confusing and time-wasting
- causing extra work and administration
- resulting in areas of low service levels and high irritation
- resulting in inconsistent pricing
- preventing consolidation of deals
- preventing consolidation of information
- hindering forward development generally.

## Case study insight

### When 'division' really means division

A company had a lot of business and an excellent relationship with a key customer. The customer asked to buy a product made by the supplier's sister division, which the supplier was happy to arrange. However, when the key account manager rang the sister organization, they said, 'We can't supply your customer: we only sell through distributors.' This did not seem important to the key account manager, but he said, 'OK, we'll buy it from you and sell it on.' Astonishingly, the reply was, 'We can't do that: you're not one of our distributors!'

Eventually, the key account manager resorted to physically buying the product from a retailer, at a consumer price, and selling it to the customer at trade price. That day, he learned that organizational structure is more important than serving customers in some companies.

Failure to integrate the customer interface and the customer offer across divisional and country boundaries and across internal functional boundaries stops suppliers from bringing new and innovative value to customers in a world of mature markets where differentiation is hard to find. Such suppliers are effectively turning their backs on one of the few opportunities many of them have and opting for continuing commoditization, with the poor returns that normally yields. And why? Because battling against internal 'turf wars' is just too hard and too dangerous.

> Battling against internal 'turf wars' is just too hard and too dangerous.

## External customer boundaries

While some of an organization's KAM is dedicated to prospective key customers, most is focused on existing customers. These are often customers with whom a substantial amount of business is already transacted, but who have scope to offer more because they are a large multidivision or multinational company. In many cases, the relationship with one particular part of the customer is excellent, and so the business has reached saturation there, or is approaching it. The supplier should logically choose one of two strategies:

- **Proactive maintenance**: Set targets at current levels, and work on margin and contribution rather than volume and development.

- **Development strategy**: set targets for growth, by definition with other parts of the customer, and work on opening up the relationship and the business in these new areas.

If the supplier is seeking growth from this customer, it must sell outside its familiar part of the organization. This is neither comfortable nor easy. It normally takes a great deal of effort, persistence, and ingenuity in working out how the existing relationship can be used to deliver benefit to the new part of the customer, given that it will already have an incumbent supplier.

It seems really strange, then, that suppliers very often give their key account managers no incentive at all for this effort. Why not? Because, however underdeveloped the relationship is, the territory 'belongs' to someone else in the company even though the customer may not have consented to this ownership.

---

### Case study insight

#### The price of 'principle': how to prevent growth

A supplier's company in Germany had a wonderful relationship with the German operation of a large multinational. The key account manager, and his counterpart in the customer, thought the relationship could potentially be extended into the customer's French operations, where it was dealing with a French competitor at the time, but not receiving the kind of benefits that the German partnership had achieved.

Exploratory contact with the supplier's French subsidiary established that it would be pleased to accept the introduction and approach the customer's French operation: but also that France did not pay rewards to key account managers from other countries, and was firmly opposed to setting any such precedent. The key account manager passed on the information requested, but he had no confidence that the business would be gained without his involvement to factor in all the benefits that had been set up in Germany – as so it proved. France handled the customer as a new lead, and nothing came of it.

---

In theory, extra reward drives extra effort. So, presumably, no reward generally gets no effort. Salespeople have traditionally been paid bonuses in addition to basic salary, which are intended by companies to steer them towards delivering the required results (although that is not always what happens). So it seems curious that when suppliers want key account managers to achieve something particularly difficult and time-consuming, for example, penetrating a new part of the customer's business, they are not prepared to incentivize it by even as much as they reward normal business.

> Very little cross-boundary business development actually happens, in spite of the vast amount of talk about it.

Very little cross-boundary business development actually happens, in spite of the vast amount of talk about it; but often, it is only talk. Suppliers need to realize that if they do not follow through a cross-selling strategy to its logical conclusion, and take action to facilitate it at all points, it will fail to happen. If organizational boundaries get in the way, there are two choices: get rid of them, or identify the barriers and create an effective work-around.

---

### CHECKPOINT

#### Crossing boundaries in your company

- Do your company's key account managers have resource from other functions unarguably allocated to their customers?

- Do you know what and how much each of your key customers buys from any part of your company/group?

- What percentage of your company's sales go to customers buying from other parts of your company/group?

- Do you know how much your company/group has of each of your key customers total relevant spend?

### 11.1.2 Considering the customer's structure

Before designing an organizational structure to support KAM, it makes good sense to consider the customer's structure and behaviour. Ideally, the supplier's structure should mirror that of the customer. If it does, then it will be easier to align contacts, negotiate deals, match up information and so on. Figure 11.2 represents four variations of the ways in which supplier

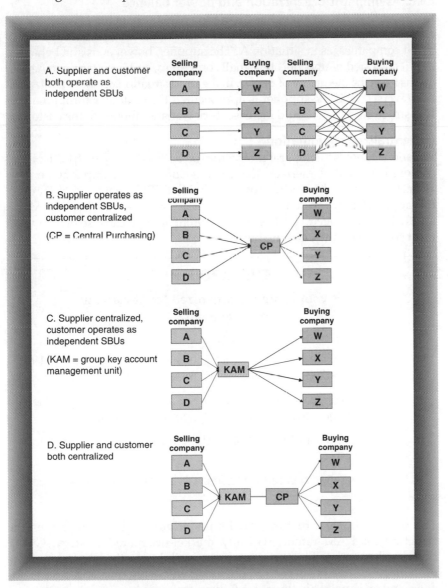

**Figure 11.2**
The interaction between different supplier and customer organizational structures.

and customer SBUs might do business together, which will depend to a great extent on the degree of centralization in their structures. Each lettered box represents a different SBU, defined either by geographical location or division, or both.

## A: Decentralized and autonomous

In situation A both sides have decentralized structures and act autonomously in their dealings with suppliers or customers. As both sides operate in the same way, this sounds appropriate, and if they work together exclusively as in the simple version of A, it could be. However, it quickly becomes inappropriate when SBUs start to interact with additional parts of their counterparts' business, as the alternative version shows. This demonstrates how easily autonomous forms of organizations can cause expense, confusion and waste.

## B&C: Asymmetric organization and power balance

In approach B, the customer has decided to reap the benefits of being a large customer and leverage its size, rather than behaving like a collection of small companies, as in situation A. The supplier, however, is still behaving as if it consisted of unconnected small companies, and is suffering in negotiations from the inequality of power. In the third situation, C, the organization has reversed, and the supplier is approaching the customer through a unified structure, which should increase its power and interest to the customer.

## D: Centralized coordination

Situation D shows a comparable structure on both sides in which both organizations have central interfaces that can develop a relationship together, and still acknowledges the existence of the individual SBUs behind both. Through this approach they can deliver what many customers require from KAM (i.e. an efficiently managed, consistent, transparent offer). It can also deliver what most suppliers want (i.e. more business).

---

### CHECKPOINT

#### How is your company organized for key account management?

- Draw boxes for each of the SBUs in your company and name them, as in Figure 11.2, and do the same for your customer's organization. Link them up according to how they relate to each other.

- Does your company offer the customer key account management through a single point of contact with appropriate authority?

- Does the customer offer central purchasing through a single decision-making point?

- Is your company organized to maximize its leverage with the customer?

---

The organizational structure and its underlying philosophy drives the structure for KAM rather than any market-orientated strategy. Group Boards who operate by giving total responsibility to the chief executives or managing directors of their SBUs, along with a big reward for performance, and an equally big threat for failure, feel unable to intervene in those businesses in any way in case their intervention is held responsible for poor performance. This philosophy hinders corporate initiatives, including cross-boundary KAM.

Not only does the corporate structure affect the implementation of KAM, it even affects the identification and recognition of the customer. Look at all the potential relationships in the first situation in Figure 11.2, where both sides are decentralized. If you are in supplier SBU A, do you count the various customer SBUs as one customer, or as four? Presumably, supplier SBU B also thinks it has four customers, and so do the others. The group may easily believe that it has 16 customers, whereas, in reality, it has no more than four, or even just one. Should there be a different key account manager for each relationship? Should each relationship have a different strategy and a separate plan as well? That is the logical outcome that suppliers should confront before setting up their KAM organizations and hence allocating 'ownership' of customers.

It is exactly the issue of uncoordinated viewpoints that prevents suppliers from answering the simple but crucial question, 'Which is your group's biggest customer?' This very important question takes some companies weeks and months to answer, and they are often surprised at the outcome. (Look out for customers who have different names in different places or in different markets: you may fail to recognize their importance to you if your management information systems do not pick up and aggregate all their data.)

---

### Case study insight

**The mystery of the most important customer**

A supplier in the construction industry had several divisions focused on different areas of expertise. Its key customers were prime contractors and heavy-spending government departments like the Highways Agency and the Environment Agency. Traditionally, it analysed its results by project rather than customer. When it changed its management information system it found that its biggest customer across the group was the Ministry of Defence, because although it was not the biggest in any division, it did business with all of them, whereas most customers were heavily involved with one or two at the most. This discovery was a surprise to everybody, including the Board!

---

In summary, the customer's structure is a major factor in how the supplier should structure itself. Since any supplier has not one but many customers, it will need, at least, a flexible structure in order to approach each in an appropriate way. Companies tend to like tidy organograms that people with a helicopter view can get their heads round, but suitability rather than tidiness should not be the first consideration in dealing with key customers.

### 11.1.3 Global vs local

The assumption is often made that global accounts must automatically be key accounts, but this is not necessarily so. In some businesses, most large customers operate globally and require global management, but not all of them qualify to be key accounts. According to Professor George Yip:

> Global account management is an organizational form and process by which the worldwide activities serving a given multi-national customer are coordinated by one person or team within the supplying company.
>
> (Yip and Madsen, 1996)

Note that this definition does not say that the customers are necessarily strategically important to the supplier, which is an intrinsic part of the definition of KAM. For example, probably the majority of customers of freight forwarding and logistics companies shift goods all over the world, but they are too numerous all to be counted as key.

On the other hand, where most of a supplier's customers are geographically limited, it is often those who have pushed their business out round the world who provide the most opportunity and the greatest challenge. So for these suppliers, being global or at least multinational is a mandatory criterion for their key accounts. Really, it is the growth and strategic importance of these customers rather than their global reach, as such, that makes them a key account.

> The real difference between key account management and good account management is the amount of investment the supplier will make.

The real difference between KAM and good account management is the perceived size and potential of the relationship, and hence the degree of commitment and amount of investment that the supplier will make. There is no intrinsic reason why substantial, stable relationships should be key accounts, even if they are global: but if being global means bigger business then the two may converge in practice. Again, the customer's structure has to be taken into account, as in Figure 11.3, which charts the kind of KAM that should apply according to the geographical spread of supplier and customer.

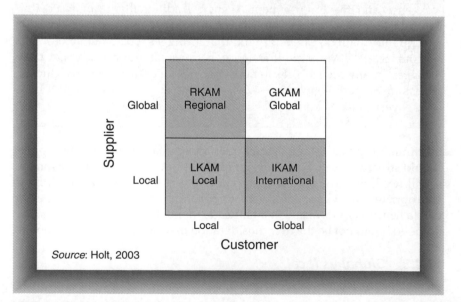

*Source*: Holt, 2003

**Figure 11.3**
Matching local and global structures.

For a local supplier with a local customer, local – probably national – account management is fine. A global supplier with a global customer might have a lot to do to manage the relationship, but the match is good and it should work well. The more challenging issues arise from situations in the other two boxes, which represent mismatched organizational structures.

If the customer is global while the supplier is still organized locally then, at least, the supplier needs to institute some kind of international KAM to respond to it. This can work provided that the key account manager has a clear position in the company's structure and a strong remit for the role, and that senior management deal decisively with the territorial issues. Where authority is still vested entirely at local level, it is often exceedingly difficult to get the agreement of all the countries that need to buy into the deal. International account managers have to negotiate internally with individual country managers at the same time as they are negotiating externally with the customer, and may find themselves in a very difficult position, with maximum responsibility and minimal authority.

If the customer is a multinational rather than a global company, in other words, it is still making decisions on an individual country basis, then a global supplier can address it at regional level. Regional KAM is probably easier to control and manage than truly global relationships, which involve an additional level of complexity. The countries in the major regions of the world obviously have their distinctive characters, but they also share features in common with other countries in their region, and dealing with them at this level may allow a supplier to leverage scale and achieve economies of scale, while stopping short of the complexity of global relationships.

The major barrier, perhaps, to global customer management is suppliers' fear of customers' demands for globally harmonized prices, which they anticipate being the lowest price paid anywhere. In fact, organizational structure plays a major part in creating barriers to global pricing. Suppliers are better able to offer global pricing, if they must, where they have set up some kind of an overarching global structure for managing key customers with genuine decision-making capability and authority over regional or local SBUs.

> Organizational structure plays a major part in creating barriers to global pricing.

---

### Case study insight:

#### Compensating for a mismatched organizational structure

In one 'global' supplier, different countries not only had different costs, but also different margin expectations and even different cost models. Its global customers used their negotiating power to win very competitive prices, so it was quite possible that the price agreed in the global deal delivered below local target margins in some countries. This then showed as low-margin or even loss-making business on the country's books so, not surprisingly, country managers were not keen to agree to this kind of price level. In order to gain local approval, which was needed before the deal could go ahead, the country had to be compensated for apparent 'losses'.

> This was achieved by setting up a global profit and loss account that was owned by the global account manager, alongside the country profit and loss account, and transferring compensation to a pre-agreed level to the country's account, to make up the deficit. This approach, although rather tortuous, was more successful than earlier alternatives.

Generally speaking, suppliers' country-based SBUs still 'own' the income and the costs of business that is delivered to parts of the customer within their territory, even if the deal has been negotiated at a global level. However, customers tend to prefer in-country billing as well, because of issues like local VAT and tax, and their own accounting systems. If pricing were not resolved to the satisfaction of the country as well as the customer and global account manager, it could have major impact on the service support received by the customer on the ground. Indeed, poor support for global customers in countries where they are a minor player is problematic anyway, where the structure allows autonomy to SBU heads. There are three main options to solve the problem:

- Coercion: pulling authority on the country manager, if it can be done.

- Central billing: taking the business away from the country (the ultimate threat).

- Combined business development and compensation: driving more business out of the deal for the country where possible, compensating for losses or low margins where necessary.

Combined business development and compensation is the best choice, since only this solution is likely to result in real cooperation and an adequate level of service for the customer. On the plus side, global account managers who have demonstrated the potential achievable by bringing business to the country from their customer have gained some stunning results from the country's subsequent cooperation.

In summary, there are complex and subtle issues with important consequences that should receive very careful thought when the structure for global, regional or local KAM is developed.

## 11.2  Organizational structures and their implications

### 11.2.1  Key account management in traditional structures

We suggested at the beginning of this chapter that, in KAM, the willingness to work across a structure is at least as important as the structure itself. Without contradicting that view, it is true that some organizational structures are distinctly KAM-unfriendly, and are a major cause of failure in KAM initiatives. It must be the responsibility of those at the top to set up an organizational structure with the minimum of barriers to KAM inherent in it, if they genuinely support this approach to customers. Since KAM is essentially a cross-boundary activity, it will frequently encounter barriers, foreseen and unforeseen. If the key account manager is not to be overwhelmed, the amount of obstruction needs to be kept to a minimum.

Sadly, ambivalence is as common as wholehearted support from the senior management team. KAM often starts with a single champion, who does not alone have the power to make the structural adjustments necessary for success. The rest of the Board may sit on the fence, passing resolutions stating that, if the initiative 'proves itself', consideration will be given, at some unspecified time in the future, to formalizing its position in the structure with a wider remit.

The organizational structure through which KAM is delivered has a major effect on the supplier's ability to implement strategies like global pricing, or standardized service offerings, or consolidated information management, for example. It also has a significant effect on suppliers' costs. Resources are wasted through duplicating effort, and cost savings fail to materialize if they require a critical mass, because they cannot consolidate activity or amass the volume from several geographies.

With a traditional country-based structure, the supplier is more or less incapable of having a unified view of the customer, so it is very often alarmingly ignorant of this customer's position in the marketplace; how it is changing; how much business it gives the supplier and hence the supplier's dependency on such customers; and how much this customer costs the supplier as well.

Consider the structure in Figure 11.4. It shows a traditional country-based organization which is led by the country managing director, reporting to a regional director who may or may not be on the main board. The managing director has a number of directors reporting to him or her, one of which is the sales director: key account managers then report to this position. In some cases, key account managers report to a key account director, who reports to the sales director.

You can see that in a structure like that in Figure 11.4 the key account managers, and the customers they represent, are anything from four to six levels away from the Board. It is most unlikely that the Board will know anything about the strategies of these customers, or even those of their own company for these customers. The decisions they make will not be informed by this crucial part of the marketplace, so they run the risk of being out of alignment with the leaders in it.

This is not what key customers sign up for when they enter into a relationship with a key supplier. Indeed, it is not unusual for key customers to insist on proof that their key account manager has access to the group Board when they commit to the relationship. However, it is most unlikely

Some organizational structures are distinctly KAM-unfriendly.

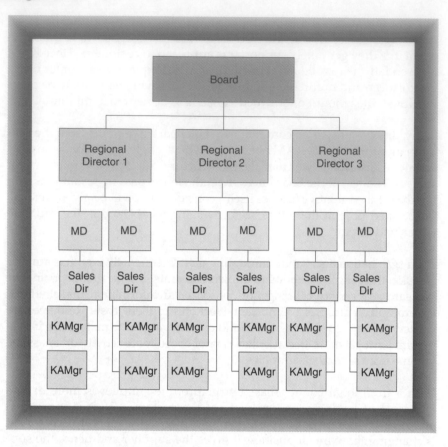

**Figure 11.4**
Traditional country-based structure.

that a key account manager in a structure like that in Figure 11.4 would get anywhere near the Board. In this kind of set-up the key account manager can normally only draw on the resources of his or her own country, which may not be suitable or sufficient for the purpose. Any activity of the customer outside the geographical boundary is problematic, often so much so that it is denied or ignored, if at all possible. It is certainly not considered as an opportunity.

## Case study insight

### How a regional structure masked the real identity of a key customer

Among the customers of a supplier to the luxury goods industry were two companies owned by the same parent. However, they had different names, operated in different parts of the world and, while there was some overlap in activities, one was largely a retailer while the other's main activity was manufacturing and wholesaling. For various reasons, but particularly because the headquarters of the two companies were in diametrically different parts of the world, they were managed by two different key account managers. Both customers were treated as borderline key accounts, and both key account managers felt they could develop the business more if they had more resources, but the business case for neither customer individually justified greater investment.

In fact, these two companies were really the upstream and downstream activities of the same business. Regardless of what they were called or where they operated, they should have been managed by the same key account manager. He would have been able to draw up a more comprehensible and comprehensive view of the customer's operations, and make a strong business case for supporting them at a key account level.

### 11.2.2 Centralized key account management organizations

In an alternative form of organization better suited to key accounts, a dedicated unit is created which is independent of country or division. Dedicated, independent KAM units will focus on a consolidated view of the customer in a way that country-based structures do not, and probably do not want to either. Such units generally have resource of their own, such as market experts and financial analysts, and buy in additional services from the rest of the organization, as they need them. The importance of key customers is made clear by their proximity to the Board, as Figure 11.5 shows.

> The importance of key customers is made clear by their proximity to the Board.

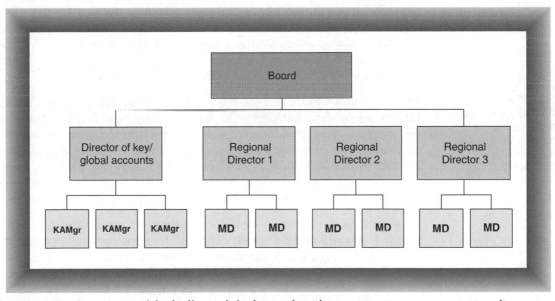

**Figure 11.5** Structure with dedicated, independent key account management unit.

This kind of structure is often driven by the need to deal with global customers (though not exclusively), as companies recognize that they have issues like global consistency of service and global pricing that nation-based organizations do not handle well. The chances of identifying appropriate strategies for key customers, agreeing them with the customer, and monitoring them are much higher within a dedicated unit than when key accounts are owned by country or product units and dispersed through the company.

One of KAM's main wins is growth gained by extending a good relationship with a customer into new areas of its organization. This route to growth alone offers major rewards. The strategy for a key account managed by a dedicated, independent unit should give a great deal of attention to such opportunities. However, in key accounts managed from a country or division home base these kinds of opportunities are often not addressed for a whole variety of reasons, including lack of knowledge, mismatched culture and a narrow interpretation of self-interest overriding the company's interest, and so on.

> One of KAM's main wins is growth gained by extending a good relationship with a customer into new areas of its organization.

Customer profitability should be easier to observe overall from a dedicated unit. In this form of organization measurement of cost to serve is easier, and hence understanding and management of customer profitability is also potentially better. Inconsistencies can be seen and addressed; synergies can be spotted and the consequent opportunities explored. However, it is still not always easy to coax systems and countries into providing the necessary information.

In the end, however, regardless of who handles the development side of the relationship with the customer, ultimate success or failure depends on what is actually received, and delivery on the ground is still the province of the operational side of the traditional organization. While the key account manager strikes the high-level deals centrally with the customer, it falls to the local organization to make it work, and that is likely to include the local salesforce as well as operations, logistics, customer service and so on. As one key account manager said, 'We have to get them (the local organization) happy. It's all about service in the end, and they deliver it.'

> Unless targets are clarified, simplified and aligned, the supplier will probably succeed only in frustrating its own ambitions.

We cannot stress too highly the importance of understanding the different targets set by different people in the company who have various and diverse goals and agendas, which will impact on the development and execution of the customer's business. Suppliers that have put several target-setting mechanisms in place find they collide horribly with each other around key customers. Unless targets are clarified, simplified and aligned, the supplier will probably succeed only in frustrating its own ambitions.

As a compromise between local ownership of customers, as depicted in Figure 11.4, and a dedicated unit divorced from any particular affiliations, as depicted in Figure 11.5, suppliers sometimes implement a structure that gives account leadership to one particular part of the business on a customer by customer basis, as illustrated in Figure 11.6. So, for example, the French SBU may lead on a customer that has its headquarters in France, while the Italian SBU leads on key customers based in Italy. The decision on who will lead may also be based on the location of the bulk of the customer's business with the supplier. In other words, a customer that spends most with the supplier in Germany will be managed from Germany, even if the customer's head office is in Rome. This approach can be applied on a divisional basis as well as geographically. If the freight-forwarding part of a supplier sells more to a customer than its logistics and assembly division, the lead key account manager for this customer will be in the freight-forwarding division.

Some customers apply a similar policy in their buying structures so that, in a manufacturer of cars, trucks and buses, for example, the lead buyer for valves for may be in the trucks SBU, in which case the supplier might choose to lead its approach for this particular customer from the SBU that has the best relationship with the customer's truck division.

Though they may not be recognized as such at the time, these approaches are awkward compromises that should be seen as transition stages towards a dedicated, independent unit. They are, nevertheless, rather popular. They are believed to have the advantages of the dedicated unit in terms of the consolidation of views and of strategies. However, as Figure 11.6 suggests, the supplier has not made any radical changes to the pre-existing structure, and therefore it works in much the same way as it did before. The key account manager is somehow supposed to make the 'dotted line' links work, in spite of the very mixed and unclear mandate they have been given.

> These approaches are awkward compromises that should be seen as transition stages towards a dedicated, independent unit.

In fact, after some initial progress that may come from ironing out anomalies, further business development often fails to materialize. The SBU

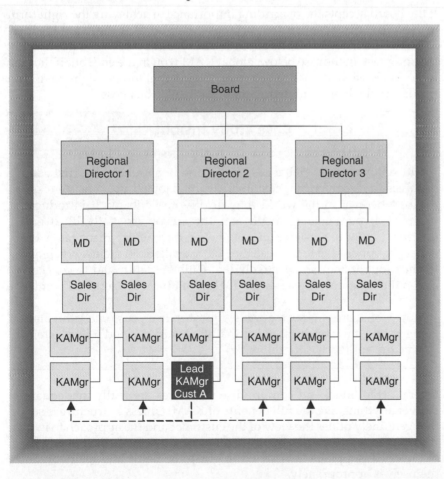

**Figure 11.6**
Compromise structure with designated lead key account manager.

hosting the key account manager still exerts a strong gravitational pull, which has several unfortunate effects:

- The host SBU requisitions resource that was meant for the relationship, to apply it to its own purposes.

- The key account manager remains in a familiar 'home', and is then not forced to learn and offer to the customer the capability of the supplier as a whole.

- Trying to reconcile the conflicting demands of the host SBU and the group as a whole from this position is a no-win situation that causes wear-out in key account managers.

These compromise structures arise from a mixture of concerns, which are real if not necessarily praiseworthy or valid:

- perceived loss of territory or importance for country or divisional managers

- concern that key account managers become distanced from the 'real' business

- reluctance to add to central costs in decentralized businesses.

If the Board accepts the overriding importance of achieving the right form of customer management for each customer, none of these are insuperable, but the first – concerns about territory and power – is undoubtedly the strongest. In the case below, global KAM won in the end, but if the customer backlash had not been so clear, the internal forces might have won the day, to the long-term detriment of Citibank's business.

---

### Case study insight

#### Pitched battle: country managers vs customers

Citibank has many global customers, and it was one of the first companies to recognize that customers wanted joined-up, consistent service wherever in the world they dealt with Citibank. It introduced global account management, and the customers really liked and responded to the programme. However, the country managers were deeply opposed to it, because they felt it challenged their sovereignty. They fought back so effectively that Citibank felt it had to concede, and the programme was shelved. The country managers had won!

However, there was such a wave of protest from customers threatening to take their business away, that the Board decided it had to reinstate the approach. (Buzzell, 1985)

---

Overall, traditional and compromise structures are really inadequate to deliver anything like the full benefits of KAM. Unless a structure is set up that genuinely unites the view of the customer and the approach to it, then the outcomes will be disappointing, not because the principle is wrong, but because suppliers have failed to grasp the nettle and really organize themselves appropriately.

So far we have discussed the structural sources of difficulties in handling each key account, but the structure also has an effect on whether the supplier is in control of the whole portfolio of its most important customers, which is considered in the following section.

## 11.2.3   Portfolio management

A supplier's key customer portfolio should be managed like a share portfolio (Figure 11.7 and Chapter 2). Some customers are there for growth, and others for current income. Some customers are high risk, but may pay off with high returns: they should be balanced by others that are low risk, which then offer lower, more secure returns. The customers in which investment is appropriate should be carefully selected against a business case for each that takes at least the next three years into account, and if a customer is not responding well, investment may be switched to a more promising customer. The portfolio should be varied and well balanced, and the portfolio overall should perform to expectations, not necessarily any particular customer.

> The portfolio overall should perform to expectations, not necessarily any particular customer.

**Figure 11.7**
A supplier's portfolio of customers.

Where a separate KAM unit exists, so that key customers can be recognized and managed as a group, this kind of approach is possible. Valid comparisons and carefully calculated trade-offs are made to optimize the use of the supplier's resources of time and money. However, in the traditional or compromise structures shown in Figures 11.4 and 11.6, this is more or less impossible. Funds allocated at country or divisional level will be applied by the SBU managing director. Each may have a different view of how much to invest in customers against their other priorities, and how to invest it.

The company below had taken management of its key customers as a portfolio very seriously by having the KAM unit report to the Board via the finance director.

> ## Case study insight
> ### Managing key customers as an investment portfolio
> A supplier acknowledged a distinction between key account management and normal sales activities by creating a separate department for it reporting to the finance director, rather than the sales and marketing function. This positioning helped key account managers to get the support they needed with financial information and financial modelling, and establishing that the numbers checked out. This reporting structure was driven by the recognition that a decision in this area could add or wipe off £millions in profits for the company.

*Resource allocation and management are an integral part of key account management.*

Resource allocation and management are an integral part of KAM. Suppliers need to apply the following elements as working concepts all the way through the important chain of decisions that finally agrees which customers are fully backed with resource and which receive less:

- **Customer categorization**: A view of key customers as a group, subcategorized according to their potential.

- **Forecasting**: An ability to forecast outcomes and model the responses to different levels of resource, given the customer's position in the portfolio.

- **Value-based prioritization**: A process that compares the potential values of customers, and agrees customer priorities based on strategy and balance in the portfolio.

- **Resource allocation**: A process of allocating resources in line with strategy and the optimization of the portfolio.

*If there is no specific supra-SBU mechanism nobody in the company has control over the most important single group of customers.*

Companies may or may not be able to plot and view their key customers as in Figure 11.7. Anyway, just having a view of them is not enough to qualify as effective portfolio management. In fact, if there is no specific supra-SBU mechanism for approving and controlling the application of resource, you can take it that there is no control. Such mechanisms generally sit alongside dedicated KAM units, and we do not find them in devolved SBU-based structures. As a result, in many cases nobody in the company has control over the most important single group of customers and, potentially, source of income.

In fact, there are three levels at which suppliers make decisions that have an impact on key customers: at the level of the contract, at the level of the customer and at portfolio level (Figure 11.8). At contract level, most companies have in place reasonably clear decision-making processes for approving which they will bid for, although most could and should use better and more explicit evaluation criteria. However, the customer dimension is often omitted and decisions are made based only on the contract. You should be asking more than just 'Does this look like a profitable contract in its own terms?' when it may consume resource that would be better applied to another customer and more aligned to the overall portfolio strategy. You should be asking 'Is this contract profitable and does winning it further our strategy?'

**Figure 11.8**
Decision-making
levels.

---

## CHECKPOINT

**Do you check all three levels to make decisions on contract acceptability?**

1. Contract decision level:
   - Will this contract be profitable for us?

2. Customer decision level:
   - Does this contract fit customer strategies?
   - Is the plan for the customer valid in their terms and viable in ours?

3. Portfolio decision level:
   - Does the plan for the customer fit with portfolio strategies?
   - Can it be resourced?
   - Does it make an appropriate contribution to portfolio objectives?

---

Using a matrix like that in Figure 11.9 might help you see that you should at least consider less attractive contracts with attractive customers, where you want to develop the relationship, for example. You might also want to reconsider taking an apparently attractive contract with an unattractive customer, as experience shows that these often do not turn out well, or even profitably in the end, and may divert scarce resources from the use intended for them.

Both the broader, portfolio-level view and the narrower, contract-level view should be operated, but the customer should be the pivotal decision-making level that informs decisions at the lower and higher levels. Furthermore, suppliers' decisions at contract level and at customer level should be linked together and guided by decisions taken at portfolio level. Our research showed that such processes are frequently absent, and without the processes to implement it, real portfolio management does not exist.

> Without the processes to implement it, real portfolio management does not exist.

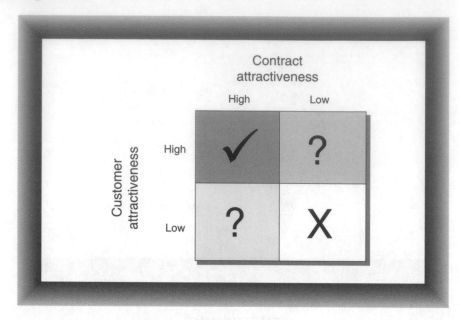

**Figure 11.9**
Assessing
opportunities.

### 11.2.4 Target alignment

Misaligned
targets bedevil
implementation.

Target alignment or, more commonly, target misalignment is one of the most difficult issues in implementing KAM. Targets, and who sets them and how, epitomize all the unresolved issues around customer 'ownership', profit and loss responsibilities, rewards and more. Misaligned targets bedevil implementation, but however obvious this is from an external perspective, companies clearly have real difficulties about putting coordinated targets into practice, since conflicting targets seem to be the norm.

Conflicting targets that are problematic for KAM are set at all levels in the organization:

- SBUs/divisions
- Internal functions/departments
- Individuals, key account managers and others.

'I don't focus on
overhead
contribution. When
I'm incentivized on it,
I'll do it.'

It is fairly common to make national companies and other internal service delivery units into profit centres, and hence set profit targets for them. Targeted, profit-seeking divisions and internal support departments cause real issues in managing key customers, for example, by trying to claim parts of the key customer's business as 'theirs'; or by spending more time on 'their' customers (lower tier customers with less business and simpler needs); or worse, by pushing up prices to achieve their profit targets. In effect, part of the profit has been detached from the customer and kept by the division or department. If the key account manager cannot secure a price premium, which is tough when competing for key customers, the profitability of the account appears worse than it really is, leading to misinterpretation of the situation and potentially bad decisions.

> ## Case study insight
>
> ### Manufacturing company removes barrier to competitiveness
>
> A European manufacturing company had several production units in Europe, which made different products that were sold through its national sales and marketing companies. In an effort to focus efficiency and cost-cutting measures, it made its production units into profit centres. The production units priced their products on a cost-plus basis at a level that allowed them to reach their profit and loss targets. Based on these prices, the national companies were losing bids too often, especially with key customers, because they were uncompetitive when they priced to meet the additional profit targets they also carried.
>
> Volumes went down. So the production units raised their prices to cover their heavy overheads on the lower volume but, obviously, this situation could not continue. The directors reinstated the production units as cost centres rather than profit centres, and kept the national sales companies as profit centres. They were now able to work with transparent pricing that could meet the needs of key customers.

There are numerous drivers of misaligned targets, as shown in Table 11.1 together with the effect each can have, so perhaps the fact that they conflict so often should come as no surprise.

Targets are taken to represent the ultimate manifestation of strategic intent, so they act as the guidelights for those who implement strategy; and when they are mismatched with strategy, implementation will be compromised. Staff believe that their targets indicate what the company really wants them to do, in a way that any amount of rhetoric does not. If they are also rewarded on achieving those targets, then that clinches any argument: fulfilment of targets, if at all possible, is what the company will get. If those targets, taken across the organization, point in different directions, then confusion and conflict are what the company will get. Only if they are aligned, will it make the progress it seeks.

Targets act as the guidelights for those who implement strategy.

| Driver | Effect |
|---|---|
| Aspirations | A supplier may set a high-level target for its business overall, roll it out to all customers and apply pressure to achieve it to everyone, even where it is inappropriate for specific customers |
| Ownership | Targets are given to individuals or groups of individuals: the emphasis on their responsibility for meeting their targets also means that they do not take any responsibility for meeting anyone else's target |

**Table 11.1**
Drivers of misaligned targets and their effects.

**Table 11.1**
(*Continued*)

| Driver | Effect |
|---|---|
| Time span | Key customer targets should be medium/long term, which is often at odds with the short-term targets normally applied to salesforces, or to demands on SBUs, especially those closely watched by investment analysts |
| Customer definition | Ambitious targets for key customers as a whole may mean nothing to SBUs with only a small part of the customer which expect to fulfil their ambitions through other customers |
| Business mix | Suppliers can set production targets according to the needs of their manufacturing/operating units, which apply pressure to sell what they produce that may be at odds with what the customer wants to buy |
| Metrics | Targets may be set in terms of volume, revenue, gross margin, costs or contribution in different parts of the business: different metrics implies different behaviour |
| Target-setting processes | Target-setting may be started at the top or the bottom: top-down generally aligns itself with corporate ambition, but has no guarantee of feasibility, while bottom-up is aligned with market forces but may fall short of corporate requirements |

## Summary

Key account management is essentially a boundary-crossing initiative. If it fails to cross boundaries, both external ones in the customer and internal boundaries in the supplier organization, then it is probably an unjustifiable expense. It is certainly a wasted opportunity.

However, suppliers seem to lack the conviction and confidence to remove the barriers to make KAM work effectively, and leave it to individuals to use their powers of influence and persuasion to overcome them. In fact, key account managers will need all their reserves of influence and persuasion on legitimate targets anyway. For the supplier to duck the issues that it alone can address, such as alignment of targets, is an abdication of its responsibility that sets a poor example throughout the organization.

Although the customer's organization clearly plays a part, the most difficult problems in KAM are caused by the supplier's own organization. You would think that such issues could easily be solved if the solution lies in the supplier's hands, but their persistence shows clearly that is not the case. Suppliers might be able to resolve the issues either by adopting a more appropriate structure, or by installing processes that work across the existing structure, but very often they do neither. If they find it difficult to retain key account managers working under a burden of organizational misalignment, they should not be surprised.

# 12 The origins of key account management

While key account management (KAM) has a great deal of its origins in sales, the philosophy has come a long way from there, and this chapter tracks the development of KAM in academic research and in practice. Needless to say, the two are often not synchronized, and while research has established best practice some considerable time ago, many companies lag well behind, even now. Perhaps understanding the origins of the KAM philosophy will help you to appreciate why KAM is interpreted differently in different companies which are operating different evolutions of the concept.

The identification of the decision-making unit (DMU) in industrial buying was an important breakthrough in the 1960s. It established the complexity of the industrial buying decision compared with a consumer decision, and demonstrated the importance of developing relationships with multiple contacts in the customer who had different interests and viewpoints. Most salespeople, however, had only a single contact in each customer and, at that time, were not adept at developing more.

The Industrial Marketing and Purchasing Group developed the concept of interacting with the customers and developing relationships aimed at customer retention as a deliberate strategy. There has been much debate about when relationship marketing is and is not appropriate, but there is at least general agreement that it is not for all customers, even if which customers are suitable is disputed. Relationship marketing looked longer term and introduced the idea of customer lifetime value, secured through high levels of customer satisfaction.

The KAM philosophy fundamentally believes that collaboration with customers is better for both than confrontation, and seeks to overcome the traditional view of buyer–seller relationships as adversarial. The suspicion has always been that the financial interests of the organization will be threatened by the other party, but evidence suggests that:

● Adversarial behaviour adds costs (e.g. 30 per cent in the construction industry)

- Collaboration creates opportunities for saving costs
- Suppliers do not know how much they make from their customers anyway.

The drivers of KAM are numerous, from globalization and political pressure for corporate responsibility to the speed of change in business, but all factors ultimately tend to give ever larger customers increasing choice and power. Successful KAM carries with it the risk of increasing business dependence, but as the marketplace consolidates few can withstand the trend.

Suppliers and key customers will become increasingly committed to each other in integrated supply chains which can deliver better, faster and cheaper, and which compete with other integrated supply chains rather than individual competitors. In spite of some high profile casualties of interdependent buyer–seller relationships, it is hard to envisage a return to hands-off exchanges that cannot respond to the requirements of today's customers.

# Introduction

This chapter is important in that it puts key account management (KAM) in a historical context and traces its evolution from a sales-push approach to what it is today: a partnership between supplier and customer with the purpose of delivering superior value propositions to the ultimate consumers. KAM has evolved from the principles of customer focus and relationship marketing in business-to-business markets. It is distinguishable from key account selling by its emphasis on long-term, mutually beneficial relationships between selling companies and buying companies which are rooted in the realization of opportunities for profit enhancement for both parties. KAM is a management approach adopted by selling companies aimed at building a portfolio of loyal key accounts by offering them, on a continuing basis, a product/service package tailored to their individual needs. Where appropriate, technical, social and process links are built up between supplier and customer.

Defining the appropriate KAM approach and integrating it as a process is a significant challenge for selling companies. It is a challenge not least because different accounts demand different approaches and processes. The success of KAM is largely determined by the key account. Key accounts are those customers in a business-to-business market that are identified by selling companies as being strategically important. However, what constitutes strategic importance to the selling company? Revenue and volume are easy to measure, but accounts can be both big and unprofitable. Success also depends on the strategic importance to the customer of the selling company and what it supplies. The degree of receptivity demonstrated by the customer to a partnership approach is also influenced by the skills of the supplier in meeting the customer's needs. Those skills have to be

> Key accounts are those customers in a business-to-business market which are identified by selling companies as being strategically important.

consistently demonstrated not just at the single point of contact represented by the key account manager, but at every point of contact between the two organizations.

Peter Drucker recognized the importance of customer dynamics in his early works in the 1950s, whilst specific study of the topic began in the 1960s. 'What the customer thinks he is buying, what he considers "value" is decisive – it determines what a business is, what it produces and whether it will prosper' (Drucker, 1955).

## 12.1   Historical foundations

### 12.1.1   The decision-making unit

The origins of KAM are rooted in the history of industrial marketing. The first theoretical breakthrough in analysis of the relationships between selling companies and buying companies was the concept of the decision-making unit (DMU), which was developed in the 1960s by Robinson, Farris and Wind (1967) of the American Management Association. This notion was valuable because it ensured consideration of the way in which buying decisions are made within buying organizations. It demonstrated that there was more to successful selling than clever negotiations with a purchasing professional, so that understanding the motivations and roles of all the people involved in the purchasing decision became a relevant selling skill. The idea of the DMU encouraged managers who had been resistant to 'soft' methodologies to recognize the importance of people in the dynamics of trade.

The decision to purchase in a complex organization involves those with purchasing and financial expertise, those with technical expertise and those with hierarchical leverage. In some cases, the purchasing department may even be excluded from the purchasing decision. The number of people in the DMU is likely to be a factor of:

- The cost of the purchase

- The complexity of the product

- The inherent degree of risk.

The degree of risk will be particularly high if the product is new. Thus, if a selling company's product is strategic to the buying company, then it is probable that a significant number of buying company personnel will have an interest in new purchases.

In contrast, research at the time suggested that salespeople were heavily reliant on single contacts within buying companies and were not influencing the customer's whole DMU. In Table 12.1 the direct relationship between company size in terms of the number of employees and DMU size is contrasted with the average number of contacts made by salespeople over a defined period.

| Number of employees in customer | Average number of buying influences (people in the DMU) | Average number of contacts made by salespeople |
|---|---|---|
| Under 200 | 3.42 | 1.72 |
| 201–400 | 4.85 | 1.75 |
| 401–1000 | 5.81 | 1.90 |
| Over 1000 | 6.50 | 1.65 |

**Table 12.1** Contrasting the number of buying influences and number of contacts made by salespeople

It followed that identifying and influencing all the people involved in the buying decision should be a mandatory selling activity, regardless of the salesperson's persuasiveness. Selling required research, the ability to make constructive contacts at senior levels in the customer organization, and tailoring the selling role and selling message to decision makers with differing interests and needs.

Despite this progress in recognizing the complexity of purchase decision making, sales management specialists tended to present the human interactions in selling and negotiation as an adversarial interface. Advice to sales professionals was (and often still is) centred on their personal communications and negotiations with the customer, and there was no discussion of the role of the salesperson's colleagues in building and maintaining relationships with customers. The approach of purchasing management specialists was equally flawed by a concentration on adversarial approaches.

As different supply chain relationship opportunities opened up in the late 1980s and early 1990s, the concept of the DMU soon became insufficient in helping selling companies achieve their objectives.

> Identifying and influencing all the people involved in the buying decision should be a mandatory selling activity.

> The approach of purchasing management specialists was equally flawed by a concentration on adversarial approaches.

### 12.1.2 Relationship marketing

Soon after the theory of the DMU was first promulgated, the Industrial Marketing and Purchasing Group (IMP) advocated the simultaneous analysis of buyer–seller relationships, an 'interactionist' approach. Their model highlighted the interaction process, participants, environment and atmosphere. Relationships were deemed to represent both a valuable resource and an investment, providing an effective information channel and serving to increase economic and technological efficiency and to reduce uncertainty.

The IMP's work was followed by the concept of relationship marketing. It contrasted traditional approaches to sales and marketing, which became known as the transactional focus, with the relationship focus which seemed more appropriate to the market conditions of the 1990s. Relationship marketing seemed to build on the quality movement in operations management by presenting an ideal based on building customer satisfaction through quality, service and value.

The transactional focus concentrated on single sales, product features, tactical campaigns, discontinuous customer contact, limited commitment and a view of customer service and quality as being the concern of specialist departments (Table 12.2). The relationship focus embraced customer retention as a deliberate strategy through continuous customer contact, delivering benefits, a long-term outlook, high commitment and an expectation that all staff would deliver service and quality. Strategic intent and shared internal values became part of the product and services offered.

**Table 12.2**
The different characteristics of transactional and relationship marketing

| Transactional focus | Relationship focus |
|---|---|
| Single sales | Lifetime value of a customer |
| Product features | Satisfaction of customer needs |
| Tactical promotional campaigns | Strategic marketing |
| Short-term reward structure | Varied reward structure |
| Only in contact with a customer during the sale | Continuous customer contact |
| Limited points of contact/influence | Contacts and influence from the boardroom to the shop-floor |
| Salesperson guards his or her access to the customer | Team approach to intercompany communications and activity |
| Limited commitment | Extensive commitment |
| Special department for 'after-sales service' | After-sales service involves the whole team |
| Quality is policed by quality control | Quality involves the whole team |

*Source*: Payne, 1993

There has been much debate about what circumstances made relationship marketing appropriate. In 1985, Barbara Jackson (as quoted in Kotler, 1997) argued that the investment was most worthwhile in industries where customers would have long-term horizons and high switching costs, such as buying capital equipment. Customers buying commodities might still be best served by a transactional approach.

In 1991, Anderson and Narus presented the idea that it was the nature of the individual customer that should be the deciding factor in relationship approaches as some customers value high service levels, brand values and long-term relationships with suppliers while others do not. When making buying decisions, some customers take into account more than just the price: time and hassle may be significant factors as well as a variety of benefits that could loosely be called 'value'.

Studies of the relationship between customer retention and lifetime profitability started to suggest that, where at all possible, a long-term approach was likely to deliver significant benefits to the selling company. The cost of attracting a new customer is estimated to be five times the cost of keeping a current customer happy. A study by Bain and Company (Reichheld, 1996) indicated that companies could improve profits anywhere from 25 to 85 per cent by reducing customer defections by 5 per cent (Figure 12.1).

> Companies could improve profits anywhere from 25 to 85 per cent by reducing customer defections by 5 per cent.

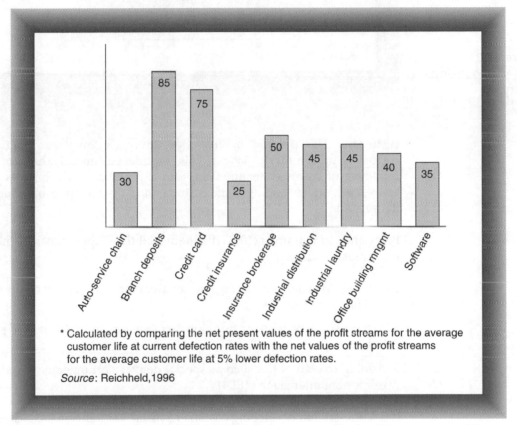

* Calculated by comparing the net present values of the profit streams for the average customer life at current defection rates with the net values of the profit streams for the average customer life at 5% lower defection rates.

*Source*: Reichheld, 1996

**Figure 12.1**   Reducing defections by 5 per cent boosts profits by 25 per cent to 85 per cent.

In the past, companies sought to erect exit barriers to deter customers from switching suppliers. Measures included loss of discounts and refusal to service multisupplier installations. Such negative reinforcement only served to ensure that customers who defected never returned. In contrast, relationship marketing seeks to retain customers by improving their satisfaction. It embraces all that companies do to understand valued customers and to improve their offerings to them.

> Negative reinforcement only served to ensure that customers who defected never returned.

The ideal is to convert prospects and customers to 'advocates' who praise the company and encourage others to buy from it. The relationship marketing ladder of customer loyalty shown in Figure 12.2 emphasizes the two main marketing tasks of attracting new customers and retaining existing

**Figure 12.2**
Ladder of customer loyalty.

*Source*: Payne, 1993

customers. The creation of customer advocates involves progressing customers up the loyalty ladder. This is achieved through the successful fulfilment of customer requirements and expectations, which necessitates an in-depth understanding of the customer and their relative importance to the supplier.

Berry and Parasuraman (1991) distinguished three approaches to enhancing customer value:

1. Adding financial benefits such as loyalty discounts, better credit terms and financial services.

2. Adding social benefits such as club membership, theatre trips and sports links.

3. Adding structural ties such as special delivery arrangements and electronic data interchange (EDI).

It is assumed that developing customer satisfaction delivers the customer's lifetime value. To calculate customer lifetime value, multiply the annual customer profitability (revenue less the costs to service that customer) by the number of years they are likely to need the product or service. In fact, customers tend to become increasingly profitable over time. Figure 12.3 demonstrates how customer retention contributed to increased profits in a number of service industries.

The benefits to be gained from better customer relationships were seen to vary by industry. In industry-to-industry markets where there are fewer and larger customers to be won and lost, the potential for developing partnerships with customers became a new focus of attention.

> In the 1990s, marketing was redefined as building and sustaining customer relationships.

Thus, in the 1990s, marketing was redefined as building and sustaining customer relationships. Analogies were drawn with courtship and marriage in order to emphasize that a fundamental element of the new

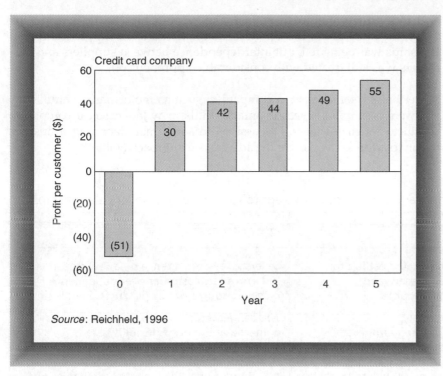

Source: Reichheld, 1996

**Figure 12.3**
How much profit a
customer generates
over time.

concept was ensuring long-term relationships with customers. A correlation between customer retention and profitability was seriously explored for the first time.

Relationship marketing can be clearly identified as a major breakthrough in terms of a marketing-led contribution to company prosperity. However, 30 years of growth markets meant that companies could get away with being production-led and technology-led. The difficult market conditions of the 1990s were going to force dramatic change.

## 12.2    The arrival of key account management

### 12.2.1    The KAM philosophy

Until recently, KAM was often dismissed or downgraded to key account selling and selling to major or national accounts. 'Account manager' has often been regarded as a euphemistic term for 'salesman'. However, some companies moved beyond sophisticated selling towards customer retention through integrated processes and enhanced value delivery. These 'partnership' arrangements became a benchmark for KAM best practice.

The belief that companies can best satisfy their customers by being tough on suppliers has declined in the last 10 years, although it persists in some industries. A few business analysts claim that US and UK business cultures are adversarial and there is not enough trust between organizations and individuals within them to make partnerships work. During the 1980s, the influence of the Japanese 'keiretsu' model of supply chain relationships was being felt, but interdependence between suppliers and customers was still treated with considerable apprehension.

| Some manufacturing industries began to address the risks of the adversarial approach. | Nevertheless, some Western companies, such as motor parts manufacturers, were beginning to see advantages in the way Japanese car companies conducted their business. Discussions in some manufacturing industries began to address the risks of the adversarial approach (Table 12.3). |

**Table 12.3** The risks inherent in the alternative approaches to buyer–seller relationships

| Adversarial | Interdependent |
| --- | --- |
| Sellers and buyers are constantly jostling for advantage and relationships between companies are inherently unstable. | Sellers' over-dependence on a few customers is mirrored by customer over-dependence on single source of key products/services |
| *This can lead to:* <br> ● Lack of trust resulting in frequent, costly supplier switching/customer churn <br> ● Unequal power relationships are exploited <br> ● Sellers and buyers have no chance to learn from each other or 'best practice' <br> ● Price is the main focus of attention, at the expense of value <br> ● Advances in technology may not be advances in fulfilling customer needs <br> ● Waste from duplicating technical skills <br> ● Purchasing skills cannot evolve <br> ● Tailored offerings are rarely available | *This can lead to:* <br> ● Inertia and lack of flexibility <br> ● Unequal power relationships are perpetuated <br> ● Influence over the way the companies are run is legitimized <br> ● Complacency on price <br> ● Technology may stagnate <br> ● Loss of independent skills in each company <br> ● Decline in purchasing expertise <br> ● Dedicated plant cannot be re-used |

Whether more sophisticated approaches were driven by exhortations from industry leaders about partnerships or by the practicalities of market conditions is debatable. In the 1980s models were developed both by marketing and purchasing academics (Ford, 1980; Dwyer *et al.*, 1987; Lamming, 1993) in order to explain the way in which relationships between particular buyers and sellers evolve over time. These models indicated that each exchange is not only affected by market considerations of price and the fit of the product/service to the need, but also by relational and process factors.

The relational development model of Millman and Wilson (1994) was explored in Cranfield research (McDonald *et al.*, 1996). Further quantitative research (McDonald and Woodburn, 1999) modified the concept of an evolution of relationships to an analogy with Maslow's (1943) hierarchy of needs, which was not dependent on time. The importance of recognizing different stages of relationship development is discussed in Chapter 3.

The extent to which a relationship between buyer and seller can develop will be dependent on anticipation of mutual benefit. As early as 1982 and 1986, academics had been working to develop ways of discerning different types of customers and their relative attractiveness to suppliers, and of determining the value of the selling company's capabilities as perceived by customers (Fiocca, 1982; Yorke, 1986). This would mean that 'key' customers could be defined and the relative strategic importance of any particular customer to the selling company could be identified.

Our research (Woodburn and McDonald, 2004) discovered that few companies were able to measure even the relative profitability of their accounts because most management accounting systems were unable to facilitate the allocation of costs to individual customers. However, many suppliers have become increasingly concerned about the profitability of their largest accounts, as mounting evidence has shown that they are often making a loss on them (see Chapter 6).

Nevertheless, there is growing evidence that partnership reduces costs. Up to 70 per cent of the costs in a company can be associated with supply chain issues, so there is plenty of opportunity for improvement and a need to focus on smart solutions. From a 1995 survey, Partnership Sourcing Limited (1996) reported that in 75 per cent of buyer–seller partnerships costs had been reduced and in 70 per cent quality had improved.

> There is growing evidence that partnership reduces costs.

## Case study insight

### Partnership from the viewpoint of buyers

In his report 'Constructing the team', Sir Michael Latham said that it is generally accepted in principle that partnering can deliver significant benefits to customer and supplier. Market research conducted by Galliford plc indicated that 75 per cent of purchasing professionals in the construction industry would agree that partnering is the future. As a response, Galliford developed a system specifically for managing construction projects on a partnership basis. The system incorporates a comprehensive set of performance measures. George March, chief executive of Galliford, commented that partnering had to be more than a philosophy; it had to be tangible, transparent, structured and measurable. (Anon., 1995)

Even after objective considerations of mutual benefit have been established, the potential for a 'partnership' KAM approach is still constrained by other factors. The receptivity of the customer to KAM is obviously paramount. The sophistication of purchasing practices may depend on:

- the degree to which the company has developed the purchasing function,
- the size of the company,

- the depth of change in the market, and

- the company's values.

Many chief executives talk about partnership, but in reality they are unwilling to undertake the investment and culture change it requires. Further, the selling company may not be equipped for integrating their processes with those of their customers. The strategic value of the product or service needed has to be taken into account along with the relative power of each party. A supplier may need to reconfigure an offering or the process by which it is delivered in order to improve its value.

Wilson and Croom-Morgan (1993) proposed a problem-centred model in order to assess whether the operational synergy possible at the highest levels of KAM/supplier partnership can be achieved. In addition to the product need, the selling company must address the process need: reducing the hassle factors inherent in incorporating their products/services into those of the buying company. Solutions such as just-in-time delivery, packaging and palleting, consignment stock management, EDI and sub-assembly have all been used to transform buyer–seller relationships from being transactional to being interdependent.

Wilson and Croom-Morgan (1993) also discussed ways in which the selling company can meet the 'facilitation need' of the buying company by being on-site or accessible by telephone or e-mail to help the customer use the product or service. In the Cranfield research (McDonald *et al.*, 1996) buying decision makers expressed strong preferences for 'suppliers who are easy to do business with'.

Closer relationships between buying and selling companies require a broader range of skills from those who are responsible for managing the value interchange. Consequently, sales representatives graduate to consultative selling to general business management. The origins of KAM may have been in sales, but companies now have key account managers reporting directly to general managers. The purchasing profession has also graduated from price negotiation to value delivery to strategic management.

> If there is an association ... between achieving short-term gain and career progression, win–lose scenarios will dominate thinking.

Each profession now has the opportunity to manage a variety of approaches to supply chain relationships and the risks inherent in them. However, the determination for achieving the benefits must be driven from the top of the organization and be reflected in the firm's systems, including reward and career development structures. If there is an association in the sales or purchasing professional's mind between achieving short-term gain and career progression, win–lose scenarios will dominate their thinking.

> Partnerships between unequals are unlikely or unstable.

The wide range of buyer–seller relationships is portrayed in Figure 12.4. At one end of the spectrum, there are big league global buying–selling dyads pursuing the leanest supply and achieving synergy and integration. Where power, risk and trust are in balance between buyer and seller,

Source: McDonald and Rogers, 1998

**Figure 12.4**
The spectrum of
buyer–seller
relationships.

partnerships of equals can be highly successful. Partnerships between unequals are unlikely or unstable (Krapfel, Salmond and Speckman, 1991), although some larger companies may emulate the Japanese model of 'benevolence through loyalty' in order to develop smaller suppliers.

At the other end of the spectrum, smaller players in smaller economies who may not be highly attractive or 'key' accounts to any of their suppliers are forced to adopt tactical approaches to supply chain issues in order to survive. In the middle of the relationship range there are moderate degrees of preference, including longer term contracts accompanied by some nervousness over single sourcing and/or over-reliance on a few customers.

The word 'partnership' has become rather discredited by overuse in inappropriate situations, but the essential philosophy is still very valuable when judiciously applied.

### 12.2.2   Driving forces

KAM in selling companies and partnership sourcing in buying companies are now well-established approaches to the management of value in the supply chain. They are not universally appropriate, but they have proved to be a considerable leap in progress. However, that progress has not been based solely on recognizing the objective benefits of a more cooperative business philosophy. Those benefits might have been realizable years ago. Instead, it is the way in which markets and economies have changed which has provided the driving forces for change.

As mentioned in Chapter 1, Cranfield produced a report called *Marketing, the Challenge of Change* (McDonald *et al.*, 1994) for the Chartered Institute of Marketing, which was commissioned in the light of criticism of the marketing department and what it delivered. The researchers identified that problems did indeed exist with the use of marketing as an add-on to selling. Such an approach was proving inadequate. Marketing as a philosophy was the driving force for industry leadership. However, it was not being embraced through altruism or a recognition of the genius of the gurus who recommended it, but because the business environment demanded it. The same factors were identified when researching the driving forces behind the trend towards KAM. These change drivers are:

- Rapid change

- Process refinement

- Market maturity

- Customer power

- Globalization.

The adversarial culture in the UK construction industry is believed to add 30 per cent to costs.

Partnership is perceived as being a worthy concept, which is difficult to attack, although people may argue about what it really means. All political parties in the UK have exhorted businesses to be more partnership oriented. Many politicians and senior civil servants believe that adversarial relationships between buying and selling companies are bad for overall industry competitiveness. For example, the adversarial culture in the UK construction industry between architects, contractors and subcontractors is believed to add 30 per cent to costs. Common sense dictates that the interests of all parties in a project are legitimate: unprofitable suppliers are risky and unprofitable customers are also very risky. Therefore, KAM and partnership sourcing are encouraged by expert opinion.

Governments have tried to encourage responsibility in supply chains by legislation designed to protect employees and customers. Throughout the USA and Western Europe legislation has become increasingly influential in supply chain management. For example, quality and traceability have been powerful reasons for partnerships in the manufacturing industry. It is certain that legislation will force the traceability issue wider and wider.

Globalization is a driving force for relationships.

Besides legislative imperatives, globalization is a driving force for relationships. Consumers around the world have more choice and lower prices. In industry-to-industry markets the opportunities for buying from anywhere for anywhere are almost universal, but providing a consistent

## Case study insight

### US employment law applies throughout the supply chain

In the USA, buyers have been put under legal as well as moral pressure not to buy from suppliers who violate US labour laws, whether they are based in the USA or other countries such as Latin America or Asia. A 50-year-old law holds buyers liable for suppliers' illegal labour practices. Raids in California revealed Thai refugees in barbed wire encampments producing goods for major department stores. It is not uncommon in the USA for the law to require companies to police their sources of supply, even when those sources are outside US borders. (Hancock, 1998) level of service worldwide to key accounts is a task selling companies still have to work very hard to fulfil. In the 1970s, the way most multinational companies operated resulted in the company logo being the only commonality between their geographical operations (and sometimes even that was altered). Opening up the boundaries of business has helped suppliers to realize the extent to which they can grow with their key customers if they are able to meet the challenges presented successfully. Going global may also, in the long term, be an opportunity for spreading risk.

In the past few years, different leagues of supply chain activity have been identified and these are outlined in Table 12.4. Companies with global scope want to deal with other companies with global scope and local companies tend to deal with others who know their cultural markets.

| League | Operational level |
|---|---|
| Premier League | Global |
| First Division | Regional |
| Second Division | National |
| Third Division | Local/niche |

**Table 12.4**
Leagues of supply chain activity

We know that global businesses represent approximately one-third of the private sector worldwide. The concentration of global buying companies seeking global selling companies in order to ensure consistency of supply worldwide means that it will be increasingly difficult for geographically restricted players to move up to the 'premier league' except via the minor element of 'benevolence through loyalty' in the system. That minor element could be critical to companies vying for promotion. The cost reductions that can be achieved through partnership will make the company more competitive and, therefore, better equipped for expanding to a larger geographical scale. Creation of alliances with more influential players in their supply chain will be an alternative route to league promotion for ambitious small companies.

End consumers still perceive variety and choice in the economy and most are still highly dependent on local companies and the public sector for a high proportion of their weekly spend. Global economies of scale are attractive in many industry segments, but global firms do not dominate every segment.

In the global premier league, an increasing number of opinion leaders come from the Far East. These new giants are mostly manufacturing companies whose distinctive competence is making things smaller, cheaper, faster and more reliable. Relationships between buying companies and selling companies are perceived to be part of the business culture of the Far East, and Japanese companies have influenced best practice around the world. Many award-winning US and European companies have adopted partnership sourcing. It is therefore easy to conclude that partnering relationships will become a mainstream concept in global business and demand KAM responses. Companies operating on a global scale need to transcend geographically narrow definitions of business culture and adopt best practice.

Partnership is an enduring theme of best practice and KAM complements it. The challenge for selling companies is to keep 'raising the bar' of account management achievement in order to realize business growth in the future.

### 12.2.3   Implementing key account management

Flagship selling companies have the following topics on their KAM agenda.

#### Monitoring and measurement of relationships

Research by Kearney and UMIST (in Nolan, 1996) has indicated that the foundation stone of improving performance in relationships with customers is monitoring and measurement. Each relationship must be measured at the transactional and process level and at the strategic level. Attention to detail is a quality attitude which is universally welcomed by customers and it helps in establishing an aura of integrity and professionalism.

#### Continuous and proactive improvement of products/services

Measurement is linked to continuous improvement of the product or service on which the company's identity is based. The best of professional relationships will not be able to survive deterioration in the competitive position of the selling company's core offering. In addition to continuous improvement, it is helpful to be the initiator of dramatic breakthroughs in technology or service delivery. Buying companies like to see their chosen suppliers acquire prestige alongside discovering better ways of fulfilling their needs.

#### Training and development of employees

The pioneering selling company must also invest in the training and development of the whole customer-focused team, not just the key account manager. Assigning multiple levels and functions for staff with objectives related to particular customers' needs will weave the philosophy of KAM into the whole fabric of the company.

#### Integration of processes and systems through collaborative associations with customers and other suppliers

One of the technical specialisms that the selling company needs to acquire is an understanding of processes, whole supply chains and transfer of value. All selling companies should consider how they might expand their scope of activities with customers. The customer may also require a supplier to work together with other key suppliers to solve a particular problem such as systems integration. Proactively presenting new, integrated solutions to customers would be even more attractive to them. Apart from anything else, it reduces the fear of monopoly associated with single sourcing if the single source is, in effect, a variety of consortia (perhaps but not necessarily with a common leadership).

## Case study insight

### Systems integration in the computer industry

Computer companies in the late 1980s/early 1990s had to migrate from promoting their proprietary systems in isolation to providing complete solutions for customers. This meant that they had to work together with other suppliers of information systems and services on what were usually called systems integration projects. In the first instance, they had to establish tactical alliances with companies who might in other circumstances be competitors, in order to gain mutual benefit from fulfilling a customer need. In some cases, these relationships developed into strategic alliances

## Summary

The concept of KAM has evolved from academic exploration of the DMU and relationship marketing. As a profession, KAM has become distinct from key account selling, encompassing the management of integrated processes with customers in order to deliver enhanced value. As KAM has developed, so has the purchasing professional. Partnership sourcing is a mirror-image concept complementary to KAM.

As discussed in Chapter 1, the future of relationships between companies in the same supply chains will depend on their mutuality in terms of understanding, interest, investment and commitment. From mutual benefit between two partners in a buyer–seller dyad, the future of KAM is destined to evolve into the value management of several companies in the supply chain, which will be in competition with other supply chains. The simplistic concept of buying and selling as being the buyer–seller transaction will be considered history and KAM and partnership sourcing will be seen as stepping-stones towards integrated value management.

# Further reading

## General

This is a list of publications and research reports from the authors which address numerous aspects of key account management. As we have drawn on them in several chapters they are noted here and not repeated in the additional references under each individual chapter.

McDonald, M. and Rogers, B. (1998). *Key Account Management – Learning from Supplier and Customer Perspectives*. Butterworth-Heinemann.

McDonald, M. and Woodburn, D. (1999). *Key Account Management – Building on Supplier and Customer Perspectives*. Financial Times Prentice Hall.

McDonald, M., Millman, A. and Rogers, B. (1996). *Key Account Management – Learning from Supplier and Customer Perspectives*. Cranfield School of Management Research Report, Cranfield University.

McDonald, M., Rogers, B. and Woodburn, D. (2000). *Key Customers: How to Manage Them Profitably*. Butterworth-Heinemann.

Woodburn, D. and McDonald, M. (2001). *Key Customers. World-leading Key Account Management: Identification and Development of Strategic Relationships*. Cranfield School of Management Research Report, Cranfield University.

Woodburn, D., Holt, S. and McDonald, M. (2004). *Key Customer Profitability – Making Money in Strategic Customer Partnerships*. Cranfield School of Management Research Report, Cranfield University.

## Chapter 1: The crucial role of key account management

Hancock, S. (1998). Fair's fair. *Purchasing and Supply Management* 5 November.

McDonald, M., Ryals, L., Dennison, T., Yallop, R. and Rogers, B. (1994). *Marketing, the Challenge of Change*. Cranfield University.

Porter, M.E. (1980). *Competitive Strategy*. The Free Press.

Porter, M.E. (1985). *Competitive Advantage: Creating and Sustaining Superior Performance*. The Free Press.

Wilson, C. (1998). *Profitable Customers: How to Identify, Develop and Keep Them*, 2nd edn. Kogan Page.

## Chapter 2: Selecting and categorizing key customers

Fiocca, R. (1982). Account portfolio analysis for strategy development. *Industrial Marketing Management* 11: 53–62.

Zolkiewski, J. and Turnbull, P. (2000). Relationship portfolios – past, present and future. *Proceedings of the 16th Annual IMP Conference*, University of Bath.

## Chapter 3: Relationship stages

Christopher, M. (2005). *Logistics and Supply Chain Management.* Prentice Hall.

Dunn, D.T. and Thomas, C.A. (1994). Partnering with customers. *Journal of Business Industrial Marketing* 9(1): 34–40.

Maslow, A.H. (1943). A theory of human motivation. *Psychological Review* 50(4): 370–96.

Millman, A.F. and Wilson, K. (1996). Developing key account management competences. *Journal of Marketing Practice: Applied Marketing Science* 2(2): 7–22.

Scott, C. and Westbrook, R. (1991). New strategic tools for supply chain in management. *International Journal of Physical Distribution and Logistics Management* 21(1): 23–33.

## Chapter 4: Developing key relationships

Dunn, D.T. and Thomas, C.A. (1994). Partnering with customers. *Journal of Business & Industrial Marketing* 9(1): 34–40.

Håkansson, H. and Snehota, I. (1995). Analysing business relationships, in Håkansson, H. and Snehota, I. (eds) *Developing Relationships in Business Networks.* Routledge, pp. 24–29.

Millman, A.F. and Wilson, K. (1996). Developing key account management competences. *Journal of Marketing Practice: Applied Marketing Science* 2(2): 7–22.

Morgan, R.M. and Hunt, S.D. (1994). The commitment-trust theory of relationship marketing. *Journal of Marketing* 58: 20–38.

Scott, C. and Westbrook, R. (1991). New strategic tools for supply chain management. *International Journal of Physical Distribution and Logistics Management* 21(1): 23–33.

## Chapter 5: The buyer perspective

Anderson, J.C., Hakansson, H. and Johanson J. (1994). Dyadic business relationships within a business network context. *Journal of Marketing* 58: 1–15.

Buzzell, R.D. and Gale, B.T. (1987). *The PIMS Principles: Linking Strategy to Performance.* The Free Press.

Ellram, L.E. (1991). Supply chain management. *International Journal of Physical Distribution and Logistics Management* 21(1): 13–22.

Krapfel, R.E., Salmond, D. and Spekman, R. (1991). A strategic approach to buyer–seller relationships. *European Journal of Marketing* 25(9): 22–37.

Millman, A.F. and Wilson, K.J. (1994). From key account selling to key account management. In *Tenth Annual Conference on Industrial Marketing and Purchasing.*

Olsen, R.F. and Ellram, L. (1997). A portfolio approach to supplier relationships. *Industrial Marketing Management* 26: 101–13.

Perrien, J., Ricard, L. and Landry, C. (1999). *Proceedings of the Ninth Biennial World Marketing Congress.* Sage Publications.

Porter, M.E. (1985) *Competitive Advantage: Creating and Sustaining Superior Performance.* The Free Press.

Turnbull, P.W. and Valla, J.P. (1986). *Strategies for International Industrial Marketing.* Croom Helm.

Williamson, O.E. (1985). *The Economic Institution of Capitalism: Firms, Markets, Relational Contracting.* The Free Press.

## Chapter 6: Key account profitability

Davidson, H. (1998). *Even More Offensive Marketing.* Penguin.

Haigh, D. (2005). Brand finance. *Marketing Magazine* 1 April.

Millman, A.F. and Wilson, K.J. (1994). From key account selling to key account management. In *Tenth Annual Conference on Industrial Marketing and Purchasing*.

Pascale, R.T. (1990). *Managing on the Edge: How Successful Companies use Conflict to Stay Ahead*. Viking.

Peters, T.J. and Waterman Jr, R.H. (1982). *In Search of Excellence: Lessons from America's Best-Run Companies*. Harper & Row.

Reichheld, F.R. (1994). Loyalty and the renaissance of © marketing. *Marketing Management* 12(4): 17.

Reichheld, F.R. and Sasser Jr, W.E. (1990). Zero defections: quality comes to services. *Harvard Business Review* September–October, 105–11.

Ryals, L. (2002). Key account profitability. PhD thesis, Cranfield University.

Storbacka, K., Sivula, P. and Kaario, K. (2000). A strategic perspective on the most valuable customers. *Velocity* Q2.

Wilson, C. (1998). *Profitable Customers: How to Identify, Develop and Keep Them*, 2nd edn. Kogan Page.

## Chapter 7: Key account analysis

McDonald, M. (2007). *Marketing Plans: How to Prepare Them, How to Use Them*, 6th edn. Butterworth-Heinemann.

Porter, M.E. (1980). *Competitive Strategy*. The Free Press.

Robinson, J., Farris, C.W. and Wind, Y. (1967). *Industrial Buying and Creative Marketing*. Allyn & Bacon.

## Chapter 8: Planning for key accounts

McDonald, M. (2003). *Marketing Plans: How to Prepare Them, How to Use Them*, 7th edn. Butterworth-Heinemann.

Millman, A.F. and Wilson, K.J. (1994). From key account selling to key account management. In *Tenth Annual Conference on Industrial Marketing and Purchasing*.

Pascale, R.T. (1990). *Managing on the Edge: How Successful Companies Use Conflict to Stay Ahead*. Viking.

Peters, T.J. and Waterman Jr, R.H. (1982). *In Search of Excellence: Lessons from America's Best-Run Companies*. Harper & Row.

## Chapter 9: Achieving with processes

Bonoma, T. (1985). *The Marketing Edge: Making Strategies Work*. The Free Press.

Holt, S. (2003). The role of the global account manager: a boundary role theory perspective. PhD thesis, Cranfield University.

## Chapter 10: The role and requirements of key account managers

Canon-Bowers, J.A., Salas, E. and Converse, S. (1993). Shared mental models in expert decision making teams, in Castellan, Jr, N.J. (ed.) *Current Issues in Individual and Group Decision Making*. Erlbaum, pp. 221–46.

Deeter-Schmelz, D.R. and Ramsey, R. (1995). A conceptualization of the functions and roles of formalized selling and buying teams. *Journal of Personal Selling and Sales Management* 15(2): 47–60.

Glassop, L. (2002). The organizational benefits of teams. *Human Relations* 55(2): 225–49.

Hackman, J.R. (2002). *Leading Teams: Setting the Stage for Great Performances*. Harvard Business School Press.

Holt, S. (2003). The role of the global account manager: a boundary role theory perspective. PhD thesis, Cranfield University.

Homburg, C., Workman, Jr, J.P. and Jensen, O. (2002). A configurational perspective on key account management. *Journal of Marketing* 66 (April): 38–60l.

## Chapter 11: Organizing for key account management

Buzzell, R.D. (1985). *Citibank: Marketing to Multinational Customers*. Harvard Business School.

Homburg, C., Workman, Jr, J.P. and Jensen, O. (2000). Fundamental changes in marketing organization: the movement toward a customer-focused organizational structure. *Journal of the Academy of Marketing Science* 28(4): 459–78.

Jones, E., Chonko, L. and Cannon, J. (2005) Key accounts and team selling. *Journal of Personal Selling & Sales Management* 25(2): 182–198.

Yip, G.S. and Madsen, T.L. (1996). Global account management: the new frontier in relationship marketing. *International Marketing Review* 13(3): 24–42.

## Chapter 12: Origins of key account management

Anderson, J.C. and Narus, J.A. (1991). Partnering as a focused market strategy. *California Management Review* Spring, 95–113.

Anon. (1995). Galliford puts partnering into practice. *Purchasing and Supply Management*, October.

Berry, L.L. and Parasuraman, A. (1991). *Marketing Services: Competing Through Quality*. The Free Press.

Christopher, M.G., Payne, A.F.T. and Ballantyne, D.F. (1991). *Relationship Marketing: Bringing Quality, Customer Service and Marketing Together*. Butterworth-Heinemann.

Drucker, P.F. (1955). *The Practice of Management*. Heron Books.

Dwyer, F.R., Schurr, P.H. and Oh, S. (1987). Developing buyer–seller relations. *Journal of Marketing* 5: 11–27.

Fiocca, R. (1982). Account portfolio analysis for strategy development. *Industrial Marketing Management* 11: 53–62.

Ford, D. (1980). The development of buyer–seller relationships in industrial markets. *European Journal of Marketing* 14(5/6): 339–53.

Hancock, S. (1998). Fair's fair. *Supply Management* 5 November.

Kotler, P. (1997). *Marketing Management*. Prentice Hall.

Lamming, R. (1993). *Beyond Partnership: Strategies for Innovation and Lean Supply*. Prentice Hall.

Maslow, A.H. (1943). A theory of human motivation. *Psychological Review* 50(4): 370–96.

McDonald, M., Ryals, L., Dennison, T., Yallop, R. and Rogers, B. (1994). *Marketing, the Challenge of Change*. Cranfield University.

Millman, A.F. (1993). The emerging concept of relationship marketing. *Ninth Annual Conference on Industrial Marketing and Purchasing*, Bath, UK, September.

Millman, A.F. and Wilson, K.J. (1994). From key account selling to key account management. In *Tenth Annual Conference on Industrial Marketing and Purchasing*.

Nolan, A. (1996). Purchasing failure costs £2.4 bn. *Supply Management* 14 March.

Partnership Sourcing Limited. (1996). Can David and Goliath patch things up? *Purchasing*, February.

Payne, A.F.T. (1993). *The Essence of Services Marketing*. Prentice Hall.

Payne, A.F.T. (ed.) (1995). *Advances in Relationship Marketing*. Kogan Page.

Reichheld, F.R. (1996). *The Loyalty Effect*. Harvard Business Press.

Robinson, P.J., Farris, C.W. and Wind, Y. (1967). *Industrial Buying and Creative Marketing*. Allyn & Bacon.

Sewell, C. and Brown, P. (1990). *Customers for Life*. Pocket Books.

Unger, H.G. (1995). Foreign sweatshops may cost US buyers dearly. *Purchasing and Supply Management*, December.

Wilson, K.J. and Croom-Morgan, S.R. (1993). A problem-centred approach to buyer–seller interaction. Conference on Industrial Marketing and Purchasing (IMP), University of Bath, September.

Yorke, D. (1986). The application of customer portfolio theory to business markets – a review. In *Third Annual Conference on Industrial Marketing and Purchasing*.

# Integrated fast track

For those who want to start or finish with the complete helicopter overview, we have compiled all the 'Fast tracks' of the essentials of each chapter into this rapid reprise of the content of the entire book. However, to understand more, or to find out what to do about these issues, you will need to read the chapters themselves.

## The crucial role of key account management                    CHAPTER 1

For a decade, the authors have been researching global best practice in the domain of account management, sponsored by many of the world's leading companies. The following topics in particular have been the focus of our research:

- **Key account selection:** Only a few selected customers can be included in the key account programme.

- **Classification of key accounts:** Derogatory labels like A, B, C, or gold, silver, bronze should be avoided at all cost.

- **Key account profitability:** The power of customers and their increased purchasing power has led to greater demands on the services of their suppliers. Unfortunately, many traditional accounting systems are incapable of accurately capturing all of the associated costs of dealing with major customers. Consequently, many suppliers are acting in ignorance of which customers make or lose them money.

- **Key account needs analysis:** A deep understanding of the customer's business is essential to success.

- **Strategic planning for key accounts:** Just as a three- to five-year strategy is essential for any business, so strategic plans for selected customers, signed off by the customers themselves, are also critical to success.

- **Roles and skills of key account managers:** Selling and negotiation skills are no longer sufficient on their own.

- **Other issues:** Information technology, organization structure and internal marketing all contribute to creating successful key account programmes.

The challenges that all organizations face today are:

- **Market maturity:** In most sectors, mature markets have transferred power from suppliers to customers, as suppliers compete for a share of a decreasing number of customers.

- **Globalization:** Market maturity has led to an increasing number of industries in which only a handful of truly global companies dominate the landscape. Hence, any supplier who cannot offer a seamless service in every part of the world where the customer operates, will not win the business.

- **Customer power:** With this new-found power, customers are increasingly looking to selected suppliers to give them competitive advantage by product and process development.

All these developments mean that suppliers have to be much more stringent in their key account selection criteria. They must allocate their scarce resources intelligently across their customer base, taking account of the risks associated with different kinds of customers in order to build continuous shareholder value added.

## CHAPTER 2     Selecting and categorizing key customers

Choosing the customers that your company wants to treat as key accounts ought not to be too hard, certainly when compared with some of the difficult cultural and structural issues that arise from key account management. However, many companies approach the task in a rather casual fashion first time around, and only later realize how many onward decisions are driven by their selection of key customers, and how awkward it may be to unpick inappropriate choices.

The key customers you  seek should be those that are aligned to your corporate strategy and will therefore make a major contribution to its achievement. If they do not, who will? So your portfolio of key accounts should contain these customers, and only these customers. If you dilute it with customers with dissimilar agendas, which will not respond particularly favourably to your strategies, you will be unable to demonstrate sufficiently positive results from the key account management programme, and you risk sinking the whole initiative. Undoubtedly, there will be pressures to include unsuitable accounts, but they must be resisted. Counter such pressures by adopting an objective criteria-based process, and applying it rigorously.

Whatever the size of the organization, there seems to be an almost universally appropriate number of key accounts, which is probably between 15 and 35, with 5 and 50 as the outer limits. Certainly, anything with three digits is too many. In fact, the process of selection and categorization starts with deciding, more or less, how many key accounts your company can handle.

The identity of the customer deserves careful attention. It not only determines how the customer will score against the criteria, and hence how much resource it should receive, but it also has implications about how it should be managed. Customers should be identified in their terms, not carved up according to the supplier's structure, unless it is well matched with the customer's.

Selection criteria should be chosen and their importance weighted by a senior management group, and then rolled out to be scored to people who know the customer. These criteria are applied to assess the customer's attractiveness to your company, and the data are then used on the vertical axis of the key account selection/categorization matrix to build a picture of your portfolio of customers.

To complete the picture, you need the customer's view of you as a supplier, in their terms. Obviously, that will be different for each customer, and you must resist the urge to apply a standard set of criteria on the horizontal axis. If you did that, it would only be a reflection of what you think of yourselves, and would not represent their views and differences at all. You would also, in effect, be saying that these customers are all the same and all want the same things, which is contrary to the whole philosophy of key account management, apart from being patently untrue.

The matrix identifies four kinds of key customers, to which it is appropriate to offer four generic strategies that should guide the specific strategies that are developed for each customer individually:

1. Star key customers – investment for growth

2. Strategic key customers – strategic investment

3. Status key customers – proactive maintenance

4. Streamline key customers – management for cash.

The systematic assessment approach described in this chapter enables suppliers to build a portfolio view of their customers that drives many further insights, decisions and expectations about them, which is much more realistic and powerful than the key customer lists that many suppliers use. We will refer to it frequently in the rest of this book.

## CHAPTER 3 — Relationship stages

Key account management (KAM) is very much concerned with managing the relationship with the customer, but remember that the relationship is a means to an end, that is, business development and not an end in itself. Nevertheless, it is important to understand these relationships, which vary from simple, transactional forms to intimate and complex liaisons. There is a distinct hierarchy of relationship levels which describes the progression from the simple trading stage right up to a configuration that is only a short step away from a merger. Whatever level of relationship is reached, the requirements for efficient fulfilment of basic transactions remains, although a good relationship might allow a greater period of tolerance and assistance with poor performance than a simple, easy-to-exit relationship. Ultimately, however, a customer will have to buy from the supplier who gives them the offer they need, however good the relationship.

Both the key account manager and the supplier organization need to know what kind of relationship they have with each customer, and therefore what they can and cannot do with it. Suppliers generally have delusions of intimacy with the customer, and believe that they are one stage closer than the customer does. Since the essence of a relationship is reciprocation, then the supplier can only work with the level of relationship that both parties agree on.

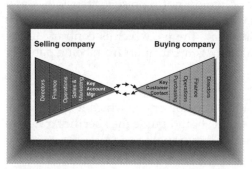

### Exploratory relationships

Suppliers need to recognize potential key accounts from the outset and treat them as such. The bigger the customer, the longer it takes. Be prepared to be patient and manage internal expectations. Monitor the signals sent out rigorously.

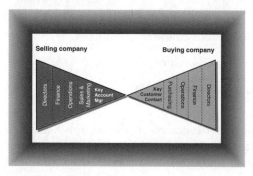

### Basic relationships

This simple, transactional relationship has benefits of efficiency, clarity and resource control alongside its disadvantages of vulnerability to competition, fragility to change, potential for bias, limited understanding of each other and limited opportunity.

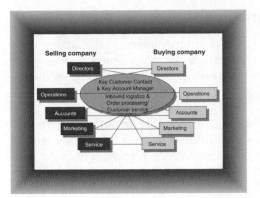

## Cooperative relationships

To be regarded as a transitional stage, this stage is hard to control and likely to be losing money. It may be a necessary rite of passage, but not a stage to prolong. Key account managers are still 'out in the cold' and 'in the dark', and the supplier is not yet trusted, so the more positive feel has yet to be translated into real advantage.

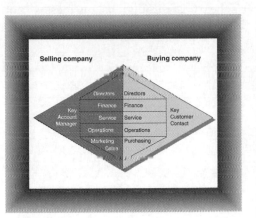

## Interdependent relationships

This is the stage to which suppliers developing KAM normally aspire with the right kind of customer. These relationships involve trust, much more exchange of information, proactive strategies based on a much deeper understanding of the customer and opportunities for joint strategic planning leading to substantial business growth.

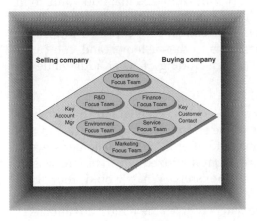

## Integrated relationships

These relationships are just short of a merger. Boundaries between the two companies are dissolved, since a high degree of trust eliminates the need for protection. *Integrated* relationships are few in number because they take a lot of dedicated resource, are not easy to put together, and tend to repel other customers in the same marketplace.

Even close relationships do not necessarily last forever, although there are some that have worked for decades. Disintegration may be driven by changes in the ownership or market position of either company, or by the supplier's failure to develop the relationship. Ultimately, the supplier has to be able to offer the customer what it wants, so a relationship, however good, cannot compensate if the supplier's product or service fails to meet the customer's needs.

**CHAPTER 4**       **Developing key relationships**

Most companies embarking on key account management (KAM) are hoping to develop their customer relationships. We hope you will do so having first decided, very carefully, which ones are suitable for development – because some are not.

But what does deciding to develop a relationship mean? How do you know where to start? Charm has very limited leverage in corporate purchasing today and, indeed, the procurement department will make sure that it does not count for much. If you want to be a key supplier, much more tangible value is expected.

In fact, the way to a customer's heart is through its business – not your business. As a minimum, the customer expects its key suppliers to understand:

- Its marketplace
- Its strategies
- What its customers want
- How it adds value in its business
- Where it makes its money.

There are no shortcuts that are likely to last, so Chapters 7 and 8 give you a systematic process to gain the deep customer understanding you need, plus a process to help you come up with strategies that add value to the customer's business. Added value (for the customer, not necessarily for you) is what gains commitment. Your company is expected to bring an on-going stream of value propositions to the customer, and you cannot possibly do that without a real understanding of what adds value and why, where and when.

Customers classify suppliers according to the potential they have to bring value to their business, in terms of the supply-side market risk and their purchasing power. If what you have to offer is, in the customer's eyes, a commodity product delivered in a commoditized way, you are wasting your time trying to build a relationship. What would they gain? Customers, like suppliers, have a limited capacity for intimacy, and they will use what capacity they have where it gives them most advantage.

Given a strong foundation of customer understanding, relationship development can be accelerated through doing a good job of mapping the people inside the customer who matter to you, and deciding with whom you want to have your relationships. You should also decide who, in your organization, will be the 'owner' of that relationship – no key account manager can or should 'own' them all. Rather, it is the key account manager's job to encourage and build a balanced set of relationships from top to bottom of both organizations, supporting the supplier's staff in working out strategies to help their counterparts in the customer organization. Rather than responding to purely personal needs, ideally, they will be adding value to the contact's working life and area of the business, which is a more robust way to build a relationship anyway.

Many people seem to believe that relationships 'just grow', but if you have good business development strategies and adopt a process of applying them through good relationship development strategies, you should really be a winner with your customers. Try picking the features of an *interdependent* relationship and working on those alongside your business development strategies. The synergistic effect of the two together should give the relationship and its outcomes some real acceleration. Having achieved the relationship your company wants, there are a few traps to be avoided. They may seem obvious when simply stated but, sadly, they appear quite frequently:

- complacency
- lapses in integrity
- leaking profitability.

Relationships with key customers can and should be developed with purpose and with process (see Chapter 9). These relationships are too valuable and too risky to leave to any less focused approach.

## The buyer perspective                                   CHAPTER 5

As buying companies seek new routes to competitive advantage and value for their customers, they now look to key suppliers to help them. Naturally, customers are far more likely to act according to their own perceptions and aspirations than to any view or objective that selling companies might wish to impose on them. A buying company has its own set of strategic decision support tools to help it select the suppliers who are important to the fulfilment of its aspirations.

First, a selling company needs to understand whether it has the opportunity of being a key supplier. The chances are small if it is one of many competitors, or it is in a weak position relative to the customer, or it supplies a product or service which does not contribute to the customer's critical path. If analysis reveals that this is the selling company's situation with this customer, the supplier should look elsewhere for its own key relationships or possibly reposition itself through developing its offer. It should not waste money and effort on trying to develop a relationship that is unlikely to succeed and bear fruit.

At the same time, the supplier should decide what this customer can contribute to its own strategic objectives, using the methods described in the following chapters. These methods require an in-depth understanding of the customer's situation, needs and strategies and, indeed, successful key account managers are those who really know how their customers operate and why.

Generally speaking, only if buyer and seller strategies are complementary in terms of products, their approach to business and to the relationship between them will it be possible to develop the relationship beyond a fairly simple level towards an interdependent or integrated stage. However, if all these elements are in place and closer involvement is achieved, the flow of benefits to both parties can be very exciting.

At less-developed stages of the relationship the cost of nurturing the relationship can easily outweigh the benefits. The range and extent of cost savings increase on both sides as trust between the two parties grows and barriers are reduced. In some situations, reducing risk by working with a known partner can allow costs to be cut, for example by eliminating duplication of processes. In other situations, reduction of costs may increase risk, for example by moving to just-in-time supply and eliminating buffer stocks. Clearly, reduction of costs and reduction of risks are closely linked and need to be managed jointly from a foundation of a thorough understanding of the partner and its concerns.

Trust is a mediator through which most interactions pass and activities will be interpreted. Care should be taken to manage the partner's perceptions, as reserves of trust may be crucial in carrying a supplier through any difficult patches in performance or in the relationship. In the end, powerful customers still call the shots.

## CHAPTER 6  Key account profitability

Marketing as a discipline has failed during the past 50 years by concentrating on promotion rather than on developing world-class marketing strategies. The result is that in most companies, marketing has been relegated to running promotional campaigns and designing T-shirts and does not deserve a place at the high table, that is, the board of directors.

The result of this sad lack of marketing leadership is the demise of many of our erstwhile famous organizations. Most of the highest earning Return on Investment plcs during the decade up to 1990 have gone into liquidation or were acquired in desperate circumstances, whilst many of the leading companies in different sectors up to the year 2000 also got into financial difficulties or were acquired.

All of this happened against a background of three major challenges that industry was facing during this period and still faces – market maturity, globalization and customer power.

The most dramatic challenge has been the massive shift of power to customers away from suppliers. Today, customers are destroying old make/sell business models, whilst technology has empowered customers to have more information about their suppliers than they have about them. Meanwhile, a new wave of business metrics and new pressures from institutional shareholders to report meaningful facts about corporate performance, combined with demands from other stakeholders for exemplary corporate behaviour, have resulted in a need for strategies other than downsizing and cost-cutting as a route to increased profitability.

Never before has the need for real marketing professionalism in relation to key account management been greater.

This raises the question of what marketing is. It is a function, just like finance, with its own professional institute and body of knowledge. The challenge is to understand the needs of customers, then to formulate strategies for meeting these needs in a way that enables the company to create long-term net free cash flows which, having taken account of the associated risks, represent a financial return over and above the cost of capital, thus creating shareholder value. This strategic imperative is quantitatively measurable using the body of existing marketing knowledge and CEOs must demand of their chief marketing officers that their strategic forecasts for their key account performances are subjected to the same rigorous due diligence as other initiatives, such as acquisitions.

Some key accounts will inevitably reduce shareholder value, but providing these are managed to increase net free cash flows and to reduce risk, this is acceptable. Overall, as long as the aggregate of the net forecast value from all key accounts is positive, having taken account of the risks and the cost of capital tied up in servicing them, then it is possible to prove to the Board and to shareholders that the key account performance is creating shareholder value continuously.

## Key account analysis                    CHAPTER 7

Correct market definition and market segmentation are essential prerequisites of successful key account management. A market is the aggregation of all goods and services that can satisfy a particular need or set of needs. Drawing a map of how goods and services flow through the value chain helps a key account manager understand the customer's business, as well as revealing ways in which you may be able to add value as a supplier.

Market segmentation is the process of breaking a market down into smaller groups of customers who share the same or similar needs. It is important at two distinct levels. First, key accounts in one segment may have different needs from those in another segment. Second, understanding how your customer's market is segmented provides much potential for helping them to succeed.

The total process of preplanning prior to producing a strategic plan for your customer is shown in the following diagram.

Steps 1, 2, and 3 should, ideally, be completed centrally to avoid duplication of effort by key account managers. Step 3 is about understanding in depth the forces that are being brought to bear on competitors in an industry. These are: customers, supplies, substitutes, potential entrants and, of course, industry competitors. A PEST analysis (political, economic, sociological, technological) is also an extremely useful way of understanding more about the customer's trading environment.

Each key account manager can now use this information to delve further into each customer's specific business processes. This includes understanding the customer's objectives and strategies, their financial ratios, how their business processes work, their buying processes, their sales history and their dealings with competitors.

One extremely useful vehicle for summarizing much of this is the traditional SWOT analysis (strengths, weaknesses, opportunities and threats), completed as if it were the customers themselves completing it.

All the CSFs (critical success factors) for the customer can now be sorted into those categories that merely help them to avoid disadvantage and, crucially, those that can create advantage for them, for clearly it is this latter group that will encourage a key customer to prefer dealing with you rather than with one of your competitors. You now have everything you need to approach the customer with your proposals for how you can help them increase sales, reduce costs, avoid costs or add value in other ways. They are usually so impressed that they are prepared to give you additional confidential information. You are now ready to prepare a strategic plan for the customers.

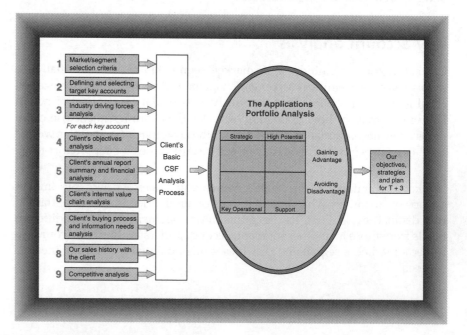

# Planning for key accounts

**CHAPTER 8**

Marketing planning is a logical sequence of events leading to the setting of marketing objectives and the formulation of plans for achieving them. The sequence is:

1. Mission statement
2. Set corporate objectives
3. Conduct marketing object
4. Conduct SWOT (strengths, weaknesses, opportunities and threats) analyses
5. Make assumptions
6. Set marketing objectives and strategies
7. Estimate expected results
8. Identify alternative plans and mixes
9. Set the budget
10. Establish first-year implementation programmes

The plan itself contains:

1. Mission statement
2. Financial summary
3. Market overview
4. SWOT analyses
5. Portfolio summary
6. Assumptions
7. Marketing objectives and strategies
8. Forecasts and budgets

All companies need to have a longer term (strategic) marketing view as well as a short-term (tactical) marketing operation. Often the most potent short-term tactic is the use of the salesforce. These can combine as shown in the matrix (left).

From this it can be seen that being good at implementation of the wrong strategy can lead to a very quick death!

Exactly the same philosophy must be applied to planning for key accounts, as sophisticated customers will only build integrated relationships with suppliers who understand this business and can help them to increase sales, reduce costs, avoid costs and create value for them on a continuous basis. As this involves committing resources to such suppliers, they insist on well-researched strategic plans which are agreed jointly.

Even in cases where suppliers do not enjoy integrated relationships, it is still essential to prepare strategic plans designed to capture the inherent value planned for customers.

In this chapter a template is provided for preparing a strategic plan for a key account. Finally, a format used by customers for preparing strategies for their key suppliers is provided.

## CHAPTER 9     Processes – making key account management work

Today, the delivery of superior customer value is as much about a company's business processes as it is about the core product or service, and yet implementation gets nothing like as much attention as it needs. If something has to be done more than once, and almost everything does recur, then there should be a process for doing it. A process can even be mapped for relationship development and, indeed, relationships might develop a lot faster if such a process were followed.

A process may be defined as 'A continuous and systematic series of actions performed in a definite manner directed to some end'. It should represent the most effective and efficient route to converting inputs into outputs. Suppliers' processes are generally designed to deliver to many customers in a standardized, replicable manner, which is good for costs but often not good for key accounts. Start by 'auditing' your processes to see which perform well for key accounts and which, from their point of view, are too slow, inflexible, unreliable, opaque, uninformative, uncosted and unsuitable for integration with the customer's processes.

While, at first sight, you may think that there are only a limited number of processes which impact on key customers, on closer examination you will see that there are far more. They can be divided into:

- **strategic** processes that involve senior management, to which key account managers contribute,

- **strategy realization** processes that add value to the supplier and customer through realizing the agreed strategy, with which the key account manager spends most of his or her time,

- **operational/transactional** processes concerned with the delivery of what has been promised.

The key account manager plays a different role in each and has different levels of 'ownership' of the process. For example, key account managers need to understand operational processes and be alerted to deviations from expectations, but should not be part of the daily machinery or they will never do anything else.

Each process should be broken down into its component steps, and the role of the key account manager and others identified at each stage. This exercise demonstrates how the process works, and also builds up a picture of what their job should be.

Senior management is responsible for a number of processes in successful key account management, and if they are not aware of that at the outset, the requirement and the means to fulfil them should be identified for them at an early stage. The key account manager's role is mostly provision of information to these processes, so he or she needs to be aware of them, how they work, and what should be contributed. The strategic processes include:

- Selecting attractiveness criteria and key customers
- Managing the customer portfolio
- Considering implications of customer strategies
- Incorporating account plans in business planning
- Allocating/prioritizing resources
- Assessing and managing risk to the company
- Sponsoring key customers
- Coordinating across boundaries
- Enabling organizational learning.

Key account managers have another set of processes with which to work. 'Developing' occurs frequently in this list, because their job is to add value to both organizations by managing change:

- Analysing key accounts, developing strategy and planning
- Developing relationships with customers
- Developing business, capturing opportunities
- Selling and negotiating
- Pricing
- Developing new products
- Customizing products and service
- Managing the product mix
- Developing marketing programmes
- Developing the supply chain
- Developing transaction handling

- Providing customer training
- Developing internal relationships
- Providing information.

Below is a simplified list of operational processes, which run day in, day out. Key account managers, whether they like it or not, are held responsible by the customer for the delivery of what they have promised, so they need a process of two-way communication with operations by which they can brief operations with information they get from the customer, and operations can brief them as appropriate, about good and poor performance.

- Selling
- Processing orders
- Manufacturing/operations
- Servicing customers
- Delivering to customers
- Collecting payment.

A good deal of sales activity belongs at this operational/transactional level, and may be carried out by the field salesforce or telesales, rather than the key account manager.

Measurement should be fit for purpose: it does not come free. Measurement is closely related to processes and is often about processes, so it fits alongside them at the three layers of the company identified earlier:

- **Strategy:** Measurement of profit to support making the right strategic decisions.
- **Strategy realization:** Measurement of value and progress to support the alignment of implementation with strategy, including the 'amount' of key account management (KAM) invested in the customer.
- **Operational/transactional:** Measurement of cost and performance to support improvements in efficiency and productivity.

Key customers in different categories, treated to different strategies, should clearly be measured differently. Performance objectives should reflect these different expectations.

## CHAPTER 10     The role and requirements of key account managers

In order to determine the role of key account managers, suppliers first need to ask themselves what they intend the role of key account management (KAM) itself to be. That should decide what its 'agents', the key account managers, have to do. The objectives for KAM and the route to achieving them should be worked out in some detail.

Normally, the prime driver will be the marketplace and leading customers in it, so the company should have a view on how KAM will work from their point of view. Specifying the role that KAM plays in the supplier's strategy is of the greatest importance, and one often underestimated or misunderstood. Initially, KAM is about making reciprocated commitments to customers, but that quickly needs to be followed by fulfilment of those commitments, so companies should anticipate the issues in operations and adapt. In fact, they will find that adaptation means changing the organization and culture, as well as plans and processes.

The question then arises of 'who does what?' Obviously, key account managers are responsible for a great deal of the activity, but the company is also responsible for supporting them, by providing resources, communicating organization-wide, tackling barriers and making decisions that are beyond the remit of the individual.

The scope of the KAM initiative will highlight the breadth of the key account manager's role. At the simplest level, the key account manager has two roles: *implementation* of a business strategy with the customer, and *facilitation* of that implementation through building the relationship. The relationship is not an end in itself, but should be employed to create and implement strategies that will develop business with the customer. These two roles go hand-in-hand: success requires both.

Exactly how the key account manager plays these roles depends on the nature of the customer and the overall strategy allotted to it. *Streamline* customers allocated a 'manage for cash' strategy should receive different treatment from *strategic* or *star* customers, so the key account manager's role must be adjusted accordingly. The first require a tough negotiator who will need to manage costs and operations rigorously, while the latter require someone to create a vision of the future and work to make it happen.

The key account team, however, can take on part of the role. The team can apply its expertise to fulfil some elements, though some, like team leadership, cannot be separated from the key account manager. Unfortunately, key account managers' experience of team-working is often very limited, and they make poor team leaders unless they receive proper training and support for this part of their role. To make matters worse, the members of the account team normally do not report directly to the key account manager, but still remain within their function or region. Nevertheless, the key account team should be an on-going group of people committed to the same objectives for the customer's business, not a project team or other transient group of people. Important customers expect team support and increasingly are getting it from suppliers.

Generally, there are two key account teams that exist simultaneously: the head office, cross-functional team, which is concerned with current delivery of commitments to the customer and also with how to adapt and develop new value; and the regional sales team, which supports customer strategic business units (SBUs) in the field and applies the deals agreed centrally.

Such a broad role demands a wide range of competencies and attributes. Regrettably, in many cases, suppliers have automatically appointed senior salespeople to the role without considering the competencies needed, and then found later that a substantial proportion of them do not have and are unable to acquire them. Indeed, 'selling' is a comparatively minor part of the role, and not one that should be used exclusively for determining the right people for the job.

To make appropriate appointments, suppliers should ideally start by establishing an 'inventory' of their key customers, categorized into four types according to the strategy selected for them. Clearly, customers should be managed by a key account manager who is suited to applying the strategy selected for each of them, i.e. an 'entrepreneur', 'business manager', 'customer manager' or 'tactician'. Once the supplier has assembled its customer inventory, it can see how many of each of four types of key account manager are needed.

Different competencies and attributes are demanded by each of these roles, although they also have some in common. Competencies are defined as behaviours required to achieve high levels of performance, whereas attributes are more about the way people think and the values they hold, though they also affect behaviour. Attributes are harder to learn and to change. The competencies and attributes that relate to each of the four roles have been worked out, so that individuals can be profiled and matched to the role they would perform best. Such an approach can be used as a foundation for a conversation with the key account manager to discuss how he or she can develop to achieve personal and organizational objectives, now and in the future.

## CHAPTER 11    Organizing for key account management

Key account management (KAM) is essentially a boundary-crossing initiative. Many of the benefits accrue from crossing boundaries, whether they are internal ones or those in the customer's organization.

- More interesting and powerful propositions with hard-to-match competitive advantage can be achieved by integrating offers from different parts of the supplier organization.

- Substantial growth can be won by developing business with new parts of the customer's organization.

Companies need a clear organizational structure, understandably, especially as they become bigger and more complex, but the structure should be used positively to enact the company's strategy, not to frustrate it. Any structure has its advantages and disadvantages, which can be offset by a genuine will to work across the structure, whatever it may be. Unfortunately, structures and their boundaries are often reinforced by a culture of ownership and defence of a territorial power base, which is not helpful in KAM. Suppliers need to be aware of how the structure can operate to produce 'blind spots', such as an inability to aggregate customer information that will obscure the identity of potential key customers; the ways in which they are organized; and how they make their decisions.

The supplier's structure is not the only consideration in deciding how to organize for KAM. Obviously, the customer's structure must be taken into account as well. For example, whether the supplier is a global or local organization, and whether its customer is global or local, produces a number of different forms of KAM.

In a traditional, country-based organization, the key account manager and hence the customer is several layers away from the top of the company, so communicating their strategies and gaining attention for their needs at a high level is very difficult, and not what key customers expect if they have been invited to participate in a strategic relationship. This form of organization also makes the management of key customers as a portfolio more or less impossible. In fact, if there is no clear process which brings them together in the same framework and authorizes the same person or people to make decisions about them, then portfolio management is not happening.

The ultimate form of organization for KAM is a central unit which has its own resources, with a director of key accounts who reports direct to the main Board rather than a national or divisional Board. Key account managers in a central unit should have the authority to make central or global deals, albeit in consultation and with a defined approval process. In all forms of organization, however, the local company or region will have to support and service the deal on the ground, so it is always important that they back it. Successful suppliers employ various mechanisms to deal with this tricky issue.

In fact, it is the company's targets that are often responsible for many of the conflicts that arise between different parts of the organization. Suppliers that can properly align their targets will avoid many of the problems frequently encountered in KAM, just by resolving that single issue.

## The origins of key account management                    CHAPTER 12

While key account management (KAM) has a great deal of its origins in sales, the philosophy has come a long way from there, and this chapter tracks

the development of KAM in academic research and in practice. Needless to say, the two are often not synchronized, and while research has established best practice some considerable time ago, many companies lag well behind, even now. Perhaps understanding the origins of the KAM philosophy will help you to appreciate why KAM is interpreted differently in different companies which are operating different evolutions of the concept.

The identification of the decision-making unit (DMU) in industrial buying was an important breakthrough in the 1960s. It established the complexity of the industrial buying decision compared with a consumer decision, and demonstrated the importance of developing relationships with multiple contacts in the customer who had different interests and viewpoints. Most salespeople, however, had only a single contact in each customer and, at that time, were not adept at developing more.

The Industrial Marketing and Purchasing Group developed the concept of interacting with the customers and developing relationships aimed at customer retention as a deliberate strategy. There has been much debate about when relationship marketing is and is not appropriate, but there is at least general agreement that it is not for all customers, even if which customers the suitable is disputed. Relationship marketing looked longer term and introduced the idea of customer lifetime value, secured through high levels of customer satisfaction.

The KAM philosophy fundamentally believes that collaboration with customers is better for both than confrontation, and seeks to overcome the traditional view of buyer–seller relationships as adversarial. The suspicion has always been that the financial interests of the organization will be threatened by the other party, but evidence suggests that:

- Adversarial behaviour adds costs (e.g. 30 per cent in the construction industry)
- Collaboration creates opportunities for saving costs
- Suppliers do not know how much they make from their customers anyway.

The drivers of KAM are numerous, from globalization and political pressure for corporate responsibility to the speed of change in business, but all factors ultimately tend to give ever larger customers increasing choice and power. Successful KAM carries with it the risk of increasing business dependence, but as the marketplace consolidates few can withstand the trend.

Suppliers and key customers will become increasingly committed to each other in integrated supply chains which can deliver better, faster and cheaper, and which compete with other integrated supply chains rather than individual competitors. In spite of some high profile casualties of

interdependent buyer–seller relationships, it is hard to envisage a return to hands-off exchanges that cannot respond to the requirements of today's customers.

Now you should have a good idea of the whole content of the book, either to whet your appetite before reading it, or to remind yourself of the entirety of what you have just read in much greater depth. Try reading it again as a reminder at a later date.

# Index